Enfin Malherbe

South Atlantic Modern Language
Association Award Study

Enfin Malherbe

The Influence of Malherbe on French Lyric Prosody, 1605-1674

Claude K. Abraham

The University Press of Kentucky

ISBN: 0–8131–1254–0

Library of Congress Catalog Card Number: 70–160042

Copyright © 1971 by The University Press of Kentucky

A statewide cooperative scholarly publishing agency
serving Berea College, Centre College of Kentucky,
Eastern Kentucky University, Kentucky State College,
Morehead State University, Murray State University,
University of Kentucky, University of Louisville,
and Western Kentucky University.

Editorial and Sales Offices: Lexington, Kentucky 40506

To my severest critic, Marcia,
this book is gratefully dedicated

Contents

Acknowledgments

I would here like to thank all those who made this work possible: the Humanities Council, the Graduate School, and the Division of Sponsored Research of the University of Florida, for financial support; Professor J. Wayne Conner, head of the Department of Romance Languages of the University of Florida, a gentleman and a scholar in every sense of the word, a true friend indeed; Professor Amédée Carrat and his entire family, for their hospitality during my stay in Paris; but most of all, my wife Marcia, for her patience, her encouragement, her great help.

Enfin Malherbe

Chapter One

Introduction

To Boileau's exultant "enfin Malherbe vint," Benoist replied with a petulant "il aurait mieux fait de ne pas venir," and the battle is still going on, sustained by an occasional biased study and consecrated by manuals that insist on facile labels. Let it be clear at the outset that this study was undertaken neither to praise nor to damn Malherbe. Rather, I set out to attempt a definition of his role by ascertaining the extent of his actual influence. It would have been child's play to suggest—and to prove with numerous examples, for nothing is easier than the piling on of literary "evidence"—that Malherbe had many followers (or none at all) who slavishly obeyed his rules. The greatest danger to this study was, in fact, the constant temptation to "prove" a trend. I hope I have resisted this temptation.

Let it be clear also that, while I consider the question of Malherbe's influence as one that demands clarification, I do not question the adequacy of the existing works on Malherbe. Everyone interested in the field would like to see a sequel to René Fromilhague's biography of the young Malherbe,[1] but that scholar's work on the poetry of Malherbe,[2] along with the much older but still viable tomes by Brunot[3] and Souriau[4] are quite adequate for our understanding of the master. In this introduction, therefore, I will limit myself to a situation of the problem, and this only insofar as it is essential to the understanding of the method used to determine Malherbe's influence.

One of the first problems that presented itself was a definition of the word influence, a fact made plain by Faguet when he states that "L'école de Malherbe, c'est Boileau, Racine, La Fontaine, Molière, qui d'ailleurs le réclament comme leur maître et suivent ses préceptes."[5] "Le réclamer" is one thing, "suivre ses préceptes" is quite another, and to be convinced of the latter one should be faced with a method more rigorous than that of Faguet. As Renée Winegarten put it, "It is not impossible for a poet to admire a way of writing and yet grow to realize that it is not meant for him."[6] In other words, "Malherbe a très bien fait, mais. . . ." This can be seen in the fact that La Serre dedicated his first work to Malherbe, calling him "le plus éloquent homme . . . [et] en France le Socrate d'Athènes,"[7] but this in a prose work by a writer who never managed to become a poet.

The second problem was one of scope: who was to be included? The answer came from a review of Souriau's book which had, to some extent, covered the versification of the giants: "Après les grands poètes, avant eux peut-être, il faudrait étudier les petits. D'abord, la règle du XVIIe siècle, en matière de versification comme en matière de langage, a été sinon faite, du moins imposée par eux. . . . Il importe donc au plus haut point de connaître ceux qui ont exercé l'interrègne, de Malherbe à Boileau, et de voir ce qu'ils ont fait de l'autorité."[8] Another danger was the possibility that the inclusion of many minor poets would weigh down my study, but that danger had to be faced if the work was to have any value. A further limitation concerns the topic. As René Bray has suggested, the influence of Malherbe is in many domains.[9] I am concerned only with versification.

Another problem was one basic to any literary research: how much of the past research on the matter is valid and how much must be swept aside? It is not surprising that Banville, like his contemporaries, found in Malherbe a ready scapegoat:

> C'était l'orgie au Parnasse, la Muse
> Qui par raison se plaît à courir vers

[1] *La vie de Malherbe* (Paris: Colin, 1954).

[2] *Malherbe: Technique et création poétique* (Paris: Colin, 1954). (Hereafter cited as *Technique*.)

[3] Ferdinand Brunot, *La doctrine de Malherbe* (Paris: Masson, 1891).

[4] Maurice Souriau, *L'évolution du vers français au dix-septième siècle* (Paris: Hachette, 1893).

[5] Emile Faguet, *Histoire de la poésie française de la Renaissance au Romantisme* (Paris: Boivin, 1923–1936), 1:307.

[6] *French Lyric Poetry in the Age of Malherbe* (Manchester: Manchester University Press, 1954), p. 101.

[7] Jean Puget de La Serre, *Le secrétaire de la cour* (Lyon: Muguet, 1646).

[8] Ferdinand B[runetière], *RHL* 1 (1894): 497.

[9] *La formation de la doctrine classique en France* (Lausanne: Payot, 1931), p. 7.

Tout ce qui brille et tout ce qui l'amuse,
Eparpillait les rubis dans ses vers.
Elle mettait son laurier de travers.
Les bons rhythmeurs, pris d'une frénésie,
Comme des Dieux gaspillaient l'ambroisie;
Si bien qu'enfin, pour mettre le hola
Malherbe vint, et que la Poésie,
En le voyant arriver, s'en alla[10]

Nor should it surprise us that Petit de Julleville thought that all the great writers of the seventeenth century, "tous, poètes et prosateurs, ont reconnu sa maîtrise et suivi, indirectement, sa discipline."[11] What is more surprising is that Souriau still perpetuated the idea: "Malherbe commence donc l'école du purisme, qui est l'une des deux moitiés de l'école classique";[12] and that Winegarten only a few years ago categorically stated, "By 1620, Malherbe's doctrine which fixed as inviolable rules some of the tendencies of the previous thirty years, was accepted by most lyric poets of any importance at Court."[13] One might open a parenthesis here to ask whether there was such a fast doctrine in 1620 and who these "poets of any importance at Court" might be, but such questions are the subjects of books yet to be written. The answer to my original problem was reached in a more arbitrary fashion, and I decided to accept with few reservations the basic statements as to the climate—intellectual and social—of the times and the poetic and personal temperament of Malherbe. The rest is, I hope, the legitimate subject of this study, a study which will deal primarily with prosody, leaving purely linguistic matters to someone better qualified and more disposed for such work.

Many years before Malherbe appeared, "de nouvelles tendances littéraires s'étaient manifestées."[14] Mythology was shrinking in popularity, poets such as Desportes were restricting their vocabulary, poetic furor was receding before the onslaught of reason. When Gosse states of Malherbe,

[10] Théodore de Banville, *Cariatides* (Paris: Charpentier, 1879), p. 184.
[11] *Histoire de la langue et de la littérature françaises* (Paris: Colin, 1897), 4:15.
[12] *L'évolution du vers français*, p. 107.
[13] *French Lyric Poetry*, p. 16.
[14] Brunot, *Doctrine de Malherbe*, p. 563.

"I recollect no other instance in the history of literature in which one individual has contrived to stem the whole flood of national taste," adding that it is "certain that through the early years of the struggle there remains no evidence of his having been supported by any associate opinion,"[15] he is disregarding the work of all but the most frequently anthologized poets. "Avant 1600 déjà, une partie de l'opinion cultivée souhaitait une poésie nouvelle, ou réformée, celle-là même qu'annonçaient Desportes, Bertaut, du Perron."[16] The only quarrel one might have with this statement is that it tends to limit the scope of this new wave to the world of poetry, whereas it pervaded all of man's endeavors. The difference between Malherbe and his opponents seems less one of a purely poetic ideal than one of basic philosophies. Tristan L'Hermite's "Promenoir des deux amants" is imbued with a pagan sentiment of nature and life reminiscent of Ronsard and totally foreign to Malherbe. Ronsard had stated that "nulle Poësie se doit louer pour acomplie, si elle ne ressemble la nature, laquelle ne fut estimée belle des anciens, que pour estre inconstante, et variable en ses perfections."[17] Malherbe, true friend and follower of du Vair, "combattait les Grecs," and to do this effectively, "il n'avait qu'à se souvenir de Sénèque pour réclamer, dans les vers français, plus de sévérité, plus de naturel, plus de raison."[18] In fact, it is precisely because Malherbe did not always go far enough in this direction that the seventeenth-century critics found fault with him. As Fromilhague suggested, "l'esthétique de du Vair n'est-elle pas exactement celle que nous laissait prévoir sa philosophie?"[19] And isn't Malherbe's esthetic a continuation of that of du Vair, that is to say, a reflection of a new tendency permeating an entire society? At the turn of the century, certain trends were discernible: "There were two parties: a liberal party, which was really reactionary and traditionalist; and a dogmatic party, which was revolutionary."[20] The quarrel between

---

[15] Edmund Gosse, *Malherbe and the Classical Reaction in the Seventeenth Century* (Oxford: Clarendon Press, 1920), p. 13.

[16] Marcel Raymond, *Baroque et renaissance poétique* (Paris: Corti, 1955), p. 153.

[17] *Œuvres complètes* (Paris: Gallimard, 1950), 2:973.

[18] Albert Counson, *Malherbe et ses sources* (Liège: Université de Liège, 1904), p. 158.

[19] *Technique*, p. 117.

[20] Elbert B. O. Borgerhoff, *The Freedom of French Classicism* (Princeton: Princeton University Press, 1950), p. 3.

these two trends had begun long before Malherbe's arrival in Paris, and the seventeenth century never stopped being aware of the conflict.

According to Borgerhoff, this argument, "begun in 1606 with Malherbe's *Commentaires sur Desportes,* continued on through the century but ceased to be vital around 1630. In this year the last edition of Ronsard until 1781 was published, and the first complete edition of Malherbe appeared. The school of Malherbe had won its battle."[21] But the battle was not begun by Malherbe in 1606. Already the young Ronsard spoke of "Le bon Poëte endoctriné,"[22] and later, in his *Abrégé de l'art poétique françois,* he gave this advice to the poet: "tu seras laborieux à corriger et limer tes vers," being opposed to "ces inventeurs fantastiques et melancholiques, qui ne se rapportent non plus l'un[e] à l'autre que les songes entrecoupez d'un frenetique," for the works must be "facilement conceues et entendues d'un chacun."[23] Peletiers du Mans, like the Ronsard of the *Abrégé,* though slightly before the *Abrégé,* suggested that "la Nature bien demande le secours e la mein artisane."[24] Perrault marveled at du Perron who, in Ronsard's time, spoke as people did a century later and was able to "se saisir par avance d'un style qui ne devoit estre tout-à-fait en usage que plus de soixante ans après."[25] In other words, long before Malherbe, and often within the thoughts of one man, two concepts coexisted, one technical and artificial, the other naïve and inspirational. In the newer of the two trends, "le souci de la clarté avait rapproché la poésie de la prose, de même que l'introduction de la raison dans la création poétique finira par éliminer à peu près complètement l'inspiration."[26]

By 1600, the battlelines were already drawn, and years before Malherbe's entrance into the arena, des Yveteaux felt obliged to defend Desportes in his "Elégie sur les œuvres de M. des Portes." In 1603, when Laudun d'Aigaliers's *Franciade* appeared, it had to be defended in the preface against the "Aristarques courtisans, . . . jeunes esprits dont le foible cerveau/ Veut produire à la Cour un langage nouveau," and who

[21] Ibid., p. 4.

[22] *Œuvres complètes,* 1:407.

[23] Ibid., pp. 997–99.

[24] Jacques Peletier du Mans, *L'art poëtique* (Paris: Belles Lettres, 1930), pp. 74–75.

[25] Charles Perrault, *Les hommes illustres* (Paris: Dezallier, 1696–1700), 2:9.

[26] Fromilhague, *Technique,* p. 93.

caused des Yveteaux to deplore the fact that they seemed to have "plus d'art que de science." These new poets were already aware of themselves. They only needed a voice to lead them, and when "enfin" Malherbe came, it was in answer to a prayer, not as a total surprise. Thus, long before the arrival of the leader-to-be, there were voices that "protègent l'esprit et l'art français contre l'invasion massive du baroquisme étranger."[27] Thus du Perron (who should be considered a rival of Malherbe, especially insofar as esthetic concepts are concerned), in remarks that are quite "Malherbian," severely chastised Ronsard's sonnets.[28] Gosse believes that at that time "conditions had brought French literature to a point where reform was useless and revolution was inevitable."[29] There was no Malherbian revolution. Rather, reformers, waging an already victorious campaign, were ready to accept the yoke of discipline. The nascent century, "knowing the cost and the danger of such discipline," enhanced its poetic consciousness by the very acceptance of it.[30] Malherbe's tenacity, will, and method made him leader of a movement that already existed. This explains why a Jean de Lingendes, while not a disciple of Malherbe, could be under the master's influence—though possibly only because he was already going in the same direction.

If Borgerhoff's suggestion that 1606 is the starting point of this quarrel cannot be accepted without qualifications (and just how public were the *Commentaires* in 1606?), 1630 as its end is even less acceptable. While this was the date of the last seventeenth-century edition of Ronsard, this poet remained quite popular. Marcel Françon demonstrated that Ronsard never ceased to appear in most of the *recueils collectifs*,[31] and while most critics found reason to condemn him, they found even more reason to praise him. Therefore, Fernand Desonay was right in stating that "Ronsard ne fut pas dédaigné au XVIIe siècle."[32]

---

[27] Pierre Colotte, *Pierre de Deimier, poète et théoricien de la poésie: Sa carrière à Paris et ses relations avec Malherbe* (Gap: Orphrys, 1953), p. 14.

[28] *Perroniana* (Geneva: n.p., 1667), pp. 283–86.

[29] *Malherbe and the Classical Reaction*, p. 5.

[30] Borgerhoff, *Freedom of French Classicism*, p. 5.

[31] "La renommée de Ronsard au dix-septième siècle, d'après les recueils collectifs du temps," FR 32 (Dec. 1958): pp. 144–46.

[32] "La réputation littéraire de Ronsard au XVIIe siècle," BBP 27 (1924): 141.

Yes, "enfin, Malherbe vint," but he came to administer the coup de grâce to an already weakened foe. Desportes in 1605 was still beloved by all, but, as a contemporary put it, he was, though "Favori d'Apollon, relique de Parnasse."[33] The rules had been evolving for some time and Desportes himself, as well as poets such as Bertaut, are to be credited with much of the trend.[34] Against lines such as Motin's paraphrase of Psalm 129,

> *Du profond de mon cœur, plein d'amères angoisses,*
> *D'angoisseuse amertume et d'un profond émoi,*[35]

an entire era was to rebel, and if "l'essentiel demeure toujours l'exemple et l'action particulière d'un homme,"[36] the role of such a man cannot be studied apart from the trend that made his achievements possible. The works of men such as Deimier, of groups such as the Piat-Maucour Academy attest to the existence of this trend dedicated to the "pureté de la langue" and the advancement of poetry in general.[37] But if before Malherbe others worked "au progrès de la langue et de l'art des vers," it is equally true that "en lui se réunissent les résultats de tout ce travail antérieur."[38] Valéry said it only too well, and Fromilhague repeated it, "tout classicisme suppose un romantisme antérieur."[39]

Malherbe was not only in reaction to Ronsard, he was fighting the omnipresent shadow of the giant whose mediocre followers used the name of the master to preserve an era that Malherbe wished to end. In fact, the basic difference between Malherbe and many of his contemporaries was that he alone was unwilling to bow to that shadow. The Ronsard whom Malherbe attacks was not the author of the already cited

[33] Antoine de Nervèze, *Essais poétiques* (Paris: Dubreuil, 1605), p. 64.

[34] See Philippe Martinon, "La genèse des règles de Jean Lemaire à Malherbe," *RHLF* 16 (1909): 62–87.

[35] *Œuvres inédites* (Paris: Librairie des Bibliophiles, 1882), p. 76.

[36] Marcel Raymond, *L'influence de Ronsard sur la poésie française* (Paris: Champion, 1927), 2:350.

[37] Michel de Marolles, *Mémoires* (Amsterdam: n.p., 1755), 1:77.

[38] Gustav Allais, *Malherbe et la poésie française à la fin du XVIe siècle* (Paris: Thorin, 1891), p. 402.

[39] "La création poétique chez Malherbe," *DSS* 31 (April 1956): 247.

passage, nor the poet who stated that "la poésie ne peut estre plaisante, vive ne parfaitte sans belles inventions, descriptions, comparaisons,"[40] but rather the Ronsard who maintained that the "fable" was everything while "les vers sont seulement le but de l'ignorant versificateur."[41] Malherbe's entire poetic art is precisely that of a versificator. Malherbe "ne cesse d'inventer des contraintes nouvelles, de captiver son inspiration dans un réseau de plus en plus serré de règles. Et ces règles, toujours plus nombreuses, toujours plus draconiennes, deviennent aussi toujours plus arbitraires. Jusqu'à lui, elles étaient pour ainsi dire postulées par la matière poétique elle-même, elles étaient l'interprétation d'une exigence interne de la poésie. . . . Avec lui, elles experiment la volonté du poète de rendre son art plus difficile."[42] This is what distinguished him from his contemporaries, this is the side of him that can be, and has been, defined, and this is the Malherbe whose influence must be sought in the works of the poets of the seventeenth century.

As I suggested earlier, the difference between Malherbe and Ronsard is more than a quarrel over the exact role of the poet. When Malherbe praises Desportes, he invariably demonstrates "une préférence marquée, presque exclusive, pour des qualités essentiellement oratoires de logique, de clarté, de force."[43] As Colotte has pointed out, "quand Malherbe arrive à Paris, . . . sa confiance en lui, en son génie, est étonnante. Il est sûr de la conception *rationnelle* de sa poésie et de son art."[44] He is less a poet than "une intelligence critique adonnée à la poésie."[45] This is the point which must be kept in mind when discussing Malherbe's lyricism.

The mythical origins of lyricism as we see it today go back to the rites of Dionysus and betray an early desire of man to involve himself wholly in the life of a god, "mais d'un dieu sacrifié, déchiré."[46] But poetry is not lyricism, for if lyricism is born of pathos, poetry is a form born of order and giving rise to order. "Le ton, l'ethos malherbien, c'est une vertu affirmative, une extraordinaire netteté et franchise d'attaque,"[47] an apol-

---

[40] *Œuvres complètes*, 2:998.
[41] Ibid., p. 1001.
[42] Fromilhague, *Technique*, pp. 28–29.
[43] Brunot, *Doctrine de Malherbe*, p. 157.
[44] *Pierre de Deimier*, p. 10.
[45] Ibid., p. 11.
[46] Marcel Raymond, *Baroque*, p. 157.
[47] Ibid.

Ionian call to life, quite distinct from the dionysiac oblivion. Thus, when Saulnier states that Malherbe "demeure un homme du XVIe siècle,"[48] pointing out that Régnier and Montchrestien were younger than Malherbe, he is splitting chronological hairs and disregarding the profound cleavage that can exist between singers still devoted to Dionysus and a craftsman in the service of Apollo. Plato, in both *Phaedrus* and *Ion,* put forth the idea that a musician who never went beyond the preliminaries of harmony was not a true musician, and that a craftsman without "demon" was not a poet. Giordano Bruno, carrying this idea one step further, suggested in *Degl'eroici furori* that there were as many sets of rules as there were poets. But for Malherbe, only a rigorous application of logic to the formulation of a valid set of rules could save French poetry from the anarchy in which it was wallowing. Thus, when Chapelain said "ce que Malherbe a d'excellent et d'incomparable, c'est l'élocution et le tour des vers et quelques élévations nettes et pompeuses dans le détail," he was judging Malherbe quite accurately. When he concluded that the result was merely "de fort belle prose rimée,"[49] he was applying criteria that Malherbe did not even recognize. If by lyricism we mean "ce que le mouvement de l'inspiration pouvait avoir de libre encore, d'indépendant et de capricieux,"[50] then Malherbe is indeed guilty of having helped to stifle it. But if by lyricism we mean something more closely associated with the outward expression of music, then the usual accusations leveled against Malherbe have no meaning.

Malherbe came to Paris not to court fame but to make his fortune. If the university was not in rebellion against Ronsard by the time of Malherbe's arrival, the court definitely was, as even a rapid glance at Bertaut's or du Perron's poetry will show. Malherbe was nothing if not practical. The best court musicians of his time used his poems for their airs. As Lila Maurice-Amour points out, more than one-fourth of his poetic production was set to music or obviously written to be so set.[51] "The practice of setting poetry to music line by line imposed formal limitations on the

---

[48] V. L. Saulnier, "Malherbe et le XVIe siècle," *DSS* 31 (April 1956): 218.

[49] *Lettres* (Paris: Imprimerie Nationale, 1880–1883), 1:637.

[50] Ferdinand Brunetière, "La réforme de Malherbe et l'évolution des genres," *RDM* 6 (Dec. 1892): 672.

[51] "Les poésies de Malherbe et les musiciens de son temps," *DSS* 31 (April 1956): 298.

lyric, and in the *air de cour* there was a tendency to end-stop the lines and to emphasize the rhyme and also to have a cadence in the middle of the line. . . . [Thus] it may even be that Malherbe's preoccupation with difficult rhyme, and his rules concerning enjambment and caesura, were formulated not out of a mere love of austerity for its own sake, but for musical consideration closely bound up with the *air de cour*."[52] Was not his dislike for *vers suivis* most likely due to an idea that they were unsuited for musical setting? Thus, in an age of progressively more elusive muses, Malherbe should be credited with, if anything, preserving the unity of song and poetry for a while longer.

As I have suggested, Malherbe is not representative of a literary current, he is its champion, for "avec des vertus et des jugements nuancés on ne fait guère triompher des doctrines."[53] Malherbe is brutal, cynical, aggressive, but that is Malherbe the doctrinaire. We should keep in mind that the seventeenth century, in commenting on Malherbe, viewed his poetry rather than his theories, which it knew only imperfectly. The danger we face constantly is one which occurs when we ask Malherbe the poet to apply rigorously the edicts of Malherbe the critic. To help the progress of a theory, Malherbe had to create a myth. To survive as a poet, he had only to be himself. "Les dangers commencent seulement au moment où le mythe envahit l'œuvre aussi, où l'on demande à l'œuvre de Malherbe d'être aussi pure et aussi unique que sa doctrine."[54]

This is not to suggest that the poet and the critic are at odds. Rather, each one "vit de sa vie propre,"[55] and the intransigent critic's commentaries should not make us fail to see a poet whose imaginativeness could be "bizarre . . . d'une manière spontanée."[56] As I have stated already, I do not believe Malherbe's theories were generally known. Racan mentions a few in his biography of the master, and Balzac, who had the famous *Commentaires* in his possession in 1653,[57] planned to copy out the best of them, but this does not prove that the seventeenth century at any time

[52] Winegarten, *French Lyric Poetry*, p. 5.

[53] A. Kibédi Varga, "Enfin du Perron vint: Malherbe ou le sens de la publicité," *RHLF* 67 (Jan. 1967): 1.

[54] Ibid., p. 2.

[55] Antoine Adam, *Histoire de la littérature française au XVIIe siècle* (Paris: Domat, 1948–1956), 1:35.

[56] R.-R. Wagner, "Le language poétique," *DSS* 31 (April 1956): 274.

[57] *Œuvres* (Paris: Billaine, 1665), 2:957.

was truly conversant with the detailed "laws" of the master. Thus, when Faguet states that "la littérature de 1615 à 1660, n'a presque aucunement subi l'influence de Malherbe. . . . Tant s'en faut que tout ait reconnu ses lois, que ses lois ont été méconnues à peu près par tout le monde,"[58] he is succumbing to the danger I spoke of and equating the two roles of Malherbe. Whether the commentaries were meant as a pedagogical tool or a polemical weapon, they had lost their importance by the time alluded to by Faguet: Desportes was dead and the literary tastes of the new era were no longer to be demonstrated. René Bray maintained that "l'œuvre essentielle de Malherbe, ce n'est pas son œuvre positive, c'est son œuvre négative."[59] I cannot agree with this echo of Faguet. Malherbe the destroyer was the strong reflection of an already existing trend. The real Malherbe was a builder, one who realized that, after the purification, order had to be established, and that, for this, examples were needed. Agrippa d'Aubigné saw this too when he said, "je demande seulement à ces Legislateurs, que pour avoir l'autorité sur le siècle que les grands Maistres de ce temps là ont prise, et qu'ils puissent estre alleguez comme ceux-là *exemplo,* que nous voyons de leurs mains des Poëmes epiques, heroïques ou quelque chose qui se puisse apeller œuvre."[60] Malherbe obliged. How much of this example was followed remains to be ascertained, and this study is meant to throw some light on precisely that subject. We are all familiar with the practice and the doctrine of Malherbe. Let us now look at the practice of the century.

[58] "La poésie de Malherbe à Boileau," *RCC,* ser. 3, 6 (1894): 163.
[59] *Formation de la doctrine,* p. 8.
[60] *Œuvres complètes* (Paris: Lemerre, 1873–1892), 1:462.

The Age of
Louis XIII

Chapter Two

Malherbe &
His 'Écoliers'

There is no doubt that Malherbe's doctrines, whether constructive or destructive, were spread by word of mouth in his own lifetime as well as later on. But when Malherbe came to Paris, he did so to court fame and fortune, with a strong emphasis on the latter, and he knew that theories alone would not accomplish this task. He enjoyed the admiration of his *écoliers,* but fundamentally "se souciait peu d'estre loué des gens de lettres," preferring the more concrete manifestations of admiration that could be secured from the "gens de la Cour."[1] We must keep in mind that it was at court that the new ideas were getting their strongest support. As Colotte points out, an *art poétique* is welcome "des doctes, des hommes graves . . . qui aiment à réfléchir et philosopher," but such a crowd could do little to further Malherbe's career.[2] And so, while a few pedants occupied themselves by theorizing, incorporating in their *arts poétiques* and *académies* many of the new tenets championed by Malherbe, the poet gravitated toward the world of "le courtisan et le mondain [qui] éliminent le docte, l'homme de cabinet."[3] Here again, Malherbe was opportune as well as opportunist: the theorists were many but the poets few. Desportes died in 1606; du Perron stopped writing about the same date, as did Bertaut when he became bishop. In 1611 des Yveteaux was exiled and Malherbe remained in sole possession of the battlefield. It was to him, the poet, that the neophytes came. The theorist continued to exist, but only to enhance the poet. How else can one explain the childish gesture reported by Racan with which Malherbe dismissed the rest of Ronsard when questioned by his disciples about those poems of the Pléiade master he had not damned?

The first evidence of Malherbian influence is usually located in the *Parnasse des plus excellens poëtes de ce temps.*[4] However, while the

"Malherbians" are very well represented (even a minor poet such as Touvant has seven poems included) the works offered show little or no influence of the master. I must also add here that the *recueils collectifs* should not be accepted without reservations, especially in matters dealing with form, for they were most unreliable when it came to the careful reproduction of an author's work. Time after time, authors publishing their work separately did so with a preface in which they claimed that they had done violence to their basic modesty only to undo the harm done their literary reputation by the carelessness of the compilers of *recueils*. Thus La Mesnardière, feeling that the reader of the *Recueil du Palais* could only be misled as to the real merit of his work which had been "entièrement défiguré" in that anthology, condescended to publish his *Poésies*.[5]

Both Touvant and Colomby are well represented in the *Parnasse*, and the critics' desire to make of this an important event in the evolution of classicism may be due to the paucity of works by these two pupils of Malherbe. What is remarkable, especially where Touvant is concerned, is that subsequent anthologies show very few major changes that might be ascribed to Malherbe. The 1607 *Parnasse* shows Touvant breaking almost every rule of Malherbe, a fact that should not be surprising considering the date. The same author is represented by five poems in the 1615 *Délices* and by four in the 1620 version of that *recueil*.[6] Though Touvant did not die until shortly before the appearance of the 1615 anthology, all the poems appearing in the *Délices* had already been published in the *Parnasse* and were virtually unchanged. His "Ode bachique" is replete with words such as *soudainement* and *froidure* which Malherbe would never have condoned. By the same token, quite some time before Touvant's death, Maynard had convinced Malherbe and his circle that six-line stanzas had to be divided 3–3; yet the bulk of Touvant's poems in that form fail to show such a break, either in 1607 or in the posthumous versions. All in all, this poet, while acknowledged by Malherbe as one

[1] Racan, *Œuvres complètes* (Paris: Jannet, 1857), 1:276.

[2] *Pierre de Deimier*, p. 21.

[3] Ibid., p. 22.

[4] (Paris: Guillemot, 1607).

[5] (Paris: Sommaville, 1656), preface.

[6] *Les délices de la poésie françoise* (Paris: Toussainct du Bray, 1615, 1620).

of his "pupils," seems to have learned but little from his master, and it is perhaps due to this recalcitrance that the anthologies subsequent to the 1620 *Délices* do not contain any of his poems.

Colomby obviously became one of the *écoliers*, a member of the French Academy, and a Conseiller du Roi thanks to his cousin Malherbe, who must also have had something to say about his nomination to the post of "orateur du roi pour les discours d'Etat," a job created for Colomby and abolished after him.[7] He was certainly no Cicero, for the *Comédie des académistes* refers to him as the "muet orateur des affaires d'Etat," and Malherbe, if we are to believe Racan, thought he had "nul génie pour la poésie." This opinion may explain why Malherbe in his letters to Colomby[8] never mentions literary matters. This may also help explain the chronology of Colomby's poetic legacy: from 1605 to 1615 he produced about fifteen poems, some of which are quite long. After that date, only a few liminary poems appeared, to praise close friends.

By the dates of his poems, their nature, and his closeness to his cousin, Colomby can easily be considered Malherbe's first student. This is not to suggest that Colomby was "Malherbian" from the time of his first poem, but his ideas, if not his capabilities, led him in that direction from the very start. After the poetic fiasco of *Les plaintes de la captive Caliston à l'invincible Aristarque*, about 300 bad lines of adulation, he published his first *poème de circonstance*, the *Discours presenté au Roy avant son partement pour aller assiéger Sedan*,[9] a poem that he reworked for inclusion in the 1607 *Parnasse*[10] and once again for the 1615 *Délices*.[11] This is the only poem that is found in so many versions, but it offers little that can be seized by the comparatist: most of the changes made between the first and second version cannot be credited with certainty to anything but the typesetter's caprice, while the changes wrought in the 1615 edition are mostly due to the fact that the subject of the poem had died. Thus, "Toy du corps de l'état grand prince tutélaire"[12] became "Miracle de nos

---

[7] François Boisard, *Notices sur les hommes du Calvados* (Caen: Pagny, 1848), p. 57.

[8] *Œuvres* (Paris: Hachette, 1862–1869), 4:72–78. Unless otherwise noted, all future references are to this edition.

[9] (N.p., 1605; and Paris: Prévosteu, 1606.)

[10] "Toy du corps de l'état. . . ."

[11] "Miracle de nos jours. . . ."

[12] *Parnasse*, 2(1607): 6.

jours, notre ange tutélaire";[13] "Qui prends plaisir aux vers" became "Si tu chéris les vers"; and so on. Only one stanza was totally reworked:

> *Si ton âme aujourd'hui justement offensée*
> *Du mépris de tes lois, résout en ta pensée*
> *D'aller punir l'orgueil d'un sujet fugitif,*
> *Tu peux, par la valeur de tes grands capitaines,*
> *Sans te mettre au péril des armes incertaines,*
> *Lui donner le trépas, ou le faire captif.* [1607]

This became:

> *Mais las! où t'en vas-tu pour exciter nos larmes,*
> *Rechercher les hasards dans la gloire des armes,*
> *Et poursuivre toi-même un sujet fugitif?*
> *Toy, qui par la valeur de tant de capitaines,*
> *Sans te mettre au péril des armes incertaines,*
> *Lui peux donner la mort, ou le faire captif.* [1615]

Here obviously the death of the king had nothing to do with the changes, the reasons for which must be sought elsewhere. Aside from an only slightly better choice of words, the stanza is strengthened mainly by an unyielding line-by-line construction, with a definite break after the third line. As I have already mentioned, it was some time before 1615 that Maynard convinced Malherbe that such a division was necessary if the six-line stanza was to be considered lyrical.

The above sample is quite typical of the sixty-nine stanzas of alexandrines. The *a a b c c b* rhymes, while not always rich (*tributaire-calvaire, honneur-seigneur*), are acceptable; enjambments, especially in the revised version, are at a minimum; and the caesura is regular. The stanzas themselves, divided capriciously in the early versions, are cut 3–3 with greater regularity, as illustrated above.

The *Délices* of 1615 contain thirteen poems by Colomby, twelve of them new ones.[14] The new harvest is quite varied. While some traits are more reminiscent of *Les larmes de Saint-Pierre*, others are a deliberate

---

[13] *Délices* (1615), p. 549.

[14] In the interval, only one poem by him had appeared, that one in the *Recueil sur la Pucelle* of 1613.

imitation of a somewhat more mature Malherbe. This is the case of the "Consolation à la Reine," obviously inspired by "Consolation à M. du Périer":

> Consolez-vous, Madame, essuyez votre face,
>   Mettez fin à vos pleurs:
> Faites que la raison domine dans la place
>   Où règnent les douleurs.
>
> . . . .
>
> Mais enfin qu'advint-il de ce deuil incroyable?
>   Le destin rigoureux
> Pour son affliction fut-il plus pitoyable,
>   Ou le mort plus heureux? [pp. 526–32]

The strophic division is as loosely woven here as it is in Malherbe's poem, a far cry from the obviously much later "Plainte de Mme de Rohan," a well-constructed, metrically sound poem in sestets, all regularly divided:

> En vain vous essayez de soulager ma peine,
> En me représentant que la nature humaine
>   Nous oblige au trépas:
> Nul mal, tant soit-il grand, à mon mal ne ressemble:
> Que je sois impassible et mère toute ensemble
>   Cela ne se peut pas. [p. 539]

The basic construction here is quite Malherbian, not only in that it is heterometric with alexandrines predominating, but that the secondary break comes between lines of equal length (12–12–6//12/12–6). The rhyme scheme, however, is far from orthodox. Not only is the rhyme *peine-humaine* barely sufficient, but Malherbe preferred the *a a b c b c* scheme to the one illustrated here; though again, a definite dating would help, since Malherbe did use this scheme in his earlier works. By the same token, a "Chanson" whose octets are divided 4–4 would benefit us much more if we could date it more precisely.

While no concrete proof can be offered either for or against any particular man's influence, a few remarks seem in order. Colomby and Malherbe, by the nature of their special relationship, were obviously in contact with each other long before the arrival of either man in Paris. Thus, while many of the aforementioned traits were already present in the *Plaintes* of 1605, this in no way eliminates them from our consideration. Malherbe's tastes seem to be reflected in many ways in Colomby's poetry, especially the shift to a more linear construction. Colomby and Malherbe seem to have shared a dislike for *vers suivis* and a preference for heterometric rather than isometric stanzas, especially in quatrains and sestets. On the other hand, Colomby's rhymes are seldom rich, and Malherbe must have been dissatisfied with his cousin's efforts in the lexical realm. The language of the younger poet is seldom *châtié*, and Malherbe's concern for the *mot juste* seems not to have touched him; witness the statement to the effect that a king

> *Ne doit rendre jamais ses valeurs prophanées*
> *Contre un petit sujet qu'il peut toujours ranger.*[15]

It might be argued that such disregard for Malherbe's dicta reflects the fact that basic linguistic reforms take longer to evolve and take hold than technical rules of versification, just as Colomby's silence after 1615 might be attributed to his unwillingness or inability to follow Malherbe in this domain. Such speculations are not, however, within the framework of this study.

Colomby was undoubtedly Malherbe's first proselyte in Paris, but it is on Maynard and Racan that the greatest attention must be focused, not only because of all the disciples they were the only ones with genuine talent, but because, with this talent, they adopted and adapted the master's lessons. That their personalities differed drastically is well known, but precisely for this reason I plan to look at them simultaneously: the contrast will not only cast light on their work, but also show how and to what extent they were influenced by Malherbe. That they were influenced by Malherbe has been amply demonstrated by René Fromilhague, to whose work I am indebted for much of this portion of the present study. That they were often criticized specifically and that at times they listened to such criticism is made obvious by the changes they wrought in successive editions of their poems.[16] But to suggest that Racan and Maynard were

---

[15] *Discours au Roy,* ll. 32–33.

[16] This has been ably demonstrated by Charles Drouhet, *Le poète François Mainard* (Paris: Champion, 1909), pp. 73–76.

docile lambs, that Malherbe "ne trouvait parmi eux aucun contradicteur redoutable," is to disregard not only Racan's statements but also his work and that of his friend. And to consecrate the error by adding, "c'est assuré-ment un phénomène digne de remarque que la docilité avec laquelle l'im-mense majorité se courbait sous cette volonté impérieuse, qui puisait toute sa force dans la raison et le bon sens. Ce public, qui dans un accès d'en-gouement et d'enthousiasme aveugle, avait tant exalté l'afféterie et les raffinements de Ronsard et de son école, rentrant à la voix de Malherbe dans la voie naturelle, brise aujourd'hui les idoles qu'il avait adorées hier,"[17] is ludicrous at best, and fails to take into account testimonials such as those of Maynard himself who, in a letter, linked together Ronsard, Desportes, and Malherbe as his favorite poets.[18]

Never servile, Maynard and Racan continuously debated and argued, sometimes convincing the usually intransigent Malherbe, more often bowing to his bullying logic. Better than any other poets or critics of the century, they sensed what was behind the new reformatory wave. They understood Malherbe and he knew it, just as he knew that it was precisely because of such understanding that Racan was repeatedly heretic. Racan admits that time and time again Malherbe was "prêt de le declarer hereti-que en poésie,"[19] yet he "préféroit Racan, pour le génie, à ses autres éléves."[20] Deploring Racan's heresy, he recognized his force.[21] Appreciative of Maynard's workmanship, "M. de Malherbe l'estimoit l'homme de France qui scavoit le mieux faire des vers."[22] It is perhaps in this context that Malherbe's famous *boutade* about poets being "arrangeurs de syllabes" should be taken. I do not view it as a limit imposed on poetry, but rather as an honest statement of fact concerning Malherbe's, and what he er-roneously felt to be Racan's and Maynard's, limitations. Was it against this verdict that Maynard rebelled after Malherbe's death, breaking many of the rules that he had obeyed until then? Was it to this judgment that he was still reacting years later when he declared to Flotte that he hated to be censured, saying, "Ie suis opiniastre en certaines choses, et croy con-

[17] Eugène Borel, *Des réformes littéraires opérées par Malherbe* (Stuttgart: n.p., 1857), p. 9.

[18] *Lettres* (Paris: Quinet, 1653), letter 194, p. 583.

[19] *Œuvres complètes*, 1:283.

[20] Malherbe, *Œuvres,* ed. Gilles Ménage (Paris: Barbou, 1722), 1:4.

[21] Ibid., p. 43.

[22] Racan, *Œuvres complètes*, 1:283.

noistre les Vers aussi finement qu'homme qui viue"?[23] It has been suggested that "par les *thèmes* qu'ils traitent ils [Racan and Maynard] annoncent des *courants nouveaux*."[24] This is undoubtedly true but, more important, it was with the deep understanding of Malherbe's rigidity and the elasticity of their own art that they made these currents flourish.

In the *Parnasse réformé*, du Bartas deplored the fact that everyone had forgotten "ce que c'est que d'expressions Poëtiques: Pourveu qu'on soit assez heureux pour rencontrer la rime et la mesure, on se persuade que tout le reste n'est rien."[25] While this is not quite fair either to Malherbe or to his two good pupils, it is very reminiscent of the *Lettre au sieur Malherbe*, a manifesto by Jacques Favereau written to defend his reintroduction of *vers irréguliers*, a strict-rhyme adaptation of *versi sciolti*. In it, he praised Malherbe only to damn his followers with heavy irony, concluding that they "s'amusent à épinocher, et pointiller sur les syllabes et paroles, au lieu de s'attacher à la substance des choses: si bien qu'aujourd'-hui, pour faire des vers à la mode, c'est-à-dire pour avoir l'approbation d'eux, la chose du monde dont il se faut le plus garder, c'est d'être poète."[26] In fact, Malherbe did attach great importance to words and to form. His concept of lyricism was Apollonian rather than Dionysiac, orderly rather than capricious, but to suggest that this concept demands that "il se faut le plus garder . . . d'être poète" is unjust. Already *La Satire du temps* had pointed out

> *Que les vers de Hardy n'ont point d'égalité,*
> *Que le nombre lui plaît plus que la qualité,*
> *Qu'il est capricieux en diable . . .*[27]

Caprice. This was Malherbe's pet aversion, one which was to lead him to excessive reactions and in which his pupils were only too often to follow him. In the *Parnasse réformé*, answering du Bartas's charge, Malherbe claims that "l'amour de l'antiquité vous a perdus," making them

---

[23] *Lettres*, letter 171, p. 504. See also letter 276.

[24] André Lagarde and Laurent Michard, *Les grands auteurs français du programme* (Paris: Bordas, 1961), 3:27.

[25] Gabriel Guéret, ed., *Le Parnasse réformé* (Paris: Osmont, 1674), p. 62.

[26] Cited by Renée Winegarten, "A Neglected Critic of Malherbe: Jacques Favereau," *FS* 6 (Jan. 1952): 32–33.

[27] Cited by Emile Roy, "Un pamphlet d'Alexandre Hardy," *RHLF* 22 (1915): 501.

prefer "l'Écumière fille" to Venus and obscurity to reason.[28] He goes on: "Je ne suis point de ces critiques severes qui condamnent jusques aux moindres libertez: Il est permis aux grands Poëtes de s'affranchir quelquefois des regles communes," but he quickly adds that too many poets have exaggerated this license by shortening words, lengthening others, changing spellings, using slang or patois just to achieve rhythm or rhyme.[29] Malherbe's attitude toward these liberties can be studied best if viewed in two separate categories: lexical and syntactical.

Malherbe repeatedly criticized lax use of words[30] and he was particularly intransigent regarding words of time, such as "mille tourmens," one of Racan's favorites. In this respect as in many others, Racan obliged during the master's lifetime only to revert to his earlier habits after Malherbe's death. Maynard, on the other hand, seems to have been convinced, switching to more specific concepts of time such as *trente avrils, sept lustres entiers,* and so forth. However, if Malherbe demanded exactness, he forbade pedantry. Thus, Desportes's "Des suppliants Némésis a souci" (Diane I, lvi) warranted "je n'eusse point usé de ce mot: il a du pédant,"[31] and "Lachésis" received the same treatment.[32] Malherbe conceded that the gods of antiquity might be personified, but recoiled before the unnecessary complications involved in calling every nightingale Philomène or the sun Phébus, a sentiment readily echoed by Deimier. By the same token, he felt that mythology was complicated enough without further inventions or erroneous documentation. He blamed Régnier for allowing France to rise into the skies to talk to Jupiter, and Desportes was repeatedly criticized for errors and inventiveness in this realm.[33] Racan could still remember in 1654 a "rude réprimande" he got from Malherbe when he mistook "Lycophron pour la ville où demeuroit Cassandre."[34] Not only did Malherbe condemn innovations and errors in this domain, but he demanded that the poet use his art to clarify "toutes ces légendes indécises qui flottent dans l'incertain du passé."[35] In his mind, the existence of an absurd

[28] Guéret, p. 68.
[29] Ibid., pp. 73–76.
[30] See his *Œuvres,* 4:253, 283.
[31] Ibid., p. 259.
[32] Ibid., p. 467.
[33] Ibid., pp. 424, 250, 254.
[34] *Œuvres complètes,* 1:349.
[35] Brunot, *Doctrine de Malherbe,* p. 172.

legend was no excuse for its perpetuation: "C'est l'opinion de tous les auteurs que les Parthes vainquent en fuyant; mais il n'est rien si ridicule," so why give credence to the myth and use it?[36]

According to his own testimonial, Racan was seventeen years old at the most when he came under Malherbe's influence. Perhaps for this reason his language follows fairly closely the dictates and examples of his mentor. Maynard was not quite as fortunate in this respect. Older by seven years, he had come into contact with literary trends diametrically opposed to those espoused by Malherbe. In his youth he had read profusely the Italian poets, particularly Tasso and the Bernesque. Even after coming under Malherbe's influence, he frequented men such as d'Urfé and Desportes. He was conversant with the ancients and particularly with such poets as Ovid, Statius, and Martial, all known for their penchant to "subtiliser la pensée, à la compliquer, à courir après l'expression rare et alambiquée."[37] Thus, while Maynard rightfully boasted of being "clair et net," he was not always able to rid himself of these earlier influences, as even a cursory glance at his "Vos drogues ne servent de rien" will show.[38] Furthermore, in at least one respect he defended his deviance from Malherbian dogma: "Pour les *Vaillans Heroïques,* i'espere que vous les souffrirez comme on souffre les amoureux passionez, et les sçauans melancoliques." He claimed to be "raui de faire un substantif d'un adjectif," following in so doing the "modernes eloquens."[39]

Maynard worked very hard, as Drouhet demonstrated by studying the manuscripts and diverse versions of poems that Maynard reworked. By his own confession,[40] we know what his creative efforts cost him, and when Flotte suggested that he might have used a "gascon" expression in one of his works, he retorted "ie suis si exact, et crois estre si sçauant en la langue Françoise, que toute l'Academie auroit de la peine à me persuader que ie fusse Gascon. Ie puis pecher contre le bon sens, mais ie croy estre assez intelligent dans la Grammaire."[41] In letter 154, he defends at great length the phrase "calme tes déplaisirs," which Flotte had attacked, and time and time again he justifies the use of certain words or the purity of

---

[36] *Œuvres,* 4:349.
[37] Drouhet, *François Mainard,* p. 450.
[38] For probable source, see Martial, Epigr. 17, Bk. XII.
[39] *Lettres,* letter 214, p. 639; letter 241, p. 726.
[40] Ibid., letter 246, for instance.
[41] Ibid., letter 164, p. 476.

his language, claiming that if his critics were correct, "depuis la mort du bon Malherbe, il ne s'est pas fait dix bons vers en France."[42]

In matters dealing with syntax, Malherbe was far less intransigent. He condemned the obscure or diffuse, and deplored the "vice de la métaphore trop continuée,"[43] but, on the other hand, his own poetry shows a marked penchant for enigmas, antitheses, antonyms, alliterations—in short, the commonplace baggage of the baroque poets. The very early lines

> Lors fuiront de vos yeux les soleils agréables,
> Y laissant pour jamais des étoiles autour,[44]

were far from being the last of their kind, and one of his last poems, the ode "Pour le roi, allant chatier la rébellion des Rochelois," is replete with antitheses and metaphors.

Here, as in the matter of lexical influence, Maynard is more interesting than Racan who, on the whole, followed his master quite closely. Maynard, though convinced of the correctness of Malherbe's ideas (and this is readily seen by his obvious attempts at emulation), was often hampered and sometimes helped by his previous contacts and vastly different temperament. Throughout his career, Maynard was torn between the Malherbian logic and the Italian exuberance. It was perhaps to this inner tension that he owed some of his greatest lines. But it was undoubtedly for this reason that he failed pitifully in the ode, the Malherbian genre par excellence. As Rapin put it in 1675, "l'Ode doit avoir autant de noblesee, d'élevation et d'emportement. . . . Elle demande . . . une imagination hardie. . . . Malherbe et Racan ont eu un genie merveilleux pour l'Ode: Malherbe a plus de pureté dans son air: et Racan plus d'élevation."[45] The odes of Maynard, on the other hand, "are less ambitious than Malherbe's and hug the shores of reflective-satirical themes. The lyrical afflatus, the backbone of character, the sense of rightness and inevitability are lacking from nearly all of the post-

[42] Ibid., letter 235, p. 715. See also letter 262.

[43] Œuvres, 4:261. On this score, it is interesting to note that Racan, who must have been aware of Malherbe's feelings, allowed one of the longest metaphors possible to take up the bulk of his vers de ballet "Pour un marinier."

[44] Ibid., 1:3.

[45] René Rapin, Réflexions sur la poétique (Paris: Barbin, 1675), pp. 157–61.

Malherbian odes. Little remains save the form and the formulae, the outer shell of the ode."[46] Maynard's failings in this genre are especially obvious when we compare his efforts with those of Malherbe on the rare occasions when both treated an analogous subject.

On the occasion of the death of Henry IV, every poet worthy of the name voiced his grief. Maynard's ode, in contrast to Malherbe's *stances,* is sadly lacking in Rapin's desired "élevation et emportement," as witnessed by this stanza:

> *Doncques les Parques obstinées*
> *Ont changé nos plaisirs en dueil,*
> *Et fait arriver les journées*
> *Du grand Henry dans le cercueil.*
> *Donc ceste valeur sans seconde,*
> *Ce Roy qui fit trembler le monde*
> *De l'un jusques à l'autre bout,*
> *A fait par sa fin deplorable*
> *Voir qu'il n'eust rein de perdurable*
> *Que sa gloire que vit partout.*[47]

What little force there is at the beginning of the stanza is rapidly dispelled by the awkward conceit of the last lines, unfortunate remnant of Maynard *italiénisant.* The *stances* of Malherbe, prompted by the same event, but on which the author lavished so much care that he never really finished them, show a far greater sense of the grandiose:

> *Enfin l'ire du ciel, et sa fatale envie,*
> *Dont j'avois repoussé tant d'injustes efforts,*
> *Ont détruit ma fortune, et sans m'ôter la vie*
> *M'ont mis entre les morts.*[48]

The antithesis, terminating in one of the more fortunate *chutes* in all of Malherbe, accentuates rather than detracts from the desired tone set earlier in the stanza.

Maynard's ode "Au roy Henry le Grand" is equally unsuccessful in

[46] Winegarten, *French Lyric Poetry,* p. 109.
[47] *Poésies* (Paris: Garnier, 1927), pp. 266–67.
[48] *Œuvres,* 1:178.

26

capturing the Malherbian elevation. Written in ten-line stanzas, it scarcely contains a single *dizain* that is not marred in one way or another. The last six lines of stanza 24 are a fair indication of the tone of the entire poem:

> *La victoire est toute preste*
> *De te couronner la teste,*
> *Et de voler au devant*
> *De ton indomtable armée,*
> *Qui desja semble affamée*
> *Des richesses du Levant.*

Add to this absurdities such as "nos troubles sont calmes" (stanza 25), ambiguous lines such as these from the same stanza:

> *Nous avons sous ta conduite*
> *En la honte de la fuitte*
> *Assez veu les ennemis,*

chevilles such as "je voy desja, ce me semble," and the picture of a truly bad ode is complete.[49]

Malherbe had a definite affinity for antitheses and conceits, as did all the poets of his time, but as Drouhet points out, most of Maynard's more tasteless endeavors in that realm can be traced directly to the Italians, and particularly to men such as Fulvio Testi, whose

> *Cosi mentre aspettando il cor di sole*
> *Odio il di, bramo notte e mi conviene*
> *Per verdere il mio sol fuggire il sole.*[50]

led to Maynard's epigram to Cloris which closes with these lines:

> *Que mon sort est capricieux!*
> *Pour voir le soleil qui m'éclaire,*
> *Il faut que je ferme les yeux!*[51]

---

[49] *Poésies,* pp. 231–33.
[50] *Rime* (Modena: Cassiani, 1617), p. 37.
[51] *Poésies,* p. 63. It should be noted here that this poem, however precious

Maynard repeatedly tried to imitate the Italians on themes such as "La belle matineuse." In fact, one gets the impression that with a minimum of creativity and invention, he was copying anything that was "à la mode." Whenever Maynard is precious, he is trite and commonplace; his originality must be sought elsewhere, and here again, one must agree with Drouhet, who saw in this phenomenon merely one more proof of the fact that "la nature de son talent" was fundamentally "robuste et sain,"[52] and incapable of adapting the Italians creatively.

If the worst examples of misused antitheses and conceits can be traced to the Italians, Maynard's more fortunate attempts can easily be traced to a willful imitation of his master. Here, in fact, Malherbe is only too often outdone, not only in inventiveness but also in structural perfection. An example of this can be found in the 1607 *Parnasse*, which contains three versions of "Victoire de la constance," one anonymous, one by Malherbe, and one by Maynard. While it is true that Maynard demonstrates, in this poem as elsewhere, that "il ne s'est défait que fort lentement d'un certain nombre d'images et de procédés de style et il n'a jamais pu complètement renoncer à un fonds d'idées et de sentiments propres aux ouvrages de ses anciens modèles,"[53] it is obvious that here the pupil was beginning to profit from the lessons of the master. The second stanza,

> *Je tiens ceste beauté qui n'a point de seconde,*
> *De qui les blonds cheveux arrestent tout le monde,*
> *Car quelle ame assez forte a jamais evité*
> *Ceste captivité?*[54]

while not as good as Saint-Amant's on the same subject, nor equal to Tristan's "Les cheveux blonds," is far superior to Malherbe's example, which only exudes the irascibility of the older man:

---

it may seem to us, was prompted by genuine feelings for a real woman. (See Drouhet, *François Mainard*, p. 352, and Pierre Lafenestre, "François Maynard," *RHLF* 10 (1903): 457–77.) For a thorough discussion of such uses of precious devices, see Philip A. Wadsworth, "Artifice and Sincerity in the Poetry of Tristan L'Hermite," *MLN* 74 (May 1959): 422–30.

[52] *François Mainard*, p. 453.

[53] Ibid., p. 370.

[54] *Poésies*, p. 208.

Enfin cette beauté m'a la place rendue
Que d'un siége si long elle avoit défendue;
Mes vainqueurs sont vaincus; ceux qui m'ont fait la loi
La reçoivent de moi.[55]

When Malherbe speaks of love, he is either imperious or "il débite les fadeurs de Bertaut ou réédite celles de Desportes ou de Régnier."[56] In this domain, the author of "La Belle vieille" is patently superior. It is surprising that in the realm of structure, Malherbe, so fond of symmetry, is again outdone by Maynard. In "Alcandre plaint la captivité de sa maîtresse," Malherbe seldom rises above the commonplace; witness the first stanza:

Que d'épines, Amour, accompagnent tes roses!
Que d'une aveugle erreur tu laisses toutes choses
A la merci du sort!
Qu'en tes prospérités à bon droit on soupire!
Et qu'il est malaisé de vivre en ton empire,
Sans désirer la mort![57]

Nor can this be excused by pointing to the date, for the ode "Pour le roi, allant chatier la rébellion des Rochelois," one of Malherbe's last efforts, shows little progression in symmetry, though the images are somewhat more forceful:

Je suis vaincu du temps; je cède à ses outrages,
Mon esprit seulement exempt de sa rigueur
A de quoi témoigner en ses derniers ouvrages
Sa première vigueur.[58]

Maynard seemed fascinated by the possibilities of antitheses and strove for perfection in their symmetrical statement. Most frequently, this perfection is found in the alexandrine, where each half of the antithesis is perfectly

---

[55] *Œuvres,* 1:28.

[56] Drouhet, *François Mainard,* p. 399.

[57] *Œuvres,* 1:158. There is an important variant, ending the second line with "tu conduis toutes choses."

[58] Ibid., p. 283.

contained in each hemistich—"La première clarté de mon dernier soleil" —a process further enhanced by the separation of the line into two separate syntactical units:

> *Tes désordres sont grands. Tes vertus sont petites.*
> *De blâmer ta rigueur, et de loüer ma foy.*
> *La vie est un grand bien, mais ce bien me tourmente;*
> *Mais que dis-je ennemy? Je suis amoureux d'elle.*

The last two examples, coming from one sonnet that contains several other examples, show this predilection verging on the abusive.[59]

Critics have repeatedly tried to see in Malherbe the ancestor of La Fontaine, and in the former's heterometric poetry the antecedent of the latter's free verse. Miss Winegarten[60] thinks that Favereau rather than Malherbe is to be credited with the rebirth of the trend, but this is perhaps giving too much credit to too minor an author. Still, she is right in denying Malherbe all credit on this score. If Malherbe's taste ran to heterometric stanzas, this was in no way detrimental to symmetry, for the schema was flawlessly repeated from stanza to stanza, since Malherbe was constantly aware of the musical possibilities of his poetry. It is from this point of view—the musical—that I would first like to look at some of Malherbe's basic poetic structures to ascertain the nature and degree of Racan's and Maynard's faithfulness to the dicta of the master.

Many of Malherbe's poems, we must remember, were intended for a specific air. Such is the case of the *stances* "Que n'êtes-vous lassées"[61] which he mentions in 1610 in a letter to Peiresc as "la chanson pour laquelle je vous avois prié de m'envoyer un certain air sur lequel j'ai pris ma mesure."[62] This song, reproduced by Verchaly,[63] shows a remarkably close union of words and music. One of the most popular songs of the century, set by many composers,[64] is his "Ils s'en vont, ces roys de ma vie."[65]

---

[59] *Poésies*, pp. 45, 42, 142, 293.

[60] "Jacques Favereau," p. 34.

[61] *Œuvres*, 1:162–65.

[62] Ibid., 3:142.

[63] André Verchaly, *Airs de cour pour voix et luth* (1603–1643) (Paris: Heugel, 1961), pp. 42–43.

[64] Ibid., pp. l–li.

[65] *Œuvres*, 1:221–22.

Its three quatrains and four-line refrain, although heterometric (8–5–8–5 and 7–7–7–6 respectively), demonstrate a form rigorously maintained from stanza to stanza and very rich crossed rhyme (feminine-masculine-feminine-masculine), the music emphasizing the regularity thus obtained.

On the union of words and music, one further point must be made: Malherbe was equally adept at writing verse intended as *récit* and as the more popular *air de cour*. From the literary point of view, the difference is obvious: while the song may have free verse, the *récit* should not.[66] Printed in the first Bataille anthology,[67] "Donc cette merveille des cieux" is a perfect example of Malherbian lyricism, uniting word and note and showing a close cooperation of musician and author: "La déclamation assez précise et qui veut se rapprocher du parlé naturel se développe dans un ambitus restraint (sixte mineure) et, à l'intérieur de chaque vers, use de notes répétées ou d'intervalles conjoints que l'ornementation enrichit sans briser la ligne mélodique. . . . Quelques notes sont prolongées pour atténuer la véhémence de la déclamation."[68] Semi-pauses between lines 1 and 2, 2 and 3, and 5 and 6 reinforce the syntactical breaks, while between lines 3 and 4 the accompaniment goes on as the vocal line holds, emphasizing the median break.[69] This distinction between *récits* and *airs* is nowhere more obvious than in the ballet, where the former are usually regular and declamatory in tone while the latter are almost invariably heterometric, with a set pattern repeated from stanza to stanza.

It is when writing poetry to be set to music that Maynard and Racan show themselves to be most creative within the framework of Malherbian discipline. In this area, in fact, the master learned from the pupils: "Au commencement que M. de Malherbe vint à la cour, qui fut en 1605, . . . il n'observoit pas encore de faire une pause au troisième vers des stances de six. . . . Il demeura toujours en cette negligence pendant la vie de Henry le Grand, . . . et je ne sçais s'il n'a point encore continué cette mesme negligence jusques en 1612, . . . tant y a que le premier qui s'aperçut que cette observation estoit nécessaire pour la perfection des

[66] See "Que n'êtes-vous lassée," written ca. 1609, and compare it with "Donc cette merveille des cieux" of the same date.

[67] *Premier livre d'airs* (Paris: Ballard, 1611).

[68] Verchaly, *Airs de cour*, p. xl.

[69] An equally good example is "Complices de ma servitude" (*Œuvres*, 1:174–77), first printed with music in the fourth Bataille anthology (Paris: Ballard, 1613) and reproduced by Verchaly, *Airs de cour*, pp. 32–33.

31

stances de six fut Maynard."[70] Malherbe was convinced immediately, but, as we shall see shortly, perhaps without comprehending fully the essence of the rule. It is distinctly possible that he saw in it little more than another difficulty to vanquish. As Fromilhague has shown, Malherbe did not like involved or complicated developments and used the stanza to express himself even in his *vers suivis,* which he organized into groups by means of syntactical structures and punctuation.[71] As Racan told Ménage in a letter dated 1654, "M. de Malherbe m'ordonnoit de fermer [le sens] de quatre en quatre, même en ma pastorale. Cette grande justesse me sembloit ridicule quand j'estois obligé de décrire des passions violentes et désordonnées."[72] In his life of Malherbe, Racan adds that "M. de Malherbe vouloit aussi que les elegies eussent un sens parfait de quatre en quatre vers, mesme de deux en deux, s'il se pouvoit, à quoy jamais Racan ne s'est accordé."[73] This is undoubtedly because Racan was the first to realize that the pauses demanded by Maynard were dictated not by a love for precision but by musical limitations: "D'abord Racan, qui jouoit un peu du luth et aimoit la musique, se rendit en faveur des musiciens, qui ne pouvoient faire leur reprise aux stances de six, s'il n'y avoit un arrêt au troisième vers. Mais quand M. de Malherbe et Mainard voulurent qu'aux stances de dix, outre l'arrêt du quatrième vers, on en fit encore un au septième, Racan s'y opposa, et ne l'a jamais presque observé. Sa raison estoit que les stances de dix ne se chantent presque jamais, et que quand elles se chanteroient on ne les chanteroit pas en trois reprises."[74] Thus Maynard consistently divided his ten-line stanzas 4–3–3, even those obviously not meant to be set to music (Odes to Flotte, to Charles de Noailles) while Racan remained true to his decision.

Even a cursory look at the strophic structure of the sestet shows the extent of the basic misunderstanding between master and pupils. Malherbe, sensing perhaps that the isometric quatrains and sestets of alexandrines were ill suited to the *air de cour,* hardly ever used the sestet. Racan, on the other hand, saw its potential for majestic lyricism and used it quite frequently, especially in his later psalms. This does not mean that

[70] Racan, *Œuvres complètes,* 1:283.
[71] *Technique,* pp. 181–90.
[72] *Œuvres complètes,* 1:356.
[73] Ibid., 1:283.
[74] Ibid.

Racan was averse to employing the heterometric sestet; he used it nearly one hundred times, in fact, and to great advantage. But the nature of the median break and its veritable reason seem to have bewildered Malherbe, especially where shorter lines were concerned, and "à partir du moment où Maynard a fait accepter à son maître la nécessité de cette césure dans le sizain en mètres brefs . . . Malherbe abandonne cette forme strophique."[75] Both Maynard and Racan not only saw the value of the break, but understood that at times it must be disregarded. Racan's "Cruel tyran de mes désirs"[76] was one of the most popular songs of the seventeenth century if one can judge by the frequency with which it was anthologized. Its thirty-six lines are divided into heterometric sestets (8–8–8–8–8–12). In most of the musical settings, as is the case in the Boesset version,[77] the second half of the first hemistich of the alexandrine is repeated—"Je conte les ennuis, les ennuis que je souffre en aymant"—giving this last line an extraordinary length. Any 3–3 division would fail to bring the stanzas into the usual balance, and Racan avoids it. The six stanzas are divided 4–2, 2–2–2, 2–2–2, 2–2–2, 1–1–2–2, and 2–2–2, the middle two stanzas being omitted from the Boesset setting. The results are felicitous, yet Racan remained, as a whole, faithful to Maynard's suggestion, though he preferred the 3–1–2 break to the 3–2–1 schema favored by Maynard and Malherbe, who both saw that the six-beat line is naturally linked to the longer preceding one,[78] especially in the popular 12–6–12 tercet.

It is not surprising, therefore, that Maynard showed the greatest originality in the adaptation of the median break. In early examples, he shows a greater affinity for the syntax of Bertaut than for that of Malherbe. Thus, "Regrets d'une grande dame," written sometime before 1607, is made up of sixteen sestets (12–12–6–12–12–6), six of which are composed of a single syntactical unit. In "Asseurance de fermeté," of the same vintage, five of the ten stanzas of alexandrines are of a single sentence each. Of the twenty-six stanzas, eleven have only one sentence and six have no median caesura whatsoever. But by 1612, he has changed radically, and "Urgande à la Reyne" has only one irregular stanza:

[75] Fromilhague, *Technique,* p. 372.

[76] *Poésies* (Paris: Hachette, 1930), 1:156–58.

[77] Verchaly, *Airs de cour,* pp. 140–41.

[78] For a statistical analysis of these predilections, see Fromilhague, *Technique,* pp. 306–7.

La gloire des combats que je leur ay veu faire
A bien desja remply l'un et l'autre Hemisphere;
Mais si de vos beaux yeux, ils ont un doux accueil,
D'acquerir . . .[79]

The main break follows line 2, with a secondary median one. However, while the other stanzas are more regular, only four of the ten stanzas are broken by more than a comma. Such was no longer the case by 1615, when Maynard wrote two items destined for a royal ballet. Both "La Nuict" and "Pour le ballet de la Princesse d'Espagne" heed the strict interpretation of the new rule, with only one stanza in each poem having a 4–2 break. Thereafter, deviations from the rule are rarer still, and nearly invariably fall into the category of the drinking song.

Speaking of the court song "N'est-ce pas trop de cruauté," Mme Maurice-Amour states that "les quatre couplets qui la composent accusent rigoureusement, pour chaque vers, le même rythme en vue de l'ajustement à une diction musicale tantôt syllabique, tantôt vocalisée, . . . et pour chaque sizain, la même pause au troisième vers permettant la reprise de chacun des deux motifs—A et B—notée sur la plupart des airs de cour de ce temps."[80] The second part of this statement deserves several comments. First, this is not true, since the third stanza has no pause at all, which should not surprise in view of the fact that the song antedates 1607. The second and more important comment deals with the thematic division of the stanza. It seems to me that the syntactical division of the second tercet was dictated as much by the nature of the air as by any other consideration. It is when writing drinking songs that Maynard most frequently uses the 3–1–2 schema, or even breaks his rule altogether by using the old 4–2 or 2–2–2 break. This is undoubtedly because such a format "suggère le schéma A-BB d'un air à boire où la reprise se fait sur les deux derniers vers en refrain."[81] Thus the very popular *air de cour* "Que d'espines, Amour . . ." remains strictly within what Fromilhague calls "les conditions de l'expression lyrique,"[82] showing a perfect union of word and music within the framework of the 3–3 break,[83] while the lively drinking song

[79] *Poésies,* p. 260.
[80] "Musique et poésie au temps de Malherbe," RHLF 56 (1956): 212.
[81] Ibid., p. 213.
[82] *Technique,* p. 304.

"Amy des morceaux delicats," a 1646 effort, is divided 2–2–2. By the same token, the earlier (ca. 1627) and more famous song "Je ne puis souffrir les esprits" is written in heterometric sestets of which the first four lines form either one or two units, the last two lines being the refrain

Je veux mourir au cabaret
Entre le blanc et le clairet.

Either of these drinking songs, having found a "condition de l'expression lyrique" proper to its genre, is eminently more singable than Racan's famous "Ode bachique," written about 1614 and divided 3–3.

As I have already stated, Racan's purpose in submitting to Maynard's suggestion was to achieve a more lyrical sestet. As he said himself, he refused to follow his colleagues when they deemed it proper to extend this rule to other stanzas. This question may seem minor, but it is not, for it goes to the heart of the basic difference between Racan on the one hand and Maynard and Malherbe on the other. Racan, sensing that the ten-line stanza was not ideal for musical setting, rejected a rule which he felt was meant primarily to help the singers. Malherbe seems to have realized immediately that Maynard was less concerned with musicianship than with musicality. Both had seen that the conventional structures were disruptive in nature and seldom lyrical. This is undoubtedly why Malherbe shunned one of the most popular forms of his day, heterometric ten-line stanzas with alexandrines. He fully realized that alternating lines resulted in chaos while any other alternative disrupted the flow of the *dizain,* witness this example from the pen of Chapelain:

Grand Richelieu, de qui la gloire,
Par tant de rayons éclatants,
De la nuit de ces derniers temps
Eclaircit l'ombre la plus noire;
Puissant esprit, dont les travaux
Ont borné le cours de nos maux,
Accompli nos souhaits, passé notre espérance,
Tes celestes vertus, tes faits prodigieux,

---

[83] For a musical analysis, see Verchaly, *Airs de cour,* pp. lii–lv; for the poetry, see Fromilhague, *Technique,* pp. 231–33.

Font revoir en nos joirs, pour le bien de la France,
La force des héros et la bonté des dieux.[84]

This poem, to which I shall return when dealing with the poetry of Chapelain, breaks all Malherbe's rules. What concerns us here is the rule dealing with the division of the ten-line stanza. The 6–4 division, a reversal of the 4–6 pattern, is acceptable, but the 4–2 division of the first part is not. The entire poem demonstrates the main reason why Malherbe avoided the form: the first six lines are octosyllabic, the last four alexandrines, and no intonation or musicianship can make a unified stanza of the ten-line total. In the ten-line stanza, be it heterometric or not, Malherbe and Maynard demanded a 4–3–3 break for the sake of a more harmonic structure. Racan rebelled, but the epithet of "heretic" must have rankled, for he used the stanza less and less during the lifetime of the master. From 1615 to 1620, Racan used it rather frequently, always dividing it 4–6, but with a median break in the second half only half of the time.[85] From 1620 to the death of Malherbe, he used it only once in his nonreligious poetry, for the "Ode à M. de Balzac." When, after 1628, Racan again used the ten-line stanza, he adhered to the ideas of Maynard, breaking the stanzas 4–3–3, but by then Maynard had gone beyond, demanding not only a secondary break, but that this break be as strong as the first. In other words, Maynard now used three distinct and separate syntactical groups.[86] This Racan refused to follow, either in the religious poems, which often still show a 4–2 break:

> *Son regard calme les orages;*
> *Il fait les montagnes mouvoir,*
> *Et donne à la mer des rivages*
> *Qui la tiennent dans son devoir.*
> *Les plus durs rochers de la terre*
> *Sont de cire pour son tonnerre.*
> *Egalement il a soûmis*
> *L'Assyrien et le Barbare,*

[84] Maurice Allem, ed., *Anthologie poétique française: XVIIe siècle* (Paris: Garnier, 1914), 1:261–62.

[85] See Fromilhague, *Technique*, p. 436.

[86] See his two odes to Richelieu, 1630 and 1633.

Et contre tous il se declare
L'ennemi de nos ennemis.[87]

or in the secular ones, where the secondary break is often very weak:

Dunquerque contre ta puissance
La prend en vain pour sa defense,
Neptune l'effroy des vaisseaux
Tremble aux éclats de ton tonnerre,
Et se resserrant dans les eaux
T'abandonne toute la terre.[88]

Malherbe obviously disliked the isometric *dizain* almost as much as the heterometric ten-line stanza, and shunned it after 1614. According to Fromilhague, this was because "il redoutait de ne pouvoir la porter à la perfection qu'il exigeait pour elle."[89] Such a hypothesis would certainly not contradict what we know of a wise Malherbe conscious of his weaknesses, but I wonder if he did not see some more basic flaw in the structure of the stanza itself. He obviously agreed with Maynard when the latter saw the need for a 4–3–3 break. But by 1614, he may readily have realized that Racan's objections were not without logic. Racan had seen that the *dizain* was simply not lyrical: heterometric, it was chaotic; isometric, it tended to become heavy. Frequent breaks, far from remedying the situation, merely hamper the flow of the stanza. Even Flotte spoke against this tendency of Maynard toward "vers détachés," and although Maynard defended himself vigorously, he convinced no one: "C'est une façon que i'affecte, et contre laquelle il y auroit bien de la peine à me faire reuolter: deuant toute la terre ie soustiendrai que c'est la bonne façon d'escrire."[90] For once, Malherbe was less stubborn. As Fromilhague states, he must have sensed that while a short heterometric stanza is full of movement, a long one "risque de tourner au désordre et de rendre difficile à saisir le rythme d'ensemble du dizain."[91]

[87] "Cantique de Judith," *Œuvres complètes*, 2:394.
[88] "Ode au Roy," *Poésies*, 1:281.
[89] *Technique*, p. 440.
[90] *Lettres*, letter 176, p. 524.
[91] *Technique*, p. 171. It is interesting to note that one of Malherbe's

Until Malherbe's time, isometric quatrains were the rage, especially those using alexandrines. Driven perhaps by his contrary spirit, Malherbe disdained the form in favor of the heterometric $a\,b\,a\,b$, 12–12–12–6 quatrain, least used until then.[92] The entire seventeenth century followed suit, possibly convinced by the quality of the master's efforts. Generally speaking, Maynard and Racan heeded Malherbe's strictures, but failed by and large to follow him in his new tendencies. Racan used the isometric quatrain of alexandrines only once in his profane poetry while Maynard wrote four of his longer poems in that form. However, many of Racan's religious poems are in alexandrine quatrains, as are at least a dozen of Maynard's epigrams. Furthermore, both Maynard and Racan shunned the alexandrine-based heterometric quatrain. Maynard used it only twice, and both poems probably antedate his liaison with Malherbe. On the other hand, both repeatedly used the isometric quatrain of less than alexandrine length, especially for their more bantering verse. Malherbe disdained this shorter form entirely, probably because of his aversion for syntactical groups carrying over more than two lines. Indeed, shorter lines make it difficult to complete a sentence within one or even two lines, and this is why Maynard and Racan were at times guilty of badly dividing a quatrain.[93]

Much has been said about Malherbe's rhyme schemes, but not until Fromilhague's study did it become plain that here also two forces were at work. One was obviously Malherbe's love of perfection, his elation at besting the difficulty itself; the other was once again one of musical values. This latter point was diagnosed by Maurice-Amour, who pointed out that if Malherbe preferred masculine rhyme schemes it was undoubtedly because these were "spécialement propres à l'intelligibilité d'un texte chanté."[94] This is true even for the ten-line stanza, where Malherbe almost invariably used an $a\,b\,a\,b\,c\,c\,d\,e\,e\,d$ scheme, b and d being masculine.[95]

---

favorite odes was his "Sur le voyage de Sedan," written in heptasyllabic *dizains*. "De la musique avant toute chose"?

[92] Fromilhague, *Technique*, pp. 140–46.

[93] Maynard, *Poésies*, p. 200; Racan, *Poésies*, 1:102.

[94] "Musique et poésie," p. 206.

[95] See "Pour les pairs de France," *Œuvres*, 1:65–67; "Sur l'attentat commis en la personne de Henri le Grand," ibid., 1:75–83. Only one long poem in isometric *dizains* uses an $a\,b\,b\,a\,c\,c\,d\,e\,d\,e$ scheme, the "Ode à Bellegarde," ibid., 1:107–17.

In this respect, while Racan followed the master quite closely, Maynard did not.

Most of Malherbe's rules of versification as derived from a study of his own poems show him to love the difficult and shun the obvious and the facile. On this score, Maynard was an apt and faithful pupil. His desire for what he called "netteté" is seen not only in his poems but also in his personal correspondence with friends such as Flotte, who was also his most severe critic. Maynard, as we have seen, often rebelled against Flotte's criticism, but his desire for perfection made him submit: "Ce que mon esprit commence, vostre censure l'acheue."[96] Having sent some poems to his friend, he admonished "ne les publiez pas iusques à ce que ie leur aurai donné vne forme raisonnable, et que vostre sage critique sera en quelque façon satisfaite," for only with "profonde meditation" and "longue patience" can beauty be reached. He constantly spoke of "limer," of hard work,[97] and was especially conscious of the difficulties presented by the need for perfect rhymes: "La servitude de la rime a fait des chevilles par tout. Ie n'en exempte pas mesme le bon Malherbe, il est si remply de bourre, qu'en certains endroits il en est insupportable."[98] It was undoubtedly because of this desire for perfection that Maynard suppressed so many of his poems. The Toulouse manuscripts are filled with poems that are badly divided and filled with padding, and whose rhyme schemes are definitely un-Malherbian.[99] Drouhet has amply shown not only that Maynard was a harsh judge of his own work but that he reworked his poetry constantly, and in analyses such as the one of "Regrets d'une grand'dame sur la mort de son serviteur," he proved by comparing various versions that Maynard had indeed been influenced by Malherbe.

For the sestet, Malherbe used at times the *a a b c c b* rhyme scheme, but much more frequently the previously shunned *a a b c b c*, a format adopted not only by Maynard but by the majority of the poets of the century, including Tristan, Théophile de Viau, and Malleville. But if Maynard can be called Malherbian, it is not because of the adoption of a

---

[96] *Lettres*, letter 231, p. 699.

[97] Ibid., letter 231, pp. 699–700; see also letters 246, 254, 276, and others.

[98] Ibid., letter 213, p. 634.

[99] G. Clavelier, "Œuvres inédites de François Maynard," 20 (1908): 225–36, 392–401, 500–511; 21 (1909): 77–85, 338–50. One particular poem of three *dizains* is divided 4–2–2–2, 4–2–1–3, and 6–1–3, with rhymes as unsatisfactory as *dequoy-ches toy*.

particular rhyme scheme, for in this respect he was frequently recalcitrant. In his treatment of sonnets, for example, Maynard was quite independent. Malherbe had been asked by Racan and Colomby to give up writing "licencieux," that is, irregular sonnets. For spite, he continued until his pupils stopped asking, then, when the whole circle grew tired of them, gave them up.[100] As Racan put it, "n'y a eu que Mainard, de tous ses ecoliers, qui a continué à en faire jusqu'à sa mort."[101] It should be said, however, that Maynard was faithful to the strictures of the master during the latter's lifetime. The six sonnets definitely attributed to that period are regular, but "tous ses sonnets publiés après 1628 sont non seulement irréguliers—encore pouvait-il sur ce point se prévaloir des exemples de son maître—mais féminins en grande majorité: trente-trois fois sur cinquante-quatre."[102]

If Maynard is to be called Malherbian, it must be because of his close adherence to the disciplined concept of rich rhymes. On the matter of polysyllabics with mute final syllables, Maynard adhered more and more rigidly to Malherbe's ideas while Racan seems to have drifted further and further from them.[103] By the same token, masculine polysyllables without the *consonne d'appui* are rare in Maynard,[104] and even these few violations have a precedent in Malherbe, who had problems with these words (*soleil, amour, toujours*). When dealing with monosyllables, Maynard is exceptionally rich, but this is a trend already discernible in his earlier poems. The *ame-flame* rhyme, for instance, forbidden and shunned by Malherbe, can be found only once, and that in Maynard's very early "Bien que vos yeux brulent mon ame," a work included in the 1607 *Parnasse*. Following in the footsteps of Malherbe, Maynard eventually limits such rhymes to the *ame-blasme, ame-infame,* and *blasme-infame* patterns. He is equally rigid in his use of the *-ème* rhymes, and if there is some freedom in his adoption of *ace-asse* and *esse-aisse* rhymes, it comes for the most part after 1628.[105]

[100] Fromilhague, *Technique*, p. 179.

[101] *Œuvres complètes*, 1:264.

[102] Fromilhague, *Technique*, pp. 178–79.

[103] Ibid., p. 530.

[104] Twenty-five out of 2,100, according to Fromilhague, *Technique*, p. 462.

[105] Ibid., p. 558. This raises another question, one that cannot be resolved:

While Maynard's practice leaves in doubt the nature of his own personal convictions, Racan's does not. As he had done when dealing with strophic composition, Racan carefully chose among Malherbe's many strictures dealing with rhymes, following some, disregarding others. Here, as in the case of the previously examined problems, he does not show caprice or iconoclasm for its own sake. Rather, he seems to have been motivated by a higher ideal, "la richesse d'expression du poète et de son art,"[106] disregarding those tenets which had been motivated by Malherbe's love of the *difficulté vaincue*, following those that contributed to the richness of his art. Thus, in dealing with the rhyme patterns of sonnets, Racan was a faithful student of Malherbe. Of his seventeen regular sonnets—*a b b a a b b a c c d e d e*—twelve are strictly Malherbian, nine masculine, and only three feminine.[107] On the other hand, one look at the fullness of his rhymes will show that he was not convinced by Malherbe's thoughts on the need for *rimes riches*. Malherbe was particularly strict, both in his own usage and in his criticism, when dealing with tonic vowels. After "Les larmes de Saint-Pierre" he shuns the rhyming of long and short [a] (*fasche-sache*), never uses and always censures rhymes that not only mix length of vowel but change the spelling (*ame-femme*), using *ame* only with *blasme*, and *flamme* with *épigramme*.[108] Racan violated all of these rules, and was particularly lax when dealing with rhymes rich to the eye, rhyming *près* with *regrets*, *Seine* with *plaine*, *nous* with *jaloux*, *estonnée* with *immoler*, *flame* with *ame*, and so forth. This last rhyme, although particularly censured by Malherbe, was used by Racan no less than eleven times.[109] Such evidence of laxness is ubiquitous, and only in his use of masculine polysyllables with *consonnes d'appui* did Racan follow Malherbe closely. In this respect, in fact, he outdid Maynard, failing to accord the *consonne d'appui* only 21 of 2,700 times.[110] It is apparent, then, that when convinced of the

---

how much of Malherbe's influence was personal and how much of Maynard's obedience was due to lack of poetic integrity?

[106] Ibid., p. 492.

[107] Ibid., p. 178.

[108] Each [m] had its value in these words, the first one making the [a] nasal.

[109] Fromilhague, *Technique*, p. 556.

[110] Ibid., p. 462.

validity of a rule, Racan could be as Malherbian as anyone. When such a conviction was lacking, not even the presence of the master could deter him from his "heresy."

Of all Malherbe's students, the one who benefited least was undoubtedly du Moustier. Not even Yvrande, an equally mediocre pupil, author of the priapic "De ce vit que tu vois" included in the 1618 and 1619 editions of the *Cabinet satyrique,* violated as many Malherbian precepts. Musically inclined, du Moustier favored the heptasyllabic line, the form of Malherbe's favorite ode, "Sur le voyage de Sedan." It is this predilection for relatively short lines, coupled with his desire for rich rhymes, that ruined du Moustier's poetry. These two factors necessitated frequent inversions and syntactical rearrangements, some of which led to a most tortuous syntax, as can readily be seen in the second stanza of "Sur la mort de . . . Henri le Grand":

> *Peuples noyons nous en pleurs*
> *Pour témoigner nos douleurs*
> *En l'incomparable perte*
> *De Henry, dont la vertu*
> *De son Empire abbatu*
> *La gloire avait recouverte.*

As might be expected in heptasyllabic lines, there is no strict delineation, no caesuras, and—a fact that should not surprise in view of the date—no median break.

Ironically, the musicality inherent in the heptasyllabic line was irrevocably destroyed by the syntax, and the rhymes so obviously sought were seldom satisfactory. Reworked for the 1615 *Délices,* the above-mentioned poem renamed "Sur le Trépas de . . . ," was not improved. In fact the rhymes deteriorated:

> *Enfin le ciel en courroux*
> *A donc lancé dessus nous*
> *Son plus grand coup de Tonnerre,*
> *Et mis notre espoir à bas,*
> *Par le tragique trépas*
> *Du plus grand roi de la terre.*[111]

The sonnet on the same subject breaks every rule of Malherbian poetry, and its tercets verge on the ridiculous:

> *Mais Dieu pour nous montrer que tout pouvoir humain*
> *N'est jamais assuré si ce n'est par sa main,*
> *Nous ôtant ce bon roi nous a fait reconnaître,*
>
> *Qu'en ce triste accident aurons recours à lui*
> *De notre jeune roi il s'est rendu l'appui*
> *Et contre nos discours en biens il nous fait croire.*[112]

His heptasyllabic "Consolation a un ami sur la mort de son frère" is not only as brutal as Malherbe's "Consolation," but fails to redeem itself in any manner:

> *Mais quoi, tant de vains efforts*
> *Ne ressuscitent les morts.*[113]

Du Moustier's syntax further deteriorates in his ode on the crowning of Louis XIII, and reaches its nadir in his "Elégie à Orante" in alexandrine *vers suivis,* a form despised by Malherbe. The rhymes are barely passable (*trahi-haï*), enjambments are plentiful, and lines such as "Vous prie si votre œil ingrat le peut permettre"[114] explain why Malherbe did not consider du Moustier among his best *écoliers.*

Malherbe acknowledged only six such *écoliers,* but there were many other poets who saw in him the leader of a new trend that they too wished to endorse. These admirers fall into two categories: those who failed to grasp the details of his art, and those who, not totally convinced, were not sufficiently orthodox to be admitted into the inner sanctum. Rosset is a perfect example of the first, Deimier of the second.

François de Rosset showed little poetic talent in his attempts to be Malherbian. His best effort is probably his ode "A M. de Silery," a 350-

---

[111] P. 921.

[112] Ibid., p. 929. Though a slight modification of the punctuation would help, the poem is obviously beyond redemption.

[113] Ibid., p. 931.

[114] *Délices* (1620), p. 702.

line poem in octosyllabic ten-line stanzas. The rhymes are, for the most part, fairly rich, enjambments rare and seldom drastic. There is no hiatus, and archaisms are relatively few and marginal:

> *Qu'un autre ébloui d'une pompe*
> *Perde le meilleur de ses ans,*
> *Après la vanité qui trompe*
> *D'un faux espoir les courtisans.*[115]

The rhyme scheme—*a b a b c c d e e d*—is that used by Malherbe at that time (1609), but the inversion cited above is detrimental to the flow of the thought, which is also hampered by a rather unfortunate choice of words. Rosset's *Paranymphes* is a later and more modern attempt. It includes an ode to Malherbe, thirteen ten-line stanzas of abject admiration totally devoid of either lyricism or discipline that are characterized by lexical errors and clumsy constructions. Enjambments abound even between stanzas, lines are frequently padded and nearly always clumsy. One can readily imagine Malherbe's reaction to such dubious praise.

Deimier's career, as poet and as critic, can be divided into three main periods: the early Provençal, the early Parisian, and the late Parisian. The first period is marked mainly by "la facilité et une abondance extrème, l'accumulation de recherches de style baroque, un archaïsme accusé":[116]

> *Beau Sein, doux paradis de fleurs blanche-pourprines,*
> . . . .
> *Beau Sein, tu es si beau de beautez si tres belles,*
> *Que les doux Amoureaux de leurs mignardes ailes*
> *T'esventillent tousjours d'un doux esventement.*[117]

The only saving grace is that Deimier soon saw the error of his ways. He came to Paris in 1605 and soon repudiated his earlier production: "J'ay tousjours détesté l'usage de ces permissions poétiques, et n'estoit que du

---

[115] *Nouveau recueil des plus beaux vers de ce temps* (Paris: Toussainct du Bray, 1609), p. 438.

[116] Pierre Colotte, "Malherbe et Deimier," in *IVe centenaire de la naissance de Malherbe* (Gap: Orphrys, 1956), p. 79.

[117] Cited by Fromilhague, *Vie de Malherbe*, p. 163.

temps que j'estois en Provence, on me disoit que cela se pratiquoit à la Cour chez ceux qui escrivoyent le mieux, et que cest avis m'estoit comme confirmé par les termes licencieux que je lisois dans les œuvres de Ronsard, . . . je n'en eux jamais usé."[118] However, he was far from Malherbian at that time, or at least not "en possession de la doctrine de Malherbe, connue de l'intérieur, comprise, acceptée, assimilée."[119] Though he dared anyone to find "un traict de licence"[120] in his *Printemps des lettres amoureuses* (1607) or in his *Amoureuses destinées* (1608), his poems are still marked by the influence of Ronsard, Desportes, du Bartas, and the Italians:

> *Clair astre de beauté qui des beautés plus belles,*
> *Portez parfaitement les graces immortelles,*
> *Et de qui le mérite étonne l'univers.*
> *O beauté! qui du Ciel nous montrez les merveilles!*
> *Dois-je pas en aimant vos beautés nonpareilles,*
> *Aussi bien que mon cœur vous dédier des vers?*[121]

Deimier's conversion took place about 1608. In his novel of that year, *Lysimont et Clitye,* he followed a poem with the remark that it was good enough to satisfy his harshest censors on the grounds that it followed the five rules required by them: "la mesure ou juste quantité des syllabes qui sont deuës aux vers, la richesse des rimes, l'elegance et la douceur des paroles, la bonté du langage, et la valeur et propriété des raisons."[122] Two years later, in his *Académie,* he demanded these very qualities of the poet, adding only invention and clarity.[123] There is no doubt that "Deimier s'est d'abord rallié pleinement à Malherbe et à son rationalisme poétique, mais . . . il n'a pu suivre sa doctrine dans le durcissement, les renchérissements, la rigidité de plus en plus marquée que l'on peut constater dans son évolution."[124]

The basic tone of Deimier's *Académie* is conciliatory. He is willing to

---

[118] *Académie de l'art poétique* (Paris: Bordeaulx, 1610), p. 167.
[119] Colotte, "Malherbe et Deimier," p. 81.
[120] *Académie,* p. 168.
[121] *Parnasse* (1607), 1:308v°.
[122] Cited by Colotte, *Pierre de Deimier,* p. 33.
[123] Pp. 20–21.
[124] Colotte, "Malherbe et Deimier," p. 87.

follow Malherbe in all ways where reason is involved, but rebels at the thought of gratuitous refinements and "superstitions."[125] He repeatedly points out that these "superstitions" are contrary to the spirit of the new trend, and that a good poet *must* reject them. Obviously, Deimier foresaw "les dangers pour la poésie d'un rationalisme outrancier et exclusif."[126] This in no way makes an *arriéré* of him. Like Malherbe, he refused to acknowledge the supremacy of the ancients: "Hormis en la doctrine de la foy, il est honneste et requis en toute science et discipline, de disputer et de croire par raisons et demonstrations, et non point par la seule force des authoritez."[127] Like Malherbe, he saw the advantages of art: "Le Poëte qui n'escrit que par art, composera d'ouvrages beaucoup plus propres et agreables que ceux de l'autre qui ne sera riche que de ce que la Nature aura decoré son esprit."[128] But, unlike Malherbe, Deimier refused to allow these rules to stifle the spirit, giving paramount importance to invention, this "Idée ou dessein qui porte une conception nouvelle, laquelle prend son origine en l'imagination que l'entendement entretient en soy, pour parvenir à la fin d'un sujet que la volonté s'est proposé."[129] This idea was far from new, having been borrowed from Peletier du Mans,[130] but it was to be taken up by later theorists and incorporated into most of the *arts poétiques* of the century. François Colletet, for instance, was to shamelessly plagiarize from the *Académie,* often without a single change, in the preparation of his oft re-edited *Ecole des muses.* And when in 1671 Richelet belittled Deimier's work, saying that it contributed little or nothing, he merely demonstrated that by then Deimier's theories were common practice.

Nowhere is this more evident than in Deimier's statements regarding rhyme. Whereas Malherbe loved the *difficulté vaincue,* Deimier was definitely reluctant to condemn facile rhymes lest poetry be entirely sterilized by difficulties, a situation where "il ne faudroit plus accompagner de rimes les vers, afin de ne commettre ce vice."[131] Allowing

[125] Pp. 327–29.
[126] Fromilhague, *Technique,* p. 127.
[127] *Académie,* pp. 105–06.
[128] Ibid., p. 13.
[129] Ibid., p. 222.
[130] Lucy M. Gay, "Sources of the *Académie de l'Art Poétique* of Pierre de Deimier," *PMLA* 27 (1912):412.
[131] *Académie,* p. 337.

orthographic differences, he stressed the importance of sound, but even there he was conciliatory, almost apologetic. He chastised excessive freedom in this domain: "Les belles rimes doivent avoir au moins une mesme consonnance pour principe de leur sylabe," but allowed far more freedom than Malherbe, and when he spoke of monosyllables he categorically stated that "la reigle de leur union est plus libre."[132] One look at his *La Royale liberté de Marseille*,[133] especially at the last poem, "Prière pour le roi," will show that he believed and followed his own dicta. In subsequent chapters, we will see to what extent the rest of the century did likewise.

[132] Ibid., pp. 321, 324.
[133] (Paris: Perier, 1615).

Chapter Three

Rambouillet

"L'Hôtel de Rambouillet fut une institution nécessaire [qui] . . . vint à son heure."[1] Malherbe too came at the right time, and so it should not be surprising that "L'Hôtel de Rambouillet a eu le mérite de l'apprécier et de le mettre en valeur."[2] This does not mean that the Chambre Bleue became the birthplace or even the home of any particular theory. We must remember that to amuse herself, the sickly and often morose Madame de Rambouillet gathered around her young aristocrats of very diverse tastes whose one common trait was a liking for good literature. Professional writers soon joined these noble amateurs in a mutually profitable gathering. It was therefore a very fluid group with relatively few faithful "members," though many writers kept a more or less constant contact with the witty hostess. The bulk of Voiture's letters are an attempt to keep such a contact while on various missions abroad, and many of Balzac's letters betray somewhat the same desire though on a broader basis, namely, to keep abreast of what was going on in the literary world as a whole.

Almost every poet of merit, and many without, became at one time or another associated with the Hôtel de Rambouillet, and since Malherbe was one of the first to frequent it, it has become customary to visualize the critic sitting in judgment over his contemporaries. There is undoubtedly some truth to this, but his influence was surely more limited than is usually thought. This limitation is twofold, the most obvious element being chronology: the poets usually associated with Rambouillet are Malherbe, Voiture, Desmarests, Chapelain, Malleville, Scudéry, Montausier, Sarasin, Godeau, Corneille, and Ménage, to name only the more famous. To these, one might add Chandeville, Philippe and Germain Habert, and Petit. But Malherbe died in 1628, and at that time Sarasin, Godeau, Corneille, Ménage, Petit, and Germain Habert had not yet been presented at the Chambre Bleue. Of the others, only Voiture could be considered an "habitué," having been introduced about 1624 or 1625 at the latest. As Magne has pointed out, the years of glory of the famous Hôtel did not begin until 1635.[3] By then, Malherbe was dead and Desmarests and Chapelain, at forty, were considered old by the younger crowd. I do not wish to suggest that in the early years of the *salon* Malherbe was the only poet in attendance. Rather, I believe him to have been the only poet of any merit who was of the seventeenth century and not merely a vestige of the sixteenth. Therefore, concerning Malherbe and the other seventeenth-century poets, there was no personal contact to speak of at the Hôtel de Rambouillet, and even less influence. What influence he did have on the poets who amused Arténice need not be sought in or explained by the personality of the master. Not the man, but his poetry, collected and published shortly after his death, was to be the subject of discussion in the Chambre Bleue. There is no doubt that it was admired. To what extent it was followed remains to be seen.

The other limitation is more difficult to pinpoint. Renée Winegarten speaks of "two traditions, one deriving from Malherbe, one from Marot."[4] Sarasin, in the second canto of his *Dulot vaincu,* put it as well as anyone:

> Marche sévèrement le Poème Tragique,
> Suivi de son cadet, le Poème Comique,
>
> . . . .
>
> Enfin, ce que la France admire de Bons-Vers
> S'y trouvent tous rangés en des postes divers.[5]

At Rambouillet, both veins found their admirers. Marino, though "fort ignorant,"[6] was extremely popular; Voiture, in spite of some rather tasteless jokes, was too "aimable" not to be readily forgiven. Malherbe, on the other hand, could be his own worst enemy: his irascible nature, coupled with an embarassing speech defect, made him the butt of many a jest. Balzac,

[1] Albert Delplanque, *La Marquise de Rambouillet et Malherbe* (Paris: Lethielleux, 1925), p. 57.

[2] Ibid., p. 95.

[3] *Voiture et les années de gloire de l'Hôtel de Rambouillet* (Paris: Mercure de France, 1912).

[4] *French Lyric Poetry,* p. 76.

[5] Jean-François Sarasin, *Œuvres* (Paris: Champion, 1926), 1:472–73.

[6] Jean Chapelain, *Opuscules critiques* (Paris: Droz, 1936), p. 504.

a frequent admirer, considered him "le plus mauvais récitateur de son temps. Nous l'appelions l'Antimondory; il gâtait ses beaux vers, en les prononçant," spitting at least six times in reciting four lines of poetry.[7] Two trends, therefore, coexisted at the Hôtel de Rambouillet, but not always as amicably as Sarasin suggested. Scudéry's admiration for Malherbe was not without reservations, and he went so far as to refer to him as "vostre grand Malherbe."[8] "Their" Malherbe, in turn, had little regard for those poets cultivating a lighter muse, and when Balzac showed him Voiture's sonnet on Urania, "à dire le vray, il en fut surpris. Il s'estonna qu'vn Aventurier (ce sont ses propres termes) qui n'avoit point esté nourri sous sa discipline; qui n'avoit point pris attache ni ordre de luy, eust fait si grand progrés dans vn païs, dont il disoit qu'il avoit la clef." At that time, Balzac himself thought it a great sonnet, an opinion which he changed only slightly later on.[9]

Regarding the nature and balance of this coexistence, two basic theories have been advanced. On the one hand, it is affirmed that "on peut dire approximativement qu'entre 1605 et 1610 le nouveau règne se prépare, de 1610 à 1615 il s'annonce; en 1625 il a vaincu l'opposition. Après 1630, date de la publication posthume des œuvres de Malherbe, l'Auguste est, sauf pour les irréconciliables, devenu Divin."[10] While not unanimously accepted, this view has been only too often repeated. On the other hand, some recent critics, echoing Maynard's lament, see the fortunes of Malherbe declining radically shortly after his death. Maynard, in his "Lettre à Flotte," had indeed spoken of attacks on Malherbe:

> Sa doctrine est si malmenée,
> Que ses épaules ont gâté
> Plus de bois que sa cheminée.

But it must be noted that the much older Maynard (the poem was written in 1639) is here complaining about the abused *doctrine* and nothing else.

---

[7] *Œuvres* (1665), 2:683.

[8] Georges de Scudéry, *Autres poésies,* bound in with *Le trompeur puni* (Paris: Sommaville, 1635), p. 126.

[9] Balzac, *Œuvres* (1665), 2:582.

[10] Brunot, *Doctrine de Malherbe,* p. 525.

Unlike Renée Winegarten, I am not convinced that Malherbe was eclipsed in the 1630s, or that this eclipse was due to his writing in a serious vein while the vogue was for lighter verse.[11] It is true that Malherbe had captured "dans le genre serieux le vrai genie de la Langue Françoise," as Boileau put it in his *Réflexions . . . sur Longin*,[12] and that, on the other hand, he was quite inept in the genres made popular by the poets whom Pellisson characterized as "galants," but Voiture never drove Malherbe out of fashion. To be sure, there was a definite revival of the "badin" in the 1630s, but I do not see it as the result of a struggle that doomed the "grands genres," as Winegarten suggests when she claims that this shift to the *badin* went hand in hand with "a trend in seventeenth-century French thought: the decline of the heroic ideal."[13] Nor can I agree when this critic blames the decline on the swing from Stoicism to Epicureanism, thanks chiefly to Gassendi.[14] As the *recueils collectifs* amply demonstrate, Malherbe remained in vogue quite some time after his death. Furthermore, most of the great poets of the 1630s and 1640s, and many minor ones as well, simultaneously cultivated both muses, the *badine* and the *sérieuse;* witness Corneille, Saint-Amant, Sarasin, to mention but a few. The heroic ideal was, in fact, to die out eventually and Gassendi to prevail, but not during the reign of Louis XIII. For the demolition of the hero, to borrow a phrase from Bénichou,[15] one must wait for the heyday of Jansenism.[16] Whatever slight decline in the vogue of Malherbe may have occurred shortly after his death is undoubtedly due to two facts: the absence of the formidable personality, and the lack of urbanity, of "cet air fin, délicat et spirituel"[17] in his works.

Generally, the revival of the *badin* was a broad phenomenon which has been fully investigated and needs no further comment. Voiture, one of its most adept champions, took personal credit for some of its specific

[11] *French Lyric Poetry*, p. 58.

[12] *Œuvres complètes* (Paris: Gallimard, 1966), p. 524.

[13] *French Lyric Poetry*, p. 59.

[14] Ibid., p. 60.

[15] Paul Bénichou, *Morales du grand siècle* (Paris: Gallimard, 1948), p. 86.

[16] It should also be pointed out that Gassendi's first work on Epicurus was not published until 1641.

[17] Charles Perrault, *Parallèle des anciens et des modernes* (Paris: Coignard, 1688–1697), 3:189.

manifestations and can therefore rightly serve as a starting point for this investigation of the various moods prevalent at the Hôtel de Rambouillet.

As I have already pointed out, Malherbe reluctantly admitted that Voiture was capable of writing a good poem. The admiration was not reciprocal, and Voiture went so far as to state that he preferred four lines by Mme de Rambouillet to all of Malherbe's output.[18] Such statements must, of course, be taken with more than one grain of salt, but they reveal a basic difference in attitudes toward the craft, in what Renée Winegarten has rightly called "criterion of taste":

> *From Voiture stemmed a group of poets which, though loosely knit, had far more cohesion than what passes for the school of Malherbe after the death of the master. The conformity of ideas among these poets is all the more remarkable when it is considered that most of them regarded poetry less as an art than as a social accomplishment. After the advent of Voiture, the new poetry established its own criterion of taste, for it could no longer be judged according to Malherbian standards and demanded new standards of criticism.*[19]

I am not convinced that Voiture had anything resembling a "school," but the concept of the role of poetry was, for the bulk of the poets, closer to Voiture's than to Malherbe's. Chapelain thought Voiture's elocution "lâche et négligée, quoique naturelle," a trait which he felt carried over into his writings;[20] Faguet conceded that Voiture could be serious, but never in his poetry.[21] One look at the careful composition of his sonnets will dispel this idea, and Boileau, who repeatedly praised Voiture in the highest terms, saw this only too readily: "Voiture, qui paroist si aisé, travailloit extrêmement ses ouvrages."[22] Voiture, it might be said, was the first master of the "impromptu à loisir," the first—at Rambouillet, at least—to make a hard task look easy. With him, the *artifice* became *naturel*.

At the Hôtel de Rambouillet, as in other literary gatherings, the

---

[18] *Œuvres* (Paris: Charpentier, 1855), 1:139.
[19] *French Lyric Poetry*, p. 69.
[20] *Opuscules critiques*, p. 386.
[21] *Histoire de la poésie française*, 3:65–76.
[22] *Œuvres complètes*, p. 4.

general opinion seems to have been "on devient poète par l'étude des règles," as Chapelain repeatedly said, but even the most ardent Malherbians saw the inherent dangers of such a school. Thus Balzac, a staunch admirer of Malherbe,[23] deplored a poetry that could have a "régularité exquise," but "ne vous semblera pas bien naturelle."[24] In his second *Discours,* Balzac spoke of a "je ne sais quoi" which goes beyond the rules, and in his rejoinder to Scudéry's attack on *Le Cid,* he suggested that "il y a des beautés parfaites qui sont effacées par d'autres beautés qui ont plus d'agrément et moins de perfection."[25] While Malherbe considered himself an arranger of syllables, Balzac, in the fifth *Discours,* stated that true eloquence "n'a que faire de compter scrupuleusement les syllabes, ni de se mettre en peine de placer les dactyles et les spondées, pour trouver le Secret de l'Harmonie," a secret that is innate and cannot be learned.[26] Chapelain, who considered himself Malherbe's successor, thought him a great technician but a bad poet,[27] yet refused to blame him for what he called the sterility of the century. He also refrained from speaking against Malherbe's rules, for "ce serait s'opposer en vain au torrent."[28]

But if there was such a "torrent," it did not impress some of the lighter poets at Rambouillet.[29] Of these, Voiture took particular pleasure in violating many of the master's rules. He not only wrote rondeaux, elegies, ballads, *épîtres,* triolets, all forms frowned upon by Malherbe, but prided himself in having written rondeaux "qui ont mis les beaux esprits en fantaisie d'en faire."[30] Whether or not Voiture was taking too much credit is difficult to say, but a definite vogue of these archaic forms undeniably occurred at that time. Saint-Amant, speaking of them in his "Pétarade aux Rondeaux," remarked: "Comme du blasme on passe à la

[23] See his letter to the Bishop of Aire, 20 Sept. 1623, or those to Bois-Robert of Aug. and Sept. 1623.

[24] *Lettres choisies* (Paris: Courbé, 1647), 1:346.

[25] Ibid., p. 400.

[26] *Œuvres* (Paris: Lecoffre, 1854), 1:280.

[27] *Lettres,* 1:18, 636.

[28] Ibid., 2:210.

[29] Though Chapelain was not much older than most of the faithful of the Hôtel, his attitude seems to have alienated him from an entire clique that considered him old-fashioned.

[30] *Œuvres,* 2:314.

loüange!"[31] Nor was this vogue of short duration, since in 1650 Courbé published a *Nouveau recueil de divers rondeaux,* an anthology which, by the way, contained several rondeaux by Maynard, the not-too-faithful disciple who had succumbed to the temptation of the fad.

Voiture did not limit his iconoclasm to indulging in forbidden forms. In one of his more irreverent songs he deliberately mocked not only Malherbe's distaste for vague numbers but also his strictures on facile rhymes and easy versification:

> *Quand nous fûmes dans Etampe,*
> *Nous parlâmes fort de vous,*
> *J'en soupirai quatre coups,*
> *Et j'en eus la goutte crampe:*
> *Etampe et crampe vraiment,*
> *Riment admirablement.*[32]

The bulk of Voiture's production is in songs, ballads, rondeaux, and other archaic or generally non-Malherbian forms. It would be useless to see in them a desire to follow or break rules, just as it would be futile to analyze for such purposes the Spanish poetry or the "vers en vieux langage" of the versatile Voiture. He did, however, occasionally indulge in more orthodox genres where he showed a special predilection for quatrains and sestets. Here some comments may be warranted.

Generally speaking, Voiture disregarded Malherbe's concepts of rhyme in all but a few instances, the exceptions being some very carefully evolved sonnets. The most obvious failing is a negligence regarding the homophony of the *consonne d'appui: doux-vous, trésors-corps, peint-teint,* with a particular predilection for *foi-moi.* However, this is not the only rule he breaks; almost every stricture of Malherbe is disregarded: compounds rhyme with their root (*durer-endurer*); grammatical endings are used for facile rhymes (*ingratitude-servitude,* but particularly adverbs in *-ment*); homophones and homonyms are very frequent partners, though at times badly matched (*venus-Vénus*); and long sounds are made to rhyme with short ones (*peine-éprenne*), the most frequent violations being *âme-*

---

[31] *Œuvres* (Paris: Didier, 1967), 2:202.

[32] *Œuvres,* 2:344. His own comments on the richness of these rhymes (2:148) are equally irreverent.

flamme and *extrême-même*. Frequently rhymes are for the eye alone (*mer-abîmer*), but sometimes they fail even in this respect (*l'air-égaler*).[33]

In the realm of structure, Voiture is equally un-Malherbian. I have already mentioned his predilection for archaic and irregular forms, but even in his use of quatrains, sestets, and *dizains* he is highly unorthodox. Until Malherbe, the isometric quatrain with *a b b a* rhymes was in vogue. As we have already seen, Malherbe preferred the heterometric *a b a b* construction. Voiture wrote eleven poems in quatrains,[34] seven of which are isometric, a definite reversal of a trend, though the bulk of these isometric poems use the *a b a b* rhyme scheme preferred by Malherbe. None of the heterometric poems use patterns found in Malherbe. What such statistics reveal is simply that, while Voiture may have started a new trend in courtly poetry, he did so while relying almost entirely on archaic forms. This theory gains credence with even a cursory look at Voiture's use of the sestet, his favorite single form.

Here, as in the study of the quatrains, statistics form only a framework for the picture, but a useful one. While Malherbe consistently moved away from the isometric sestet, eight of Voiture's twelve poems in sestets are of that type. Of the other four, two are octosyllabic except for the last line, which is alexandrine. This particularly clumsy form was never used by Malherbe and need not be discussed here. The other two merit some comments. Both "L'Amour sous sa loi" and "Ce n'est pas sans raison" are extremely free in their make-up; both are obviously songs, the last two lines of the first stanza being a refrain present in all subsequent stanzas:

> *L'Amour sous sa loi*
> *N'a jamais eu d'amant plus heureux que moi;*
> *Béni soit son flambeau,*
> *Son carquois, son bandeau!*

[33] All of these samples are taken from only a few pages (ibid., 2:277–96), but they are by no means all the violations on these pages. In "Je sens au profond de mon âme" (2:292–96), the *âme-flamme* rhyme is found four times, *âme-femme* once, *blâme-flamme* once, along with rhymes such as *fasse-face*, *extrême-même*, and so on. Ironically, Voiture's use of the *rimes normandes* does not oppose him to Malherbian practice, but the entire century was to censure such rhymes.

[34] The "Romance espagnole" is also in quatrains, but I do not consider it as falling within the realm of this study.

> *Je suis amoureux,*
> *Et le ciel ne voit point d'amant plus heureux.*[35]

and:

> *Ce n'est pas sans raison*
> *Qu'on dit que je vous admire,*
> *Et pour moi je n'en puis dédire*
> *Monsieur de [Saint-Brisson].*
> *Coralte, vos beaux yeux forcent toutes les âmes*
> *A brûler, à brûler de leurs flammes.*[36]

In these two songs, the syntactical break is quite logical, bowing to the demands of the refrain. However, this cannot be said for the much longer "Je sens au profond de mon âme." Of its twenty-three stanzas, twelve are cut 3–3; five 4–2, 2–4, or 2–2–2; six are without any syntactical break whatsoever. Even if one discounts the capricious punctuation of the day, the results are often curious:

> *La mauvaise me tient ravie*
> *Mon âme, mon cœur et ma vie:*
> *Car chez elle se vint sauver*
> *Le voleur de cette dépouille;*
> *Mais j'espère tout retrouver,*
> *Si tu permets que je la fouille.*[37]

Throughout the poem, enjambments such as the ones above further add to the chaotic impression left by the varied breaks.

Voiture's poems in ten-line stanzas reinforce the idea already presented. Voiture used the *dizain* only six times; three of these occasions are single-stanza *placets* and a fourth is a two-stanza fragment. All are isometric, either octo- or decasyllabic. The two octosyllabic poems are relatively Malherbian, with only the first stanza of the fragment "La plus adorable personne,"[38] composed of one syntactical unit, deviating from

[35] *Œuvres*, 2:334–35.
[36] Ibid., p. 340.
[37] Ibid., p. 296.
[38] Ibid., p. 306.

the orthodox 4–6 break. The four decasyllabic poems, on the other hand, are totally un-Malherbian, not only in their very nature (Malherbe never used this particular form) but in their inner structure, their rhyme scheme, the quality of the rhymes, the vocabulary, grammar, and so forth. Two of the *placets*, "Plaise, seigneur, . . ." and "Prelat passant . . ." as well as the longer ballad "Vous vous trouvez toujours dessus vos pieds,"[39] have a highly unorthodox *a b a b b c c d c d* rhyme scheme and break either 4–6, 6–4, or 5–5. The demand for three words rhyming together was obviously too much for Voiture, who resorted to such combinations as *roc-choc-troc, estoc-croc-troc, Maroc-Enoc-troc,* and *coq-froc-troc,* or even *réprime-s'imprime-s'imprime.* This is obviously Voiture-burlesque at his best—or worst—and hiatuses such as "longtemps y a" contribute as much to the generally slap-dash impression, as do clumsy inversions such as "Il ne lisoit Metamorphose aucune" or the cacophony present in a passage like "rendez les péchés effacés/ De ce cocher. . . ."

Only in his sonnets did Voiture show how carefully he could compose. The bulk of these are quite Malherbian, and I have already mentioned Malherbe's surprise over the success of this "adventurer." What is perhaps most interesting in Balzac's relation of the event is not Malherbe's surprise but his blindness to everything except matters of pure technique. Voiture obviously worked hard on this poem, perhaps too hard: as Balzac points out, the content became lost in the quest for structural perfection. Since Malherbe saw only the form, he failed to note flaws that did not escape Balzac's analytic mind: in lines 7 and 8, Voiture goes from "bénir son martyre," the height of Stoicism, to a much lesser "n'oser murmurer contre la tyrannie," a regression rather than a progression, and Balzac concludes, "Voilà quelle est l'importance de la musique des vers. L'esprit trompé par le plaisir de l'oreille, et attentif au son des paroles, est détourné de toute autre attention. Il s'attache de telle sorte aux nombres et aux mesures, qu'il en oublie tout le reste."[40] Voiture, in his attempt at being Malherbian—consciously or otherwise—had gone overboard.

I have already stated that two trends coexisted at the Chambre Bleue. But if Malherbe ruled supreme and unchallenged over one until his death, Voiture was not as fortunate. Renée Winegarten has spoken of a "cohesive

[39] Ibid., pp. 426–29.
[40] *Œuvres* (1665), 2:584.

group" stemming from Voiture,[41] but there are several indications that, as early as 1627, Voiture's supremacy was challenged sufficiently to make him lash out in no uncertain terms.

In the last years of Malherbe's life and in the years immediately following his death, there is no doubt that, numerically at least, the *badin* predominated at Rambouillet. Voiture was rapidly becoming the favorite when, in 1627, there appeared a dashing young man from Malherbe's home town. Even though this young poet won all the hearts around him because of his "beauté . . . qui n'avoit rien que de Grand et de Noble," and because "l'on eust dit qu'il estoit venu au monde en sçachant le monde, tant il agissoit sagement et galamment tout ensemble,"[42] there is no mention of him in any of Malherbe's writings. This is indeed strange when one considers that Pherecide, as he is known in *Le Grand Cyrus*, was none other than Eleazar de Sarcilly, Sr. de Chandeville, nephew of Malherbe. He was sixteen when introduced into Rambouillet by Mme de Grancé.[43] In no time at all he won the hearts of all the ladies present, including "the Lioness," Mlle Paulet, though he always remained within the bounds of the proprieties expounded in the famous salon. It was, in fact, because he was equally adept at *galanterie* and *vers galants* that he won at least one skirmish in his war with Voiture. While the latter was in Spain,

> *il ne prenoit pas plasir que M. Godeau et M. de Chandeville, grand garçon bien fait et nepveu de Malherbe, c'est-à-dire versificateur, se fussent si bien mis dans l'esprit de Mlle Paulet, et peut-estre de Mlle de Rambouillet, en son absence. Il luy fit une insolence le propre jour qu'il revint de Flandres. . . . En la remenant le soir, il ne put s'empescher de luy parler de Chandeville, et l'appelloit cet Adonis, et y mesla peut-estre quelque mot de Venus. La Lyonne se mit en fureur; ils furent deux ans sans se voir; enfin il y retourna, mais elle ne luy a jamais pardonné.*[44]

[41] *French Lyric Poetry*, p. 69.

[42] Madeleine de Scudéry, *Artamène ou le Grand Cyrus* (Paris: Courbé, 1650–1653), 7, bk. 1:536–37.

[43] Pierre-Daniel Huet, *Les origines de Caen* (Rouen: Maurry, 1706), p. 367.

[44] Gédéon Tallemant des Réaux, *Historiettes* (Paris: Gallimard, 1960–1961), 1:494.

The extent of Voiture's jealousy was readily discernible in a letter from Madrid to Mlle Paulet in which he contemptuously referred to his rivals.[45] According to Godeau, one of the targets of Voiture's invective, this jealousy was only too justified, for Chandeville was supplanting Voiture in all the better literary circles.[46] Ironically, shortly after the writing of the letter in question (March 1633) Chandeville died and Godeau gave up profane pursuits, poetic and other.

Between 1627 and 1633, however, there can be no doubt as to Chandeville's popularity. Chapelain in 1670 claimed that Chandeville "n'y [Rambouillet] a eu que peu d'accès . . . ayant eu son attache principale à Mlle Paulet et à l'hostel de Clermont,"[47] but this recollection of an old man is contradicted by many contemporary testimonials—Huet, Sauval, Godeau, Voiture himself, the Scudérys, to name just a few. It was Mme de Rambouillet who attached him to the person of the Cardinal de La Valette, and it was Chandeville who, according to Georges de Scudéry's preface to Le vassal généreux, introduced him into the salon of Mme de Rambouillet. Nor was Chandeville's reputation limited to a few salons, for Sauval, speaking of the popularity of his works, also points out that "il étoit si estimé à la Cour, et des gens de Lettres, que sa mort fut generalement regretée,"[48] a sentiment echoed by Pelletier:

> Que ta mort, Chandeville, a fait verser de larmes,
> Quand la cour tout en deuil, au milieu de ses charmes,
> Fit voir de son regret le juste sentiment.[49]

This popularity survived him. He had stated his intentions regarding his own poetic production in a preface to Scudéry's Trompeur puni, and, "mon dessain n'estant pas qu'on voye iamais mon nom imprimé ailleurs que dans ses liures,"[50] he destroyed the bulk of his poems shortly before

[45] Œuvres, 1:102.
[46] Bibliothèque de l'Arsenal, Ms. Conrart, 22:843.
[47] Lettres, 2:703.
[48] Henri Sauval, Histoire de Paris (Paris: Moette et Chardon, 1724), 1:327.
[49] Cited by Armand Gasté in his edition of Eléazar de Sarcilly, Sr. de Chandeville, Poésies (Caen: Le Blanc-Hardel, 1878), p. xv.
[50] Included in Chandeville's Diverses poésies (Paris: Courbé, 1639).

his death. Scudéry managed to save a few which were published in 1639 and again in 1643 by Courbé. Sauval stated that "Ses ouvrages, à la verité, ne chargent pas trop la main, mais Courbé qui les a imprimés ne s'en est pas plaint."[51] A further testimonial to the popularity of these few poems is the frequency with which most of them found their way into the *recueils collectifs* of the century.[52] The Scudérys, as might be expected, praised him eloquently if not judiciously: "Il faisoit des Vers si beaux, si touchans, et si passionez, qu'il estoit aisé de voir qu'il n'auoit pas l'ame indifferente: et ceux du Grand Therpandre son Oncle, qui a tant eu de reputation, n'estoient pas plus beaux que les siens."[53]

In the preface to Scudéry's *Trompeur puni,* Chandeville speaks very highly of Malherbe and Racan, suggesting that without them "nostre Siecle n'auroit pas la gloire, de voir surpasser les Anciens Poëtes Latins," but he goes on to say that it is only in Scudéry "que paroist mieux qu'en aucun autre, cet entousiasme, et cette eleuation d'esprit, qui a fait appeller la Poësie diuine: Ceux qui n'ont pas ce feu Celeste, se peuuent bien nommer versificateurs, mais non pas Poëtes." Generally speaking, though, this most *précieux* of poets followed the basic strictures outlined by his famous uncle. This is not meant to suggest servility, for Chandeville is highly original within the framework of Malherbian rules. But even this tendency can be considered Malherbian, as Fromilhague has pointed out: Malherbe constantly strove for originality, neglecting forms preferred by his predecessors and going so far as to abandon any when "il n'y avait plus d'originalité à affirmer—quant à la technique s'entend."[54]

Malherbe used the sestet more than any other form: forty-two times, including twenty-seven major poems. As we have already seen, while isometric octosyllables predominate in his earlier attempts, he later on prefers heterometric structures, especially those combining alexandrines with octosyllabic lines, seeking diversity in the possible combinations of these two lengths. Of the 480 lines of poetry left by Chandeville, 240 are sestets, all heterometric. Except for the eighteen lines of the song "Je suis content . . . ," which uses a 10–10–4–6–10–6 combination, all these sestets

[51] *Histoire de Paris,* 1:327.
[52] See Frédéric Lachèvre, *Bibliographie des recueils collectifs de poésies publiés de 1597 à 1700* (Geneva: Slatkine, 1967), 2:187–89.
[53] *Le Grand Cyrus,* 7, pt. 1:538.
[54] *Technique,* p. 372.

combine alexandrines with octosyllabic lines.[55] Of all the combinations used by Chandeville, only one can be found in Malherbe: "Mon cœur es tu si foible, et si peu genereux," in 12–12–8–12–8–12 *a a b c b c* masculine sestets is in a form used once by Malherbe. If in spite of his metrical innovations—or because of them—Chandeville can be called Malherbian, a glance at the inner structure of his sestets will only reinforce that opinion. Of the forty stanzas involved, all but eight contain at least two syntactical units with a major break after the third line. Of the exceptions, two seem to be the result of the printer's capricious use of punctuation; three are composed of one syntactical group with a weak break after the third line; the remaining three comprise the song "Ie suis content, malgré la tirannie," which deserves special comment. Here is its first stanza:

> Ie suis content, malgré la tirannie,
> Du vieux ialoux de la belle Ismenie,
>   Le Roy des Dieux
>   Qui gouuerne ma vie,
> Pour m'obliger, encor qu'il n'ait point d'yeux,
>   Trompe ceux de l'enuie.[56]

Obviously the punctuation is highly capricious. If one is to make sense of this stanza, the comma ending the first line must be deleted and the stop ending the second line strengthened. If the punctuation is corrected in all three stanzas, the result is a poem with a definite 2–4 break. In view of the title—"Chanson"—and of the unorthodox combination of lines, is it too much to suggest that musical considerations prevailed here?

Structurally, Chandeville was equally Malherbian in all his other poetic endeavors. Although he indulged in *vers suivis* (two elegies totaling some 120 lines) the rhymes are flat, with, as Malherbe demanded, "le sens fermé" every two lines (every four lines in a few exceptional cases) and with only one enjambment that Malherbe would have censured:

---

[55] The madrigal "I'approuve la discretion," of doubtful authenticity and unpublished until 1878, is completely free, changing structure from stanza to stanza. "Que mon audace est insensée" departs slightly from the basic formula, using an 8–8–12–12–12–6 combination.

[56] *Diverses poésies*, p. 21.

Ce Tonnerre grondant qui brisa tous obstacles,
Les feux du Firmament, ny tant d'autres miracles,
Ne preuvent pas si bien une Diuinité
Aux esprits de ce temps, comme vostre beauté.[57]

In matters of rhyme, Chandeville has few lapses. His *consonne d'appui* homophony is generally good, with only *doux-vous* a repeated violation. There are relatively few commonplace rhymes, *pas-trépas* and *fers-enfers* being the only noticeable ones. In his entire production I can find only three rhymes specifically censured by Malherbe: *faite-parfaite, extreme-mesme,* and *flame-ame.* Ironically, neither *ame* nor *flame* is ever found except in conjunction with the other. The rhyme scheme of the sestets is quite Malherbian, *a a b c c b* and *a a b c b c* each being used in four poems, but the two sonnets fail in that realm. All in all, however, the conclusion is inevitable: the rival of Voiture, the friend of Scudéry, the darling of the *galant* world was a budding Malherbian when he died at the age of twenty-three. Like his uncle, he was mourned and admired. But imitated?

Of all the poets at Rambouillet at that time, Scudéry felt closest to Chandeville, who had introduced him into this literary circle perhaps as early as 1627, referring to him as a man "de qui je regrette sensiblement la perte et chéris la mémoire uniquement."[58] Yet, two other poets, because of factors both chronological and poetical, may be considered as peers of Scudéry: Malleville and the older of the Habert brothers, Philippe.[59] Both Malleville and Philippe Habert were at Rambouillet, both were members of the group known as the *Illustres bergers,* and both were among the first members of the Academy.

Pellisson thought that the approximately 270 alexandrines of Habert's *Temple de la mort*[60] were among the very best in all French literature.

---

[57] Ibid., p. 3.

[58] Georges de Scudéry, *Le vassal généreux* (Paris: Courbé, 1636), dedication.

[59] Philippe Habert died rather young and the authorship of all the poems attributed to him is uncertain. Only "Le temple de la mort" seems definitely to be by him, and even that work's first edition is bound (at the Bibliothèque Nationale, at least) with *La métamorphose des yeux de Philis en astre* (n.p., 1639) by his brother Germain.

[60] First edition, n.p., n.d; second edition by Sommaville, 1646.

Malherbe would not have agreed, for these *vers suivis* have all the bad traits that characterize the early *précieux* poetry of Philippe's brother Germain. In spite of an outward mechanical regularity, the poem gives an impression of chaos. This is perhaps due to the constant changes in moods which, unfortunately, do not prevent a certain monotony from pervading the entire work.[61] Many of the frequent enjambments seem purposeless and the language is frequently archaic:

> *Au creux de ce vallon dès l'enfance du monde,*
> *Est un temple fameux . . . .*[62]

All in all, the poem is not only un-Malherbian, it is bad beyond description and one wonders how the poet's reputation was acquired.

Malleville is patently superior but even less Malherbian. Less, because while Habert's violations are undoubtedly due to a lack of ability, Malleville's are far more basic in nature. This becomes particularly obvious when one views the rhymes used by Malleville. Violations such as *flame-ame, blasme-dame, mort-effort-transport-fort* are frequent, as they are in the bulk of the poetry analyzed so far. To resolve this fundamental question, one need only recall that, while Malherbe forbade and shunned such rhymes, Deimier did not. It was Malherbe's nature to abhor poetic license, just as it was Deimier's to grant it. Malleville and his friends chose to follow the easier path, and their choice is reflected not only in matters of rhyme but elsewhere as well. On the matter of syllable count, for instance, Malherbe allowed few liberties. He accepted the use of *avec* before a vowel and *avecque* before a consonant, but refused to condone arbitrary choices—*jusque-jusques, donc-doncque-doncques, encor-encore-encores, guère-guères*—for the sake of meter. Malleville used all of these at one time or another.

The hiatus is fairly frequent in the poetry of Malleville,[63] but I am convinced that we are dealing with something other than poetic license

---

[61] It should be remembered that this fear of monotony caused Malherbe's distrust of *vers suivis*.

[62] Ll. 13–14.

[63] Maximilian Lierau, in *Die metrische Technik der drei Sonettisten Maynard, Gombauld und Malleville, verglichen mit derjenigen Fr. Malherbes* (Greifwald: Abel, 1882), p. 10, counted forty-eight occurrences in some 6,000 lines.

in this case. It is obvious that Malleville did not always compose with the same degree of craftsmanship. Some of his poems are very carefully done, others show the greatest laxness imaginable. Every instance of hiatus that I noted occurred in poems that showed carelessness in other respects as well. In these poems, expletives are frequent and obvious: "Il n'est rien de si beau qu'elle est."[64] Enjambments occur with near regularity, but by far the most disturbing manifestation of this carelessness is obscurity, often the result of inexplicable inversions:

> La terre de ses fleurs n'est point si redevable,
> Et la faveur du Ciel qu'a celle de ses pas,
> Et de mille beautez qu'on ne connaissait pas,
> On en voit en ses yeux le portrait véritable.[65]

That example, however, is not nearly as obscure as this one:

> . . . ce miracle du monde,
> Qui du Roi de nos cœurs rend l'état florissant.[66]

Some examples of obscurity are of the type that made Verlaine curse the tyranny of rhymes:

> Le ciel qui l'environne éclatte de saphirs,
> L'air est tout de parfums, et rien que les Zephirs
> Au chant des rossignols n'accordent leur haleine.[67]

How does a sky explode with blue dots (sapphires), and of what nature is the "accord" between song and breath? At times, the unraveling of difficulties demands the careful rereading of more than one stanza; witness these tercets of a Malleville sonnet:

> Mais dedans le transport où mon âme s'égare,
> Quand je me représente une chose si rare,
> Que même le désir n'y peut rien ajouter,

[64] *Poésies* (Paris: Courbé, 1659), p. 6.
[65] Ibid., p. 3.
[66] Ibid., p. 42.
[67] Ibid., p. 5.

Je ressens une peine à nulle autre seconde,
C'est qu'étant si parfaite on ne peut éviter
D'avoir en la servant pour rival tout le monde.[68]

At first glance, one might think that the perfection belongs to the "peine à nulle autre seconde."

But, as I have already suggested, Malleville is not always so careless. The majority of his sonnets are very much "dans les règles," and Maurice Cauchie, though he thought a literary analysis of Malleville's work to be superfluous,[69] could not refrain from exclaiming "Quoi de plus achevé, par exemple, qu'un sonnet comme celui-ci?" when referring to "Quel crime ay-je commis."[70] In his choice of metrics, Malleville usually chose forms consecrated by Malherbe. Thus, the majority of his sonnets are alexandrine with an *a b b a a b b a c c d e d e* masculine rhyme scheme. Many of his ten-line stanzas, particularly those fashioned for the *Guirlande de Julie,* are isometric octo- or decasyllabic, almost all with a major break after the fourth line and a secondary one after the seventh, and using the Malherbian *a b a b c c d e e d* rhyme scheme. All of these poems are marked by fairly careful craftsmanship and by a seeming desire to remain within certain rules of poetics, though here again it must be understood that Deimier's ideas may have been applied, rather than Malherbe's. The homophony of the *consonne d'appui* is constantly violated, long vowels are made to rhyme with short ones, adverbs are abused. In the sonnets, syntactical groups begun in one stanza frequently run on to the next, either in the quatrains or in the tercets, though it must be said that the results are usually quite fortunate. In short, Malleville applies poetic license whenever a stricter appliance of the rules would destroy or hamper the mood he is trying to create.[71]

It is true that, physically at least, Scudéry spent little time at the Hôtel de Rambouillet. Nevertheless, he remained in touch and frequently submitted his work to its august gathering: "Depuis qu'un

[68] Ibid., p. 10.

[69] *Documents pour servir à l'histoire littéraire du XVIIe siècle* (Paris: Champion, 1924), p. 76.

[70] Ibid., p. 55.

[71] It should be added that this experimentation was not always successful. "Sur un mal d'yeux," using 8–8–8–12–12–12 sestets (ibid., p. 39), gives an unfortunate impression of alternating octosyllabic and alexandrine tercets.

homme qui meritoit beaucoup, puisqu'il méritoit vostre estime; Ie veux dire mon cher et parfait Amy, feu Monsieur de Chandeville . . . m'eust donné l'honneur d'estre connu de vostre Maison, ie fis vœu de ne mettre iamais rien au iour, qui n'en fust premier iugé digne dans l'Hostel de Ramboüillet."[72] As is well known, he was a swashbuckler, and his rodomontades frequently crept into his poetry. Except for this one reservation, his poetry is akin to that of Malleville and Chandeville. As a result, he was very popular in and out of the Hôtel de Rambouillet, though his most avid fans, men such as Hardy, Rotrou, Balzac, were somewhat older than he. Balzac, devoted to most of Malherbe's ideas, saw many defects in Scudéry's work, but admired him nevertheless and claimed to have been one of the first to recognize his merits.[73]

In *Clélie*, the author states that du Bartas, having written at a time when the language was still far from perfect, "ses ouurages paroistront bien tost auoir quelque chose de vieux dans le stile," while Malherbe has "changé la langue de son païs [and . . .] seruira d'authorité à tous les Poëtes de la nation," his poems being "magnifiques et naturels," full of majesty and *douceur,* harmony and *justesse.*[74] Georges de Scudéry, whether he was the author or not, was willing to claim the authorship of this opinion, thus adding his name to the long list of admirers of Malherbe. But, according to Chapelain, Scudéry did not possess that which he admired so in Malherbe, though he amply compensated for his lack of *savoir* and *jugement* with the purity of his French and a "naturel qui est beau."[75] Maurice Cauchie three centuries later went much further in his praises, calling Scudéry's 1649 collection of poems "un des meilleurs de la première moitié du XVIIe siècle."[76] As we shall see shortly, Scudéry's admiration of Malherbe had no effect whatsoever on his own production, Cauchie went too far in his attempts to rehabilitate his subject, and Chapelain, not too surprisingly, came very close to the truth.

It is difficult to determine whether Scudéry lacked *savoir*, or whether his ardent nature merely made him disregard it, but his most

---

[72] *Le vassal généreux,* lettre.
[73] *Œuvres* (1854), 1:454.
[74] Madeleine de Scudéry, *Clélie* (Paris: Courbé, 1660), 4, pt. 2:858–59.
[75] *Opuscules critiques,* p. 359.
[76] "Les premières poésies de Scudéry (1631–1636)," *MdF* 299 (1947): 59.

obvious failing is, as Chapelain put it, a lack of judgment. The results frequently show him to be closer to the spirit of the decried du Bartas than to that of the admired Malherbe, who certainly would not have hesitated to strike out "France qui doit t'accroître autant que l'univers" as nonsensical, and

> *Mais confesse à genoux, France, aussi bien que moi,*
> *Que ta grandeur consiste en celle de ton roi*[77]

as absurd.

Skirting the commonplace with unbridled rodomontades such as

> *Moi qui suis fils d'un capitaine*
> *Que le monde estima jadis,*
> *Je fais des vers bien plus hardis,*
> *Ma Minerve est bien plus hautaine.*
> *La naissance m'inspire au sein*
> *L'ardeur d'un généreux dessein,*
> *Qui n'est point dans ces âmes basses.*
> *Et je diray (s'il m'est permis)*
> *Que le ciel m'a donné des grâces*
> *Qu'il ne despart qu'à ses amis.*[78]

Scudéry demonstrates, beyond *jugement* or *savoir*, a serious lack of self-discipline. While the mechanics of good Malherbian poetry—syntactical breaks, rhyme schemes—are frequently adhered to, the spirit is not. Expletives are to be found with appalling frequency, whether in superfluous parentheses such as the one above or "Je fus (pour les quitter) aux rives de Marseille,"[79] or in redundant phrasings whose only excuse for existence is the requirement of line:

> *Le sort, l'iniustice, et l'enuie,*
> *Ont assez trauersé sa vie;*

---

[77] *Le sacrifice des Muses* (Paris: Cramoisy, 1635), p. 111.

[78] Cited by Georges Mongrédien, *Madeleine de Scudéry et son salon* (Paris: Tallandier, 1946), p. 15.

[79] *Le sacrifice des Muses*, p. 111.

> *Mais il surmonte apres sa mort,*
> *Et l'aueugle iniustice, et l'enuie, et le sort.*[80]

One of the passages quoted by Cauchie in his attempted rehabilitation of Scudéry is the following, taken from the rather late "Stances à Philis":

> *Philis, ce sont vos yeux qui l'ont fait possesseur*
> *D'une âme si bien défendue.*
> *Qu'il la traite avecque douceur,*
> *Puisqu'elle s'est rendue;*
> *Elle obéit, elle en reçoit la loi:*
> *Qu'il n'y soit plus tyran, mais roi.*[81]

This is a poor choice for rehabilitation indeed. The penultimate line contains some obvious padding. Much worse is the fact that the stanza is barely recitable due to the strange rhythmic pattern. Nor is this an exceptional case:

> *Un extase si doux m'emporte, en t'écoutant*
> *Ajouter aux beaux vers de nouvelles merveilles.*[82]

With its bad caesura and enjambment, this passage is as unacceptable as the halting second line of the following quatrain:

> *Mais si son œil, d'un trait farouche,*
> *Me défend de la chercher,*
> *La douleur n'ouvrira ma bouche*
> *Que pour bénir ma plaie en adorant l'archer.*[83]

Insufficient rhymes abound in Scudéry's poems, for he, like his friends, was obviously more in agreement with Deimier than with Malherbe, but the quest for rhymes contributed at times to the problem presented above (or vice-versa?):

[80] *Le cabinet de M. de Scudéry* (Paris: Courbé, 1646), p. 223.
[81] "Premières poésies," p. 70.
[82] *Le cabinet*, p. 237.
[83] Ibid., p. 201. The other stanzas of this poem are 8–8–8–12.

Que s'il faut contenter ce désir curieux
Et vous dire quel est cet aimable visage,
Voyez-en le portrait regardant dans mes yeux.[84]

Note that if the first line of this tercet is to have its proper syllable count, *curieux* must be considered as trisyllabic; for the same reason, *yeux* is monosyllabic.[85]

If by the nature and quality of his rhymes Scudéry differs but little from the non-Malherbian poets already discussed, there is another aspect of his production, one particularly apparent in the *Poésies diverses,* that shows him to be even more akin to those poets most readily labeled baroque in recent years. Scudéry "n'est pas un disciple de Théophile, il ne l'a jamais approché, mais il l'admire et le plaint."[86] It was Scudéry who, in 1632, published the first "definitive" edition of Théophile's works, having previously taken a dangerous stand in defending the libertine poet during his times of trouble.[87] Scudéry, however, goes beyond admiration and courageous devotion to a memory in writing poems such as "Le miroir enchanté."[88] Whether he was consciously imitating Théophile or not is impossible to say, but the shocking realism of these verses, their evocative power and vivid imagery definitely recall and improve upon Théophile's frequently anthologized ode "Un corbeau devant moi croasse."

I cannot agree with those who consider the love poems of 1649, written when Scudéry was forty-eight years old, as nothing more than the nostalgic relations

Des ridicules aventures
D'un amoureux à cheveux gris.[89]

[84] *Poésies diverses* (Paris: Courbé, 1649), p. 255.

[85] Malherbe condemned the rhyming of a diaeresis with a synaeresis but was not always able to avoid it himself. In all probability, Malherbe would have censured the awkward *-dant dans* of the last line.

[86] Antoine Adam, *Théophile de Viau et la libre pensée française en 1620* (Geneva: Slatkine, 1966), p. 378.

[87] See Frédéric Lachèvre, *Le procès du poète Théophile de Viau* (Paris: Champion, 1909), 1:341–46, 512–18.

[88] *Poésies diverses,* p. 156.

[89] "Au lecteur."

Whether in the fairly regular sonnets or in the less successful odes and *stances,* a new Scudéry emerges. "La tempête," the first poem in the collection, is replete with conceits, antitheses, excessively long metaphors —in short, the baggage of all the baroque poets since the generation of du Bartas. This is true for many of the poems in the collection. Furthermore, repeated attempts at musicality through syntactical and rhythmic variations abound. At times, the results are prosaic and insipid, for not all subjects lend themselves to these procedures;[90] more frequently the results are quite fortunate, particularly in the shorter poems, as can be seen from this sonnet ending:

> *Elle ne s'émeut point; ils sont toujours émus;*
> *Ils courent; elle est fixe; et mon esprit confus,*
> *Voit la mère paisible et les enfants superbes.*[91]

Elsewhere, Scudéry's preciosity, conceits, and imaginary landscapes recall the Tristan of the "Promenoir." This is the case with subtle poems such as "Le Printemps"[92] and with the longest ode in the collection, the 800-line "Les Muses":

> *Là, mille et mille Nayades,*
> *Parmi des objets si beaux,*
> *Laissent tomber en cascades*
> *Le mobile argent des eaux.*[93]

This is a far cry from Malherbe.

During the last decade of the reign of Louis XIII, the Hôtel de Rambouillet was truly in its glory. This was a decade that also saw a still greater polarization of literary ideals. With Chandeville dead, Scudéry far from Paris, and Godeau gradually withdrawing, Voiture became the uncontested leader of the mundane side in spite of his frequent trips abroad. With Malherbe dead and Balzac in retirement, Chapelain, un-

[90] See for instance "Ode sur l'Immaculée conception de la Vierge" (*Poésies diverses,* pp. 102–04), or "Ode à Mme la comtesse d'Harcourt" (ibid., pp. 105–11), both pentasyllabic.

[91] Ibid., p. 3.

[92] Ibid., p. 175.

[93] Ibid., p. 117.

doubtedly the most learned of the Rambouillet faithful, became their heir. It would be difficult to attribute the differences between the two "camps" to any one factor or group of factors, but we should note that the self-styled Malherbians were not of the same age as those less involved with criticism and the science of poetics. Chapelain and Desmarests were born in 1595; Godeau, torn between the two poles until his conversion, was born in 1605, one year before Corneille; of all the other poets worthy of mention, Montausier, born in 1610, was the oldest. One therefore gets the impression that a group of young men, in the presence of two older men of opposite temperaments, rendered all due respect to Chapelain, while rallying around the lovable and jovial Voiture.

Chapelain was convinced that he was "l'héritier de Ronsard et l'émule de Malherbe."[94] The date of his entrance into Rambouillet is uncertain (some experts suggest 1627) but his reputation was made much earlier. When in 1620 Marino requested an opinion of Malherbe and Vaugelas, they referred him to Chapelain "qui savait aussi bien qu'eux l'italien et mieux encore la Poétique."[95] Chapelain was undoubtedly impressed by this gesture, but less so by Marino who, in his eyes, "se connaissait à guère de choses."[96] He felt that Marino's forte was "dans le lyrique, et quand il a voulu en sortir, il s'est toujours trouvé audessous de ce qu'il s'était persuadé et qu'on attendait de lui."[97] On this score, Chapelain never changed his mind, and as late as 1673 he still maintained that Marino, though quite imaginative and lyrical, "était fort ignorant."[98] Yet this opinion should not be overemphasized. Chapelain deplored one extreme without falling into the other. His own production was not always up to his own expectations, but his judgment of others was usually quite just, and he was one of the first to realize that Corneille's *Cid* was a masterpiece, with or without rules:

> *Corneille est ici depuis trois jours. . . . Il ne fait plus rien et Scudéry a du moins gagné cela, en le querellant, qu'il l'a rebuté du*

[94] Antonin Fabre, *Les ennemis de Chapelain* (Paris: Fontemoing, 1897), 1:3.

[95] Paul Pellisson and P.-J. Thoulier d'Olivet, *Histoire de l'Académie Française* (Paris: Didier, 1858), 2:128.

[96] *Opuscules critiques*, p. 397.

[97] Ibid., p. 401.

[98] Ibid., p. 504.

*métier et lui a tari sa veine. Je l'ai autant que j'ai pu réchauffé
et encouragé à se venger et du Scudéry et de sa protectrice en
faisant quelque nouveau Cid qui attire encore les suffrages de tout
le monde, et qui montre que l'art n'est pas ce qui fait la beauté.*[99]

It was undoubtedly in this spirit that he told Mlle de Gournay that
Malherbe "tournait mieux les vers ni que moi ni que vous-même. Mais je
vous dis aussi qu'il ignorait la poésie."[100] Is this why, although he knew of
Malherbe's thoughts on the subject, he preferred *vers suivis* to stanzas?[101]
Is this why, although he consistently criticized Malherbe's lack of poetic
qualities, he thought of Maynard as the best of poets and "nostre
maître"?[102]

For two decades preceding the appearance of his *Pucelle,* Chapelain
enjoyed the highest of literary reputations, thanks to his critical dicta
and a few well-conceived poems. Among the latter, one may mention three
sonnets that Balzac considered the best he had ever seen,[103] and even more
so, his *Miserere*[104] and the famous ode to Richelieu.

The sonnets, containing lines such as "Amoureux chevalier, que
mille hauts faits d'armes,"[105] verge on the cacophonic and do not speak
highly for Balzac's sincerity. The *Miserere,* a poem of twenty-two heterometric ten-line stanzas combining octosyllabic sestets with alexandrine
quatrains, has but a few good moments. At times, a certain imagistic
realism enhanced by a series of sharp contrasts makes one forget the non-
Malherbian construction. Unfortunately, these passages are rare, while
insipid clichés are far more frequent. Commonplaces such as the following
may bring to mind Malherbe, but if so, it is the Malherbe of the weaker
passages of "Les larmes de Saint Pierre":

> *Fay de mes pleurs une Piscine*
> *Où mon vieil homme despoüillé*

[99] Ibid., pp. 401–02.
[100] Ibid., p. 372.
[101] *Lettres,* 2:274.
[102] Ibid., 1:599.
[103] *Œuvres* (1665), 2:673.
[104] (Paris: Camusat, 1637).
[105] *Poésies choisies de Messieurs Corneille, Bensserade,* . . . *4ᵉ partie*
(Paris: Sercy, 1658), p. 420.

Des crimes dont il est souillé
Renaisse à ta grace divine.[106]

Chapelain could have found better examples, even in Malherbe.

Between the bad sonnets and the equally bad *Miserere,* Chapelain wrote his masterpiece, the *Ode à Mgr le Cardinal Duc de Richelieu.*[107] It had three editions in his lifetime, was included in many *recueils collectifs,* was greatly admired by Huet and Rapin, and even Boileau condescended to call it "une assez belle Ode."[108] In this respect, the mortal enemy of Chapelain was kinder than Collas, who called the ode a "triste chef-d'œuvre, tout à fait incapable . . . de sauver la réputation de son auteur du naufrage de la *Pucelle.*"[109] Further belittling the subject of his book, Collas states: "Héritier de Malherbe, Chapelain l'est dans son ode, si on entend qu'il applique consciencieusement les procédés du maître; mais de l'héritage il n'a pris que cela; il a laissé le meilleur: ce don lyrique. . . ."[110] While as a whole the ode is rather dull, this is not its main failing as a Malherbian legacy, since its very form is in violation of the master's every idea on form.

As I have already stated, Malherbe, fearing chaos, disliked heterometric ten-line stanzas. In fact, he wrote only two poems using that form, both starting with alexandrines and ending with shorter lines. He preferred isometric ten-line stanzas and used mostly octosyllabic lines, though he soon abandoned such long stanzas altogether. Chapelain's ode is made up of ten-line stanzas, each composed of an octosyllabic sestet followed by an alexandrine quatrain. Thus while Malherbe, in accord with Maynard, insisted on a 4–6 break, this ode contains a visual, formal 6–4 division. Yet structurally Chapelain did divide most of his stanzas 4–6, with a secondary break after the seventh line. Thus, in spite of the visual and formal aspects, Maynard's 4–3–3 stricture is heeded. What is noteworthy about this procedure is that, as a result of this syntactical arrangement, the octosyllabic lines are linked to the alexandrines and the pitfall Malherbe feared is avoided:

[106] Stanza 3.
[107] (Paris: Camusat, 1633).
[108] *Œuvres complètes,* p. 6.
[109] Georges Collas [Carl Felix von Schlichtegroll], *Jean Chapelain* (Paris: Perrin, 1912), p. 113.
[110] Ibid., p. 114.

Ebloui de clartés si grandes,
Incomparable Richelieu,
Ainsi qu'à notre demi-Dieu,
Je te viens faire mes offrandes.
L'équitable siècle à venir
Adorera ton souvenir
Et du siècle présent te nommera l'Alcide:
Tu serviras un jour d'objet à l'univers,
Aux ministres d'exemple, aux monarques de guide,
De matière à l'histoire et de sujet aux vers.

If anything, this effect is enhanced on the rare occasions when Chapelain allows a single sentence to fill the entire stanza:

Mais bien que sous ton grand génie
Le courage et le jugement
De notre heureux gouvernement
Composent la douce harmonie,
Bien que tes superbes lauriers
S'égalent à ceux des guerriers
Dont les siècles passés racontent les miracles,
N'attends pas toutefois que je chante aujourd'hui
La prudente valeur, qui malgré tant d'obstacles
T'a rendu des humains le refuge et l'appui.

This keen sense of rhythm and harmony is nowhere more obvious than in Chapelain's judicious use of carefully balanced antitheses:

Tu n'en as que la fleur, nous en avons le fruit:
Recevant les faveurs, aussitôt tu les verses,
Et le bien que te cherche, en même temps te fuit.

The refining of this sense of balance in a double confrontation, one within the line, the other within the hemistich, is apparent in the following:

Et, sans que sa vigueur soit jamais affaiblie,
Qu'on cède, ou qu'on résiste, il va d'un même cours.

After that, oxymora such as the one suggesting that in Richelieu's love for his subjects and willingness to sacrifice himself for them "Il n'est point de tourment qui ne lui semble doux" can only appear as bombastic commonplaces that spoil an otherwise sound poem.

At Malherbe's death, only Desmarests was old enough to have established any literary contacts, and by the time the "années de gloire de l'Hôtel de Rambouillet" rolled around, he was too busy with Richelieu and the newly-founded Academy to spend much time at the salon. While the more serious Chapelain thought of him as "un des esprits faciles de ce temps," he also considered him "inépuisable et rapide dans l'exécution, aimant mieux y laisser des taches et des négligences que de n'avoir pas bientôt fait."[111] On the other hand, the younger, less learned members of that coterie soon discovered that *galanteries* were not his forte. As a result, at the Hôtel in the 1630s there were two men, Chapelain and Voiture, representing two diametrically opposed concepts of poetry, both looking for a following but surrounded only by very young men, some nearly a full generation younger, with only Godeau and Corneille bridging the chronological gap, and Corneille's presence in the salon was, at best, infrequent.

Godeau, at the beginning of this period, was still very much the jolly dwarf, as Magne described him, not averse to secular poetry. In 1633, the *Nouvelles muses des Sieurs Godeau, Chapelain . . .*[112] appeared. The title of the anthology, by including his name, implies a certain popularity, since the sales of such volumes depended on the reputation of the authors featured. If Chapelain was trying at this time to wear Malherbe's mantle, Godeau was not. "Divines sources de la Gloire," typical of the Godeau poems included, is as un-Malherbian as possible. The octosyllabic ten-line stanzas have every syntactical break imaginable, enjambments abound, as do bad rhymes, the most frequent violation being nonhomophonic *consonnes d'appui*. Godeau's contributions to the *Guirlande de Julie* are of the same ilk: the eighteen heterometric lines of "La tulipe" defy analysis, and only one rhyme—*souvent-vent*—can be considered acceptable. "Le narcisse" is no better as to rhymes, though the heterometry of this sestet is Malherbian. All in all, it must be said that when Godeau abandoned this type of poetry for more

---

[111] *Opuscules critiques,* p. 361.
[112] (Paris: Bertault, 1633).

pious endeavors, Voiture's "camp" lost very little. By that time, the still younger members had decided what avenue to follow.

Of these younger poets, Charles de Montausier is the most difficult to situate. When he entered the famous salon, he was barely twenty years old, but his portrait, as drawn by Magne, shows him to be ill-suited for the amusements of the Hôtel de Rambouillet: "Le cadet, Charles, marquis de Salles, c'est au contraire la maussaderie, la rudesse, la lourdeur, la brutalité, le pessimisme."[113] During this period the young man spent most of his time at the wars and seldom came to throw cold water on the happy group. For many years, it was he who encouraged Chapelain and defended him against all comers. He was the only one not bored by the *Pucelle,* which he sincerely admired.[114] Time and time again, Chapelain referred to Voiture as the man Montausier thoroughly disliked,[115] a dislike that is easy to understand: "Montausier sent instinctivement que la grâce de Voiture s'oppose, dans l'esprit de Julie d'Angennes, à sa rudesse et lui nuit."[116] The situation was, in fact, delightfully ironic: Montausier's worship of Julie, though far from secret, remained unspoken, and only Chapelain's prodding brought the young lover out of his shell.[117] From his military post in Alsace, Montausier sent some of his typically heavy lines to the woman he adored, and Julie, who could be cruel in her pranks, charged Voiture with the reply. It must be admitted that Montausier's erotic declarations were hardly in tune with the poetic tastes of the "Divine Julie":

> Je ne sçaurois vous dire assurément
> Combien encor mon triste éloignement
> Me causera de fâcheuses journées
> Car, jusqu'ici, mes volontés bornées
> Ne m'ont permis de vivre librement.
> Ceux qui sur moy règnent absolument
> De demeurer m'ont fait commandement.

[113] Emile Magne, *Voiture et les origines de l'Hôtel de Rambouillet* (Paris: Mercure de France, 1911), 1:193.

[114] Magne, *Voiture et les années de gloire,* pp. 84–86.

[115] *Lettres,* 1:367, 539.

[116] Magne, *Voiture et les années de gloire,* p. 151.

[117] Ibid., p. 156.

Rompre leurs liens qui sont mes destinées,
Je ne sçaurois.[118]

For once, Maynard and Voiture could agree on the merits of a poem. The latter, commanded by Julie, wrote a reply which, though sarcastic, gave some hope:

Je veux qu'on soit à moi parfaitement,
Et, quand je fais quelque commandement,
Je n'entends pas que l'on me vienne dire:
Je ne saurois.[119]

At any rate, Montausier refused to give in and wrote a sonnet which Magne considers "peut-être sa meilleure œuvre poétique, . . . sa profession de foi amoureuse":[120]

Aimez, servez, bruslez avecque patience
Ne murmurez jamais contre vostre tourment,
Et ne vous lassez point de souffrir constamment:
Il n'est rien qui ne cède à la persévérance.

Si vous estiez troublé de la vaine créance
Qu'on a beaucoup de mal et peu d'allègement,
Apprenez qu'il n'est point de tel contentement
Que de voir, à la fin, triompher sa constance.

Lorsqu'une belle main daigne essuyer vos pleurs
Un moment de plaisir paye un an de douleurs;
Le repos est plus doux qui vient après la peine.

Pour estre bien aimé, soyez bien amoureux,
Mesprisez le mespris et surmontez la hayne,
Enfin, soyez constant et vous serez heureux.[121]

[118] Cited in ibid., p. 156.
[119] *Œuvres*, 2:325.
[120] *Voiture et les années de gloire*, pp. 156–57.
[121] Ibid., p. 157.

What is remarkable in this sonnet is not its fairly Malherbian nature, despite some facile rhymes, but that its general tone demonstrates a change in Montausier. Some time before, possibly as early as 1633, he had asked some friends to contribute to what was to become the *Guirlande*.[122] He must have realized that Julie would respond more readily to the honey of the *galants* than to the vinegar of the *pédants*. The sonnet above and the poems that follow may not be as successful as one might wish, but they do show that, in spirit at least, Montausier had joined the "corps," the inner circle of the Hôtel. He contributed to the *Guirlande* and asked the better poets to join him. Many did, but Voiture was not among them, though it is impossible to ascertain whether he refused to collaborate with his enemy or was never asked to do so.[123]

Although most of Montausier's poems were never published, he enjoyed a certain popularity if one can judge by the frequency with which his name appears in the various *recueils* of poems and songs. This popularity is in itself a mystery for, as I have suggested, it was only with utmost difficulty that he achieved a partial success in gallantry. On the other hand, as we shall soon see, Chapelain's sympathy for the young man must have been due to the latter's inclinations and not to his fortunate emulation of Malherbe. If Montausier's personality was perhaps in some ways reminiscent of Malherbe's, his poetic output, early or late, was not. It is not only all too frequently heavy and plodding, but totally lacking in what Chapelain had called *savoir*.

Of the twelve sonnets mentioned by Magne,[124] only four are in alexandrines, the rest octosyllabic. The rhyme scheme is generally Malherbian, though there are exceptions. The full extent of Montausier's un-Malherbianism can best be seen in "Désirs incertains":

> *La douleur me rend le teint blême*
> *Quand on me traite rudement;*
> *Mon inquiétude est extrême*
> *Quand on me traite doucement;*

[122] Chapelain, *Lettres*, 1:46.

[123] Later on, when Julie became ridiculous in her resistance to the marquis, Voiture changed his stand and, by voicing his new sentiments, consecrated the conversion of Montausier.

[124] *Voiture et les années de gloire*, pp. 374–79.

Tantôt ami, tantôt amant,
Je ne me connais pas moi-même,
Et je ne sais pas seulement
Si je souhaite que l'on m'aime.

Souvent je suis las de souffrir,
Et souvent je crains de guérir,
Tant mon incertitude est grande.

Faisant tous les jours mille vœux,
Je ne sais ce que je demande:
Amour, dis-moi ce que tu veux.[125]

Note that the rhyme scheme is *a b a b b a b a c c d e d e*, and that practically all of Malherbe's dislikes are well represented: *a* contains a short rhyming with a long as well as two homophones; three of the four *b* rhymes are adverbs; *e* is made up of two monosyllabic homophones. It is a pity that Alceste was not asked to comment on this sonnet, which is, as Faguet states, "dans le goût d'Oronte";[126] unfortunately, it is typical of Montausier's taste as well.

The various madrigals that Montausier wrote for the *Guirlande* are no better. "Zéphyre à Julie" is heterometric, combining octosyllabic lines with alexandrines, but in a way that suggests *vers libres* rather than anything Malherbian. Its fourteen lines are divided into three uneven groups (4–2–8) and the rhymes are as poor as the ones already examined. Some constructions are quite clumsy; others result in cacophony—"Que celles que l'on met. . . ." Still others show that Montausier had not entirely succeeded in shaking off his pedantic past—"L'eau dont Permesse les arrose."[127] The other madrigals, though shorter, do not improve. But one poem of this type, probably written at the same time, has some fortunate passages and deserves attention. It is "A des rossignols qu'il entendait chanter," rescued from the obscurity of the Conrart manuscripts by Paul d'Estrée. Here is the first stanza of this song, which the critic rightfully described as having "une certaine délicatesse de touche":

[125] Paul d'Estrée, "A travers les manuscrits de Conrart," *RHLF* 2 (1895): 89–107.
[126] *Histoire de la poésie*, 3:137.
[127] Allem, *Anthologie*, 2:88.

Rossignols, dont la douce voix
Trouble le silence des bois
Où je demeure,
Vous êtes heureux en amour,
Vous chantez la nuit et le jour,
Et moi je pleure.[128]

This particular combination of lines was never used by Malherbe, who would not have totally approved the structure either. In subsequent stanzas, rhymes are often unsatisfactory and enjambments occur. Commonplaces are exploited, as in the last stanza:

. . . loin des divins appas
Sans qui ma vie est un trépas,
Toujours je pleure.

Yet, one cannot help but agree with Faguet who, in spite of some strong reservations—which I share—felt that the *chute* was "très bien trouvée," and that the song was, as a whole, "charmante et d'un joli tour."[129]

As I have said, Montausier's idea of a floral offering to Julie d'Angennes not only was accepted with alacrity by the "corps," it became his passport to membership. Most of the contributors have already been discussed, but one remains. Germain Habert, five years younger than Montausier, was a member of the fortunate few, of the "corps." Despite his youth, he was one of the first members of the Academy. It was therefore natural that Montausier would ask him to participate in the creation of the *Guirlande*.

Habert is one of the more interesting faithful of the Chambre Bleue. As *précieux* as any member of the "corps," he was at home at the Hôtel. He also frequented the salon of the somewhat less fashionable Mlle de Gournay,[130] an unyielding foe of Malherbe. Yet poetically he could be quite Malherbian. His "Métamorphose des yeux de Philis en astres" is of a remarkably limpid versification. The subject, of course, is not of a type happily treated by Malherbe, but Habert was versatile. In his paraphrases

[128] D'Estrée, "A travers les manuscrits," p. 92.
[129] *Histoire de la poésie,* 3:136–37.
[130] C.-P. Goujet, *Bibliothèque françoise* (Paris: Mariette, 1740–1756), 16:215–20.

of psalms, for instance, one recent critic sees in him not only a conscious follower of Malherbe, but one who chooses those psalms "dont le ton est le plus magnifique."[131] It is difficult not to agree with this critic when she astutely remarks that if the alexandrines of these paraphrases are at times massive, they are nevertheless "animés d'un souffle puissant qui les emporte jusqu'au bout sans défaillance."[132]

Habert composed these three paraphrases about 1637, when he was only twenty-two years old, but their merits are undeniable. The language was undoubtedly influenced by his mundane penchant and more *galant* poetry, and these influences at times spoil otherwise powerful passages:

> *Ouy sans doute, Seigneur, ta feconde science*
> *Est un vaste ocean, sans rivage et sans fonds,*
> *Dans les sacrez détours de sa grandeur immense,*
> *Je m'égare toûjours, toûjours je me confonds.*
> *Quand je passe la nuit dans cette noble étude,*
> *A la fin pour tout fruit de mon inquietude*
> *Je connois ma faiblesse et ma témérité,*
> *Je tombe à chaque pas; et l'errante courriere*
> *Qui dans un char brillant ramene la lumiere,*
> *Me rencontre et me laisse en cette obscurité.*[133]

The last two and a half lines are shockingly out of place. Their pedantry and "baroquism" weaken the impression of sincerity in the preceding lines. At times, however, the combination of artifice and sincerity can be quite fortunate:

> *Et quand je descendrois dans le plus creux de l'onde,*
> *Où s'eteint chaque jour la lumière du monde,*
> *J'y serois découvert par celle de tes yeux.*[134]

Structurally, Habert is equally successful. The heptasyllabic quatrains of Psalm 84 are of extreme regularity, and the alexandrines of Psalms 49

[131] Paulette Leblanc, *Les paraphrases françaises des Psaumes à la fin de la période baroque* (Paris: Presses Universitaires de France, 1966), p. 117.

[132] Ibid., p. 122.

[133] Cited in ibid., p. 122.

[134] Ibid.

and 138 form ten-line stanzas that are most Malherbian. The major break is invariably 4–6 with a secondary break almost always after the seventh line.[135] The regularity of the caesuras, the perfect balance of the lines, everything contributes to a lyricism that Malherbe could only have admired:

> *Non, si de ton courroux, j'excite la tempeste,*
> *L'aube ni le couchant, le midy ni le nort,*
> *N'auront point pour cacher ou défendre ma teste*
> *D'abysme assez profond, ni d'azile assez fort.*[136]

Is it any wonder then that Chapelain[137] and Balzac admired him, that Maynard said of him, "jamais . . . la poësie françoise n'a parlé si hautement,"[138] and that both Sorel and Guéret credited him with having contributed as much as anyone to the establishment of Malherbe's reforms?

Still, it would be wrong to think that Habert was always so Malherbian. Perhaps he thought of paraphrases as exercises in proficiency and virtuosity, and thus lavished much care on their composition. His *stances* are much freer. Not only do they lack the grandeur of movement and flowing lyricism so present in the paraphrases (a defect that could be explained partially by the subjects) but they are technically and poetically much weaker. Like the "Métamorphoses" written about 1639, the *stances* all too frequently fail to take flight not because of the subject matter but because of weaknesses that a more careful craftsman could have avoided.

The *stances* "C'est souffrir trop longtemps"[139] fall into this category. While they are always correct as to number, the rhymes are seldom more than sufficient, and enjambments are frequent and often lead to a chaotic structure. The *stances* "Sur le jour de l'an"[140] are no better. The mixture of diverse moods is at times funny, more often painful. The isometry of

---

[135] In the above-cited *dizain*, such is obviously the case despite capricious punctuation which, although probably the work of a careless typesetter, I did not dare alter.

[136] Leblanc, *Paraphrases*, p. 122.

[137] See for instance his letter to Godeau, 18 Feb. 1638.

[138] Drouhet, *François Mainard*, p. 313.

[139] *Poésies choisies. . . . 5ᵉ partie* (Paris: Sercy, 1660), pp. 367–68.

[140] Ibid., p. 235.

the quatrains is thwarted by these shifts: as the author moves from the commonplaces of *précieux* love to most physical declarations, the tone changes, but what is meant to break the monotony only brings about disorder. The form itself of these quatrains, being isometric, is one which Malherbe had shunned in his later years. The rhyme pattern is Malherbian, but the quality of the rhymes is not: the presence of monosyllabic homophones (*prix-pris*) or homonyms (*point-point*), of long sounds rhyming with short ones (*peine-étrenne, âme-flamme*), the frequent absence of homophony in the *consonnes d'appui*, all give an impression of careless composition. This lack of polish is equally present in the elegy "Dieux! à qui me plaindrai-je?"[141] as the first two lines show:

> *Dieux! à qui me plaindrai-je? Et dessous quel visage*
> *Ferai-je voir au jour mon malheur et ma rage?*

Bad caesuras, enjambments, expletives (*dessous*), and unfortunate choices of words (*rage*) abound.

Much the same can be said of Habert's contributions to the *Guirlande de Julie*. Two alexandrine sestets, "La rose" and "Le narcisse," not only use a form abandoned by Malherbe, but show little imagination in the rhymes (*vœux-feux, vous-doux*), and "La rose," in spite of its brevity, boasts an unfortunate leonine combination:

> *Et je crains qu'aujourd'hui la rose ne finisse*
> *Par ce qui fit jadis commencer le narcisse.*

Another version of "Le narcisse" appears in the *Guirlande*, also attributed to Habert, and it is even more interesting. A heterometric ten-line stanza of a type never used by Malherbe—12–12–12–8–8–12–12–12–8–12, *a a b c c b d e e d*—and broken 3–3–4, it has unusually rich rhymes except for the *soleil-pareil* duo to which Malherbe could not have objected. The caesuras are perfect. Yet, it can only be described as an utter failure:

> *Je consacre Julie un Narcisse à ta gloire,*
> *Lui-même des beautés te cède la victoire,*

---

[141] Ibid., pp. 363–66.

Etant jadis touché d'un amour sans pareil;
Pour voir dedans l'eau son image
Il baissait toujours le visage,
Qu'il estimait plus beau que celui du Soleil:
Ce n'est plus ce destin qui tient sa tête basse,
C'est qu'en te regardant il a honte de voir
Que les Dieux ont eu le pouvoir
De faire une beauté qui la sienne surpasse.[142]

This failure can only be ascribed to overly-precious, stilted imagery and needless inversions and expletives. In short, Habert, like most of his friends, was capable of carrying on Malherbe's mission. Like his friends, he chose not to.

[142] *Ibid.*, 2ᵉ *partie* (1653), p. 229.

Chapter Four

The Academy

Little doubt can exist as to Richelieu's intention when he first forced the young Academy to accept his patronage. But we must remember that the authors who formed its nucleus were not all of a kind, and that few, in fact, had written anything that could be considered of an "official" nature. As L.-A. Bergounioux has pointed out, all the members of the Conrart group—all that is except Gombauld, who considered himself "le représentant officiel de la doctrine du maître et le chef de son école poétique" —were quite young.[1] The first meetings at Conrart had no set purpose other than to bring together some of the brilliant young men of the capital. Neither the eventual gate-crashing by older men such as Gombauld and Bois-Robert, nor the subsequent opportunism of Richelieu played any role in the formation of that nucleus. It is therefore difficult to see how and why so many critics have insisted on the regulatory nature and official capacity of the Academy. During the first decade of its existence, a decade that was also the last of Louis XIII's reign, it was a particularly heterogeneous group with diverse leanings and tastes.[2] It is precisely because of its heterogeneity that the Academy is a logical milieu for the study of Malherbe's influence.

Of the original immortals, only the following can be associated with any poetic endeavors: Bois-Robert, Chapelain, Colletet, Desmarests, Godeau, Gombauld, Gomberville, L'Estoile, Laugier de Porchères, Malleville, Maynard, Méziriac, Arbaud de Porchères, Racan, Saint-Amant, Serisay, and, as of 1636, Baro.[3] Of these, Maynard and Racan have been amply discussed already. The other fifteen, the subjects of this chapter, form a strange mixture of diverse personalities—a group of men both assiduous and lazy, pedantic and frivolous, and, as will be seen, Malherbian and un-Malherbian. Nor can a correlation be made from one category to the other: neither Balzac nor Voiture, at opposite ends of the literary spectrum, could be bothered to attend the meetings of the august assembly. It

85

is, of course, quite possible that literary ideas had little to do with their reluctance to attend. Voiture, in Gaston d'Orléans's employ at the time, might well have feared an official organization to which he might owe, to use Balzac's words on this matter, "une obéissance aveugle."[4]

Many of these poets—Arbaud de Porchères, Godeau, Gombauld, and Gomberville in particular—claimed to be disciples of Malherbe, but it is nearly impossible to ascertain to what degree these claims were sincere, since Malherbe was universally admired and it had become a trick of the trade to associate one's name with that of the master, whether that association had been acknowledged by him or not. The basic question thus remains: to what degree did these disciples actually follow the dictates of Malherbe?

One of the most interesting of these cases is that of François d'Arbaud, sieur de Porchères. Cousin of Malherbe by marriage, Arbaud de Porchères always professed to be a disciple of the master whose works he eventually published. If Malherbe never acknowledged him as a disciple, he nevertheless loved him enough to will him one half of his library, a substantial part of the poor man's total wealth.[5]

In 1622, Arbaud de Porchères published a paraphrase of psalms whose popularity led to at least two later editions, in 1633 and 1636. In the preface the author lays claim to intentions and qualities that would make of him a definite follower of Malherbe. Paulette Leblanc right-fully states that "sa paraphrase ne contient que de rares hébraïsmes très connus de tous, les images sont acclimatées au goût de l'époque, tout ce qui pourrait être insolite est abandonné."[6] What does such a para-phrase look like? A fragment of Psalm 132 will show us:

---

[1] *Marc-Antoine Dominici* (Paris: Boivin, 1936), p. 360.

[2] The members disagreed violently on the occasion of their first task, the examination of Corneille's *Cid*.

[3] Jean Baudoin was also among the first members, but his early poetry seems to have been appreciated only by himself. Only in the *Second livre des Délices* (1620) do a sizable number of his poems appear; this is not surprising since he was the editor of the volume.

[4] *Œuvres* (1665), 1:727.

[5] Racan inherited the other half, and the two poets seem, in fact, to have been close friends if one can believe the expression of warm sentiments that appear in some liminary poems they traded.

[6] *Paraphrases*, p. 107.

Ainsi qu'en la chaude saison
L'eau qui peint au matin les herbes,
Fait que nos collines superbes
Produisent des fruicts à foison:
Ainsi la paix dont est unie
Vne si sainte compagnie
Comble leur famille de biens;
Et Dieu, d'où leur vient ceste grace
Dans la gloire promise aux siens
Leur garde une éternelle place.[7]

Gone are the frequent proper names and the hyperbolic tones of the original, but gone also its majesty. To be sure, the poem is quite Malherbian in many respects: the rhyme scheme, the choice of the form itself (octosyllabic *dizains*) and the clear 4–3–3 break must have pleased the poet's cousin, but what about the actual results? Rhymes such as *grace-place, unie-compagnie,* and cacophonic passages such as *dont est unie* are not above reproach. But if Porchères falls short of the mark, it is not because of such trivialities. Although Leblanc considers this psalm "noble à souhait" and a "très joli poeme,"[8] I find it overly abstract, stilted and, above all, totally devoid of either the breadth or breath that Malherbe could have given it. This last shortcoming is particularly obvious in poems in which Porchères tries to express strong feelings such as love or hate, or deep thoughts:

Ce n'est pas d'auiourd'huy Prouidence supréme,
Que les iours de ma vie inconneus à moy-mesme
    Te sont conneus à toy;
Et soit que ie trauaille, ou que ie me repose,
    Tu preuois mieux que moy
Tout ce que vainement mon esprit se propose.[9]

How right Leblanc is to state that for this "talent un peu grêle, . . . le grand lyrisme n'était point fait."[10]

[7] Ibid., p. 108.
[8] Ibid.
[9] Ibid., p. 109.
[10] Ibid.

In all his poetic efforts, Porchères obviously tried to follow in his cousin's footsteps, and his ode to the king, published in the *Parnasse Royal*,[11] is fairly successful:

> *Grand Roy, que la France a veu naistre*
> *Pour achever de la guérir,*
> *Et que la Terre aura pour maistre*
> *Quand tu la voudras conquérir;*
> *Reçoy de bon œil en hommage,*
> *Ces vers où je peins ton image*
> *D'un crayon si vif et si beau,*
> *Que le pourtrait du plus grand homme,*
> *Qu'ait mis au jour la vieille Rome*
> *N'esgalera point ce Tableau.*

Goujet, citing this stanza, adds, "Tout le reste de cette Ode sent bien un vrai disciple de Malherbe."[12] The ode is quite Malherbian in plan and in execution, and only with the *beau-tableau* rhyme could one find fault. However, not all of Porchères's efforts were equally fortunate. His sonnet "Ministre glorieux du plus grand Roy du monde," though composed according to the dictates of Malherbe, is a pitiful failure; witness this quatrain:

> *Louis qu'avec tant d'heur ta conduite seconde*
> *A vu par tes conseils ses rebelles défaits,*
> *Et l'étranger contraint de rechercher la paix*
> *Après l'avoir battu sur la terre et sur l'onde.*[13]

The rhymes, while not rich, are satisfactory, but the tortured syntax could only have made Malherbe shudder with horror.

Foremost among the many poets who tried to find a niche under Malherbe's vast mantle was Antoine Godeau. In the preface to his *Paraphrase des Pseaumes de David*[14] he professes great admiration for Malherbe and claims to work very hard on his poems. But the reader

---

[11] (Paris: Cramoisy, 1635).
[12] *Bibliothèque françoise*, 16:165.
[13] *Sacrifice des Muses*, p. 164.
[14] (Paris: Camusat et Le Petit, 1648).

has every right to doubt the sincerity or the powers of introspection of the poet. Chapelain spoke highly of his "pureté et facilité,"[15] considering him among the very best, but because of his elegance rather than his force or regularity. Godeau himself admitted this later in life, in one of his "Epîtres morales":

> Des mes plus jeunes ans j'ai goûté les douceurs
> De l'Art victorieux de ces divines sœurs;
> Sans étude, sans peine, en leurs bois solitaires
> Elles m'ont enseigné leurs célestes mystères.[16]

In the following epistle he speaks of

> l'ardeur de cette vive flamme,
> Dont naissant, je reçus les rayons dans mon ame.

Needless to say, neither the rhyme nor the idea is very Malherbian. Careless in his composition, he often allowed his friends (Balzac and Chapelain in particular) to make corrections for which he had neither the inclination nor the diligence. It was perhaps this frame of mind which made him say some years later, when speaking of assuming the duties of his bishopric in Grasse, "Paris a mon estime, et Grasse a mon amour."[17] Godeau's full understanding of all that Malherbe stood and fought for is further put in doubt by one of his comments on the latter's work:

> Nous pouvons appeler ses pièces d'amour odes aussitôt que stances, puisque tout ce qui peut être chanté peut aussi recevoir ce nom. Et si quelqu'un s'étonne que celles qui le portent ne soient pas divisées par strophes, antistrophes et épodes, il doit considérer que cette distinction seroit inutile, l'usage que nous en faisons étant bien différent de celui des anciens, qui se servoient de ces mots pour signifier les divers tours de leurs dances aux environs de l'autel, pendant lesquelles ils avoient accoutumé de chanter.[18]

[15] Opuscules critiques, p. 363.
[16] Ep. 17, Poésies chrestiennes (Paris: Le Petit, 1660), 3:105.
[17] Ibid., p. 442.
[18] "Discours sur les œuvres de M. de Malherbe," in Malherbe, Œuvres, 1:382.

Malherbe would not have agreed to this qualification, for he "croyait apparemment que l'ode ne convenait qu'à de grands sujets,"[19] calling *stances* what others might have called *odes amoureuses*. It may be such basic misinterpretations that led Godeau astray, and this in turn might well be why, by 1695, Boileau judged him quite harshly. Calling him a "Poete fort estimable," he nevertheless had to conclude that Godeau "n'a rien qui remuë ni qui échauffe." This is what led him to conclude that Malherbe's reputation could only grow while that of Godeau was all but dead.[20] Maucroix, in answer to Boileau's judgment, cited a few good lines of Godeau, but fundamentally agreed, adding this damning thought: "il ne varie pas assez. C'est toujours la mesme figure."[21] This is indeed Godeau's major failing as a pupil of Malherbe, for the latter's main search, throughout his poetic career, was for originality.

If Godeau's theories were not as Malherbian as he thought them to be, what of his production? Unfortunately, it must receive the same judgment. The first edition of Godeau's *Œuvres chrestiennes*[22] had a tremendous success, particularly at court, and was followed by a second volume four years later. Neither shows much that can be attributed to Malherbe's influence.

In his choice of stanza forms, Godeau is not often Malherbian and is frequently unfortunate, particularly when, on rare occasions, he tries to experiment. As Fromilhague has amply demonstrated, Malherbe preferred the isometric ten-line stanza to the heterometric. Godeau did not follow him in this, but chose combinations never used by Malherbe for obvious reasons. Psalm 148 is composed of stanzas of nine octosyllabic lines and one alexandrine:

> *Messagers du Dieu des batailles*
> *De qui le bras victorieux*
> *Dans l'assaut le plus furieux*
> *Défend nos plus foibles murailles,*
> *Guide des Hebreux esgarez,*

[19] Houdar de la Motte, cited by Winegarten, *French Lyric Poetry*, p. 104.
[20] *Œuvres complètes*, p. 796.
[21] François de Maucroix, *Lettres*, ed. by Renée Kohn (Paris: Presses Universitaires de France, 1962), p. 176. On this point, see the very astute remarks of Professor Kohn in her critical notes, particularly pp. 288–93.
[22] (Paris: Camusat, 1633).

> Beaux Astres qui les retirez
> De leurs tenebres criminelles,
> Anges, dans vostre heureux sejour,
> Loüez les bontez immortelles
> De celuy qui vous brusle et vous nourrit d'amour.[23]

The form does not hamper the lyrical intent, but it is far from Malherbian. In fact, its élan is mainly due to the violation of another Malherbian stricture: the entire stanza is made up of a single syntactical unit, giving it a rather breathless *emportement* which the length of the last line slows down. His paraphrase of Psalm 67 uses another combination unknown to Malherbe:

> Lève toy lumière du monde,
> Soleil de iustice et d'Amour,
> Il est temps de rendre le iour
> Après une nuit si profonde.
> N'as-tu pas veu couler les pleurs
> Que nous donnions à nos douleurs?
> N'as-tu pas ressenti nos peines?
> Veux-tu permettre encor à ces Rois furieux
> D'espuiser le sang de nos veines,
> Comme ils ont espuisé toute l'eau de nos yeux?[24]

Not only is the result chaotic, but the rhythm and basic unity of the *dizain* are completely destroyed. The forty-three stanzas that follow are no better. Psalm 19, in *Institution du Prince Chrestien*, uses an 8–12–12–12–12–8 construction, one which was shunned by Malherbe for obvious reasons, making it difficult to agree entirely with Renée Winegarten when she asserts that Godeau "adhered to the musical conceptions of lyricism held by Malherbe and hoped to have his psalms set to music."[25] It is difficult to imagine a reaction more negative than the one Malherbe might have had, had he been obliged to judge the lyrical properties of the above stanzas, or of Psalm 103, made up of two isometric ten-line stanzas of eight

---

[23] Leblanc, *Paraphrases*, p. 154.
[24] Ibid.
[25] *French Lyric Poetry*, p. 41.

consecutive octosyllabic lines and two alexandrines, the first one broken 2–2–6, the second 4–6. Nor would his opinion of the 12–8–12–8 quatrain, frequently used by Godeau, have been much kinder.[26]

As far as the rules governing rhymes are concerned, Godeau was no more Malherbian than in other matters. It is true that he followed the *âme-blasme* demand to the point where a rhyme that is a Malherbian commonplace is at least as common in his own works, and this may have had much to do with Maucroix's condemnation, but elsewhere Godeau cannot be accused of following too closely in Malherbe's footsteps: his *consonne d'appui* is frequently weak (*feux-orgueilleux, voix-françois, tours-secours, yeux-cieux*), and some of his rhymes are completely unacceptable:

> *Mortels dont l'esprit curieux*
> *Veut tout connaître et tout comprendre,*
> *Et qui n'étant qu'un peu de cendre,*
> *Pensez souvent être des Dieux.*

Note that in this extract from the "Hymne sur la naissance du Seigneur," [kyriø] (diaeresis) is made to rhyme with [djø] (synaeresis) if the isometry of the lines is to be kept. The sonnet "Sur la résurrection des hommes" is equally bad on that score, adding to these deviations from doctrine a definitely non-Malherbian rhyme scheme, padding ("En sortiront un jour et si clairs et si beaux") and archaisms such as *froidure*.[27]

Godeau was not the only poet at the Academy to devote himself to furthering Malherbe's reputation. Another fervent partisan was Marin Le Roy de Gomberville.[28] A friend of Maynard, Gomberville wrote a preface for the latter's works in which his Malherbian leanings are made explicit. But Gomberville, like Godeau, either did not fully comprehend the nature of Malherbe's creativity or was merely paying lip service to a vogue when he professed to be his disciple.

Malherbe had understood that, to make his new regime viable, it was

---

[26] Louis XIII did have Godeau's psalms set to music and even had them sung on his deathbed, but that would have done little to soften Malherbe's blows.

[27] Ironically, this is one of Godeau's sonnets most frequently anthologized.

[28] See in particular Goujet, *Bibliothèque françoise*, 17:342–43.

necessary to "rompre le 'charme,' frapper l'opinion, lui signifier qu'un coup d'état s'opérait et que la poésie changeait de maître."[29] Malherbe's search for novelty was therefore more than an intellectual game; for him, the "difficulté vaincue" was much more than an esoteric toy. Not so for Gomberville, and Philip Wadsworth was right in his assessment of that poet:

> The experimental spirit reveals itself very clearly in the pattern of his verse. To vary his means of expression he essayed a wide range of unusual forms such as an irregular sonnet, a poem in dialogue, and many kinds of refrains. He combined different meters to create striking effects, using lines of seven, five, three, and two syllables. These intricate, difficult stanzas were a hindrance to writing good poetry, but that did not matter. Like a boy who strains a new toy to the breaking point Marin Le Roy wanted to feel out the possibilities which versification could offer.[30]

Clearly Malherbe had to accept a rather large legacy from the Renaissance poets; no new regime has ever been able to start with a perfect *table rase.* Gomberville, however, was much too eclectic to be considered a good "Malherbian." Courting fame at a very early age, by the time he was twenty-one "he counted over fifty lyrics to his credit and had already won recognition as a capable writer of verse."[31] Brienne went so far as to call him "un trés-grand Poëte."[32] He started to imitate Malherbe very early in his career, but his verse, "which deals exclusively with the subject of love, abounds with conventional Renaissance gallantry and with learned mythological comparisons."[33] Not only did this self-styled Malherbian fail to reject the Pléiade to this extent, but he also professed a deep admiration for the works of Théophile de Viau, particularly his "Le Matin" from which he borrowed on at least two occasions.

[29] Fromilhague, *Technique,* p. 627.

[30] "Marin Le Roy de Gomberville: A Biographical Sketch," *Yale Romantic Studies* 18 (1941):59.

[31] Ibid., p. 58.

[32] Goujet, *Bibliothèque françoise,* 17:348.

[33] Wadsworth, "Gomberville," p. 58. As we shall see shortly, there are some exceptions to this devotion to erotic poetry.

Nor are these general trends the only reservations, for Gomberville failed even more pitifully in applying his master's rules. Whether in his erotic poetry or in his occasional verses, Gomberville suffers from a total lack of *souffle*.[34] While his vocabulary and choice of strophic structures are within the framework of Malherbian practice, his tortured syntax and barely sufficient rhymes are not and go a long way towards explaining why Malherbe never acknowledged him as one of his *écoliers* or even echoed Brienne's praise. Throughout his career,[35] Gomberville abuses adverbs, nouns ending in *-ment*, and proper nouns to achieve a rhyme. The *consonne d'appui* is all too frequently neglected (*sort-effort* being one of his favorite combinations) and he joins most of his contemporaries in disregarding Malherbe's stricture against the *âme-flamme* rhyme, using it so frequently as to make it one of his commonplaces. In sonnets, where the poet must find four words that rhyme, Gomberville's inventive gifts frequently fall short and he resorts then to a duplication that Malherbe could only have condemned: thus, in "Sur l'exposition du Saint Sacrement," the *a* rhyme is *terre-guerre-pierre-guerre;* the *b* rhyme, an unimaginative *-té* combination, is better; but *c* is the unacceptable *cieux-yeux, d* is *âme-flamme,* and *e* the insufficient *transports-corps*.[36]

Gomberville's syntax ranges from the nearly flawless to the unintelligible. Goujet was right to quote the sonnet "Cesse d'aimer le siècle . . ." as a particularly good one, and the last two lines could have been written by Malherbe:

> *Si Dieu ne rend ton corps esclave de ton ame,*
> *Ton ame est pour jamais esclave de ton corps.*[37]

But what would Malherbe have said of the syntax of all the Gomberville sonnets in *Elogia*, riddled with *chevilles* (entire hemistiches are at times repeated for no purpose other than filling in) and with a syntax so in-

---

[34] This is especially obvious in those of his poems included in the *Sacrifice des Muses*, pp. 184, 193, 194.

[35] For late evidence of this neglect, see his sonnets in *Elogia Julii Mazarini Cardinalis* (Paris: Vitré, 1666).

[36] Allem, *Anthologie*, 1:361–62. I might add that I did not find a single satisfactory rhyme involving *corps* in all of Gomberville's works examined, but the obvious difficulty involved must be kept in mind.

[37] *Bibliothèque françoise*, 17:345.

volved that in at least one case the resulting meaning is the very opposite of the one proposed by the author?[38] It is especially in the occasional poetry, where he has the obvious examples of Malherbe to follow, that Gomberville is furthest removed from his model. Abstractions such as

> *En m'échauffant le cœur éclaire-moi les yeux,*
> *Et ne sépare plus ta clarté de ta flamme*[39]

are very frequent. Other poems use forms quite ill-suited to the noble intent:

> *Tandis que le bruit de la guerre*
> *Trouble tous les peuples d'effroy,*
> *Et que les armes de mon Roy*
> *Vont conquérir toute la terre,*
> *Dans ce dur repos où m'a mis*
> *Le pouvoir de mes ennemis,*
> *Qui tient ma fortune abbatue,*
> *Grand et divin Armand, permets que dans mes vers*
> *Pour toy j'élève une statue*
> *Qui dure pour le moins autant que l'univers.*

This statue, composed of thirteen such stanzas, had to be rescued from well-deserved obscurity by a most generous critic.[40] The following poem, which contains at least as many traits that are irreconcilable with Malherbe's teachings and examples, is cited here only to show the distance that separated Gomberville from the master he was trying to emulate:

> *Après que ton grand cœur et ta haute sagesse*
> *Ont travaillé long-temps au bien de l'Univers,*
> *Tu suspens tes travaux et tes projets divers,*
> *Et viens te reposer aux rives du Permesse:*
>
> *Là tu répans sur nous l'immortelle richesse,*
> *Qui te couvre le front de Lauriers toujours verds,*

[38] See, for instance, "Sonnet," p. 8.
[39] Allem, *Anthologie*, 1:362.
[40] Wadsworth, *Gomberville*, p. 68.

Et tu fais triompher nostre scêne et nos vers
De la scêne et des vers de l'une et l'autre Gréce.

Invoque qui voudra comme un des immortels
Ce fantôme, à qui Delphe érigea des Autels,
Et l'aille consulter sur les bords de son onde:

Pour moy je ne tiens plus ce spectre pour un Dieu,
Et veux par mes écrits apprendre à tout le monde,
Qu'il n'est point d'Apollon que le grand Richelieu.[41]

Unlike Gomberville, Jean Ogier de Gombauld seems to have understood Malherbe's basic principles and was undoubtedly much more successful in continuing his work. However, we must be careful in ascertaining the actual importance of Malherbe in Gombauld's development. Much evidence points to Gombauld's genuine admiration for and conscious imitation of Malherbe's work, but chronology cannot be disregarded, and his first collection of sonnets, for instance, are obviously of a vintage that makes any Malherbian influence impossible.

At Rambouillet, Gombauld was called "le Beau Ténébreux," and if the physical part of that appellation does not suggest Malherbe, the mental one does. In the Chambre Bleue he was considered something of an arbiter of matters poetic but seems to have had only limited intercourse there, perhaps because his somber nature clashed with the prevailing mood. This nature, however, apparently did not prevent him from trying to "passer par tous les genres d'écrire,"[42] though it did indeed prevent him from succeeding in the lighter ones. This is especially obvious in his epigrams where his attempts at humor frequently seem heavy-handed and fall flat:

L'apollon de nos jours, Malherbe, ici repose;
Il a vécu longtemps sans beaucoup de support.
En quel siècle? Passant, je n'en dis autre chose.
Il est mort pauvre. Et moy, je vy comme il est mort.[43]

[41] Goujet, *Bibliothèque françoise*, 16:21.

[42] Jean-Ogier Gombauld, *Epigrammes* (Paris: Courbé, 1657), "Au lecteur."

[43] Cited in [Viollet le Duc], *Catalogue des livres composant la bibliothèque poétique de M. Viollet le Duc* (New York: Franklin, 1965), 1:528.

In his one serious attempt at writing an ode in the Malherbian manner, "A Monseigneur le Chancelier," Gombauld was equally unfortunate, the resulting twenty-one ten-line stanzas of octosyllabics abounding in obscure mythological references, expletives, and unsatisfactory rhymes.

Years ago, Lydie Morel, in what remains the most thorough examination of Gombauld, came to the conclusion that his sonnets were his best works.[44] There are, to be sure, exceptions, and there are times when Gombauld's attempts at elevation cause him to lapse into the grandiloquent and the obscure:

> Faites voir, grand Prélat, aux mortels éblouis
> Le règne de celui qui fait régner Louis,
> Et défendez sa cause, où lui même préside.[45]

The "Panégyrique,"[46] on the other hand, is pompous, in the best sense of the word, and does indeed recall the grand style of Malherbe. Published collectively in 1646, the sonnets are representative of nearly every period of Gombauld's poetic evolution. The early "Sonnets de Phillis" cannot be compared with anything written by Malherbe after "Les Larmes de Saint Pierre":

> Je m'étais proposé de vivre en vous servant,
> Mais puisque mon amour excite votre haine,
> C'est chérir ma disgrace, et mourir en vivant.[47]

But even these early, very baroque poems are for the most part metrically sound,[48] and with few exceptions are forcefully and clearly phrased. "Sur la mort de Monsieur de Montmorency," written probably in 1632, recalls Malherbe's poems on analogous subjects with the commonplaces of stoicism, the platitudes on the universality of death, but also with the controlled fire that is Malherbe's hallmark on such occasions. Shortly

---

[44] *Jean Ogier de Gombauld: Sa vie, son œuvre* (Neuchâtel: Delachaux et Niestlé, 1910), passim.

[45] *Sacrifice des Muses*, p. 21.

[46] Ibid., p. 185.

[47] *Poésies* (Paris: Courbé, 1646), p. 59.

[48] Reading Lierau, *Metrische Technik*, one can only come to the conclusion that Gombauld was the equal of Maynard in this particular respect.

thereafter, during the years I am examining here, Gombauld began to reject the "errors of his youth." These transitional years not only are marked by a spiritual conversion, but also witness a technical perfection:

> Erreur de ma jeunesse, agréable manie,
> Amour plein d'imprudence et de témérité,
> Ta loi sur mon esprit a trop d'autorité;
> J'en serai le vainqueur, elle en sera bannie.[49]

The rhymes, the syntax, the balance in the construction, everything in this quatrain bespeaks the greatest care and skill. A later "Sonnet chrétien," the oft-quoted "La voix qui retentit de l'un à l'autre pôle," ends with a notably strong tercet:

> Que les cieux les plus hauts, que les lieux les plus bas,
> Que ceux qui ne sont point, et que les morts entendent,
> Mon âme, elle t'apelle, et tu ne l'entens pas.

Alain Charmois was perhaps too kind in saying "je sais peu de pages aussi belles" after quoting these lines, but he was not altogether wrong in praising the clarity, the "construction ferme," and the "justesse d'emploi des mots les plus simples."[50] It is indeed in his judicious use of words not beyond the grasp of the "crocheteurs des Halles" that Gombauld comes closest to Malherbe's concept of creativity:

> Reçois ton fils, ô Père, et regarde la croix
> Où prêt de satisfaire à tout ce que je dois
> Il te fait de lui-même un sanglant sacrifice.[51]

Such austerity of expression is omnipresent in the sonnets of that period, and lines such as

> Sans toy mes actions ne font que t'offenser.
> Ma parole à toute heure accuse mon penser
> Et sans toy je n'ay point de véritable joye[52]

[49] Allem, Anthologie, 1:65.
[50] "Ogier de Gombauld," MdF 305 (1949):652.
[51] Ibid.
[52] Ibid., p. 653.

not only show Gombauld as an "artisan du vers" and an able emulator of Malherbe, but as a thinker who, "avant la lettre," had a fine grasp of the Pascalian concept of the grandeur of man. We are in the presence here of the very antithesis of preciosity. Unfortunately, these lines were penned by a man who, because of his age and his personality, could have but little influence on the more mundane young authors of the Academy.

Ironically, the much younger Claude de L'Estoile (1597–1652) could have been much more influential, but failed to be so. He can be easily situated at court during the early or mid-1620s, partly by the numerous ballets that he wrote, partly by the memoirs of the time. His ballets were quite popular at court, so it is not surprising that Richelieu, whose literary values left much to be desired, asked him to be one of the "five authors." It was therefore natural that he should become one of the early members of the Academy.

According to one critic, "L'Estoile, like most of his generation, underwent the forceful influence of Malherbe. . . . Particularly in matters of versification is L'Estoile a disciple of Malherbe. Restraint is the characteristic of his verse form, even when, as in his earlier love poetry, the thought breaks through the bonds of cold generalities."[53] This critic, in one of his few harsh remarks, concludes that "Malherbe had cast his cold shadow across the poet's page."[54] According to Parker, then, L'Estoile, "like most of his generation," is a "disciple of Malherbe." If this were indeed true, then he would be, as we shall soon see, a remarkably bad one. However, there is too much testimony to the contrary, both in the works of L'Estoile and in the comments that it elicited. To be sure, a few of his poems can be considered "dans les règles," but most of these were composed quite late in the poet's life.[55] The great bulk of L'Estoile's poetic output could only have been considered "licencieux" by Malherbe, and was so considered by his contemporaries. As Pellisson put it, L'Estoile spoke "contre la servitude de la rime, et se venge de tout le mal qu'elle lui a jamais fait souffrir."[56] Unfortunately, the rhyme is not the only complaint he might have had. It is true that poets writing libretti for

[53] Richard Alexander Parker, *Claude de L'Estoile, Poet and Dramatist, 1597–1652* (Baltimore: Johns Hopkins University Press, 1930), p. 29.

[54] Ibid.

[55] See, for instance, the moving sonnet "A sa Sainteté" in *Nouveau recueil des plus belles poésies* (Paris: Loyson, 1654).

[56] *Histoire de L'Académie Française*, 1:75.

ballets were given little time to complete a job for which they received scant reward and even less attention, but L'Estoile was equally careless in writing occasional poetry. The following song, set to music by Boesset about 1642, illustrates this point:

> Objet dont les charmes si doux
> M'ont enchaisnés sous vostre empire,
> Lorsque je suis absent de vous
> Mes pleurs tesmoignent mon martyre,
> Et quand je revoy vos appas,
> Un excez de plaisir me donne le trespas.[57]

The 8–8–8–8–8–12, *a b a b c c* combination was never used by Malherbe, and the 2–2–2 break makes its structure even less Malherbian. This is a typical court song, and the effect of languor derived from the heterometry of the last two lines is readily perceptible, but it is precisely this, coupled with commonplaces such as the refrain, that makes it difficult to think that Malherbe's cold shadow had even flitted across L'Estoile's pages.

L'Estoile, going well beyond Malherbe's "crocheteurs," had demanded understanding of his poetry from any of his servants, "même les plus rudes et les plus grossières."[58] Yet it is in direct contradiction of such intentions that he wrote lines such as

> Beauté beau tresor de ces lieux,
> Chere Cloris dont les beaux yeux
> Font desirer
> Plus que l'on ne doit esperer.[59]

Obviously, the verse form is not the least Malherbian aspect of this poem published in 1627, or of the following, published three years later:

> Il est vray vous estes si belle
> Qu'après vous il n'est rien qui me puisse ravir;
> Mais cessez d'estre si cruelle,
> Ou ie cesse de vous servir.

[57] Verchaly, *Airs de cour,* pp. 196–97.
[58] Pellisson, *Histoire de L'Académie Française,* 1:247.
[59] Parker, *Claude de L'Estoile,* p. 30.

. . . .
Ie fuy les beautez plus divines
Quand le moindre mespris est parmy leurs appas:
Mesme à cause de leurs espines,
Les roses ne me plaisent pas.[60]

One more comment must be made regarding L'Estoile's poetry: while it may be argued that Malherbe was or was not a perfect "arrangeur d'idées,"[61] there can be no doubt that he had a strong notion as to the structural unity of any poem made up of stanzas. L'Estoile did not. In his "O cruelle aduanture" of 1627, the first quatrain has an *a b b a* rhyme scheme whereas the next one has *a b a b*. What is still more disturbing, especially if one accepts Malherbe's concept of lyricism, is that L'Estoile frequently changes rhythmic patterns from stanza to stanza, even in songs. The drinking song "Que i'ayme en tout temps la tauerne!" is made up of octosyllabic sestets rhyming *a a b c b c*. These stanzas are, fittingly enough, composed of short syntactical units, but without any consistency: one breaks 4–2, others 3–3, with every conceivable secondary break. But the greatest fault one can find in this song which first appeared in the *recueil* of 1627 and was also included in the "Ballet de la Douairière de Billebahaut") is that it is unsingable: no rhythmic pattern links the various stanzas. Thus, the last two lines of stanza five

Ie le prens, apres i'en suis pris;
Ie le porte, et puis il m'emporte

cannot be sung to the same music as the last two lines of stanza seven:

Car ie les ietteray dehors
S'ils ne s'accordent bien ensemble.

Parker, in defense of L'Estoile, states that "Malherbe never would have indited a stanza like this:

[60] *Recueil des plus beaux vers de Messieurs de Malherbe, Racan,* . . . (Paris: Toussainct du Bray, 1630), p. 885.
[61] See Philip A. Wadsworth, "Form and Content in the Odes of Malherbe," *PMLA* 78 (June 1963):194.

Respect qui m'impose ta loy,
Ha! mon plus grand mal vient de toy
Quand ie meurs d'amour et de foy,
Tu veux que ie me taise,
Mais Respect en depit de toy
Il faut que ie la baise.''[62]

I beg to differ: even if the punctuation is blamed on indifferent typesetting and is corrected, the breaks remain 2–2–2, a phenomenon rarely seen in the late poetry of Malherbe; the 8–8–8–6–8–6 scheme is not to be found in Malherbe; the rhyme scheme is, at best, original; and the rhymes are totally inadequate. Even after 1630, when L'Estoile wrote more and more occasional poetry, his production did not allow for too favorable a comparison, as the following lines, unfortunately only too typical, clearly demonstrate:

C'est là qu'on oit gronder les torrens furieux
Capables d'entrainer les plus forts edifices:
C'est là que tous les monts s'éleuent iusqu'aux Cieux
Et que iusqu'aux Enfers vont tous les precipices.[63]

The alexandrine quatrains particularly shunned by Malherbe, and rhymes such as *furieux-Cieux* [fyriø-sjø], militate as much against the poet as do lines such as "Et rougit pour l'Espaigne et de sang et de honte,"[64] which Malherbe could only have condemned in the name of sanity in form and content.

Of the so-called or self-styled disciples of Malherbe, only two succeeded to any degree, and one of these—Porchères d'Arbaud—only rarely. Gombauld, on the other hand, can be said to have fallen under the spell of Malherbe's intentions. This can be discerned in his work, but the influence of that work, its popularity, or, for that matter, the popularity and influence of its old and "ténébreux" author on the rather heterogeneous assembly is impossible to ascertain. Chapelain, it will be

[62] *Claude de L'Estoile*, p. 30.
[63] Ibid., p. 33.
[64] Ibid.

recalled, spoke highly of him, but with hesitation: "Il paraît soutenu et élevé."[65] Boileau, years later, was no kinder.[66]

Besides these disciples, there were, at the Academy, several poets who considered themselves, if not followers of Malherbe, then his legitimate heirs. Of these, four deserve special mention: Méziriac, Desmarests de Saint-Sorlin, Colletet, and Chapelain.

Claude-Gaspard Bachet de Méziriac died in 1638, and therefore spent relatively little time at the Academy. The bulk of his poetry appeared in the *Délices* of 1620 and bespeaks highly varied tastes. However, in the last years of his life he was held in high esteem as a grammarian, whereas most poets had by then echoed the sentiments of Malherbe, who called him "M. de Miseriac." Méziriac, in an early critical preface, voiced a strange mixture of archaic and novel thoughts: "Nostre but a esté de faire chansons faciles, simples, et intelligibles à toutes sortes de personnes, nous ne les auons point voulu releuer par conceptions hautes, et paroles ampoulees, ni les farcir de ces monstrueuses pointes que la plupart des poëtes modernes affectent si curieusement."[67] Unfortunately, the results are cleansed of any biblical tone without acquiring anything in return. Paulette Leblanc considers the following lines "tout chrétiens." One may wonder at the orthodoxy of the second half of the stanza:

> Car ton Fils, de sa grace,
> T'a pour notre race
> Plus que satisfait,
> Payant une amende
> Beaucoup plus grande
> Que notre forfait.[68]

But what is most objectionable here is the lack of breath and grandeur that is to be expected in a "De Profundis," a lack that goes a long way toward explaining Malherbe's epithet. Also to be noted is the *grace-race*

---

[65] *Opuscules critiques*, p. 353.

[66] *Art poétique*, II, IV. See also Furetière's *Nouvelle allégorique*, in which Gombauld is described as a great legislator of poets, but no great poet.

[67] Claude Gaspar Bachet de Méziriac, *Chansons devotes et sainctes* (Dijon: Guyot, 1615), "Au lecteur."

[68] Leblanc, *Paraphrases*, p. 55.

rhyme, typical of Méziriac, unacceptable to Malherbe. In fact, of all the people whose learning was held in high esteem at the Academy, few could be considered as un-Malherbian. His rhyme schemes, the quality of his rhymes,[69] clumsy, often cacophonic constructions,[70] and inconsistencies in thought (poems dealing simultaneously with Christ and with "Dieux"[71]) all show that Malherbe could have had no influence whatsoever on this respected member of the Academy. His odes, and especially those stanzas constructed like the following,

> Ce n'est pas, hommes insensés,
> Ce n'est pas là que vous pensez
> Où gît le bonheur de la vie,
> A voir éclatter en vos doigts
> Mainte et mainte pierre ravie
> Du sein des rivages Indois.[72]

should prevent anyone from suggesting that Malherbe's reign was well on its way in 1620; one look at Méziriac's "Ode au Roy sur l'heureux succès de son voyage en Languedoc," a poem so popular as to be reproduced in at least three anthologies,[73] will demonstrate that his reign was no further along when the Academy was born.

The score is not entirely negative, however. By the late 1630s some of Malherbe's ideas had taken hold, and one of the poets in whose work this is manifest is Desmarests de Saint-Sorlin, who was not only instrumental in founding the Academy but played an important role in giving it its first directions. After 1645, the date of his religious retreat, Desmarests spent most of his time on the composition of *Clovis*. Until that date, however, his work can be readily compared with that of Malherbe and, in some cases, shows distinct traces of the master's influence.

In the quality of his rhymes, Desmarests is extremely negligent. The *âme-flame* rhyme is current, as are others demanding the rhyming of a

---

[69] Long sounds rhyming with short ones and diaeresis with synaeresis are the most frequent errors.

[70] See in particular his sonnet on the death of Cardinal du Perron, cited by Goujet, *Bibliothèque françoise*, 16:8.

[71] *Délices* (1620), p. 513.

[72] Ibid., p. 517.

[73] See Lachèvre, *Bibliographie*, 1:246.

short with a long sound. There is an abuse of facile rhymes such as *-ment* and *-able*. The *consonne d'appui* is frequently slighted (*lois-bois, moy-voy*) and monosyllabic homonyms abound (*pas-pas, vœux-veux*).[74] On that score Desmarests never improved, and as late as 1669 his works were still replete with rhymes such as *David-assouvit* and *esprit-Christ*.[75]

Perhaps the most negative aspect of Desmarests's poetry is its illogical and at times nonsensical construction. Malherbe could only have shuddered at the fantasy of lines such as "Après avoir donné d'autres bords à Neptune,"[76] or meaningless oxymorons such as "insolente faiblesse."[77] At times, the phrasing verges on the tortured:

> *Sortez, tristes pensers, du profond de mon âme,*
> *Pensers, les seuls témoins de la secrète flamme*
> *Qui depuis trois hivers maîtrise ma raison.*
> *Votre foule m'étouffe, et m'emporte la vie.*
>   *J'ouvre votre prison.*
> *Soyez en liberté quand la mienne est ravie.*[78]

Elsewhere, unable to rid himself of the preciosity of the salons, he refers to Christ as "un soleil au milieu de la nuit," and to the Virgin as an "Heureux sein" who "A pu si chastement porter les fruits d'amour."[79]

While Desmarests's syntax and rhymes undeniably leave much to be desired, his ideas on the structure of the poem, of its rhythmic patterns, are extremely Malherbian. Occasionally, as in the "Discours de la poésie" that opens the *Œuvres poétiques,* he uses alexandrine *vers suivis,* but such cases are relatively rare, and when he does, the caesuras are rigorously enforced and the syntactical units confined to a minimal length, with a minimum of enjambments. The specific strophic forms Desmarests chose are seldom those preferred by Malherbe, yet the result would seem to indicate that, on this score, the two poets were not too far apart in their intentions.

---

[74] The *stances* "Apollon à Daphné" contain an unusual number of all of the above.

[75] *Prières et œuvres chrestiennes* (Paris: Thierry, 1669).

[76] *Œuvres poétiques* (Paris: Le Gras, 1641), p. 77 [*sic:* read p. 1].

[77] Ibid., p. 78 [p. 2].

[78] Ibid., p. 21.

[79] Allem, *Anthologie,* 1:279.

About 1638 or 1639, Desmarests composed six paraphrases of psalms. His favorite format for these was the octosyllabic eight-line stanza, although Psalm 96 uses a sestet of 12–12–12–12–6–12 beats with a rather fortunate *chute* and good 3–3 breaks. As can be seen by the 1669 *Prières*, the octosyllabic *huitain* remained one of his favorites.[80] In all these isometric stanzas, Desmarests adheres quite closely to the basic Malherbian precepts: the sestets are divided 3–3, ten-line stanzas 4–3–3; the caesuras are regular and enjambments rare and purposeful.

It is in his heterometric stanzas, however, that Desmarests is most inventive, most fortunate and, in a way, most Malherbian. One of the best examples can be found in the song "Du plus doux de ses traits," which had numerous editions between 1632 and 1661.[81] The three sestets are set to a typical *air de cour,* and there are two accompaniments, one for lute and one polyphonic, only one of which allows a pause between lines 2 and 3. The vocal line is the same in both versions and Desmarests's words fit the music quite well. All three stanzas break 2–2–2, though in the last two stanzas the first break is only secondary. Here is the first stanza:

> Du plus doux (bis) de ses traits Amour blesse mon cœur
> Pour l'amour de Silvie.
> Je l'ayme (bis) sans désir, aussi jamais langueur
> Ne vient troubler ma vie.
> O! bien-heureuse flamme (bis)
> Qui conservez l'amour et la paix en mon ame.[82]

Specifically, there is little here that could be considered Malherbian, yet the total effect is one of careful balance and structural harmony. The

---

[80] The octosyllabic seems to have found particular favor with Desmarests, for he used it in many isometric stanzas, such as the *a b a b* quatrains of "Apollon à Daphné."

[81] Verchaly, *Airs de cour,* p. lxiv. Its popularity was probably due, at least in part, to the beautiful air by Antoine Boesset which had found its way into Germany by 1641. Ironically, the dainty court song changed into something quite different there, and Boesset's music was published under the title "Von der Gnadenreichen Menschwerdung unsers Herren Christi."

[82] Verchaly, *Airs de cour,* pp. 164–65.

words and the music are perfectly blended to gain maximum flow from each two-line unit, particularly in the case of the last two lines, the refrain.

Much the same can be said for the five sestets of the *stances* "Pour le temps de Noël." The 8–8–12–8–8–12, *a a b c c b* pattern is not to be found in Malherbe, but cannot be faulted for that; structurally, the poem is a success. Unfortunately, it fails in every other aspect. Much the same can be said for the more ambitious "Stances à M. de Bautru." The five ten-line stanzas are marred by countless errors of versification and syntax. Yet, all in all, the result is not entirely bad:

> *Depuis que s'alluma ton funeste flambeau,*
> *Guerre, que tu nous fais d'outrages!*
> *Noble et traître métier, l'amour et le tombeau*
> *Des plus hardis courages!*
> *Bellone au milieu des combats*
> *Passe avec dédain les cœurs bas,*
> *Et s'attaque aux plus belles vies.*
> *Elle abbat sans pitié ses plus chers sectateurs,*
> *Et ne peut jamais voir ses fureurs assouvies,*
> *Sinon du plus beau sang de ses adorateurs.*[83]

The 4–3–3 division is in accordance with Malherbe's practice, and is not only syntactical but also rhythmic. Desmarests gives each syntactical unit its own distinct rhythm, weakening in the process the integrity of the *dizain*. As a result, the poem may be structurally sound but cannot be considered Malherbian by any stretch of the imagination.

Another of the self-styled inheritors of Malherbe was Guillaume Colletet. Unlike Malherbe, however, Colletet refused to reject the poets of the preceding century. "Malgré ces ignorants," he stated, speaking of his contemporaries,

> *Je viens rendre à ton nom ce qu'il a mérité:*
> *Belle âme de Ronsard, dont la sainte mémoire*

[83] *Œuvres poétiques*, p. 15.

Remportera du temps une heureuse victoire,
Et ne se bornera que de l'éternité.

In Ronsard, he saw

> . . . *le roi des grands esprits,*
> *Le père des beaux vers et l'enfant de la muse.*[84]

This admiration is shown in the very Ronsardian sonnet "La maison de Ronsard,"[85] and is especially evident in poems such as "Rodomontade amoureuse" and "Les beautés empruntées," obviously inspired by Ronsard's "Quand vous serez bien vieille." Further proof of his eclectic taste can be found in such passages as this:

> *Que Malherbe nous charme et ravisse nos Roys,*
> *Que Racan s'éternise eternisant leur gloire,*
> *Que Métel [Bois-Robert?] sacrifie aux filles de Mémoire,*
> *Qu'Urfé face parler les Antres et les Bois,*
>
> *Que l'ardant Théophile échauffe les plus froids;*
> *Que Maynard entretienne et la Seine et la Loire. . . .*[86]

As I have stated before, what matters is not what the critics said but what the poets did, and nowhere is this more obvious than in the poetic production of Colletet, who as critic was "homme d'un esprit droit et d'un jugement sain,"[87] but as poet was "plutôt né versificateur que poète."[88] At the Academy, he was considered "docte,"[89] yet Chapelain felt that "les grands mouvements lui sont inconnus, et il arrive rarement, lorsqu'il

---

[84] Allem, *Anthologie,* 1:313.

[85] Adhémar van Bever, ed., *Les poètes du terroir* (Paris: Delagrave, 1920) 2:399.

[86] *Poésies diverses* (Paris: Chamhoudry, 1656). These first six lines of a sonnet should suffice to show that even at that late date Colletet's concepts had not yet become Malherbe's.

[87] Viollet le Duc, *Catalogue des livres,* 1:492.

[88] Chapelain, *Opuscules critiques,* p. 391.

[89] Goujet, *Bibliothèque françoise,* 1:216.

s'élève, que ses pensées soient justes et qu'il ne prenne l'enflure pour l'embompoint."[90] Of course, Colletet did not agree:

> *C'est trop m'assujettir, je suis las d'imiter,*
> *La version déplaît à qui peut inventer;*
> *Je suis plus amoureux d'un vers que je compose,*
> *Que des Livres entiers que j'ai traduits en prose.*[91]

He indeed felt that he was endowed with great creative gifts. In fact, seldom did a poet so abuse the commonplace of poetic pride with so little justification. The poem in which he claims that

> *Il est vrai, j'ai l'esprit agréable et fertile;*
> *Oui, ma prose et mes vers doivent forcer les ans,*[92]

is full of expletives, poor rhymes, and countless other errors of judgment and versification, and has justly been forgotten by all but the most savant compilers. Thinking of Ronsard, Colletet stated, "Je trouve dans mes vers sa force, et son génie,"[93] but neither his contemporaries nor posterity agreed.

Colletet's poetry, be it early or late, is in constant opposition to his critical statements, and shows him to be anything but Malherbian. His early *Trébuchement de l'yvrongne* is in alexandrines *suivis* with very long syntactical units:

> *Mais insensiblement je ne m'advise pas*
> *Que la force du vin debilite mes pas,*
> *Je sens mon estomac plus chaud que de coutume,*
> *Je ne sçay quel brasier dans mes veines s'alume,*
> *Je commence à doubter de tout ce que je voy,*
> *La teste me tournoye et tout tourne avec moy,*

[90] Ibid.
[91] Cited in ibid.
[92] André Blanchard, ed., *Baroques et classiques* (Lyon: IAC, 1947), p. 84.
[93] Allem, *Anthologie*, 1:314.

Ma raison s'esbloüit, ma parolle se trouble,
Comme un nouveau Penthé je vois un soleil double,
J'enten dedans la nüe un tonnerre esclatant,
Je regarde le ciel et n'y vois rien pourtant,
Tout tremble soubs mes pieds, une sombre poussiere
Comme un nuage espais offusque ma lumiere,
Et l'ardante fureur m'agite tellement
Qu'avecque la raison je perds le sentiment.[94]

Not unlike Théophile's "Un corbeau devant moi croasse," this passage and the entire poem are the very antithesis of Malherbian poetry. Throughout the poem, whose very structure is un-Malherbian, the homophony of the *consonne d'appui* is constantly neglected, monosyllabic homonyms are made to rhyme, enjambments and bad caesuras are plentiful. There is no consistency whatsoever on matters of diphthongs; thus, *anciens* and *champions* require three syllables while *sanglier* takes up but two.[95]

Ballet libretti are always written in a hurry, and as a result the poet cannot always be held responsible for their quality, says Colletet in his *Vie d'Estienne Jodelle*.[96] This might explain the poor quality of his own contributions to the *Balet des Nations* of 1622. It does not, however, explain why there were no corrections by 1631, when the "Récit des Pescheurs" read as follows:

O vous qui presidez sur ces rives icy,
Triton, Glauque, Nerée, et vous Nymphes aussi,
Qui sous l'onde estallez vos appas, et vos charmes;
Faites qu'en nos filets, et dans nos hameçons [sic]
Tombent à ceste fois tout autant de poissons,
Que nos yeux ont versé de deluges de larmes.[97]

[94] (Paris: n.p., 1627), p. 8.

[95] See Edouard Fournier, *Variétés historiques et littéraires* (Paris: Jannet [et Pagnerre], 1855–1863), 3:127,138.

[96] Estienne Jodelle, *Les amours et autres poésies* (Paris: Sansot, 1907), pp. 25–26.

[97] Marcel Paquot, "Les 'Vers du Balet des Nations' de Guillaume Colletet," *Rev. Belge de Phil. et d'Hist.* 10 (1931):63.

By 1656, Colletet had decided to make some changes, but the improvement is, at best, debatable, the last three lines reading:

> *Faites qu'en nos filets, et qu'en nos hameçons,*
> *Nous voyons aujourd'hui tomber plus de poissons,*
> *Que nos yeux n'ont versé de deluges de larmes.*[98]

In short, whether one looks at the early poetry or the later, one finds throughout Colletet's production ample proof of a liking for *vers suivis*, for verbosity, for nonsensical images, and generally what might be called a disregard for even the most basic rules of versification. Colletet undoubtedly had a certain popularity in and out of the Academy. His contribution—five poems—to the *Sacrifice des Muses* of 1635 is exceeded only by that of Bois-Robert, the compiler. Yet, a sample of this contribution should suffice to give us an idea of the degree to which the author had fallen under the spell of Malherbe's "juste cadence" and "grace":

> *En vain tu meurs d'envie*
> *D'etouffer une vie*
> *Qui sans cesse produit des effets inouis*
> *Pour le bien de Louis.*[99]

I have already touched upon Chapelain's poetry in the previous chapter, where I noted that, with the success of the ode to Richelieu, printed in 1633 and so popular as to be anthologized that same year[100] and frequently thereafter, Chapelain became the "légitime héritier de Malherbe."[101] Most important is that, with this ode, Chapelain definitely entered into Richelieu's favor, a fact not to be disregarded when viewing his role in the young Academy, a role that has been treated sufficiently not to delay us here. Suffice it to say that his influence grew steadily. His impartiality during the famous quarrel over the *Cid* enhanced his reputation, and by the late 1630s he had become "le conseiller attitré de

---

[98] Ibid.
[99] P. 154.
[100] *Nouvelles Muses.*
[101] Collas, *Jean Chapelain*, p. 112.

presque tous les écrivains."[102] Some years later, Bois-Robert was to publicly voice such a sentiment when he considered Chapelain to be among

> *Ces grands esprits aussi pleins d'equité*
> *Que d'agremènt et de solidité.*[103]

In his criticism, Chapelain was quite Malherbian, condemning rhymes that abused proper nouns or lacked the *consonne d'appui* homophony.[104] By the same token, he blamed the vogue for "entassement d'expressions figurées" which "corrompt encore la nature de la narration et l'étouffe à force de la charger d'ornements."[105] Because Maynard had avoided these pitfalls, Chapelain praised him for the "naturel" of his epigrams.[106] He felt the need for rules and order, and in 1639 he praised La Mesnardière's *Art poétique* (although he considered it a bad one) simply because he felt the world sorely needed one.[107] And yet fundamentally he was not in total agreement with Malherbe, for he readily admitted that "l'art n'est pas ce qui fait la beauté" in a letter that leads one to think of the early attempts at defining the *je ne sais quoi.*[108] It must always be remembered, as E. B. O. Borgerhoff has pointed out, that "the *Sentiments* can be regarded as an admission of the limitations of the rules almost as much as they can be considered an application of those rules,"[109] just as Chapelain's reticence over these *Sentiments* must always be kept in mind.

Some of Chapelain's poetry has been touched upon in the previous chapter. In the period that concerns us here, the near-total of his poetic production is in the realm of circumstantial, "official" verse.[110] The reason for this is twofold: Chapelain's position in relation to the powers that be

---

[102] Ibid., p. 148.

[103] *Epistres en vers* (Paris: Hachette, 1921–1927), 1:40.

[104] *Opuscules critiques,* p. 411.

[105] Ibid., pp. 412–13.

[106] Ibid.

[107] Ibid., pp. 414–15.

[108] *Lettres,* 1:367.

[109] *Freedom of French Classicism,* p. 36.

[110] Typical titles are "Ode pour le retour de Monsieur," "Sonnet pour la naissance du Dauphin," "Sonnet sur la mort du duc de Saxe-Weymar," "Sonnet sur la naissance du duc d'Anjou," "Sonnet sur la prise d'Arras."

demanded it, but so did the popular taste. The Court was neglecting "toutes ces sortes de poésie ancienne" which had gone out of favor; as a result, if a poet wished to have the approval of the public—"et mon avis est qu'il ne faut jamais se donner la peine que pour plaire"—he had no choice but to write sonnets or odes, particularly the latter.[111]

It would be wrong, however, to consider these odes Malherbian. The stanzas are consistently broken into separate units (a practice already noted in the ode to Richelieu, and one to which Chapelain adhered throughout his career), thus destroying the unity and the flow in form and in content. Every possible type of facile rhyme can be found (too frequent proper nouns, adverbs, monosyllabic homonyms). In short, while Chapelain may be considered a somewhat better poet than either Méziriac or Colletet, with him, as with them, the critic had reasons which the poet did not know.

The foregoing poets have, at various times, been classed as *doctes,* as learned, and their critical output has usually been allowed to overshadow their versification. This is not altogether wrong and in this respect my conclusions are in complete accord with past critical judgment. Such is not entirely the case with those poets at the Academy who are usually called "précieux" or "frisés" or by any number of epithets meant to convey a certain degree of condescension and disdain. Most of these poets could—and did—have their moments of serious composition, and some of them did remarkably well.

François Le Métel de Bois-Robert made his mark in the literary world at a very early age.[112] At Rambouillet in 1627 he undoubtedly met Malherbe, but most of his time was obviously spent gaining and keeping the good graces of Richelieu. Yoshio Fukui readily makes of him a Malherbian, using as proof the fact that his poetry was included in "Malherbian" anthologies, and that a sonnet in *a b b a a b b a c c d e e d*

---

[111] *Opuscules critiques,* p. 395.

[112] I am reluctant to go along with Yoshio Fukui, *Raffinement précieux dans la poésie française du XVIIe siècle* (Paris: Nizet, 1964), p. 79, who asserts that between 1615 and 1620 Bois-Robert, along with Théophile and Saint-Amant, "s'imposèrent au monde poétique." Let us keep in mind that the young poet's first published poem did not appear until 1616, and that by 1620 only the fourteen poems in the *Cabinet des Muses* had been added to it.

was reworked to follow the more acceptable *e d e* scheme; but we must keep in mind that the *Cabinet des Muses* contained works by poets such as Régnier and Théophile,[113] and that the revised sonnet conformed to a standard that could hardly be credited to Malherbe. In fact, as Fukui points out, the tone of the sonnet ("Grands monts qui menacez . . ."[114]) is far more reminiscent of Théophile and of Saint-Amant than of Malherbe.[115]

Bois-Robert's early poetry can be divided into two major categories, the official and the *badin*. Much of the latter is of an erotic nature and is therefore difficult to compare with anything written by Malherbe, who was particularly unfortunate in that domain. From the purely technical point of view, most of these efforts are fairly correct. "Amour naissant," made up of *a b a b* alexandrine quatrains, is quite regular and shows a remarkable sense of balance, from the opening line, "Je ne sais point encor, Philis, si je vous aime," to the last one, "Vous me diriez bientôt, Philis, si c'est aimer."[116] Yet, one of the most popular songs of this period, Bois-Robert's "Que servent tes conseilz," is anything but regular. It was given at least four different musical settings between 1628 and 1661, and gave rise to several clever parodies.[117] It is composed of five heterometric sestets of a type never used by Malherbe: 12–8–8–8–12–8, *a b a b c c*, the last two lines being the refrain. Because of the refrain, there is a definite 4–2 break, a phenomenon already discussed. The rhymes (*réclame-ame, lieu-dieu, dard-départ, tort-mort*) are far from Malherbian, as are lines such as "Qu'afin que le regret me tuë."

In Saint-Evremond's *Comédie des Académistes*, Bois-Robert states:

> *Que le stile élevé me paroît incommode!*
> *Je n'ai pas le talent qu'il faut pour faire une Ode.*[118]

That statement, however, is not entirely true, and Bois-Robert's serious poetry is on a par with most of that written at the time by the other members of the Academy, a statement which in no way should be con-

---

[113] In the later *recueils*, "independents" such as Tristan also found a place.
[114] *Cabinet des Muses*, p. 534.
[115] *Raffinement précieux*, pp. 90–91.
[116] Blanchard, *Baroques et classiques*, p. 70.
[117] Verchaly, *Airs de cour*, pp. lxi, 148–49.
[118] (Paris: Charavay, 1879), act 3, sc. 1.

strued as unreserved praise. Chapelain considered some of Bois-Robert's lines so good that even Malherbe, he thought, "avec sa plus docte lime," could not have improved them.[119]

In the earliest odes, Bois-Robert shows that his ideas on the genre are not those of Malherbe, for he frequently calls *ode* what the latter would have called *stances*. His "Ode sur les lettres de Monsieur de Balzac," published at the head of the *Lettres du Sieur de Balzac*,[120] is, however, very much in line with Malherbe's concept and tone. The octosyllabic *dizains* are each broken into two distinct paragraphs after the fourth line, and the second paragraph is always cut by a secondary break after the seventh line. The rhymes are not always satisfactory, and some are too facile, but the *a b b a c c d e d e* scheme is orthodox by any standards.

Three years later, Bois-Robert published his paraphrases of seven Psalms of David. They are equally regular, even Malherbian. In the letter to the reader, he condemns Desportes for his obscurity and claims to have written something far more intelligible than the original, yet faithful to its spirit. He is, in fact, rather successful, and Psalm 101, written in the 12–6–12–6 form made famous by Malherbe's "Consolation," is quite poignant, though, like that well-known poem, it could be accused of displaying a sincerity more artistic than personal:

> *Il faut que mon offense à tes yeux soit bien noire*
> *Pour estre ainsi priué,*
> *Pour estre ainsi décheu de ce haut point de gloire,*
> *Où i'estois esleué.*
>
> *Le plus beau de mon âge est passé comme une ombre.*
> *Ie me sens defailly;*
> *Dans mes adversitez souffrant des maux sans nombre,*
> *Ie suis desia vieilly.*
>
> *Mais toy, Pere eternel, tes ans n'ont point d'espace*
> *Qui leur soit limité,*
> *Et ton Nom glorieux passe de race en race*
> *A la postérité.*[121]

[119] *Opuscules critiques*, p. 417.
[120] (Paris: Toussainct du Bray, 1624).
[121] Verses 14–16, cited in Leblanc, *Paraphrases*, pp. 114–15.

In the *Sacrifice des Muses* of 1635, which Bois-Robert edited, the most diverse poets of the time were represented. The place of honor, of course, went to the compiler himself, who included fourteen of his poems. These ranged in tone and workmanship from the fairly regular "Stances"[122] to the far-from-stately

> *La Renommée a prévenu*
> *Le désir que j'avais d'étendre*
> *Votre mérite, et de vous rendre*
> *Aux deux bouts du monde connu.*[123]

While these poems are anything but Malherbian, the nature of the "Stances à la Vierge" of 1642 is debatable. These are twelve sestets of five alexandrines followed by a six-beat line and using the orthodox *a a b c c b* rhyme pattern. While Malherbe never used this particular combination of lines, he combined these two lengths on nine occasions, each one different.[124] It is therefore obvious that Bois-Robert's "Stances" should not be considered a deviation but rather an innovation in an area where Malherbe never ceased to seek novelty. The inner structure is equally regular. Each alexandrine is a well-balanced unit with a good caesura, and the 3–3 break is well established except in stanza four, where the punctuation is ambiguous:

> *D'un repos assuré ma retraitte est suiuie,*
> *Il n'est point de jaloux qui veille sur ma vie,*
> *Dans ces lieux de silence, et de paix amoureux,*
> *Si quelque vent souspire, ou si quelque eau murmure,*
> *Ce n'est point par enuie, ils suiuent leur nature,*
> *Et me souffrent heureux.*[125]

Only one objection could be raised in this poem: the rhymes are frequently facile, commonplaces such as *vie-envie, orages-naufrages* occurring throughout.

---

[122] Pp. 28–29. Written in alexandrine sestets, *a a b c b c*, they are marred by enjambments and poor rhymes, with excessive padding.

[123] P. 47.

[124] Fromilhague, *Technique*, p. 196.

[125] *Autres œuvres poétiques* (Paris: Besongne, 1647 [*sic*: read 1646]), p. 2.

The "Stances à la Vierge" might be called Malherbian, but it is impossible to determine whether this was due to chance or to intention. Only too frequently, Bois-Robert penned official poems which, in one way or another, are un-Malherbian. One such poem, on the death of Richelieu, begins with an enjambment:

> O pavvre Estat, que je déplore
> Ta perte, et tes maux infinis.[126]

Another poem on the same subject is in alexandrines, and while its rhythmic balance is superior, its rhymes—appas-bas, Rois-loix—are not.[127] His poem on the fall of Perpignan is made of ten octosyllabic lines without a single break.[128] And so, in spite of some signs of what might be considered "Malherbianism," Bois-Robert cannot really be considered "Malherbian," and his poetry is anything but proof of the growing influence of the master.

It must always be kept in mind that the Conrart group, at the outset, was made up of very fashionable young men, and that therefore the Academy's image in the eyes of many was based as much on their reputation as on that of their more learned colleagues. In other words, in looking at the poetry created at the Academy, and in judging the poetic aura that it radiated, one cannot neglect names such as Baro and Malleville, to which one might add Laugier de Porchères.[129]

Although Balthazar Baro is better known for his contribution to L'Astrée and possibly for some rather bad plays, he also wrote some

---

[126] Autres œuvres poétiques (Paris: Courbé, 1659), p. 293. It should be added that octosyllabic huitains were not Malherbe's favorite, since he used them only three times.

[127] Autres œuvres (1646), p. 44.

[128] Ibid., p. 38.

[129] There is a tradition among historians of the Academy of also including among the "frisés" the name of Germain Habert. He was obviously well thought of in that milieu. It was he who drafted the first version of the sentiments on the Cid; and it was he who gave Richelieu's funeral oration at the Academy, where he also spoke for Séguier when the latter sought entry into the group. In the period under examination, however, his poetic output was nonexistent. Much the same can be said of his brother Philippe, who was killed in 1637 and was publicly mourned by the Academy. (See Goujet, Bibliothèque françoise, 16:3.)

poetry, much of it circumstantial. The *Second livre des délices* of 1620 contains thirteen of his poems, all bad, with poor rhymes, cacophonic passages such as "C'est parce que je ne crois pas," or archaisms such as "j'absente ces lieux."[130] At that time, however, Baro had not yet reached his twentieth birthday. Among these early poems were the *stances* "A son Altesse de Savoie," composed of alexandrine sestets. They not only share all the faults mentioned above, but are also remarkable in that there are no real 3–3 breaks in the entire poem. In 1632, on the occasion of the death of Henri de Schomberg, Baro wrote an ode of twelve octosyllabic *dizains,* some broken 4–6, some 4–3–3, some not at all. The rhymes are seldom satisfactory, often poor: *Caron-Acheron, mort-effort, fatal-Cazal;* obscure references such as

> *Celui qui fit un cimetière*
> *Des rivages de l'Eridan*

abound. In short, the poem is anything but Malherbian.

By 1635, however, Baro seems to have come into contact with some of Malherbe's ideas. His *stances* to Richelieu, "Grand Duc, c'est aujourd'huy que nos cœurs sont contents,"[131] are composed of ten alexandrine sestets, a definitely non-Malherbian form, but all are broken 3–3, the rhyme scheme is the orthodox *a a b c b c,* the rhythm is never violated. If there is still no sign of poetic instinct, at least some of the basic rules of the trade are beginning to be felt. His last effort in the genre (only a ballet and an insipid love poem were to follow) is the long ode to Richelieu, *Contre l'auteur d'un libelle.*[132] It is composed of eighteen octosyllabic *dizains,* a form used by Malherbe but not his favorite by any means. The syntactical construction is quite orthodox, with a break after the fourth line; the last six lines are generally, though not always, divided 3–3. The major objection is to the rhymes. Though the scheme is orthodox and most of the rhymes superior to those of the preceding poems, one has the definite impression that "ce bijou d'un sou" is responsible for most of the defects of the poem. Obscure proper names abound, as do strange epithets—"Dieu tutélaire," that is, Richelieu. Totally unacceptable inversions such as "Chastes sœurs qu'on va violant" can only be explained

---

[130] Pp. 361, 363.
[131] *Sacrifice des Muses,* p. 178.
[132] (Paris: Camusat, 1637).

by a need for a rhyme. The resulting impression is that Baro may have discovered Malherbe's rules but was far from understanding them or being able to implement them.

The most famous of the "frisés" was undoubtedly Malleville, whose presence at Rambouillet has been discussed. His popularity at the Academy cannot be questioned, but he seems to have been on the fringe of the mainstream. Most of his poems written during the years that concern us dealt with the commonplaces of love. Like Tristan L'Hermite, he frequently sang the praises of fair ladies, on occasion celebrating a woman beautiful "encor qu'elle soit noire." He indulged in all the fashionable forms, and for this very reason he must be considered as having existed on the fringe of the academic current, for there rondeaux and other *moyenâgeux* poems, however popular they may have been in the salons, were rapidly being discarded and despised.

Most of these lighter poems cannot be considered Malherbian. For example, the "Chanson, à la louange de l'eau, à un fameux buveur," written for his friend Colletet, is composed of five-line stanzas; the rhyme scheme is *a a b a b*, *a* being masculine octosyllables, *b* feminine hexameters; the majority of the stanzas have only one syntactical unit; many of the rhymes would have been considered facile by Malherbe (*dryades-naïades*), others insufficient (*beau-l'eau-berceau*), and still others totally unsatisfactory (*jour-séjour*).

But if such are the poems that are most frequently quoted, they are not the ones that matter here. As of 1633, Malleville was trying his hand at paraphrases of psalms or, as he called his first such attempt, "Méditations." Highly artificial in these efforts, Malleville represents a world that believed "que l'esprit était capable de tenir lieu de tout le reste."[133] These meditations are seldom faithful to either the letter or the spirit of the original, but rather represent to the poet what variations are to most composers: a formal exercise where artifice and virtuosity are to be demonstrated. As Leblanc points out, amplifications and periphrases are of the essence. Thus "Adhaereat lingua mea faucibus meis,/ si non meminero tui" of Psalm 136 becomes

> *Ie consens de languir en d'eternelles gesnes,*
> *De voir multiplier le nombre de mes chaisnes,*

[133] Leblanc, *Paraphrases,* p. 168.

Et de mes ennemis l'insolence augmenter:
Ie consens que le Ciel à mes desirs s'oppose,
Et qu'il tienne ma bouche eternellement close
Si ie l'ouure iamais que pour te regretter.[134]

By the same token, the single word "flevimus" becomes

Nous fismes dans le fleuue un fleuue de nos larmes,
Et meslames au vent celuy de nos soupirs.[135]

Prolonged imagery and periphrases can be found throughout; witness this description of the passing of the Red Sea:

De ses Rubis fondus de son pourpre liquide
La Mer fit un cristal et vermeil et solide
Qui borda d'Israël le chemin glorieux.[136]

Antitheses are to be found with equal frequency:

Ie sentis en frayeur changer ma hardiesse,
En fontaines mes yeux, en trouble mon repos,
Ma pompe en deshonneur, mon plaisir en tristesse,
Et mes chants de triomphe en ces tristes propos.[137]

In all of these psalms, and particularly in Psalm 136, which Malleville reworked extensively for the 1649 edition of his works, there is evidence of careful craftsmanship and of a sense of poetry akin to the one expounded and exemplified by Malherbe. This is not the work of a "frisé" or "parfumé," as he is sometimes called, but rather a set of well-crafted poems. Paulette Leblanc, subjecting these to the most careful analysis they have yet undergone, speaks of solidity, of good "sonorités," of an "emploi harmonieux de rythmes connus."[138] The correctness of such a

---

[134] Ibid.
[135] Ibid., p. 169.
[136] Ibid.
[137] Ibid.
[138] Ibid., p. 171.

judgment is particularly apparent when one looks at Malleville's Psalm
126:

> De quelque fondement que ton art et ta peine
> S'efforcent d'affermir la maison que tu fais,
> Miserable mortel, la cheute en est certaine,
> Si les mains du Seigneur n'en soustiennent le faix.
>
> Si de l'esprit de Dieu les veilles eternelles
> Ne defendent le fort à ta garde commis,
> C'est en vain que tes soins posent des sentinelles,
> Tu ne le peux garder contre tes ennemis.
>
> Bien que deuant le jour ton labeur recommence,
> Tu consumes ton corps pour accroistre ton bien,
> N'attens pas de cueillir le fruit de ta semence,
> Si le bras du Seigneur n'accompagne le tien.
>
> Le soin de t'enrichir auance ta ruine,
> La douleur est le pain que tu reçois des cieux;
> Et sans un doux rayon de la grace diuine
> Tu ne sçaurois secher les larmes de tes yeux.[139]

Not all the rhymes are acceptable, but neither the construction, nor the
tone of this poem—nor of any of the others of its type—could have been
faulted by Malherbe.

Ironically enough, it was Malleville who introduced Honorat Laugier
de Porchères into the Academy. Ironically, for no man could be less like
Malleville than this antique leftover from the sixteenth century. Born
about 1560, Laugier de Porchères did have some poems included in
various *recueils* of the turn of the century, but whereas Malleville was
précieux, Porchères was *ridicule* at best:

> Ce ne sont pas des yeux, ce sont plustot des dieux;
> Ils ont dessus les rois la puissance absolue.
> Dieux, non; ce sont des cieux, ils ont la couleur bleüe,
> Et le mouvement prompt comme celuy des cieux.
>
> Cieux, non; mais . . .

---

[139] Stanzas 1–4, cited in ibid., pp. 170–71.

This indecision is mercifully resolved in the last line: "Des yeux, des dieux, des cieux, des soleils, des esclairs."[140] His more solemn poems show that in that domain he also failed to equal his young friend, and poems such as "De Sponde, ton malheur . . ." or "Sur la mort de Polemandre" have some balance in construction, but little else. There is no question here of Malherbian influence, as chronology would prevent such a linking (Laugier de Porchères nearly silenced his already sterile muse after 1607), but rather of a reflected judgment of Malleville.

There were other minor poets at the Academy, all defying judgment. Jacques Serisay, for instance, had several poems in the various Sercy anthologies. Most of them show a certain regularity of form that could be considered Malherbian. Thus his "Songe d'Alidor" is composed of nineteen sestets, using an *a a b c c b*, 12–12–6–12–12–6 scheme, with rather good rhymes and sound metrics, as this sample shows:

> Sur la fin de la nuit je vous ai vue en songe,
> Et tandis que Morphée avec ce doux mensonge
> Traversait mon repos,
> J'ai cru que vos faveurs couronnaient ma constance,
> Et que sans vous porter à trop de résistance,
> Vous teniez ce propos.[141]

Note that the enjambment—lines 2–3—accentuates the *chute,* thus strengthening the median break. However, if Serisay can be considered Malherbian in form, his frequent use of a language that is anything but "châtié" and his syntactically tortured lines negate any positive contribution he might have made.[142]

As I have suggested, it is perhaps among these *précieux* poets that one finds the greatest influence of Malherbe, however slight it may be. While poets such as Chapelain censured Malherbe, whom they tried to supplant, others, such as Baro and Malleville, consciously or not, tended to follow in his footsteps in many respects. Baro, as time went on, became more and more Malherbian, at least in tone and construction. Much the same can be said for Malleville's serious poetry. What is in-

---

[140] Paul Olivier, ed., *Cent poètes lyriques, précieux ou burlesques du XVIIe siècle* (Paris: Havard, 1898), p. 106.

[141] *Poésies choisies . . . , 4ᵉ partie*, p. 316.

[142] See, for instance, his "Elégie," in ibid., *5ᵉ partie*, pp. 376–79.

teresting here is his protection of a silent relic of times past. Was it a cruel—or generous—hoax? Equally interesting is the fact that until the founding of the Academy, only six of his poems found their way into the various *recueils*, all in 1633. But from 1639 to 1658, fifty-five appeared, almost all in a light vein. During that same twenty-year span, Malherbe was represented by only four! The question that arises then concerns not so much Malleville's Malherbianism as the fortunes of the entire idea. It seems, from the various facts and poems examined, that Malleville did indeed see the necessity of certain rules Malherbe had advocated, particularly when creating poems of a more serious nature; that he gave these works due care in reworking them for the edition of his works; and that the popular appeal of these was, at best, limited. In short, in the last years of the reign of Louis XIII, a "poète de ruelle" such as Malleville could indulge in some serious work, but his fame had to rely on the *précieux* platitudes at which, it must be added, he was far more adept. To what extent such an observation holds true for a genuinely great poet will be seen shortly.

Of all the poets of the first half of the century, none has been better served by modern scholarship than Saint-Amant. The work of Gourier, Lagny, Mazzara, Roberts, to name but a few of the most recent contributors, should suffice to illustrate this point. It is therefore my purpose here to present his poetry only insofar as it will establish the degree to which the author followed in the footsteps of Malherbe.

The bulk of Saint-Amant's poetical production falls within the period discussed in this chapter and coincides with the first years of the Academy. In 1621 an "Ode à Théophile" was published with the works of the latter; in that same year, a madrigal found its way into the liminary poems accompanying G. B. Andreini's *Centaura*. Several other works came out during the next few years, but it was not until 1629 that the first edition of the *Oeuvres* appeared, published by Pomeroy. The number of subsequent editions attests to its genuine success. These "continuations" and "augmentations" were published regularly until 1651. Except for a small flurry in 1658, "the last ten years of Saint-Amant's life were rather austere ones, and they were less productive poetically."[143]

[143] Samuel L. Borton, *Six Modes of Sensibility in Saint-Amant* (The Hague: Mouton, 1966), p. 15.

The proper perspective in dealing with Saint-Amant demands not only a chronological division but also, in view of his versatility, a separation of the total production into constituent types, for "chaque genre de poésie commande le style."[144] This variety in expression and sensibility has not escaped the modern critics. It occupies a large part of Bailbé's study and is explicit in the very title of Borton's book. Saint-Amant himself took great pains to make his reader aware of this "art . . . divers."[145] He readily admitted that his mind "saute de pensée en pensée," and that he was "tantost chagrin, tantost joyeux."[146] Balzac failed to consider this and thus found fault[147] where Théophile, Faret, and Chapelain did not.

Balzac particularly disliked Saint-Amant's use of archaisms, but, as Francis Bar has pointed out,[148] these were not sins of omission but strokes of genius: in almost every case, they occur in purposefully burlesque poems where they are part and parcel of the comic apparatus and are meant to make us laugh. If Saint-Amant "sort du bon usage," it is invariably "à dessein."[149] Thus, in the "Poète crotté," a poem replete with gems such as "Ores besoin de Lanterne,"[150] the author parodied Ronsard effectively by use of archaisms:

> Je cours l'hazard d'au coing d'un Bois
> Jetter seul les ultim'abbois;
> Accravanté de lassitude,
> De trop jeusner, de marritude,
> Et qui plus est . . .

a parodic effect which, as Bar points out,[151] is made even more apparent in lines such as these:

---

[144] Jacques Bailbé, "La couleur baroque de la langue et du style dans les premières œuvres de Saint-Amant," *FrMod* 29 (1961):43.

[145] *Œuvres complètes* (Paris: Jannet, 1855), 1:30. Since the excellent Lagny edition is not yet complete, I have been forced to use this older edition for many references.

[146] *Œuvres complètes*, 1:33, 27.

[147] *Œuvres* (1665), 2:493.

[148] Francis Bar, *Le genre burlesque en France au XVIIe siècle: Etude de style* (Paris: D'Artrey, 1960), pp. 213–14.

[149] Idem, "Fins et moyens de l'archaïsme chez les burlesques du XVIIe siècle," *CAIEF* 19 (1967):42.

[150] *Œuvres*, 2:67.

[151] "Fins et moyens," pp. 52–53.

Or'que l'Archerot enfantin
De ses vo-volantes Flamméches,
R'innove en mon sang mille bréches. . . .[152]

In his later years, Saint-Amant was to be even less ambiguous, and spoke of "Bartas, un donne-ennuy."[153] Characters intended to be ridiculous are made to sound so ("C'est de moy de qui je parle"[154]), while in a military poem, an expression such as "vous leur sangle le morion" seems quite appropriate and *juste*.[155] All of the ingredients of the burlesque poetry, be it the vocabulary or the versification, contribute, by their very nature, to the Rabelaisian effect desired. In that sense, the intrinsic value of the word is as great in Saint-Amant—who saw the necessity of "prendre les mots au sérieux"[156]—as in Malherbe. This is obvious if one looks carefully at the "Poète crotté": nowhere are archaisms as plentiful as in the passage dealing with Mlle de Gournay. This suggests that Saint-Amant— and most writers of burlesque poetry—were not really opposed to Malherbe's concepts regarding beauty and nobility of expression: "Les tenants d'un genre qui se place aux antipodes du beau style ont été en accord profond avec les puristes à qui leurs petits vers faisaient froncer les sourcils. Les uns comme les autres tenaient les mots vieillis comme faisant tache, les mots vraiment anciens comme étranges et, hélas, la littérature du passé dans son ensemble comme ridicule."[157]

This should not be construed as a suggestion that Saint-Amant was Malherbian. For one thing, he had a thorough dislike for Malherbe and his admirers. The ode to Théophile of 1621 is an early proof of that; if further proof is needed, one has only to look at a manuscript in Con-

---

[152] *Œuvres*, 2:57,64.

[153] *Œuvres complètes*, 2:79.

[154] *Œuvres*, 2:69.

[155] *Œuvres complètes*, 1:175. Since the language of poetry is not the subject of this study, the reader is referred to the excellent studies by Bar cited above. Suffice it to say that Saint-Amant felt the words had to be "propres, justes et significatifs" (ibid., 2:147), and that Faret was therefore quite right in admiring his "elocution nette et vigoureuse" (ibid., 1:9). What, in truth, is more appropriate than the delightful "D'an en an" put in the mouth of the "Poète crotté"?

[156] Robert Garapon, *La fantaisie verbale et le comique dans le théâtre français* . . . (Paris: Colin, 1957), p. 342.

[157] Bar, "Fins et moyens," p. 57.

rart's handwriting, described by Frédéric Lachèvre,[158] in which the pseudonyms Thibault and Colin of a 1629 epigram are replaced with the original names:

> Balzac se dit être Mercure
> Et l'orgueilleux Maynard nous jure
> Qu'il est aussi bon Apollon
> Que Boccan est bon violon.
> Ces deux autheurs, pour la folie,
> La fraude, la mélancholie,
> La sottise, l'impiété,
> L'ignorance et la vanité,
> Ne sont rien qu'une mesme chose,
> Mais en ce poinct ils sont divers,
> C'est que l'un fait des vers en prose,
> Et l'autre de la prose en vers.[159]

To be entirely fair, however, we must decide this issue not by taking the poet's declarations at face value but by analyzing his output, particularly that part of it which can be considered of a lofty nature. This is not always easy, for the very classification is difficult to apply. Much of Saint-Amant's poetry is "heroi-comique," as the subtitles of poems such as "Le Passage de Gibraltar" suggest. Although he rejected the "fadezes" of Berni, Saint-Amant believed in pleasing, "laissant les espines aux Sciences," and concentrating on "la joye."[160] Unwilling to write poetry that would make only the "crocheteurs" laugh, he wrote in such a way that the heroic was "admirablement confondu avec le Bourlesque."[161] This is what he always liked, insisting on having his "coudées franches."[162] In these mock-heroic poems, he frequently used forms shunned by Malherbe (decasyllabic *vers suivis*, nine-line stanzas of octosyllables) and the language often falls from the nearly sublime to the very vulgar:

[158] *Glanes bibliographiques et littéraires* (Paris: Giraud-Badin, 1929), 2:138–47.

[159] Ibid., 2:143.

[160] *Œuvres*, 2:155–56.

[161] Ibid., 2:157.

[162] Ibid.

L'Impunité, sa sœur, et le Courroux sanglant,
Courroux soi-mesme s'aveuglant,

. . . .

. . . et l'on y voit la Rage
Qui ne peut parler qu'en beuglant.[163]

From the time of his "coup d'essai," as he called it, Saint-Amant had spoken of a "poësie/ Pleine de licence et d'ardeur," full of "fureur" and in which there can be no question of "contraindre la liberté/ Du demon qui m'a transporté."[164] But is the poetry of Saint-Amant truly an example of "L'art d'Apollon sans nulle estude," as the author would have us believe?[165] There are many variants to his poetry. Some of these are circumstantial. In 1623, when Montmorency was his patron, he wrote:

> *Invincible Heros, mon unique Mecene,*
> *Reçoy ces nouveaux fruits qui naissent de ma veine.*[166]

By 1629, Retz had entered the picture, and a change was needed:

> *Invincible Heros, dont la valeur m'etonne,*
> *Reçoy ces nouveaux fruits que ma muse te donne.*[167]

But not all changes were necessitated by timely references. When he changed "Nous perdons temps de retiver" into "Nous perdons le temps à rimer," he effectively "a supprimé un verbe vieilli, modifié un vers peu harmonieux."[168]

Saint-Amant had, indeed, a remarkable sureness of technique. Aware of form, he wrote well and seldom had to rewrite, though he obviously did it when he felt the need. Fundamentally, however, he could not follow in Malherbe's footsteps because the very concept of his poetry is different. Both authors could be considered *précieux* if one accepts René Bray's

---

[163] *Œuvres complètes,* 2:366.
[164] "La solitude," ibid., 1:26–27.
[165] Ibid., p. 27.
[166] "L'Arion," ibid., pp. 73–82.
[167] Ibid., p. 81.
[168] Jean Lagny, *Le poète Saint-Amant* (Paris: Nizet, 1964), p. 72.

basic definition, which sees in a *précieux* someone "qui cherche à se donner du prix, le paon qui fait la roue et jette au soleil l'éclat irisé de ses plumes."[169] Malherbe saw that peacock as a symbol of pomp and circumstance, of order and regularity. Saint-Amant focuses on its variety, its ever-changing nature, its fundamentally pictorial effect. It is true that "le tempérament baroque de l'auteur s'exprime principalement par un désir de mouvement, qui préside à la composition de ses pièces, par un souci d'intensité . . . enfin par une recherche de l'ostentation et de la surprise,"[170] but one must not forget that Saint-Amant's greatest innovation was his ability to write poetry that is "essentiellement descriptive."[171] To be sure, he is *précieux*,[172] but his is a special kind of preciosity. Not satisfied with Malherbe's stately idea of grandiose expression, he wanders from idea to idea, from image to image, demonstrating in the process his mastery of sounds, as in "La solitude," and a lexical color and richness unequalled in his time. Alain Seznec has made a thorough study of what may yet be Saint-Amant's greatest deviation from Malherbian practice, one that transcends lexical matters: the rhythmic gymnastics he uses to mold form and content into a single, coherent whole. Quoting these lines from "L'Arion,"

> *On leve aussitost l'ancre, on laisse choir les voilles,*
> *Un vent frais et bruyant donne à plein dans ces toilles;*
> *On invoque Thetis, Neptune et Palemon,*
> *Les nochers font jouer les ressorts du timon,*
> *La nef sillonne l'eau, qui, fuyant sa carriere,*
> *Court devant et tournoye à gros bouillons derriere,*[173]

Seznec points to the obvious élan of the second line and the virtuosity displayed in the last, concluding: "The movement is expressed by the accentuation: 1/5 division in the second hemistich which accelerates *fuyant sa carrière* followed by the regular 3/3 *court devant et tournoie,* these two hemistichs elegantly surrounded by two hemistichs which

[169] *Anthologie de la poésie précieuse* (Paris: Nizet, 1957), p. 10.

[170] Bailbé, "Couleur baroque," pp. 43–44.

[171] Ibid., p. 44.

[172] See Richard A. Mazzara, "Saint-Amant, Avant-Garde *Précieux* Poet: 'La Jouyssance,'" BSTCF 4 (1963):58–63.

[173] *Œuvres complètes*, 1:74–75.

answer one another, 2/4 then 4/2. Hesitation, sliding, balancing, and disequilibrium are suggested. Alliterative sonorities echo each other perfectly."[174] There is in Saint-Amant, particularly in lines such as those of stanza 44 of "Le contemplateur," a "multiple-sense imagery," one that goes beyond the purely visual to create an "almost surrealistic picture."[175] This imagery, this ecstasy of the senses is not evoked but, as in "Le melon," is directly conveyed by the structure. Thus, the form becomes a weapon in a most un-Malherbian arsenal.

There remains the question of the strophic forms used by Saint-Amant, and to better analyze these, I find it necessary to divide the years leading up to 1643 into three main periods. The first such period lasted until 1629 and contained the works of the edition of that year along with a few liminary poems not then collected.[176] The second period, spanning the years 1629–1631, gave birth to the eight poems of the *Suite des Œuvres*. The last period, 1631–1643, saw its culmination in the publication of the *Seconde Partie des Œuvres*. The strophic repartition of these three periods, given here in detail to show the tremendous inventiveness of the poet, is shown in the table.

The most salient fact presented by this breakdown is the variety of forms used by Saint-Amant. For his elegies, he preferred alexandrine *vers suivis*, while his drinking songs are invariably heterometric. One of these uses lines of three different lengths—four if one counts the ejaculatory "Vivat!":

> *Ainsi chantoient au cabaret*
> *Le bon gros Sainct-Amant et le vieux pere Faret,*
> *Celebrans l'un et l'autre à son tour*
> *La santé du comte de Harcour.*
> *Vivat!*[177]

---

[174] "Saint-Amant, le poète sauvé des eaux," *Studies in Seventeenth-Century French Literature Presented to Morris Bishop* (Ithaca: Cornell University Press, 1962), p. 40.

[175] Imbrie Buffum, *Studies in the Baroque from Montaigne to Rotrou* (New Haven: Yale University Press, 1957), p. 160.

[176] Technically, this period should be subdivided into two parts, the earlier one ending about 1625; however, the chronology of many early poems is nearly impossible to establish, making a further breakdown inadvisable.

[177] *Œuvres complètes*, 1:181.

What is almost equally obvious is that Saint-Amant used few of Malherbe's favorite forms. Approximately half of the total output is in *vers suivis*, shunned by Malherbe; the five- and nine-line stanzas cannot be found in Malherbe, who wrote only one eight-line stanza; the sonnet, never a Saint-Amant favorite, was almost totally abandoned after the earliest period. Only in two places can a comparison be made: the heterometric sestet and the isometric ten-line stanza.

If one looks at the early poems of Saint-Amant, one is struck by the relative lack of metrical gymnastics. It was not until the "Chanson à boire" of 1623 that he began to innovate, and this tendency grew as time went on. Structurally, "La solitude," Saint-Amant's avowed "coup d'essai," is quite Malherbian, as we shall see; "Bacchus" and "La Nuit" (1623–1624) are not. The rhythmic innovations were eventually to find their culminating point in the "rythme brisé"[178] of the later burlesque poems.

The earliest heterometric sestets deserving study are those of the "Plainte sur la mort de Sylvie," written about 1618 and set to music by Richard and Bouzignac in 1637.[179] As the first stanza demonstrates, nothing about this poem is Malherbian:

> *Ruisseau qui cours après toy-mesme,*
> *Et qui te fuis toy-mesme aussi,*
> *Arreste un peu ton onde ici*
> *Pour escouter mon dueil extresme;*

[178] Françoise Gourier, *Etude des œuvres poétiques de Saint-Amant* (Geneva: Droz, 1961), p. 228.

[179] Verchaly, *Airs de cour*, pp. 180–81.

NOTES TO TABLE

[1] The VS number includes two epigrams of 12 and 14 lines. To this list, two short madrigals, one for the first and one for the last period, should be added.

[2] Two mixed poems of VS, one with 4-line stanzas, one with 8-line stanzas

[3] One mixed poem of VS and 6-line stanzas

[4] One mixed poem of VS of 8 and 12 syllables

[5] One mixed poem of VS and 1 4-line and 12 6-line stanzas

[6] One of these is a fragment of a letter, the other two are youthful fragments, both later disavowed.

[7] A poem combining two or more forms is listed under each but counts as only one in totaling.

| | | Saint-Amant | | | | | | Malherbe | |
| | | Period I[1] | | Period II | | Period III | | | |
Strophic Division	Length of Line	Poems	Total Lines	Poems	Total Lines	Poems	Total Lines	Poems	Total Lines
Vers suivis	12	8[2]	1,084	1[4]	220	5	456	3[6]	199
	10					3	980		
	8	11[3]	1,022	2[5]	700				
4-line	12	1	4					4	100
	8	2	72	1[5]	4			9	64
	12–6	1[2]	24					8	484
	8–9–13	1	24						
5-line	7			1	75				
	8					1	15		
6-line	8	5[3]	208					21	720
	10–8–6	2	132						
	12–10–8–6					1	42		
	12–8	2	42			1	180	6	342
	12–6	2	54					9	360
	12–8–6	1	6						
	10–8			1	18				
	8–6			1	156				
	7–3			1[5]	72				
8-line	8	2[2]	136			1	152	1	8
	7	1	8						
9-line	8	1	18			1	603		
	8–12					1	45		
	7–5					1	18		
10-line	8	5	1,010	1	60	6	270	11	1,210
	7	1	600					2	280
	12–8	1	180						
Sonnets	12	9	126	2	28	2	28	26	364
	10					2	28		
TOTAL[7]		53	4,750	8	1,333	25	2,817	100	4,131

Puis, quand tu l'auras sceu, va-t'en dire à la mer
Qu'elle n'a rien de plus amer.[180]

While Malherbe frequently used a combination of eight- and twelve-beat lines, he never used fewer than two alexandrines in such stanzas. In this first stanza the break is 4–2, while in the other two it is 6–0 and 2–2–2. The rhyme scheme—*a b b a c c*—was one Malherbe never used in heterometric sestets.

The long (ninety-six lines) poem "La nuict" was not published until much later, but two of its stanzas were set to music by Etienne Moulinié in 1624, and several such settings followed in rapid order, attesting to its popularity.[181] Like the previous example, this poem demonstrates Saint-Amant's lyrical powers. There is a certain fluidity and André Baunier was right in speaking of "musiques, parfois éclatantes," which have "des douceurs charmantes,"[182] although Malherbe might have had reservations about passages such as "Que quand . . . quitte." But other facets of this poem would not have suited Malherbe, and they are far more important, as can be seen by the two stanzas set to music:

Paisible et ténébreuse nuit
Sans lune et sans étoiles,
Renferme le jour qui me nuit
Dans tes plus sombres voiles.
Haste tes pas déesse, exauce moy,
J'ayme une brune comme toy.

J'ayme une brune dont les yeux
Font dire à tout le monde,
Que quand Phoebus quitte les cieux
Pour se cacher sous l'onde,
C'est le regret de se voir surmonté
Du doux esclat de leur beauté.[183]

[180] *Œuvres complètes*, 1:103.
[181] Verchaly, *Airs de cour*, p. lx.
[182] "Un grand poète Louis XIII: Saint-Amant," *RDM* 43 (1918):220.
[183] Verchaly, *Airs de cour*, pp. 142–43. Note that in the *Œuvres complètes* (1:95) there are some interesting variants, all pointed out by Verchaly.

Once again, the 3–3 break demanded by Racan is abandoned for the 2–2–2 format so well suited to the *air de cour*. The combination of lines of six, eight, and ten beats was never used by Malherbe, and the *a b a b c c* rhyme scheme he used only once, in a poem built with the following meters: 10–9–7–10–8–11![184] The first rhyme of the first stanza is unacceptable, being a monosyllabic homonym; it is particularly clever in view of the pun resulting in the third line, but nonetheless un-Malherbian, as are the *moy-toy* and *yeux-cieux* rhymes. In the other stanzas, unacceptable rhymes are at least as frequent, with failing *consonnes d'appui* being the major fault.

"Le Poète crotté," written during the second period, contains twelve sestets, most of which are composed of only one syntactical unit. Metrically, however, each one is divided into two units:

> *Belle, qui dans un grabat*
> *Sans rabat,*
> *Toute seule, et toute nuë,*
> *Estends à present ton corps,*
> *Si ne dors,*
> *Las! oy ma desconvenuë.*[185]

Each half-stanza has a three-beat line bracketed by two seven-beat lines, each half ending with the same rhyme. Such a combination, needless to say, was never used by Malherbe.

Much later in his career, Saint-Amant wrote a very serious ode to the king and queen of England, using a heterometric pattern that Malherbe had used, the 8–8–8–12–8–12 one. Only the inconsistent breaks keep this long (thirty sestets) poem from being Malherbian in tone and structure. But even in this major effort, Saint-Amant failed to conform to the basic rules of Malherbian poetry. As far as rhymes are concerned, the *consonne d'appui* is rebellious as often as not, and proper nouns abound, as do facile rhymes such as first conjugation verbs. As suggested by the variety in breaks, the syntax is frequently tortuous, involving a great number of parenthetical clauses. There are few such efforts in the works of Saint-

---

[184] "Chère beauté, que mon ame ravie," *Œuvres*, 1:247–48.
[185] *Œuvres*, 2:65–66.

Amant, who must surely have felt that his pen was not made for them. The tone and the thoughts are elevated, but there is no lyricism, no unity. Such is not the case of the "Plainte de Tirsis," written about the same time. Its structure—8–12–8–6–10–6—cannot be found in the works of Malherbe since it involves a definite cleavage of the sestet. Syntactically, there are various breaks, but none 3–3, and it is precisely this further deviation from Malherbian doctrine that saves the poem: while the metrics of the poem seem to suggest a 3–3 division, the syntax bridges the gap and unites the two parts:

> *Un Ruisseau plein d'inquietude,*
> *Murmurant sur le dos d'un aspre et vieux Rocher*
> *Du mal qu'il avoit à marcher*
> *En un chemin si rude,*
> *Representoit le lamentable cours*
> *De ses penibles jours.*[186]

While one might question the content, the form is viable, even successful. It clearly shows that, with experience, Saint-Amant was seeking new modes of expression, and that he was far more successful in these endeavors than in his more conventional ones.

The octosyllabic *dizain* was undoubtedly Malherbe's favorite, especially for serious occasional poetry. It would seem that at first Saint-Amant saw the merits of such a choice, for he used it for his most serious early poems, "La solitude" and "Le contemplateur," though the former used an *a b b a c d c d e e* rhyme scheme shunned by Malherbe. Every stanza of "La solitude" has a 4–6 break, as do all but nine of the forty-six stanzas of "Le contemplateur."[187] The success of these poems has been established and further comments are certainly not warranted. What is interesting to note is that as Saint-Amant evolved his own concept of poetry he deviated more and more from these conventions. As the chart shows, he used the octosyllabic ten-line stanza only once during his second period, and that for the very burlesque "Tombeau de Marmousette." In the last period he used it six times, although three of these efforts

---

[186] Ibid., p. 128.

[187] Much the same conformity can be observed in "L'Andromède," written in heptasyllabic *dizains* (*Œuvres complètes*, 1:44–62).

are light-hearted epigrams. The other three poems, though longer, are equally burlesque, and the diverse rhyme schemes used show that the poet was not particularly worried on that score. These schemes range from the orthodox *a b a b c c d e d e* to the very original *a b a a b c c d c d*. The latter is found in "Le cidre," which illustrates a further deviation from form:

> *Comte, puis qu'en la Normandie*
> *Pomone fait honte à Bacchus,*
> *Et qu'en cette Glace arrondie*
> *Brille une lumiere esbaudie*
> *De la couleur de nos escus:*
> *Chantons, à la table où nous sommes,*
> *A la table où le Roy des hommes*
> *Nous traitte en chers et francs Voisins,*
> *Que le Jus delicat des Pommes*
> *Surpasse le Jus des Raisins.*[188]

Note that the rhyme scheme here consecrates the syntactical 5–5 division. Metrically, "Le cidre" may be written in the form Malherbe favored but surely there can be no other connection.

As time went on, Saint-Amant became more and more independent of what might be called Malherbian trends. This is obvious not only in the realm of pure form, but also on another level. Malherbe had opposed dithyrambic outbursts, historic invention, anything but the clearest of constructions. How can such ideas be reconciled with these lines describing the queen of Poland?

> *Un rare objet, que le ciel mesme adore,*
> *Une deesse, un miracle charmant,*
> *Dont sur la terre est le seul digne amant*
> *Le plus auguste et le plus grand monarque*
> *Qui sous l'arctique ait fait luire la marque*
> *Qu'au front des roys grave le roy des dieux,*
> *En ton sejour va monstrer ses beaux yeux.*[189]

---

[188] *Œuvres*, 2:224–25.
[189] *Œuvres complètes*, 1:408.

Malherbe had demanded exactness, particularly in matters of time. Yet, in his serious poetry, Saint-Amant preferred words such as *maint* or *mille et mille*, reserving for his more burlesque poems more exact denotations such as *six mois et demy*.[190] But most of all, it was by his colorful style, by his search for the surprising and the ostentatious that Saint-Amant sought distinction. Malherbe might have shuddered at lines such as "A faire vivre Amour au milieu de la mort,"[191] but Saint-Amant considered them jewels in his crown.[192]

In his *Histoire de la poésie française*, Emile Faguet said, "Il y a certainement, de 1615 à 1640, toute une école, ni très unie sans doute, ni très cohérente, très difficile à nommer d'un seul mot, mais qui est, d'une façon évidente, en état de réaction ou tout au moins d'insubordination vis-à-vis de Malherbe."[193] The degree of cohesion—and insubordination —of the authors who remained *en marge* of the "establishment" during these years will be studied in the next chapter. What should already be obvious is that even in the milieus that should have been under the influence of Malherbe, there was no "school." To be sure, no great anti-Malherbian trend can be discerned—some personal antagonism at the most—but by the same token, there is no established camp of followers, no club of admirers or, more important still, of disciples. A few of his personal friends, Maynard and Racan in the forefront, persevered, but they all too frequently attested to their failure to convince and to gain a following. At the Academy as in the Hôtel de Rambouillet in the last years of the reign of Louis XIII, Malherbe was not dead but he was in definite hibernation.

[190] Ibid., p. 166.
[191] Ibid., p. 71.
[192] For further examples of very clever uses of antitheses and oxymora, see particularly "Elégie pour Damon" and "Plainte sur la mort de Sylvie" (ibid., pp. 99–102, 103).
[193] 2:288.

Chapter Five

Independents

Until now, this study has centered around various milieus or groups that were easy to distinguish and to isolate. Obviously a large number of poets have not yet been touched upon, and these defy such easy classification. Still, in order to make the discussion less chaotic, I have arbitrarily classified some of these poets, using as a standard some traits or genres they had in common. The first of these "subspecies" is that of the satirists, a type particularly active at the turn of the century. Many satirists were openly hostile to Malherbe. Others were not, but, like Auvray, considered themselves disciples of Ronsard and of the love poets of the past century. What concerns us here is not what these poets thought of Malherbe but whether or not they emulated him in any way. It might be argued that satirists, by their very nature, were bound not to follow in Malherbe's footsteps. It should nevertheless be kept in mind that he expected his teachings and examples to be followed even in satirical poetry.[1]

Auvray wrote almost all of his poems in isometric lines, with the bulk of these being *vers suivis*. Even in his satires, he is unable to shake off a basically religious background, though his religious ideas suffer from some strange juxtapositions. As a matter of fact, he seems unable to sustain any idea or tone for very long without debasing it in one way or another. Thus in one passage he likens France to a virgin:

> *L'ignorant ne pouvoit aborder ceste belle*
> *Sans fondre à ce Soleil la cire de son aisle;*
> *Ceste Vierge n'aymoit que les plus vertueux.*[2]

As though this strange mixture of images were not enough, he tells of the court of this virgin, where any presumptuous fool is readily accused of "avoir pissé dessus le rost."[3] Such radical changes in tone and mood are frequent in Auvray's work and inevitably show a complete lack of taste. It is easy to be shocked by lines such as the following without necessarily being *précieux*:

> *Comme s'y pourmenoit mon ame épouvantée,*
> *Elle y vid une croix nouvellement plantée,*
> *Construite, se sembloit, de trois sortes de bois,*
> *Un homme massacré pendoit sur cette croix,*
> *Si crasseux, si sanglant, si meurtry, si difforme,*
> *Qu'à peine y pouvoit-on discerner quelque forme,*
> *Car le sang que versoit son corps en mille lieux*
> *Deshonoroit son front, et sa bouche et ses yeux,*
> *Toute sa face estoit de crachats enlaidie,*
> *Sa chair en mille endroits estoit toute meurtrie,*
> *Sa croix de toute parts pissoit des flots de sang,*

and so on for scores of lines without break or relief.[4] Before this deliberate and powerful painting of horror, Le Hir suggests that "on songe certes à la puissance dramatique d'un Grünewald."[5] True, but while such biblically inspired horror may have suited the palette of a gothic master, it is totally absent from the works of a Poussin. Furthermore, lines such as "Sa peau sanglante estoit cousuë avec ses os" not only are out of taste but are badly balanced and contain frequent examples of hiatus. The first lines of the poem, in fact, tell all that needs be told about Auvray's poetic sensitivity:

> *En extase je tombe, et sans sentir je sens*
> *Une insensible main qui dérobe mes sens,*[6]

as monosyllabic homonyms are made to rhyme, and the reader is confronted with the ridiculous "et sans sentir je sens une insensible

---

[1] Racan, *Œuvres complètes*, 1:342–43.

[2] Fernand Fleuret and Louis Perceau, eds., *Les satires françaises du XVIIe siècle* (Paris: Garnier, 1923), 1:181.

[3] Ibid.

[4] "La pourmenade de l'âme dévote," cited by Yves Le Hir, "Sur un poème d'Auvray," *ECl* 35 (1967):335.

[5] Ibid., p. 339.

[6] Ibid., p. 335.

main. . . ." Such nonsense is found throughout this poem, and un-Malherbian rhymes (*corps-discors*, *calcul-Hercul'*, *difforme-forme*) seem to win out over acceptable ones.

In his stanzas, Auvray is no more Malherbian. He prefers octosyllabic lines, as did Malherbe, but there the similarity ends. His rhymes are invariably bad, with the main faults being facility (adverbs in *-ment* and verb forms), lack of a *consonne d'appui* consonance, bad assonance (*air-voler*) and frequent changes in rhyme schemes in mid-poem.[7] Hiatuses such as *peu à peu* and alliterative effects such as "de tant d'objets dignes d'amour"[8] are to be found everywhere. In his edition of the *Banquet des Muses*, E. H. Balmas considers Auvray "un disciple attardé de Ronsard et des poètes d'amour du XVIe siècle."[9] But even these might have been tempted to disown

> . . . *l'Intendant du Ciel leurs exploits et leurs gestes*
> *Un jour controllera, ouy grands Princes vous estes*
> *Créez pour vos vasseaux, vos vasseaux ne sont pas*
> *Exprez crées pour vous (bien qu'ils . . .*

or "Arrabes Arrabins," "ne vous lassés jamais ces billonneurs punir," and

> *Angoulevent, angoule-vin*
> *Esprit de vin, esprit divin.*[10]

Never would Malherbe have allowed, as Auvray did, "les grandes figures infernales réduites . . . à des personnages de taverne."[11]

Régnier, thanks to a verve and a spirit which are in their very essence the antithesis of everything Malherbe stood for, was the greatest satirist of the times. His satires, be they early or late, all show that he did not apply any of the rules he might have derived from a careful reading of the works of a man he despised: enjambments are frequent; sentences are very long, often running on for more than ten lines; and rhymes such

---

[7] Allem, *Anthologie*, 1:190–95, for instance.
[8] "Le tableau de l'aurore" (ibid., p. 193).
[9] (Milan: La Goliardica, 1953), p. lvi.
[10] Ibid., pp. 31, 29, 45, 77.
[11] Ibid., p. lviii.

as *page-page, avant-devant, conçoit-foit* (*sic,* read *fouet*) can be found as readily in the late satires as in the early ones.

Not counting his "Epitaphe" and several little insignificant pieces, Régnier wrote seven poems in stanza form and as many sonnets. The rhymes in all of these are as poor as those already noted in the satires. For the sake of rhyme, old words (*pensement*), forged words (*Parnassin*), verb forms, and adverbs are abused. [iø] is often made to rhyme with [jø], as are short with long sounds (*surpasse-grace, ame-Madame, ame-flame*). Régnier wrote one poem containing two octosyllabic quatrains (*a b b a* and *a b a b*) and one octosyllabic sestet; another is made of alternating isometric and heterometric quatrains (alexandrine *a b a b* and 12–12–12–6 *a a b b*; a third poem contains heptasyllabic sestets (*a a b c c b*); the remaining four poems use octosyllabic sestets, all but one with the *a a b c c b* scheme. As the chronology would suggest, the question of 3–3 breaks does not enter the picture.[12]

Régnier wrote one octosyllabic and six alexandrine sonnets. The octosyllabic one, dating from 1610, is free in the quatrains (*a b b a b a a b*) but Malherbian in the tercets (*e d e*). All the alexandrine sonnets are in *a b b a . . . e d e*. While I would be reluctant to draw a conclusion from such skimpy evidence, it might be suggested that in this particular endeavor, considered by most poets of the time to be the ultimate test, Régnier saw the need for a certain subservience to formality.

What thus seems implicit in the works of Régnier is very plainly stated by one of his heirs, Jacques Dulorens, self-styled spokesman of the satirists:

> *Chaque genre de vers est sujet à sa loi.*
> · · · · · · · · · · · · · · ·
> *Je n'ai pas tant besoin d'un style relevé,*
> *Pour faire le crayon d'un sot sur le pavé.*[13]

Calling himself "libertin" in matters of poetry,[14] Dulorens felt that "un style relevé" spoiled some types of poems and he demanded only the right

---

[12] Ironically, in only one poem—the early "Quand sur moi je jette les yeux" (*Œuvres complètes* [Paris: Belles Lettres, 1965], pp. 220–24), written at the age of thirty—is there anything approaching consistency in breaks.

[13] *Satyres* (Paris: Sommaville, 1646), p. 138.

[14] Ibid., p. 141.

to "de long et de travers, dire ma ratelée."[15] Some years later he echoed this statement with the following lines:

> Il suffit en riant que je morde ou je pique,
> Sans qu'à me rendre net mon esprit s'alambique;
> Bon pour celui qui croit avoir seul en cet art
> Ce qu'avaient Théophile, et Malherbe, et Ronsard.[16]

Throughout his work, easy rhymes, enjambments such as ". . . c'est son doi/ Qui fist cet univers, qui vous a fait un roi'"[17] prove indeed that he "n'a point de methode."[18] Some of his lines have eleven beats, some have thirteen, and many are badly split: "N'est que du bœuf, et l'autre est de la venaison."[19] Yet, in spite of his protestations to the contrary, and despite the evidence of such carelessness, Dulorens did rework his poems, as a few examples will show.

The following lines were published in 1624:

> Race de tant de Rois, l'Hercule de la France,
> De qui Mars aujourd'hui relève sa vaillance,
> Qui en vostre jeune age avez tant exploité,[20]

and in the 1633 edition, they read as follows:

> Race de Saint Louis, Victorieux monarque
> Dont les moindres exploits sont dignes de remarque,
> Qui dès votre jeunesse avez tant mérité.[21]

By the same token, in 1624, Dulorens wrote:

> Mais conte moi, Monsieur, comment nous a traîtés
> Celui qui vous avait hier au soir invités,

---

[15] Satyres (Paris: Alliot, 1633), p. 36.
[16] Satyres (1646), p. 156.
[17] Sat. II.
[18] Ibid.
[19] Satyres (1646), p. 153.
[20] Satyres (Paris: Villery, 1624), p. 9.
[21] P. 25.

> *Si son vin était bon, et si l'as agréable,*
> *Fais-moi part quand et quand de vos propos de table.*[22]

In 1633, these lines were changed to:

> *Mais conte-moi, Monsieur, comment vous a traîtés*
> *Celui qui vous avait l'autre soir invités,*
> *Tu me feras plaisir, si tu l'as agréable,*
> *Fais-moi participer à vos propos de table.*[23]

And by 1646, they read as follows:

> *Mais conte-moi, Monsieur, comment vous a traîtés*
> *Celui qui vous avait hier au soir invités,*
> *Et tu m'obligeras, si tu l'as agréable,*
> *De me faire aussi part de vos propos de table.*[24]

While these examples do not show a tendency toward discipline, they demonstrate an attempt to remove archaisms and to smooth out chaotic lines, particularly where a hiatus occurs. Whether or not this is a direct effect of Malherbe's influence is impossible to say; it does show, however, that even self-styled rebels could, as time went on, submit to some of the more obvious and general rules that were becoming prevalent.

This contradiction between the statements of a poet and his actual production is nowhere more obvious than in some of the works of Berthelot. Whereas poets such as d'Esternod would exclaim

> *La bacchante fureur la raison me surmonte . . .*
> *Je vous prie, excusez ma muse Rodhomonte,*[25]

and prove by their "verbalisme incorrect, mais extraordinaire, qui se grise de lui-même ou laisse aller les mots en liberté," by their "éloquence cahotique"[26] that this was indeed so, Berthelot did not.

---

[22] P. 165.
[23] P. 41.
[24] P. 143.
[25] Claude d'Esternod, *L'espadon satirique* (Paris: Fort, 1922), p. xxiv.
[26] Ibid., pp. xxxi–xxxii.

Much biographical material has been cited by critics to show that Berthelot thoroughly disliked Malherbe, and every anthology of seventeenth-century poetry includes at least one example of Berthelot's parodies of Malherbe, the most popular of which are probably "Quand Polydor . . . ,"[27] "Réponse à la chanson du Sieur Malherbe,"[28] and especially "De toutes les laideurs Francine est la plus laide," obvious parody of Malherbe's "Il n'est rien de si beau comme Caliste est belle." All this is a well-known aspect of literary history. What is of interest here, however, is whether or not, in these anti-Malherbian poems and elsewhere, Berthelot chose to follow or to disregard the examples set by Malherbe.

In his satires, Berthelot uses a language that is far from *dégasconné,* enjambments are plentiful, and the sentences overly long. Thus, the first ten lines of "L'adieu de Berthelot," in spite of commas distributed haphazardly by a capricious typesetter, must be said "d'un trait." Rhymes all too often rely on the usual facile procedures, including the abuse of proper nouns and an occasional twisting of grammar:

> *Seulement je désire vivre,*
> *Un jour de tous ennuis délivre.*[29]

In most of his *vers suivis* (satires, elegies, and, curiously enough, an "ode" of one twenty-line sentence) Berthelot shows himself quite immune to Malherbe's influence. What of the sonnets and stanzas? His earlier efforts are replete with examples of bad structure:

> *Mais pourquoi leur fait-on ce massacre entreprendre*
> *Dequoi servent les coups,*
> *Le temps n'est pas venu que l'agneau se doit rendre*
> *En la gorge des loups.*[30]

The punctuation here is far from satisfactory, of course, but that is obviously not the problem. As time goes on, however, Berthelot seems more

---

[27] *Le Parnasse des poètes satyriques* (Paris: Sommaville, 1622), p. 145.

[28] *Œuvres satyriques* (Paris: Bibliothèque Internationale d'Edition, 1913), pp. 17–18.

[29] Fleuret and Perceau, *Satires françaises,* 1:21.

[30] *Parnasse* (1607), p. 392Vo.

careful on this as well as on other matters. While his rhymes are not always perfect, they are seldom unacceptable by Malherbian standards, the only consistent failing being that of the *consonne d'appui*. The breaks of his *huitains* vary, but most of his sestets follow the 3–3 pattern, particularly the "Réponse à la chanson du Sieur de Malherbe":

> *Etre six mois à faire une Ode,*
> *Et donner des lois à sa mode,*
> *Cela se peut facilement;*
> *Mais de nous charmer les oreilles,*
> *Par ses merveilles des merveilles,*
> *Cela ne se peut nullement.*[31]

His sonnets, notwithstanding a rare enjambment, are regular in every way and lead one to wonder how posterity would have classified Berthelot had he not lampooned Malherbe.

Whereas satirists are generally dismissed as being totally outside the framework of any study of lyric poetry of this period, some poets usually included in such studies must be excluded from a discussion of Malherbe's influence for simple reasons of chronology. Men such as du Perron, Bertaut, Aubigné, La Ceppède, Isaac du Ryer, or Audiguier, however late the date of their publications may range, had already shaped their literary destiny by the time Malherbe came to Paris. Therefore, there is no need to discuss them here. But some men in this category have, for reasons beyond my comprehension, been called "Malherbian" by recent critics, and I therefore feel it necessary to deal with them here, however briefly.

Jean de Lingendes died at a very young age and early in the century (1616), but he was not quickly forgotten. His *Changemens de la bergère Iris* of 1605 had seven editions between its first appearance and 1623.[32] One of his poems, set to music by Boesset, so pleased the Cardinal de Retz "qu'il la fit répéter plusieurs fois à Lambert qui la chantait devant lui."[33] He was very well represented in the various *recueils* during

---

[31] *Œuvres satyriques*, p. 18.

[32] *Œuvres poétiques* (Manchester: Manchester University Press, 1916), pp. xvii–xix.

[33] Lachèvre, *Bibliographie*, 1:226.

his lifetime, and occasionally until 1692. Goujet, commenting on his favorite form, the *stances*, pointed out their "facilité et douceur," but rightly accused them of being "toutes montées sur le même ton" and therefore boring.[34]

There can be no question of Malherbian influence on the earliest works of Lingendes, but according to Yoshio Fukui, after Malherbe's arrival and success in Paris, Lingendes wrote *stances* and odes which "reflètent très nettement l'influence grandissante de Malherbe qui, d'ailleurs, l'a compté au nombre de ses disciples."[35] It is true that Lingendes's poems were included in *recueils* which Fukui considers "Malherbian," and Lingendes contributed in 1612 to the *Romant des Chevaliers de la Gloire,* a collective work to which Malherbe and Maynard also contributed, but this does not give a reliable indication of the influence. The ballet *entrée* by Lingendes included in the *Romant* is in unbroken sestets with strangely chaotic lines, such as "Ne peut souffrir, ô grand Princesse." The "ô" is obviously padding; what is less obvious is the motive for its inclusion, since correcting the gender of "grand" would satisfy the demands of the line.

Nor should too much of a case be made for Lingendes's inclusion in certain *recueils*. It must be kept in mind that publishers are in the business of selling books, and that Lingendes was extremely popular, witness the numerous editions of his *Changemens de la bergère Iris.* In fact, this poem alone can help us to ascertain the degree of Malherbe's ascendency over Lingendes. It was first written in 1605 but had several editions during the poet's lifetime. What efforts did he make to change its non-Malherbian features, such as the numerous enjambments, particularly between the third and fourth lines of sestets, or breaking up one-sentence stanzas? None. By the same token, none of the many objectionable rhymes (*tu-teu*) were corrected in the later versions.

A look at the various *recueils* can only reinforce the above observations. The 1607 *Parnasse,* for instance, includes "Les vanitez de Floride." These *stances* are 12–12–6–12–12–6, *a a b c c b.* In his entire career, Malherbe used that form only once, and that in 1610. Add to that rhymes such as *pourueuë-veuë, armes-armes,* and *flames-ames,* and it becomes obvious that Malherbe had not yet made his mark. The 1609

[34] *Bibliothèque françoise,* 14:287–89.
[35] *Raffinement précieux,* p. 55.

Nouveau recueil had many poems by Lingendes, most of which were re-edited several times before the poet's death. How do they conform, in their original version or in later ones, to Malherbian examples? "D'où vient que sans effort" is in a form (12–12–6–12–12–6) not yet used by Malherbe, and with a rhyme scheme (*a a b c b c*) that he never used in conjunction with that meter. "Les portes d'Orient . . ." is in 12–12–12–6, *a b a b* quatrains, which Malherbe did not use until 1620. The same meter, with an *a a b b* scheme, as illustrated by "Tirsis près d'un ruisseau . . . ," had been used only once by Malherbe. The sonnet "Pour Mlle du Mayne" is quite irregular, using a scheme never found in Malherbe: *a b b a a b a b c c d e e d*. Only the "Elégie pour Ovide" and "Cognoissant vostre humeur," both written in the form made famous by the "Consolation à M. du Perier," can be considered Malherbian in that respect. Needless to say, this aspect of these poems remained unchanged in subsequent editions.

What of the rhymes? In the original versions, the *consonne d'appui* is lacking more often than not, and rhymes such as *pourueuë-veuë, faux-deffaux, abismer-mer, renommer-mer, point-point,* and a plethora of adverbs in *-ment* can be found in every stanza. Few variants appear in later editions, fewer still concerning rhymes, and even in these there is no improvement. Thus the barely acceptable *loisible-impossible* rhyme is changed after a few years to *possible-impossible*.[36] In addition to these factors, one must also mention the frequent uses of padding—"Attans, mon cœur (dit-elle), vne autre . . ."[37]—which are never corrected in later versions.

One might argue that Lingendes simply refused to bother supervising reeditions of his earlier poems. But this would not explain the "Ode à la Royne," one of his last poems. The basic structure is acceptable, being octosyllabic ten-line stanzas, *a b a b c c d e e d,* but that is all. A few are broken 4–6, but most of the stanzas have no break at all, thus displaying eighty-syllable sentences. The *consonne d'appui* is lacking as frequently as before, proper names are used very frequently for rhymes and even then do not always succeed (*monter-Iupiter*); other unacceptable rhymes, such as *jour-sejour, elles-aisles,* abound. Malherbe has often been accused

[36] P. 152.
[37] P. 136.

of "rhyming prose," but nowhere in his work can one find such strangely unpoetic lines:

> *Puis que sans me donner la peine*
> *De chercher plus auant la haine*
> *Que nous te voulons reprocher,*
> *Personne ne peut contredire*
> *Que l'Espagne ne te retire*
> *Tous les soirs chez elle à coucher?*[38]

The equally late song "Si c'est un crime que l'aymer," whose popularity I have already mentioned,[39] is no better as far as the rhymes are concerned and cannot even be considered Malherbian in form since its sestets are composed of three octosyllabic lines followed by a refrain of three hexasyllabics.

Nicolas Vauquelin des Yveteaux, because of the role he played in establishing Malherbe in the king's good graces, has also been frequently called Malherbian. This appellation, like that of Lingendes, deserves closer scrutiny. Was he, as Georges Mongrédien suggests, "neutre, indifférent, en théorie," even though the same scholar tells us that "chez lui, plus de hiatus, plus d'enjambements, des césures généralement régulières, plus de ces rimes trop faciles . . ."?[40] Furthermore, what is meant by "generally"? Is there a poet whose lines are not "generally regular"?

As a matter of fact, in his choice of forms as in his handling of them, Vauquelin reveals himself as a very erratic poet. At times he seems to reflect the newer trends; at others he strongly reminds the reader of poets long out of fashion. His sonnets, be they early or late, are almost evenly divided between the *e e d* and the *e d e* rhyme scheme. In his isometric stanzas, the octosyllabic line seems to replace the alexandrine so prevalent in his first collection (1606) but the heterometric stanzas are frequently of a type unknown to Malherbe. By the same token, the inner structure

---

[38] P. 188.

[39] See also Verchaly, *Airs de cour,* pp. lvii–lviii, and Lingendes, *Œuvres poétiques,* p. xxxix-xl.

[40] *Etude sur la vie et les œuvres de Nicolas Vauquelin* (Geneva: Slatkine, 1967), p. 216.

of these stanzas is seldom Malherbian; witness the variously balanced lines and erratic breaks of the following sestet:

> C'est beaucoup d'heur quand il arrive
> Qu'on trouve le port dès la rive;
> Car, puisque aussi bien le vaisseau
> Doit périr, c'est notre avantage,
> S'il advient qu'il fasse naufrage
> Avant qu'il fasse encore l'eau.[41]

The syntactical breaks, be they in sestets or octets, seem to follow no pattern whatsoever. The rhymes are consistently good, with only rare lapses (pas-pas being a recurring one), but this can be noted in the pre-1606 poems as well as in the later ones, and should therefore not be attributed to the influence of Malherbe. In short, Vauquelin was Malherbian in only one respect, the rhymes, and he was that before Malherbe reached the scene.

Critics have, from time to time, described the early recueils, such as the Parnasse of 1607 and the Délices of 1615 and 1620, as Malherbian. While it is true that Malherbe and his avowed disciples played major roles in the composition of these, this fact should not blind anyone to the presence of many writers who failed to follow in the master's footsteps. Honoré d'Urfé, if one judges by the number of his poems included in the various recueils of the time, was one of the most popular poets around.[42] His inclusion in the anthologies cannot, however, be attributed to his allegiance to Malherbe; witness this sonnet quatrain:

> Espoirs qui me trompez, et qui ne pouvez être,
> Pensers, qui tourmentez sans cesse mon repos,
> Désirs, qui me brûlez jusqu'au profond des os,
> Travaux, que sans pitié je vois toujours accrestre,[43]

As the first quatrain of a sonnet, this passage cannot stand on its own; the second hemistich of the first line is not only a "bourre" in the Malherbian

[41] Allem, Anthologie, 1:54–55.

[42] Lachèvre, Bibliographie, 1:183. Forty-six poems are included in the 1620 Délices alone.

[43] Délices (1615), p. 477.

sense, but its verb is, at best, badly chosen. The spelling of *accrestre* was no longer acceptable at that date. As it stands, this quatrain is simply not Malherbian. Throughout these anthologies, the poems of d'Urfé use a very involved language, poor rhymes, complicated inversions, and strangely juxtaposed verb sequences as in this excerpt:

> *Donc aujourd'hui mourra, pauvre amante affligée,*
> *Celui dont les beautés sont cause que tu vis.*
> *S'il advient, c'est qu'Amour te veut rendre vengée*
> *Au dépens du cruel qui fuit quand tu le suis.*[44]

Or this passage from the sonnet "Sur la mort de Henri le Grand":

> *Quand enfin des Français celui qui tout dispose*
> *Voulut qu'en son midi se couchât le Soleil,*
> *Et que jamais depuis l'on n'en vit le réveil,*
> *Ainsi disait Marie au cercueil qu'elle arrose.*[45]

The very popular song "Outré par la douleur," set to music by Louis de Rigaud, is no better. Many of its quatrains are quite obscure, and the last one verges on the cacophonic:

> *Réduit en cet estat elle ne peut connoistre*
> *Qu'elle, n'y quelle elle est.*
> *O pourquoy faut-il estre*
> *Lors que tout me déplaist?*[46]

Opposed to the satirists and to the poets just discussed were the members of two groups, the "Illustres bergers" and the Piat-Maucours Academy. These were not homogeneous groups and never constituted literary schools as such; rather, they should be viewed as poets gathering regularly because of certain common tastes. According to Fukui, all the members of both groups were "puristes" and Malherbian,[47] but these appellations deserve closer analysis. Fundamentally, most of the "Illustres

---

[44] Ibid. (1620), p. 10.
[45] Ibid., p. 13.
[46] Verchaly, *Airs de cour*, pp. 136–37.
[47] *Raffinement précieux*, p. 109.

bergers" tended to abstract their love, something Malherbe never did.[48]
Some, such as Molière d'Essertine, had a sensitivity "toute semblable
à celle de Théophile."[49] But even on the purely technical side, most of the
poems issuing from these two groups fail to withstand comparison
with the ideas of Malherbe, as we shall see.

Most of these poets had other literary ties and, as such—that is, as
frequenters of the Chambre Bleue or the Academy—have already been
considered. Only two others need concern us here: Marbeuf and Frénicle.

As late as 1628, Marbeuf, in a poem replete with rhymes such as
frons-affrons and with octosyllabic sestets having every break imaginable,
exclaimed, "Courtisans ne me lisez pas." He maintained that he was
"rustique et sauvage,"[50] and that

> *Mon humeur pleine d'apreté,*
> *Blâme vostre delicatesse,*
> *Car elle a trop de propreté*
> *Et moy trop peu de politesse.*[51]

His "purism" can therefore be put in doubt, as can his "Malherbian"
tendency, which is certainly not manifest in these lines:

> *Et la mer et l'amour ont l'amer pour partage,*
> *Et la mer est amere, et l'amour est amer,*
> *L'on s'abyme en l'amour aussi bien qu'en la mer,*
> *Car la mer et l'amour ne sont point sans orage.*[52]

His sonnets are almost all in the *e e d* scheme rejected by Malherbe, and
many of the rhymes are unacceptable in other ways, frequently failing in
regard to the *consonne d'appui*, use of proper nouns (*Pantheon-Actéon*),
simple and compound words (*robe-derobe*), and [jø-iø]. His strophic

---

[48] Frénicle, on the other hand, does not do this either. See, for instance,
his "Ode à M. Malleville."
[49] Adam, *Théophile*, p. 242.
[50] Cited in Goujet, *Bibliothèque françoise*, 15:172.
[51] Cited by Fukui, *Raffinement précieux*, p. 110.
[52] *Recueil des plus beaux vers de Messieurs de Malherbe, Racan, . . .*
(Paris: Toussainct du Bray, 1627), p. 261.

compositions are no better. His "Anatomie de l'œil" in *a b a b* alexandrines is full of technical jargon; it is doubtful that "la divine Julie" would have appreciated "les petits nerfs optiques" or even "l'iris jointe à l'urée."[53] Generally speaking, his rhymes are weak, the breaks inconsistent, and even the choice of forms may at times be considered unorthodox: the "Chant royal," for instance, is in decasyllabic eleven-line stanzas, *a a b a b c c d e d e,* the last line being a refrain. There is one poem, nevertheless, that deserves closer attention: "Le tableau de la beauté de la mort," both by its subject and its form—12–6–12–6, *a b a b*—brings Malherbe's famous "Consolation" to mind. In tone, it may be considered quite good, but its rhymes are barely acceptable, and the balance of the lines frequently leaves much to be desired: "Enseignent que la mal de la naissance est pire." Furthermore, the inner structure varies from stanza to stanza, some having a linking of lines 2 and 3 while others have a definite median break:

> *La mort n'est qu'une femme ainsi qu'Hylas la nomme;*
> *Hylas, c'est donc à tort*
> *Que ton jeune courage étant au cœur d'un homme*
> *Craint la main de la mort.*
>
> . . . .
>
> *Tu te laisses à tort abuser à l'envie*
> *De l'immortalité;*
> *Penses-tu préserver le verre de ta vie*
> *De la fragilité?*[54]

Whereas the last stanza might be considered Malherbian, the first one is obviously not.

The early efforts of Nicolas Frénicle were very "gaillards," but after the trial of Théophile, he, like so many of his friends, turned to "la bergerie galante et poétique."[55] His popularity is difficult to estimate: by 1629 there were three editions of his works, but only one poem in a *recueil collectif.* His earliest statements about his poetic ideas deal with poets who "préfèrent tousjours la rime à la raison":

[53] Lachèvre, *Bibliographie,* 4:150.
[54] Allem, *Anthologie,* 1:280–85.
[55] Lachèvre, *Bibliographie,* 1:193.

Je connoy des rimeurs dont le foible courage
Met la bonté des vers seulement au langage.

. . . .

Tous leurs écris ne sont que matières frivoles
Où la conception s'accomode aux paroles.[56]

Antoine Adam has amply proven that when Frénicle said these words, he was a disciple of Théophile.[57] During the second period of his production, that which Lachèvre refers to as "galante," Frénicle indulged in the usual pastoral genres, particularly favoring the elegy. He refrained, however, from following the other "Illustres bergers" in abstracting love. Whether in so doing he is Malherbian is difficult to say. But when, after 1636, he spent most of his time writing religious poetry, his style was such that Paulette Leblanc believes Frénicle "révère Malherbe et ne renie point Ronsard."[58] He had always displayed a lyrical gift, writing "vers harmonieux dans une langue très pure et très souple,"[59] but in the religious poems, particularly the psalms, in spite of what may be described as a certain incoherence, he showed himself to be "un vrai lyrique."[60]

If the strophic forms Frénicle chose for his psalms cannot often be traced to Malherbe, his search for novelty in that domain could readily be likened to Malherbe's. For his 150 psalms, Frénicle used 123 different forms, including alexandrine *vers suivis*. Many of these were rewritten, some quite extensively, between 1625 and 1661. The rhymes are improved, as is the flow of the lines, but even if one must grant these efforts a certain "souffle," they lack the cohesion and coherence that typifies Malherbe's serious efforts:

> *Que les temples magnifiques*
> *Retentissent de cantiques,*
> *Loüez Dieu de cent façons,*
> *Et que son pouvoir supréme*

---

[56] *Premières œuvres poétiques* (Paris: Toussainct du Bray, 1625), p. 95.

[57] *Théophile*, pp. 243–44. See also Fukui, *Raffinement précieux*, pp. 125–27.

[58] *Paraphrases*, p. 220.

[59] Maurice Cauchie, "Les églogues de Nicolas Frénicle et le groupe littéraire des 'Illustres Bergers,'" *RHPh* 30 (1942): 115.

[60] Leblanc, *Paraphrases*, p. 220.

Soit de mesme
Le sujet de vos chansons.[61]

Lyrical, yes, but not Malherbian.

Anthoine Brun, or Le Brun, as he is sometimes known, was extremely popular about 1620 if one judges by the number of his poems that found their way into the *recueils* of that time. A friend of Saint-Amant,[62] he founded an academy, not unlike that of Piat-Maucours, whose faithful were the contributors to *Les muses en deuil.*[63] Many of its members—Méziriac, Gomberville, and Colletet in particular—were among the most popular poets of the capital. This group was especially attached to the writing of sonnets, and in this respect Brun is quite representative. His early production is orthodox, but, like his friends, he indulged more and more in the "sonnet licencieux," preferring *a b a b* quatrains. What marks him as being totally outside of either Malherbian influence or the main tendency of his colleagues is his excessive love of ostentation made manifest by numerous hyperbolic metaphors:

> *Receuant dans ton sein cet obiect adorable*
> *Bon Dieu que tes desirs doiuent estre contens:*
> *Car auiourd'huy la mer ne t'est point preferable*
> *Puis que tous ses tresors t'arriuent en vn temps.*
>
> *Si quelques mons errans la rendent admirable*
> *Regarde ces tetons sur tes ondes flotans:*
> *Ou bien si du Soleil la retraitte honorable*
> *Ces yeux t'en fourniront deux bien plus éclatans.*
>
> *D'ailleurs si du corail quelquesfois elle accouche,*
> *Ne peux-tu pas monstrer le pourpris de sa bouche,*
> *Si des perles aussi, considere ses dents:*
>
> *Et si pour rendre en fin la mer bien plus altiere*
> *L'on te dit que Venus sortit de là dedans*
> *Alors il te faudra monstrer ma Dame entiere.*[64]

---

[61] Ibid., p. 221.

[62] See the latter's "La vigne."

[63] *Les Muses en deuil en faveur du sieur Brun* (Paris: Toussainct du Bray, 1620). See also Lachèvre, *Bibliographie*, 1:83.

[64] *Délices* (1620), p. 1130.

Small wonder that his popularity declined sharply after the early 1620s and that he was unable to join his friends at the Académie Française.

Two poets, Théophile de Viau and Tristan L'Hermite, have frequently been called either opponents of Malherbe or independents, with Théophile's "Malherbe a très bien fait . . ." quoted to justify the classification. There is no denying the classification of these two as non-Malherbian if not anti-Malherbian, but this separation might well be made on grounds even more fundamental than mere technical subservience to certain rules. Ronsard was, in many ways, pagan, but during the last years of the sixteenth century this joyful paganism had been buried under an agglomeration of pedantic "savoir." Malherbe, in the name of clarity, logic, and reason, had rejected all this in a reaction which the entire century was to sanction, and even Théophile said that

> La sotte antiquité nous a laissé des fables
> Qu'un homme de bon sens ne croit pas recevables.[65]

But while Malherbe rejected all antiquity, Théophile, Tristan, and to some extent Saint-Amant, rejected the erudition but not the atmosphere. This is readily demonstrated by poems such as "Le promenoir des deux amants." In fact, these poets reach their perfection "dans un mélange exquis d'images sensuelles qu'inspirent à la fois la nature, l'amour et la mythologie."[66] Miss de Mourgues is leery of an art that wants to imitate another, a poem that wishes to be a painting,[67] but if a painting can represent an *état d'âme*, as the impressionists wanted it to, why should a poem do less? In fact, many of the poems of Théophile and Tristan—the "Promenoir" and "Terreurs nocturnes" of Tristan and "Un corbeau . . ." of Théophile in particular—are not detailed paintings, nor do they give a great all-encompassing view of anything. Rather, they convey a particular *état d'âme* and, as in the case of the "Promenoir," a sensuality, a paganism that is the very antithesis of Malherbianism.[68] This paganism

---

[65] *Œuvres poétiques* (Geneva: Droz, 1951–1958), 1:80.

[66] Odette de Mourgues, *O muse, fuyante proie* . . . (Paris: Corti, 1962), p. 20.

[67] Ibid., p. 22.

[68] These qualities of the "Promenoir" are remarkably set off by Debussy's musical setting.

is what separates these poets from their contemporaries, and Moréas was right in saying of Théophile: "Dans un décor de toile et de carton-pâte, au milieu des *concetti* et des pointes, il trouve moyen de faire entendre parfois la voix naturalle des choses."[69]

As can be expected, Malherbe's reaction to such ideas was unequivocal. In a letter to Racan, dated 4 November 1623, commenting on Théophile's trials and tribulations, he said: "Je ne le tiens coupable de rien, que de n'avoir rien fait qui vaille au métier dont il se mêloit. S'il meurt pour cela, vous ne devez point avoir de peur: on ne vous prendra pas pour un de ses complices."[70] On the other hand, Théophile was never reluctant to praise certain aspects of Malherbe's production. In addition to the famous "Malherbe a très bien fait," one need only cite the following excerpt from the "Priere aux Poetes de ce temps":

> *Je ne fus jamais si superbe*
> *Que d'oster aux vers de Malherbe*
> *Le François qu'ils nous ont appris,*
> *Et sans malice et sans envie*
> *J'ay tousjours leu dans ses escrits*
> *L'immortalité de sa vie.*

But these sestets praising Malherbe are far from Malherbian, as can be seen from part of the very next one:

> *Pleust au Ciel que sa renommee*
> *Fust aussi cherement aymee*
> *De mon Prince, qu'elle est de moy.*[71]

Allusions to Malherbe's genuine contributions, particularly in the realm of language, are plentiful in Théophile's work, but there is always the famous "mais," which can best be interpreted as has Miss Winegarten: "Théophile questioned Malherbe's attitude to poetry and the whole foundation of his aesthetic."[72]

[69] Jean Moréas, *Œuvre en prose* (Paris: Valois, 1927), p. 408.
[70] *Œuvres*, 4:8–9.
[71] *Œuvres poétiques*, 2:130.
[72] *French Lyric Poetry*, p. 29.

Before proceeding to an analysis of some of Théophile's basic departures from the straight and narrow path traced by Malherbe, it might be interesting to point out that while Malherbe had his admirers, Théophile did not lack partisans either. As Miss Winegarten has so judiciously pointed out, subjective interpretations of contemporary opinions to the contrary, "between 1628 and 1635, nineteen editions of Théophile's works were published to five of Malherbe's, and throughout the century the balance in favour of Théophile was to be maintained."[73] Some of these contemporary opinions are quite interesting, nevertheless. Scudéry, as a friend of Théophile, was very prejudiced, which explains the strength of this statement: "tous les morts ny tous les vivans n'ont rien qui puisse approcher des forces de ce vigoureux genie."[74] In his "Tombeau de Théophile" he went still further, placing his friend above either Ronsard or Malherbe:

> Du plus hardy traict de nostre art,
> Dessus ce monument superbe
> Sera le portraict de Malherbe,
> Et plus haut celuy de Ronsard,
> Qui, s'ostant chacun la couronne
> Dont leur docte chef s'environne,
> Diront, par cette humilité,
> Qu'on ne peut refuser hommage
> A la grandeur de ton ouvrage
> Sans un excez de vanité.[75]

The same thoughts can be found expressed by Scudéry elsewhere in 1635[76] and in 1646.[77] Peiresc, who loved Malherbe "comme mon propre pere,"[78] did not, for all that, admire him unreservedly. He had serious doubts as to his merit,[79] considered his letters not worth the postage,[80] and

[73] Ibid., p. 31.

[74] Viau, Œuvres complètes (Paris: Jannet, 1856), 1:4.

[75] Ibid., p. 9.

[76] Trompeur puni, p. 125.

[77] Le cabinet de M. de Scudéry, pp. 223–29.

[78] Nicolas-Claude de Fabri, sr. de Peiresc, Lettres (Paris: Imprimerie Nationale, 1888–1898), 2:161.

[79] Ibid., pp. 45, 86, 221.

deplored his way of "examiner les choses et les conceptions si scrupuleusement et ric à rac," suggesting that "l'on a bien meilleur marché de passer
oultre."[81] Receiving an edition of Malherbe, he commented to Dupuy that
he would have preferred it had the editor published Théophile.[82] Without
being quite so harsh, Rapin in 1675 admitted that if Malherbe had a
certain purity, Théophile had "des hardiesses heureuses."[83]

Théophile wrote about 150 poems. Of these, only fourteen are
heterometric and thirteen are in isometric *vers suivis*, the latter, mostly
satires and elegies, forming the bulk of part two of the poetic works. All
the rest of his production is made up of isometric stanzas, mostly octosyllabic, although the two dozen sonnets are all alexandrine.

Most of the *vers suivis* of part one and all the subsequent ones are
alexandrine. Théophile, as Malherbe demanded, obviously tried to "fermer
le sens" at least every four lines, but he did not always succeed, particularly in the satirical pieces where a certain élan is needed and is
present thanks to the "longue haleine" allowed by seven or eight lines in
a single draft. Enjambments are frequent. As in most *vers suivis* of the
time, many rhymes are too facile (*-ment*, verb endings), others lack the
consonne d'appui assonnance, still others rely on unacceptable commonplaces (*ame-flamme*), while a large number are simply bad (*laisse-malaise,
point-point, jour-sejour, pas-pas*). Old words are relatively few (this is to
be expected, in view of his own demand for "quelque nouveau
langage"[84]), and one is tempted to think that they were chosen deliberately, usually to fit where a newer word would not have been allowed
either by rhyme or rhythm: "Ce travail importun m'a long temps mar-
tyré."[85] Ironically, the two above-quoted passages, one demanding a new
language, the other using an archaism, are from the same poem, "Elégie
à une dame."

Unfortunately, Théophile's rhymes are not much better in his
stanzas. The usual proscriptions are violated—*faux-defaux, esprit-esprit,
veux-vœux, desers-baisers, portail-crystal*, as well as the usual abuse of
-ment adverbs, verb forms, and proper nouns, the worst example of which

[80] Ibid., pp. 158–59.
[81] Ibid., 3:571.
[82] Ibid., 2:255.
[83] *Réflexions*, p. 161.
[84] *Œuvres poétiques*, 1:13.
[85] Ibid., p. 11.

is in a sonnet: *Pelion-Deucalion-Ilion.*[86] The major objection, however, is not to these lapses, however frequent they may be, or even to the use of facile rhymes. Rather, it is to the abuse of certain commonplaces. Thus, *ame* nearly always rhymes (badly) with *flamme, vie* with *envie, fer* with *enfer, jour* with *amour, sort* with *mort, vers* with *Univers.* This moon-June association becomes monotonous and after a while verges on the comic.

Théophile seems to have written all of his twenty-four sonnets relatively early in his career, and certainly none after 1622 or 1623 at the latest. Only one sonnet was published after that date,[87] but in view of its subject it must be an early one whose suppression was to be expected. All but six of Malherbe's sonnets are *a b b a . . . e d e,* and two of these six are *a b b a a' b' b' a'.* With this in mind, it is interesting to note that only eleven of Théophile's sonnets are "classical" while seven have a *d e e d* ending, two invert the quatrain scheme (*a b a b b a b a*), and four use the completely un-Malherbian *a b a b b a b a c c d e e d* scheme. On the other hand, enjambments are very few. Except for an occasional lapse—"D'un sommeil plus tranquile à mes Amours resvant"[88] or "Me dois-je taire encor Amour, quelle apparence?"[89]—the lines are free of bad inversions and are well-balanced.

Théophile used heterometric stanzas very seldom, but when he did, he used those least liked by Malherbe. The heterometric *dizain* is used only once, when two alexandrines follow eight octosyllabic lines in an *a a b c b c b c d d* scheme, without any break. The sestets are equally un-Malherbian. Théophile wrote only three poems in that form, two of which were not included in his collected works. The one included is in 8–8–8–12–8–12, *a b a b a b* stanzas without any syntactical breaks of significance. The other two attempts—8–8–12–8–8–12 and 8–8–12–12–12–8, both *a a b c b c*—can find no examples in Malherbe who, as a matter of fact, combined octosyllabic and alexandrine lines rather seldom.[90] The heterometric quatrains can be divided as follows: three poems in

---

[86] Ibid., p. 32.

[87] In 1665; see ibid., 2:219.

[88] Ibid., p. 33.

[89] Ibid., 1:133.

[90] Malherbe used the 8–8–8–12–8–12 form only twice, once in a single stanza included in a letter, though never with the *a b a b a b* rhyme scheme. Only four other poems combine lines of eight and twelve syllables, and at least one of these is of a very early vintage.

12–6–12–6, *a b a b* form; two in 8–12–12–8, *a b b a*; one in 12–6–10–6, *a b a b*; one in 12–12–12–6, *a b a b*; one in 12–12–8–12, *a b a b*; and one in 12–8–12–8, *a b a b*. A certain symmetry is to be noted; frequently in these quatrains lines of equal length are connected by the rhyme. What must also be noted is that Malherbe used only two of the above forms (the 12–6 combinations) and with different rhyme schemes. By the same token, Théophile's "symmetry" can be found only rarely in Malherbe. At times, Théophile achieves a very wide variety of effects through his use of heterometry. One can only admire the changes in mood and rhythm occurring within the framework of a single form. The "Stances à Philis," for instance, begin with a certain élan:

> Ha! Philis que le Ciel me fait mauvais visage,
> Tout me fasche et me nuit,
> Et reservé l'amour et le courage,
> Rien de bon ne me suit.

but end on a totally different tone:

> Le Soleil meurt pour moy, une nuict m'environne,
> Je pense que tout dort,
> Je ne voy rien, je ne parle à personne;
> N'est-ce pas estre mort?[91]

Elsewhere, unfortunately, such quatrains give only an impression of a lack of smoothness, of chaos, that makes Malherbe seem more consistently lyrical.

Like Malherbe, Théophile wrote the bulk of his poems in isometric stanzas, but whereas Malherbe differentiated between "ode" and "stances" mainly by the tone, Théophile did not, calling most of his heterometric poems "stances" and most of his isometric ones "odes," although "Mon espérance refleurit," in octosyllabic quatrains, was called "stances" in later editions.[92]

Théophile's octosyllabic quatrains are among his earliest and most

[91] *Œuvres poétiques,* 1:25–26.
[92] One poem, "Heureux tandis qu'il est vivant" (ibid., p. 184), is called "ode" although in *vers suivis.*

famous poems. Being of an early vintage, many of them underwent changes that tell us much about the poet's concepts. In 1619, "Le matin" had thirteen stanzas; in 1620, augmented by some new ones and two borrowed from "La nuit," it had twenty; in the 1621 edition, it was reduced to sixteen, having dropped one of the original and several of the intermediate stanzas. The variants are usually attempts to make the flow smoother and to clarify the meaning. This is particularly obvious if one compares the third stanza of the 1619 version:

> Ardans ils vont en nos ruisseaux,
> Alterez de sel et d'escume,
> Boire l'humidité qui fume,
> Si tost qu'ils ont touché les eaux.[93]

with the 1620 version:

> Ardans ils vont à nos ruisseaux,
> Et dessous le sel, et l'escume,
> Boivent l'humidité qui fume,
> Si-tost qu'ils ont quitté les eaux.[94]

By 1621, probably realizing that the stanza was hopeless, Théophile dropped it altogether. The second "ode" in this format is the equally famous "La solitude." In its original form, it consisted of three juxtaposed short odes which were augmented to enhance the feeling of illicit love. The unity of the poem is strengthened by these additions, particularly of lines 153 and the following, in which "the lines of the Ovidian myths and those of the pastoral invitation are being drawn together,"[95] closing the poem on the theme first noted at the very beginning: "Les vents qui ne se peuvent taire" of line 161 are the final echo of lines 19–20:

> Et les vents battent les rameaux
> D'une amoureuse violence.[96]

[93] Ibid., p. 195.
[94] Ibid., p. 197.
[95] Robert E. Hill, "In Context: Théophile de Viau's La Solitude," BHR 30 (1968):535.
[96] Œuvres poétiques, 1:23, 17.

It should also be noted that between these two versions, there are some important variants not always kept in mind. Thus the later "douce flamme" of Cupidon was, in the 1620 version, a "sombre flamme."[97] As in "Le matin," the variants seldom concern the rhymes, which did not seem to worry the poet particularly.

The alexandrine quartets were written later, as a whole. They are remarkably well structured, with balanced lines and no enjambments. In fact, this tendency is at times carried to extremes, leading to a dislocation of lines not too rare in Théophile's production:

> *Un arbre que le vent emporte à ses racines,*
> *Une ville qui voit desmolir son rempart,*
> *Le faiste d'une tour qui tombe en ses ruines,*
> *N'ont rien de comparable à ce sanglant despart.*[98]

All fifteen of Théophile's poems in octosyllabic sestets written before 1623 are erotic and relatively short. The Malherbian rhyme schemes for the form ($a\,a\,b\,c\,b\,c$ and $a\,a\,b\,c\,c\,b$) are used most frequently, though not exclusively. The breaks are varied, most stanzas having none at all, though here again one frequently finds stanzas of isolated lines:

> *Cloris, c'est mentir trop souvent,*
> *Tes propos ne sont que du vent,*
> *Tes regards sont tous pleins de ruzes,*
> *Tu n'as point pour tout d'amitié,*
> *Je me mocque de tes excuses,*
> *Et t'aime moins de la moitié.*[99]

On the other hand, enjambments are plentiful. All these tendencies are present in the poems of this type in part three (after 1623). In fact, many of them worsen. The rhyme schemes are now the standard $a\,a\,b\,c\,b\,c$, but these poems cannot be considered Malherbian for all that. The rhymes are at least as bad as in the earlier poems, and, as far as inner structure is concerned, not only are most stanzas without any syntactical breaks, but

[97] Ibid., p. 18.

[98] Ibid., p. 148. For the same effect, see the already-quoted last stanza of "Stances à Philis," or the famous ode "Un corbeau devant moy croasse."

[99] Ibid., 1:128.

a single sentence often takes up more than one stanza. In the "Remonstrance à M. de Vertamont," all six stanzas are really but one sentence.

An important percentage of Théophile's production is taken up by octosyllabic ten-line stanzas. The rhyme schemes, though varied, are all acceptable. As in the forms already analyzed, enjambments are frequent and the breaks varied, though most stanzas are either not broken at all or divided 4–6. These "odes" (the name is applied to all the poems in that form except one) range from the lightly erotic to the pompously occasional, from the surrealistic "Un corbeau . . ." to the pious and commonplace consolations, from "requêtes" to "remerciements," with an obvious disregard for length, tone, or structure. Few of them are ever quoted today, and their only interest for this study is the relative frequency of their 4–6 division, a trend that could be considered Malherbian.

Théophile used other isometric stanzas, though not with the same frequency. In 1618, he wrote two poems on the death of the Duchess of Nevers, both in alexandrine sestets, *a a b c b c,* with varied weak breaks or none at all. His octosyllabic *huitains* are invariably bad, the only consolation being that he used them as sparingly as did Malherbe. His "A M. de L. sur la mort de son Pere," a morbid consolation, makes Malherbe's consolations look like paragons of good taste in comparison:

> *La mort, grosse de desplaisirs,*
> *De tenebres et de souspirs,*
> *D'os, de vers, et de pourriture. . . .*[100]

The breaks of these poems are capriciously varied and the constructions in every way verge on the absurd:

> *La Parque retranchant le cours*
> *De tes Soleils bien que si cours,*
> *Rien que nuict sur toy ne devide.*[101]

The ultimate in deviation from Malherbian standards is reached in the "Ode au Prince d'Orange," a combination of alternating stanzas of six and seven octosyllabic lines.

[100] Ibid., 2:215.
[101] Ibid., 1:34.

It should not be thought that Théophile, because of some failing or other, was unable to follow in Malherbe's footsteps. In fact, he frequently demonstrated a distinct ability to deploy talents not unlike those of Malherbe. Commenting on the sonnet "Sacrez murs du Soleil où j'adoray Philis,"[102] Hélène Guedj states that "Certes, le ton du poète atteint dans cette description de Clérac détruit une grande dignité; l'alexandrin se déploie majestueusement et la forme choisie, le sonnet, impose à Théophile une concision salutaire. . . . L'alternance des vers où seule la halte à l'hémistiche est signalée et de ceux où les coupes se multiplient (deux et même trois), la suppression des articles, la densité de l'expression en font une pièce d'une telle vigueur qu'elle ne déparerait nullement un des 'récits' d'une tragédie cornélienne."[103] Nor a Malherbian ode.

A further rapprochement should be made. As Philip Wadsworth has pointed out, there is really very little "rigorous logic," or "admirable structure," or even tight "enchaînement des idées" in the odes of Malherbe; rather, "He even attained 'un ordre supérieur et cashé.' "[104] In a long study under way, D. L. Rubin is presently examining exactly this "higher, hidden order," that is, the level of image, myth, and metaphor, wherein he finds that what may seem contradictory and irrelevant in a logical scheme is nevertheless integral to a certain coherence. This is also very much the case with Théophile. As Gerhard Müller has pointed out, in Théophile there is a basic unity of the various aspects of style, if by style we understand not only language or versification but "die Gesamtpräsentation sprachlicher Kunstwerke: Thema, Motiv, Aufbau, Sprache, Vers, die Verbindung von Inhaltlichem und Formalem."[105] There may be, as De Mourgues[106] and Stone[107] have stated, some very badly coordinated passages in the works of Théophile, but never because of the poet's inability to wed form and content. Any analysis out of context, such as

---

[102] Ibid., 2:34.

[103] "Théophile de Viau, poète baroque, et le Sud-Ouest," *Baroque* A2 (1963):145.

[104] "Form and Content," pp. 190, 195.

[105] Gerhard Müller, *Untersuchung des poetischen Stils Théophiles de Viau* (Munich: Huebner, 1968), p. 15.

[106] "Reason and Fancy in the Poetry of Théophile de Viau," *ECr* 1 (1961): 75–81.

[107] Donald Stone, Jr., "Théophile's 'la Solitude': An Appraisal of Poem and Poet," *FR* 40 (1966): 321–28.

that of Stone in the case of "La solitude," may show the poem to be chaotic. But if the poem is put back into context, as it was by Robert E. Hill, then a basic unity and sense is made manifest. Treated as an isolated and insulated phenomenon, "La solitude" falls apart. Treated as a "pastoral invitation,"[108] it makes eminent sense.

Some critics[109] too often make the unity of Théophile's poems depend on a "baroquism" which in turn is often demonstrated by questionable interpretations.[110] What Stone sees in "La solitude" is a "structure . . . conceived in terms of a unity of atmosphere" but which does not "explain the poem's unfulfilled themes."[111] Hill, by careful analysis, particularly of the first thirteen stanzas, shows a "very solid construction."[112] Tracing the antecedents of the setting of this erotic invitation back to Theocritus, he aptly demonstrates that both setting and living beings in the poem can be found in models that Malherbe shunned deliberately, which were therefore far from new, but which seem "newly waxed" under Théophile's pen because they have been "pushed into new places."[113] What is particular to Théophile—and so foreign to Malherbe—is that the poem seems to be in suspension. This is because the topic demands it. As Hill points out, we are not dealing here with a sweet, gentle, and pleasant atmosphere: at the beginning of the poem we see that Venus, Diana, and Cupid will have to fight it out, and Cupid wins. But he is not a delightful cherub. He is "the cruel, Ovidian Cupid," and Théophile's invitation into this "Ovidian forest" is not to pleasure but to pain.[114] This unity is enhanced by the use of conceits which make a supernatural being, even a divinity, of the invited girl, thus making her part of the "locus amœnus."[115] But this transformation is due to the poet, and the girl is made to feel it:

[108] Hill, "In Context," p. 500.

[109] Lowry Nelson, Jr., *Baroque Lyric Poetry* (New Haven: Yale University Press, 1961), to name but one.

[110] See refutation of Nelson by Stone, "Théophile's 'la Solitude,'" pp. 323 ff.

[111] Ibid., p. 326.

[112] "In Context," p. 504.

[113] Ibid., p. 506.

[114] Ibid., pp. 529–36.

[115] Ibid., p. 533.

> *Ne crains rien, Cupidon nous garde,*
> *Mon petit Ange es tu pas mien?*
> *Ha! je voy que tu m'aymes bien,*
> *Tu rougis quand je te regarde.*[116]

She is thus made to realize that her divinity is of his creation, that here there is only a "supremely elegant proposition" based on the fact that she likes him, and that "she knows that he knows that she knows."[117] This then is an inner unity, a total one (keep Müller's definition in mind) that goes well beyond Malherbe's formal structures as analyzed by Philip Wadsworth. Théophile should be viewed not as a poet reluctant to follow Malherbe, and thus retrograde, but as one who saw a need beyond all that:

> *Il faudroit inventer quelque nouveau langage,*
> *Prendre un esprit nouveau, penser et dire mieux.*[118]

This "esprit nouveau," unfortunately, was not in keeping with the spirit of the times, and so much the worse for it.

There were some poets, however, who shared Théophile's views; foremost among them was François Tristan L'Hermite du Solier, born some ten years after Théophile.[119] In his person, French lyric poetry of the seventeenth century was to find its greatest adept of this "lyrisme épris des formes et des couleurs."[120] In that respect, he is the very antithesis of Malherbe, but not in that respect alone. As Amédée Carriat has pointed out,[121] the opposition can be seen even in the personalities of the

---

[116] *Œuvres poétiques,* 1:22–23.

[117] Hill, "In Context," p. 534.

[118] *Œuvres poétiques,* 1:13.

[119] Much ink has been spilled over the exact birthdate of Tristan. For a sensible commentary that brings all the documents available to bear on the question, see Catherine M. Grisé, "Towards a New Biography of Tristan L'Hermite," *Rev. Univ. Ottawa* 36 (1966): 294–316.

[120] Idem, "La vraie source de 'L'ambition tancée' de Tristan L'Hermite," *RLC* 41 (1967): 585.

[121] *Tristan, ou l'éloge d'un poète* (Limoges: Rougerie, 1955), pp. 53–55.

two poets. This fundamental difference led to others: "Il y eut chez Malherbe un homme soucieux des règles et des lois, il y a chez Tristan un homme soucieux avant tout de librement épancher son cœur, d'obéir à la seule inspiration. Il y avait chez Malherbe une technique, il y a chez Tristan la poésie, et pour lui sensibilité et imagination priment science et prosodie."[122] This is true to a large extent, though somewhat unfair to both poets: Malherbe, in spite of his obvious failings, was a great poet, and much of Tristan's greatness was due to the fact that he could be led by inspiration, "sensibilité et imagination," without neglecting technique. As Philip Wadsworth has so well demonstrated, seldom in poetic annals has there been such a perfect union of artifice and sincerity.[123] In Tristan's work there is a deliberate impression of naïveté made to mask a tremendous skill. There is, to use the word of René Lacôte, a "façade," but it is far from being a "pure et insincère façade."[124]

It is obvious that "Tristan was fascinated by marinistic conceits, by ingenuity, and virtuosity,"[125] but what must be even more obvious is that such virtuosity puts language to the ultimate test. Here again, the testimony of Peiresc is most enlightening: "Ces vers de Tristan pour l'Infante, quoyque d'un language un peu moings françoys *que ne se persuade,* je m'asseure, *l'autheur,* meritoient d'estres veus."[126] Whenever language is asked to convey every nuance of perception, then one goes well beyond conceits and "pointes." Saint-Amant, not Marino or Berni, should come to mind. More important still, if one thinks in terms of Tristan the "painter," then Malherbe cannot come to mind. Time and time again Tristan himself speaks of "peinture," and to achieve this end he frequently reverts (and this is perhaps his forte) to a "combination of abstract and concrete, tangible and intangible."[127] What would have been Malherbe's reaction to the imaginative description of the sea as "un grand champ

[122] Ibid., p. 88.

[123] "Artifice and Sincerity." See also idem, "The Poetry of Tristan L'Hermite," KFLQ 4 (1957): 205–11.

[124] "Tristan L'Hermite et sa façade poétique," Lettres Fr. 584 (8–14 Sept. 1955), p. 5.

[125] Valerie P. Minogue," Tristan L'Hermite in the Context of the Seventeenth Century" (Master's thesis, Cambridge University, 1957), p. 143.

[126] Lettres, 3:112. Italics mine.

[127] Minogue, "Tristan L'Hermite," p. 154.

labouré," with "des montagnes d'ombre/Auec des sources de clarté"?[128] Tristan had in addition a very "delicate sense of rhythmic harmony"[129] but he relied very heavily for his effects on alliterative processes (anaphora, alliteration, homoeoteleuton) and extended similes,[130] neither acceptable to this degree to Malherbe.

On this question of language, another point must be made. Tristan is at times *précieux*, at times burlesque and grotesque. But, as Lanson pointed out so many decades ago, the *précieux* and the grotesque are not at opposite poles. Both distort reality and go to any length to impress. As such, both are opposed to the very essence of Malherbe's beliefs. Whenever a poet indulges in either of these two moods, regardless of the form he uses, he is already well outside "la chapelle malherbienne," as Antoine Adam calls it.[131]

In spite of this, several critics have attempted to make of Tristan an "écolier" of Malherbe. Latest of these are Yoshio Fukui and K. C. Wright. Fukui is reluctant to make of Tristan a "malherbien rigoureux"[132] but is even more reluctant to dismiss the possibility of a direct influence, basing most of his argument on the fact that Tristan is among the poets included in the "Malherbian" *recueils*.[133] Wright comes to an even more unequivocal position by starting from the same premise: since the *Recueil des plus beaux vers* of 1627 is devoted, according to Toussainct du Bray, the editor, to the works of Malherbe and his "écoliers," and since this *recueil* contains a poem by Tristan, he is therefore a follower of Malherbe.[134] I have already commented on the legitimacy of this type of criticism, and there is no need to do so again. Rather, I would suggest a close look at the poem itself to determine to what extent it may be considered "Malherbian."

[128] *La mer* (Paris: Callemont, 1627), pp. 4, 7.

[129] Grisé, "The Poetry of Tristan L'Hermite" (Doctoral dissertation, University of Toronto, 1964), p. 47.

[130] For a perfect example of the latter, see stanzas 5–6 of "Les forges d'Antoigné."

[131] *Histoire*, 1:371.

[132] *Raffinement précieux*, p. 89.

[133] Ibid., pp. 89–103.

[134] "Tristan et l'évolution de la poésie lyrique française entre 1620 et 1650" (Doctoral dissertation, Edinburgh University, 1958), pp. 196 ff.

The *stances* "Enfin guéri de la folie" are composed of heterometric ten-line stanzas, 8–8–8–8–8–8–8–12–8–12, never used by Malherbe; the rhyme scheme, *a b b a c c d e d e,* was used by Malherbe only four times in octosyllabic poems: twice in epigrams, once in a fragment not collected during his lifetime, and once in an early ode (1608). Most of the stanzas of "Enfin guéri" have a 4–6 break, though not all, and the secondary breaks for the last six lines are varied or nonexistent. The rhymes are frequently lacking insofar as the *consonne d'appui* is concerned, and there are rhymes such as *pas-pas,* [iø]-[jø], *ame-flame* (three times). Add to all these factors lines such as "Mais tant et tant de larmes feintes," and the picture of a totally un-Malherbian poem is complete.

Fukui states that "la maîtrise de Tristan dans l'art de manier les strophes prouve qu'il était un digne disciple de Malherbe."[135] It seems to me that two factors are important here: the choice of forms, and the effect achieved with each. According to Fromilhague,[136] Malherbe used fifty-five different strophic forms, if one counts as different the diverse combinations of forms and rhyme schemes. Even if one takes into consideration only those poems published by Tristan before 1643, that figure is dwarfed, as the sestets alone account for the use of thirty different forms, ranging from the orthodox (octosyllabic *a a b c b c* or *a a b c c b,* alexandrine *a a b c b c*) to the highly original (9–8–10–7–12–8, *a a b c b c*), none used more than once except for the octosyllabic and alexandrine ones. One is thus led to wonder whether or not Tristan made a deliberate effort to experiment, never using a heterometric form twice, whereas Malherbe, as Fromilhague points out so frequently, not content with this type of inventiveness, put most of his effort in the fuller exploitation of a limited number of these forms.[137]

"Unequal lines, whether longer or shorter than their neighbors, will be expected to justify their inequality."[138] Heterometry may well have as one of its basic principles the freedom of invention, but Malherbe readily saw that some *chutes* were more fortunate than others, and he selected

---

[135] *Raffinement précieux,* p. 147.

[136] *Technique,* pp. 195–97.

[137] It must be kept in mind that Malherbe wrote only thirty-five heterometric poems in his whole life.

[138] Paul Fussel, Jr., *Poetic Meter and Poetic Form* (New York: Random House, 1965), p. 174.

those to demonstrate his skill: "Malherbe selected only a few of Ronsard's strophes, erecting them into stereotyped forms beyond which the poet was not to wander."[139] Might one not with at least equal justification rephrase this quotation to read "beyond which the poet had no need to wander, and would be foolish to do so"? Malherbe demonstrates his inventiveness not through versatility but by making old forms look forever new. In this respect, Tristan and Malherbe simply do not travel the same road.

The number of forms used by Tristan is, in the final analysis, only of secondary importance. What matters far more is the purpose and method of his "madness." A fine illustration is "Le miroir enchanté," first published in 1634, and written in 8–8–10–12, *a b b a* quatrains. These quatrains at first glance seem highly unbalanced:

> *Amarille en se regardant*
> *Pour se conseiller de sa grace*
> *Mes aujourdhuy des feux dans cette glace*
> *Et d'un christal commun fait un miroir ardant.*[140]

This disequilibrium has a purpose, however. The octosyllabic lines present a matter-of-fact statement; the decasyllabic line breaks the mood by presenting a hyperbole which is then developed or recapitulated in the alexandrine. We should furthermore note that throughout the poem, the instability and evanescence of an image is emphasized by the lack of balance in the form.

> *Nuit fraische, sombre, et solitaire,*
> *Sainte depositaire*
> *De tous les grands secrets, ou de guerre, ou d'amour,*
> *Nuit mere du repos, et nourrice des veilles*
> *Qui produisent tant de merveilles,*
> *Donne moy des conseils que soient dignes du jour.*[141]

[139] L. E. Kastner, *A History of French Versification* (Oxford: Clarendon Press, 1903), p. 162.

[140] *Plaintes d'Acante et autres œuvres* (Paris: Billaine, 1634), p. 127. The title did not appear until 1638, when the poem was reproduced in *Les amours* (Paris: Billaine et Courbé), p. 81.

[141] *Les vers héroïques* (Geneva: Droz, 1967), p. 155.

The first two lines are united by their brevity as well as the rhyme, but the forceful enjambment between lines 2 and 3 makes a single unit of the first twenty beats, to which the second hemistich of line 3 is added like an afterthought. Syntactically, the alexandrine might be considered to be the union of line 2 and the first hemistich of line 3. These first three lines, in spite of the punctuation, are thus a distinct unit, a separation emphasized by the recapitulative nature of the first two lines of the second half. These two lines, furthermore, definitely lack something—call it equilibrium, or even a sense of repose—which only the last alexandrine can supply. If one is to speak of unity and of composition in the poems of Tristan, it must always be thus, not in terms of form and meter, but with regard to the inner unity, to that "higher, hidden order" of imagistic or metaphoric coherence.

Until now, I have discussed poets who were "independent" insofar as they did not belong to the various groups that made up the subject matter of my first three chapters. Nevertheless, they all adhered to certain principles, however vague these might be, which allowed me to discuss them as though they too belonged to certain groups—as some actually did. There remain to be treated certain poets who were independent in even more ways. They belonged to no group, shared few tendencies with their contemporaries, and, in many cases, not only wrote but lived *en marge* of the mainstream. Some of these, in fact, made their reputation precisely by doing their utmost to be different in every way. Neufgermain, for instance, called himself the "poète hétéroclite" of Gaston and, for the sake of his daily bread, allowed himself to be the literary clown of the court of that prince.[142] Equally good-humored but equally unskilled, Adam Billaut wrote poems to amuse himself and his friends, but entertained few thoughts of his artistic merits. Some of his "chevilles" are delightful, but no "lecteur judicieux et de goût"[143] can make much of them. Such poets must, of course, be excluded from a study of this type. Those who follow are not always better, but at least they meant to be.

Poets born before 1590 but not so early as to have acquired a full poetic baggage by the time Malherbe came upon the scene are particularly

[142] See my *Gaston d'Orléans et sa cour* (Chapel Hill: University of North Carolina Press, 1963), pp. 31–38.

[143] Goujet, *Bibliothèque françoise*, 17:54.

interesting to this study, for they were seeking directions exactly at the moment Malherbe made his presence felt. Falling in this category are Schelandre, Durand, Angot de l'Eperonnière, Rosset, and Monfuron, the last three having personal ties of one type or another with Malherbe.

Jean de Schelandre, born in 1585, considered Malherbe too refined and preferred "les choses mâles et vigoureuses."[144] His language, far from "chastized," is very much of the sixteenth century, even though many of his poetic traits show that, technically at least, he was not only in agreement with Malherbe but ahead of him in some respects. Consciously virile, he "estime Bartas et Ronsard," and rejects the poets of the "nouvelle secte" who fail to realize that

> *Notre siècle est venu trop tard.*
>
> *O censeurs des mots et des rimes,*
> *Souvent vos ponces et vos limes*
> *Otent le beau pour le poly.*[145]

He yields to the "beaux esprits de ce temps," but not until he has asserted that "ma rudesse vaut bien vos modernes douceurs."[146] In this respect, he is an *arriéré*. His language is frequently in very bad taste, and the fact that he apologizes for "quelques mots grossiers"[147] does not remedy the situation. In all fairness, later works such as "Pénitence de Saint Pierre" show distinct improvements, and it may be that, however unwillingly, Schelandre was bending to the common order of things.

Technically, in spite of his grumbling at the "censeurs," he was Malherbian from the start. In fact, if one may doubt the influence of Malherbe on Schelandre it is purely because of chronology. The regularity —with only the rarest of lapses—of even his earliest poems tends to show that Schelandre did not wait to hear from Malherbe before he found the path that Boileau was to praise later. His early "Procés d'Espagne contre Hollande," in alexandrines, is very regular, with good caesuras, few en-

---

[144] Charles Asselineau, *Notice sur Jean de Schelandre* (Alençon: n.p., 1856), p. 6.

[145] Cited in ibid., p. 3.

[146] *Mélanges poétiques* (Paris: Micard, 1608), p. 249.

[147] Ibid.

jambments, acceptable rhymes. Only in one "Ode Pindarique"[148] does he harken back to times past.

Etienne Durand, born in 1585 and broken on the wheel and burned in 1618, was, on the other hand, completely *en marge* of the times. The background for his poems has been amply discussed by Frédéric Lachèvre in the introduction to his edition of the *Méditations*,[149] by Jean Tardieu,[150] and by Amelia Bruzzi,[151] and there is no need to repeat what they have already said. If, in Malherbe's wake, one may speak of a "dépérissement de la métaphore,"[152] Durand cannot be accused of being in that wake, as the very title of Bruzzi's study indicates.

In the domain of rhymes, Durand violates every rule imaginable, rhyming simple and compound, selecting badly the *consonne d'appui*, and frequently varying the scheme within a single poem.[153] But it is in far more fundamental ways that Durand is non-Malherbian. In his poetry, one finds "toutes les conventions de la poésie de cour et de la poésie amoureuse."[154] Antitheses abound, metaphors are frequently quite drawn out, and in neither case is Durand reluctant to use the commonplace ("Beauté qui me donnez cette mort immortelle").[155] His use of mythology is relatively rare and mostly clear ("Toi qu'un rocher tombant fait travailler sans cesse").[156]

His constructions, as can be seen by Sonnet XVII, are anything but Malherbian:

> *Pourquoy pour mon malheur eus-je l'œil si léger?*
> *Pourquoy le sens si prompt, et l'esprit si fragile?*

[148] Ibid., pp. 43–53.

[149] (Paris: Leclerc, 1906).

[150] "Etienne Durand, poète supplicié," in *Le préclassicisme français* (Paris: Cahiers du Sud, 1952), pp. 189–95.

[151] "Metafore e poesia nelle *Méditations* di Etienne Durand," appended to *Il barocco nella poesia di Théophile de Viau* (Bologna: Pàtron, 1965).

[152] Jean Rousset, "La poésie baroque au temps de Malherbe: la métaphore," *DSS* 31 (1956): 367.

[153] See, for instance, *Méditations,* p. 70.

[154] S. A. Varga, "Un poète oublié du XVIIe siècle: E. Durand et les 'Stances à l'inconstance,' " *Néophilol.* 39 (1955): 250.

[155] *Méditations,* p. 75.

[156] Ibid.

Que de voir, que d'aimer, et que de m'engager
A servir un bel œil d'un labeur inutile?

Pour avoir veu je meurs, mais d'une mort subtile
Qui renaist d'elle-mesme, et ne fait que changer,
Pour aimer je me vois tous les jours outrager,
Et servant je languis en ma prison servile.

L'œil, le sens et l'esprit, trop prompt, trop clair, trop vif,
M'a trompé, m'a séduict, m'a faict estre captif
D'un attraict, d'un propos, d'un amoureux cordage.

Pour avoir veu, aimé et servy son bel œil,
L'ardeur, l'amour, les fers me mènent au cercueil:
Dieux! faites pour le moins que la mort me soulage.[157]

Sonnet XXXI, commented by Colletet, is quite the same, and the lack of censure for some of the obvious deviations from Malherbian doctrine shows that the latter had not yet won over the critic.[158] Equally enlightening is the following excerpt from the famous "Stances à l'inconstance," a long poem in alexandrine five-line stanzas:

Nostre esprit n'est que vent, et comme un vent volage
Ce qu'il nomme constance est un branle rétif:
. . . .
Je te fais un présent d'un tableau fantastique
Où l'amour et le jeu par la main se tiendront,
L'oubliance, l'espoir, le desir frénétique,
Les serments parjurez, l'humeur mélancolique
Les femmes et les vents ensemble s'y verront.

Les sables de la mer, les orages, les nuës,
Les feux qui font en l'air les tonnantes chaleurs,
Les flammes des esclairs plutost mortes que veuës,

---

[157] Cited by Arnaldo Pizzorusso, "Sulla poesia di Etienne Durand," *Letteratura* 4 (1956): 38.

[158] This enlightening commentary is included in the preface of the Lachèvre edition of the *Méditations*.

Les peintures du Ciel à nos yeux incogneuës,
A ce divin tableau serviront de couleurs.[159]

Lachèvre was right in suggesting that this reveals Durand as "un des poètes sur lequel [la France] pouvait fonder de grandes espérances,"[160] but it is equally certain that he would never have found his way into the mainstream of literary life.

Rosset, Monfuron, and Angot have all been linked directly with Malherbe at one time or another, mostly for geographic reasons. Robert Angot de l'Eperonnière was born in Caen, the city of Malherbe's birth. Although known primarily for his satires, Angot also wrote a certain number of poems in stanzas and some sonnets. He also authored some *vers figurés,* the first in French excepting those by Mellin de Saint-Gelais and Panard. His satires differ little from those of his contemporaries. For the most part they are in alexandrine *vers suivis* with frequently inadequate rhymes and sentences that only too often extend well beyond the Malherbian four lines.

There is no indication of any Malherbian influence in his stanzas, either. The rhymes of his early poems are not very good and they get worse as time goes on. Most of the faulty rhymes of "La mesdisance" (1622) have a lapse in the *consonne d'appui,* but in "Contre une medisante" (1637) there are, in addition, rhymes such as *chair-toucher,* and *si haut-si haut,* and in "L'avocat infortuné" of the same year, the following rhymes can be found: *faire-affaire, parfumer-Mer, droit-droit, fosse-fausse, ame-dame, livres-livres, sac-bissac.* By the same token, the sestets of the ode "A la satyre du Sr de Courval" (1610) are all devoid of breaks. Two-thirds of the stanzas of "La mesdisance" have a median break, but "Contre une medisante" is again totally lacking, and the same can be said for the "Karesme-prenant des Muses" and for all but one sestet of "Baccanale." Only in the stanzas of Angot's paraphrases of psalms might one speak of a possible Malherbian influence, but only with great caution. His favorite form for these exercises is the alexandrine sestet, although there are quite a few sonnets. The rhyme scheme is most frequently *a a b c c b,* with the rhymes far better than in any other poem and, in most cases, at least sufficient. There are some expletives—"Hélas! comme aurions-nous, dîmes-

---

[159] *Méditations,* pp. 220–21.
[160] Ibid., p. lvi.

nous, cette envie"[161]—but not as many as in his lighter poems. The construction is generally quite good, the lines are well balanced, with strong caesuras and no enjambments. As Paulette Leblanc has pointed out, his inspiration is often autobiographical, but many of his lines are "ni bibliques, ni lyriques."[162] Rather, they show remnants of his satirical vein, still very much imbued with an outdated tone:

> Leur sein devient tout sec et leurs gorges fletries,
> Leurs tetons, tout ainsi que des pomes pourries,
> Leurs dents changent en os leurs perles d'Orient:
> Leur discours, dont Amour s'entretenoit lui-même,
> Change en tristes regretz leur bien dire suprême,
> Et ne fait qu'appeler la mort à tout moment.[163]

The commonplace of the transitory nature of things terrestrial is, of course, to be found in the Bible, and Malherbe had treated it also, but it particularly fascinated Angot:

> Ne fonde ton appui sur la faveur des Rois,
> Ni l'heur de ton salut sur un suget de verre;
> Quand ton âme s'enfuit de ton cors vne fois,
> Ton corps terrestre et lourd s'en retourne à la terre.[164]

There can be no doubt as to Malherbe's reaction to such lines.

The rhymes of Angot's early sonnets are, except for some lapses concerning the *consonne d'appui*, very good, and the rhyme scheme is the "classical" *a b b a . . . e d e*. As time went on, unfortunately, Angot became more and more careless and rhymes such as *œuvres-manœuvres, receus-culs, Soleil-pareil-œil-recueil, inconuë-reconuë, mémoire-mémoire*[165] become frequent. Padding also becomes more frequent in a form that should not have to suffer it: "Sans vous, Sire, sans vous, j'allais quitter la

---

[161] Allem, *Anthologie,* 1:124.
[162] *Paraphrases,* pp. 70–72.
[163] Cited in ibid., p. 72.
[164] Ibid., p. 73.
[165] *Le chef d'œuvre poétique* (Rouen: Boissel, 1872), pp. 17, 208, 210–11.

place."[166] Angot de l'Eperonnière had obviously not learned his compatriot's lesson.

Rosset's contacts with Malherbe date from the latter's sojourn in Provence. Many of his early poems were published separately. The "Douze beautés de Phylis" were, according to Goujet, written in love and published in anger.[167] That perhaps explains their total lack of merit. What is interesting here is that because so many of his poems were included in the "Malherbian" *Parnasse* of 1607 and *Délices* of 1615 and 1618, critics have included him with the followers of Malherbe. The following excerpt from an ode should settle the issue:

> *O Caen fertile en beaux esprits,*
> *Qui dans un si petit pourpris*
> *Dont ta muraille t'environne,*
> *Surpasses le renon vivant*
> *Dont se vont encore élevant*
> *Venouse, Mantouë, et Véronne.*
>
> . . . .
>
> *Mais aussi de ne chanter point*
> *O grand Malherbe, de tout poinct*
> *La gloire de ta rare Muse,*
> *Je mériterois droitement,*
> *Ce qu'il reçut injustement*
> *De ce tyran de Syracuse.*[168]

After reading such an un-Malherbian praise of Malherbe, I find Yoshio Fukui much too kind when he states that Rosset is of those who "ne paraissent pas être des malherbiens de stricte obédience."[169]

Monfuron, related to du Périer at Aix, probably knew and was known to Malherbe during the latter's stay in that city. In his sonnets, he is very regular, perhaps even more so than either Racan or Maynard.[170] This may have had something to do with the inclusion of some of his poems in the *recueils* during the last years of Malherbe's life. Thereafter

---

[166] Ibid., p. 13.
[167] *Bibliothèque françoise*, 15:262.
[168] Ibid., p. 266.
[169] *Raffinement précieux*, pp. 56–57.
[170] See ibid., p. 98.

he dropped completely out of sight and no one seems to have mourned that departure. It is therefore interesting to note that a poet who seems to have obeyed the strictures of the "master" was doomed to oblivion as soon as the direct protection of Malherbe could no longer be called upon.

As I have noted in preceding chapters, the "generation of '95" was the most active in the period under examination. In this section, it is represented by Saint-Pavin (1599–1670) and des Barreaux (1599–1673).

Saint-Pavin's songs and madrigals all show serious defects in craftsmanship, with rhymes and rhythm suffering from every possible error. His *stances* are all isometric (octosyllabic), the stanzas being of four, six, seven, or ten lines, with varied rhyme schemes, the scheme often changing within a poem from stanza to stanza. In his sestets, enjambments are frequent and median breaks rare:

> *Il en est mieux receu qu'un roy,*
> *Cependant s'il vient seul, je voy*
> *Qu'elle en rougit et se chagrine,*
> *Et tousjours jalouse de luy,*
> *Elle tesmoigne de l'ennuy*
> *Sitost qu'il est chez sa voisine.*[171]

The seven-line stanzas are equally irregular, but, strangely enough, the ten-line stanzas are quite regular, except for the matter of rhyme scheme, already mentioned. Enjambments are very rare indeed, and there is almost always a 4–6 break, with a secondary 3–3 break in the last six lines.[172]

In the sonnets of Saint-Pavin, again a separation must be made. His octosyllabic sonnets are full of enjambments, often even between quatrains or tercets. The alexandrine sonnets, on the other hand, are more carefully crafted. While tercets are still frequently tied together syntactically, quatrains are always autonomous and there are no enjambments to speak of. The rhymes, in richness and in arrangement, show no indication of

---

[171] Frédéric Lachèvre, *Disciples et successeurs de Théophile de Viau: La vie et les poésies libertines inédites de Des Barreaux.—Saint-Pavin* (Paris: Champion, 1911), p. 411.

[172] See particularly "Iris que les cloches me plaisent," in Denis Sanguin de Saint-Pavin, *Recueil complet des poésies* (Paris: Techener, 1861), pp. 52–53. Each of the three stanzas of the poem has a different rhyme scheme, but all are rigorously divided 4–3–3.

any possible sobering influence. In brief, if one wishes to speak of any Malherbian tendencies here, they must be limited to the realm of structure in only a few of Saint-Pavin's forms. Furthermore, because he wrote few occasional poems, his poetry is almost impossible to date, which makes the question of influence even more tenuous.

Des Barreaux wrote in every conceivable form. His *vers suivis*, mostly elegies, contain very long sentences and bad rhymes, with *âme-flâme* and [iø-jø], particularly with the use of *yeux* omnipresent. His *stances* use many different combinations of rhyme and meter, but few of these combinations can be found in Malherbe's work, and the quality of the rhymes does not favor further investigation or comparison. The few orthodox forms in his works seldom conform in regard to inner structure and coherence. Thus, there are two poems, one entitled "Jouissance imparfaite," the other "Jouissance parfaite." The latter has four stanzas, the first of which is a refrain for the other three. This refrain has eight lines, 8–12–10–12–8–8–12–12; stanza 2 has eleven lines of eight and twelve beats; stanza 3 has ten such lines, and the last stanza has twenty-seven lines. In all of these, the beat can only be maintained if rhymes such as [iø-jø] and [iõ]-[jõ] are constantly made.[173] "Jouissance imparfaite"[174] is in octosyllabic sestets, with rhyme schemes of *a b a b a b*, *a b b a a b*, and *a b a b b a*. Breaks vary from 2–2–2 to 2–4, 4–2, and 6–0. Rhymes defy description.

The sonnets of des Barreaux were his most admired works in the seventeenth and eighteenth centuries[175] and justly so. The rhymes, while far from perfect, are infinitely superior to those in his other poems. The rhyme schemes are standard, with a strange distinction to be made: most of the love sonnets have *a b b a* quatrains whereas the miscellaneous sonnets use the *a b a b* scheme. In both cases, the alexandrines are well balanced, well cut, and with only the rarest lapse to be found: "Ta seule peinture est un ouvrage immortel."[176] It thus seems that if des Barreaux took any of his writing seriously, this attitude must have been limited to the sonnets. Only there could one speak of a poet *limeur*, and even then, only relatively so.

Two more "independents" must be discussed in this chapter. Both

[173] *Disciples et successeurs*, Lachèvre ed., pp. 165–67.
[174] Ibid., pp. 159–60.
[175] Ibid., pp. 5–6.
[176] Ibid., p. 161.

are quite young when compared to those already treated, though the exact birth date of one is not known. Both wanted to enter into the main-stream of the literary world. One never made it and the other had a most difficult time of it at first.

The bulk (nearly 5,000 lines) of the poetic production of du Bois Hus is taken up by two poems, "La nuict des nuicts" and "Le jour des jours," both written in 8–8–8–12–6–12, *a a b c b c* sestets. As Jean Rousset states in his preface to Annarosa Poli's recent edition of these poems, this is "la poésie la moins sincère qu'on puisse imaginer," for du Bois Hus is "par excellence le poète de cour; . . . de la flagornerie il fait un jeu de virtuose."[177] As the title of Rousset's preface indicates, this poetry is "le triomphe de l'artifice." As such, its most interesting feature is that it is simultaneously "rigoureux et légèrement déséquilibré."[178] In her own commentary, Poli states that du Bois Hus "suit de très près les règles fixées par Malherbe dans son *Commentaire sur Desportes*."[179] Without debating whether or not the poet could have seen this commentary, can one still decide whether or not he followed its precepts? As I have shown, in the very choice of forms he did not. In the syntactical constructions (most stanzas have no break at all, and in several cases the sentence begun in one stanza is not finished until the next) he did not. Both of these considerations, however, merely mean that he was not Malherbian, not that he had not seen or heeded the *Commentaires,* since these are quite early Malherbe. By du Bois Hus's own admission, and by that of Poli, the poet refused to be a slave to rhyme.[180] Boileau would have praised him for this, but not Malherbe. In general tone, du Bois Hus insisted that his thoughts "ont gardé leur liberté toute entière."[181] Praiseworthy indeed, but not Malherbian. No wonder Bouhours abhorred all that "galimatias"[182] and the century as a whole rejected it.

The other unwilling "independent" is none other than Pierre Corneille. Unwilling to side with any school or *côterie,* he nevertheless

[177] *La nuict des nuicts. Le jour des jours. Le miroir du destin ou la nativité du Daufin du ciel* (Bologna: Pàtron, 1967), p. ix.

[178] Ibid., p. xii.

[179] Ibid., p. 364.

[180] Ibid., pp. 39–40.

[181] Ibid., p. 29.

[182] P. Dominique Bouhours, *La manière de bien penser* (Paris: Mabre-Cramoisy, 1687), pp. 466–70.

was intent on making his entrance into the literary world. Already at the time of the writing of *Mélite,* he spoke of a "naive" style, "simple et familière,"[183] and while he indicated an admiration for Ronsard, Malherbe, and Théophile, he failed to indicate what qualities in these antipodal authors he strove to emulate.[184] In 1633, he described his theory of art in these words:

> *Ars artem fugusse mihi est, et sponte fluentes*
> *Ad numeros faciles pleraque rhythmus obit.*[185]

In his "Excuse à Ariste," of the same date, he said this of his muse:

> *Son feu ne peut agir quand il faut qu'il s'applique*
> *Sur les fantasques airs d'un rêveur de musique,*
> *Et que pour donner lieu de paroître à sa voix,*
> *De sa bigearre quinte il se fasse des loix;*
>
> . . . .
>
> *Enfin cette prison déplaît à son génie;*
> *Il ne peut rendre hommage à cette tyrannie;*
> *Il ne se leurre point d'animer de beaux chants,*
> *Et veut pour se produire avoir la clef des champs.*[186]

It would thus seem that, in his earlier days at least, Corneille was definitely of an un- if not anti-Malherbian mind. As for his actual practice, Souriau went to great lengths to point out that Corneille violated practically all Malherbian rules and disregarded all of his countryman's examples.[187] Yet Corneille's contemporaries, especially critics of the "classical" period such as Boileau and de Pure, praised his efforts in just that domain, though Boileau deplored his "fautes de langue."[188]

Corneille did, in fact, violate the bulk of Malherbe's rules at one time or another, and it would serve no purpose to list these violations as Souriau has done. But in view of the sheer number of lines written by

---

[183] *Œuvres* (Paris: Hachette, 1862–1868), 1:135, 377.
[184] Ibid., p. 136.
[185] Ibid., 10:67.
[186] Ibid., pp. 74–75.
[187] *L'évolution,* pp. 130–49.
[188] *Œuvres complètes,* p. 526.

Corneille, these violations are indeed few. Ironically, some of them might be considered "légitimes au théâtre,"[189] but these are not found most readily in his dramatic works. Understandably enough, they exist in relatively larger number in the various shorter poems, both the earlier ones and those of a later period which he wrote in haste and did not always review. The most frequent of these violations deal with the quality of the rhyme. Corneille was not loath to rhyme the simple with its compound (*fait-bienfait, temps-printemps*), words of the same stem (*printemps-passe-temps*), or even monosyllabic homophones, as in the text cited above (*chants-champs*). Nor did Corneille avoid the facile, especially in these earlier years, and combinations such as *admirable-incomparable-vénérable-infatigable* or *admirable-incomparable-invulnérable-durable* are not rare. Yet most of his poems are carefully crafted, notable exceptions being his early sonnet to Richelieu and "A Monsieur DLT" from which most of the above examples were taken.[190] The only truly consistent failing is a frequent lack of homophony of the *consonne d'appui* but, as I have amply demonstrated by now, few poets were following Malherbe on that score. It might be added that in his sonnets the early Corneille seldom followed Malherbe's preferred rhyme scheme; the sonnet to Richelieu uses an *a b b a   a b a b   c c d   e e d* scheme that must have found few admirers.

Generally speaking, other defects are equally rare in Corneille and no chronological distinction can be made. Thus an occasional hiatus can be found throughout his production:

Mais c'en est un beau aujourd'hui [1640]

Où il étoit gravé d'un burin tout de flamme [1653]

On l'enfonce. Arrêtez, héros! où courez-vous? [1662][191]

Cacophonic lines are equally rare, and again cannot be attributed to anything but carelessness, without any chronological lesson:

Qu'a conservés . . . [1644]

Prépares-en enfin . . . [1647]

[189] Souriau, *L'évolution*, p. 133.
[190] *Œuvres*, 10:32, 25–29.
[191] Ibid., pp. 81, 131, 277.

Et ce que se promit . . . [1664]

Il en est en Hainaut, . . . [1678][192]

There is one respect, however, in which Corneille refused to be Malherbian. He had warned, in a passage already cited, that he had little use for musicians and that his muse simply could not adjust to their demands and requirements. Nowhere is this better demonstrated than in one of the first works Corneille wrote after his arrival in Paris, his "Récit pour le ballet du château de Bicêtre." Ironically, the vocal line of the *récit* was "dextrement jointe à celle du luth,"[193] but "le sieur Justice" must have had a difficult time with these four heterometric sestets: while their form is quite Malherbian, their structure is not. Only one sestet has a major syntactical break (4–2), while another has a secondary break after the second line; the other two sestets have no break at all and one can only surmise that Racan was not the lutist who accompanied these with such dexterity. Much the same can be said for two songs written in spite of his professed dislike for the genre:

> *Tant ma veine se trouve aux airs mal assortie,*
> *Tant avec la musique elle a d'antipathie,*
> *Tant alors de bon cœur elle renonce au jour.*[194]

Both "Toi qui près d'un beau visage" and "Si je perds bien des maîtresses" are written in heptasyllabic sestets, a form never used by Malherbe. Furthermore, the last two lines of each stanza of the first song fit the mold only with difficulty:

> *Que souvent la fiction*
> *Se change en affection.*[195]

No two stanzas of this song have the same break, and one is without any. "Si je perds bien des maîtresses" is slightly more regular, the isometry

---

[192] Ibid., pp. 98, 117, 184, 328.

[193] Ibid., p. 341.

[194] Ibid., p. 78.

[195] Ibid., pp. 53–54. The first word of this refrain varies from stanza to stanza.

being unmolested, but half of the stanzas have no syntactical break whatsoever, making it just as difficult to sing as the first song. This Cornelian tendency is equally obvious in the madrigal "A Monsieur de Scudéry, sur son *Trompeur puni*," a heterometric ten-line stanza broken 5–5, whose rhymes must have baffled even the most careful listener: the *a* rhyme is the *trépas-appas* commonplace, *b* is *-rie*, *c* is *-ni*, and *d* is *-vie*; after that, the closing *sort-mort* is a relief.

During this period, Corneille wrote one ode and one short set of *stances*. The "Ode sur un prompt amour"[196] is remarkably Malherbian (octosyllabic ten-line stanzas, broken 4–6) but fails consistently in the homophony of the *consonne d'appui*. "Stances: Sur une absence en temps de pluie"[197] is less Malherbian: the 8–10–10–8 quatrains have no example in Malherbe's work, some of the lines are badly divided ("Pour le venger, l'autre, cachant sa flamme") and some of the rhymes are unacceptable (*âme-flamme*). What is most interesting in these two poems, however, is not the content or form, but the titles. As I demonstrated in a previous chapter, not all the poets of the century understood that Malherbe considered the ode proper only for the celebration of important matters, reserving the *stances* for lesser events or erotic pursuits. Young Corneille, when naming these poems, was either unaware of this distinction or, like many young poets of the time, considered matters amorous to be of the greatest importance.

The statement by Emile Faguet quoted earlier must again be brought to mind: "Il y a certainement, de 1615 à 1640, toute une école, ni très unie sans doute, ni très cohérente, très difficile à nommer d'un seul mot, mais qui est, d'une façon évidente, en état de réaction ou tout au moins d'insubordination vis-à-vis de Malherbe."[198] As I replied earlier, there was no established camp of followers of Malherbe in the Academy or in any other "establishment." I hope I have shown here that no such following existed anywhere at any time during the reign of Louis XIII. Malherbe's entire concept of poetry was deliberately rejected, and his specific lessons (save some of the more obvious ones), although praised, were seldom if ever followed.

---

[196] Ibid., pp. 30–31.
[197] Ibid., p. 43.
[198] *Histoire de la poésie française*, 2:288.

The Age of
Louis XIV

Chapter Six

The Academy

In the years immediately following the death of Louis XIII, there were only twelve poets at the Academy: Baro, Bois-Robert, Chapelain, Conrart, Desmarests, Godeau, Gombauld, Gomberville, Maynard, Racan, Saint-Amant, and Priézac, a relative newcomer, admitted only in 1639. For all practical purposes, this number can be further reduced: Maynard died in 1646, Baro stopped writing poetry, and Priézac's poetic production was mercifully small and enjoyed little prestige, even among his peers. Because most of the others have already been discussed, they will be treated here only insofar as new developments are thought to have occurred. Thus Racan will concern us but briefly, and Gomberville and Gombauld not at all.

As far as poetry is concerned, these were not the Academy's most glorious years. Bois-Robert deplored the fact that the king showed no interest in the Academy[1] and some time later, Ménage echoed these thoughts.[2] In all fairness, it must be admitted that the group did not deserve much more. For some time, it had been vegetating:

> Elle ne va qu'à pas lents et contez
> Dans les desseins qu'elle avoit projettez.[3]

Racan and Godeau were hardly assiduous, while Voiture "cherche ailleurs de plus doux exercices" altogether.[4] Still according to Bois-Robert, the three best poets at the Academy were Gombauld, Maynard, and Chapelain. These three he considered "hors de Paralelle."[5] Considering that the first had stopped being original some time before, that the second was on his death-bed, and that the third, having written one great ode, was still promising the first canto of his *Pucelle*, is it any wonder that the young king and his minister were neglecting the Academy?

To this dearth of genuine poetic talent must be added another negative factor in the Academy's reputation during these years: great factionalism divided the republic of letters and unfortunately the praising or damning of a poet depended more often on membership in a given circle than on purely literary criteria. The Academy should have been above such squabbling; it wasn't. Much light has been shed on this particular problem by Antoine Adam in his long article on the "School of 1650,"[6] a heterogeneous group that included among its faithful many of the above-named members of the Academy and several who were to join later. In fact, adversaries of the group had a very difficult time entering the Academy; thus La Mesnardière, one of their foes, did not succeed in becoming one of the "Immortals" until 1655, and then only because the "school" had split up. This was indeed a school: "Il s'agit bien d'une Ecole littéraire, au sens le plus étroit de mot. Elle a ses maîtres. Ce sont Chapelain, Conrart, Balzac."[7] These were also the martinets of the Academy, and, as Adam pointed out, the likes and dislikes of this "cabale" were more often predicated on personal than on literary criteria. Their quarrels were, without doubt, a major contributing factor to the disintegration of the group. When Perrault read his "Siècle de Louis XIV" at the Academy in 1687, he was heralding the end of Boileau's brief reign; "on venait d'entendre le premier craquement dans l'édifice classique."[8] In 1687, in other words, there was a trend at the Academy. One may even think of such a trend some ten years earlier, when Boileau was solidly entrenching himself at its sessions, but, as Adam has pointed out, there was no such thing as a "generation of 1660," and before that the Academy was anything but homogeneous. We have already seen that the "old guard" was far from homogeneous, and, as we shall soon see, the next influx of new blood brought in Corneille, Tristan, Mézeray, Scudéry, and Charpentier, a very heterogeneous "wave" at that.

[1] *Epistres*, 1:64.
[2] *Poemata* (Paris: Courbé, 1656), p. 97.
[3] Bois-Robert, *Epistres*, 1:63.
[4] Ibid., p. 66.
[5] Ibid., p. 183.
[6] "L'école de 1650," *RHPhil* 29–30 (1942), pp. 23–53, 134–52.
[7] Ibid., p. 23.
[8] René Doumic, "Les poètes," in [Académie Française,] *Trois siècles de l'Académie Française, par les Quarante* (Paris: Firmin-Didot, 1935), p. 226.

Although there was no set trend at the Academy in the early years, certain members nevertheless considered it their duty to safeguard the purity of the language and the regularity of poetic technique. Balzac and Chapelain immediately come to mind, and rightfully so, but Racan must not be neglected in spite of his age and an oft-voiced feeling of having been left behind by the younger generation. In his later years, Racan concentrated his efforts in the composition of religious poems, but also produced two odes, a sonnet, and two madrigals of a secular nature. One of these madrigals is totally irregular, the other shows a certain attempt at regularity: a ten-line stanza composed of eight alexandrines and two six-beat lines, it has a definite 4–6 break, with a weaker 3–3 division. Unfortunately, except for *vie-envie* and *éternité-Majesté* the rhymes are barely sufficient, and the linearity, or lack of it, is very short of being Malherbian:

> *Si mon père, en naissant, m'avoit pu faire don*
> *De l'esprit poétique ainsy que de son nom*
> *Qui l'a rendu vainqueur du temps et de l'envie.*[9]

The lone sonnet of that period[10] is no better where rhymes are concerned (lack of *consonne d'appui* except in *temps-printemps*) but is perfectly structured, with remarkably well-balanced lines. The "Ode au Roy" shows the craftsman at his best, with very few lapses,[11] and the form (octo-syllabic *dizains, a b b a c c d e d e*) is the one favored by Malherbe for such poems. The 4–6 break is heeded, though the secondary 3–3 break is generally weak. Even the occasional running together of lines is difficult to fault:

> *Tu vois l'Ange qui prend le soin*
> *De les defendre de l'Envie.*[12]

The organization, the tone, the rigorous technique, all go a long way towards explaining Boileau's high regard of Racan as a writer of odes:

[9] *Poésies*, 1:264.
[10] Ibid., p. 267.
[11] Ibid., pp. 270–71.
[12] Ibid., p. 282.

> *Sur un ton si hardi, sans estre temeraire*
> *Racan pourroit chanter au defaut d'un Homere.*[13]

The "Ode à la louange de la Reine" is Malherbian in a totally different way. Imitative of Psalm 8, it is written in 12–12–12–12–6–12, *a a b c c b* sestets, a form used by Malherbe for his Psalm 128, which in turn is the basis of Racan's "Ode au Roy." Also taken from Malherbe is the idea of ending the last stanza with four lines taken from the first.[14] This very conscious imitation of Malherbe does not go so far as to influence the technique, unfortunately. The rhymes are frequently bad (lack of *consonne d'appui* homophony, *veuë-pourveuë*, [iø-jø]), enjambments are frequent, and breaks erratic.

Whereas Racan's secular poetry can be considered Malherbian in one way or another, his religious poems cannot. A tremendous variety of forms is used for the paraphrases and many of these forms had, to be sure, been used by Malherbe, but it is impossible to discern a predilection for these. Many psalms, in fact, are paraphrased in *vers suivis* with unusually long sentences.[15] The rhymes of the psalms range from the very rich to the nearly inept, the latter exemplified by the first stanza of Psalm 1, in which one finds the combination *printemps-flâmes-temps-âmes*; it would be difficult to imagine Racan doing worse. Enjambments are frequent and lines are often very badly balanced:

> *Je vais dès le matin mes prieres offrir*
> *A toy seul, qui ne peux souffrir*
> *La noire iniquité ni l'impure licence:*
> *Mon cœur n'est jamais tant du monde detaché,*
> *Ni jamais si loin du peché,*
> *Que lors qu'il est en ta presence.*[16]

Needless to say, the tortured syntax merely aggravates the problem. Simply put, while Racan could still remember the lessons of his master,

---

[13] Sat. IX, *Œuvres complètes*, p. 50.

[14] See Malherbe's paraphrase of Psalm 8, in 12–12–12–6–12–12 sestets (*Œuvres*, 1:62–64).

[15] See Psalm 77 (*Œuvres complètes*, 2:206–12).

[16] Ibid., p. 39.

as shown by his two odes, he seldom bothered to do so while composing the poems that constitute the bulk of his production during the years in question here.

There can be no doubt that Chapelain was the most respected—and insofar as he later had a voice in deciding who would enjoy financial subsidies, the most feared—of the poets at the Academy. It is therefore doubly interesting to look at the production of a man considered by many, including himself, as a worthy replacement for Malherbe. Most of his earlier poems were "d'une rare platitude"[17] and seldom Malherbian as far as the prosody was concerned. Some of these poems, in fact, seemed the very antithesis of Malherbian practice. The first lines of the sonnet "Au Dauphin" (1638) should suffice to bring this out:

> *Jeune et divin héros que le Ciel nous envoye*
> *Pour joindre un autre empire à l'empire françois,*
> *Fruit de la piété du plus juste des Roys,*
> *Et de ses jours heureux l'espérance et la joie.*[18]

The rhymes here are curious, to be sure, but no more so than the fact that this first quatrain is not a sentence. As for the third line, in view of the gossip that had accompanied the queen-mother's pregnancy, it must have ranked as one of the funniest of the generation. Did Chapelain, in his years of glory, radically alter his practice?

His "Ode pour Mgr le duc d'Anguien" (1645) would indicate that he did not. Written in 8–8–8–12–12–12–8–12–8–12 *dizains* with an *a b b a c c d e d e* rhyme scheme and varied breaks, its main feature is a plethora of *redoublements d'expression*:

> *Toi dont la force est le partage*
> *Et dont les faits passent les ans,*
> *Alexandre des temps présens,*
> *Qui du vieux Alexandre est la vivante image,*
> *Voy cette image encore et dans ce même endroit,*
> *Entre ces monts serrez, vois le nouveau destroit*

[17] *Lettres,* 1:173.
[18] Ibid., p. 300.

De la nouvelle Cilicie;
Voy du Perse nouveau le pouvoir abattu,
Voy sa frontière rétrécie
Enfin voy son audace au pied de ta vertu.[19]

These repetitions are particularly obnoxious when, as in *La Pucelle,* they are shameless padding:

Il la salüe, il part sans qu'elle luy réponde,
Sur son lit il la laisse en tristesse profonde;
Pressé de son désir et pressé de Bedford,
Il la salüe, il part et la laisse à la mort
Sans remord il la laisse . . . .

At times one might even speak of a virtuosity of expletives, be it in a single line such as "Il tombe et tombe mort sous des piles de morts," or in two parallel lines such as

Il destine Edoüard à cette heureuse couche;
. . . .
A cette heureuse couche Edoüard il destine.[20]

Padding of every type is omnipresent in the poem, and there is no attempt even to mask it:

Où, de pierres d'élite, un trésor précieux,
En même temps, et blesse, et rejouit les yeux.[21]

My intention is not to debate the literary merits of *La Pucelle.* Suffice it to say that nothing in the entire poem betrays the influence of Malherbe. The homophony of the *consonne d'appui* is frequently neglected, too frequently in fact to suggest carelessness. Chapelain undoubtedly did not feel this was a necessary restriction. As can be seen above, [iø] is made to rhyme with [jø], a common phenomenon in those

[19] Cited by Collas, *Jean Chapelain,* p. 180.
[20] Ibid., p. 248.
[21] *La Pucelle* (Paris: Flammarion, 1891), 2:97.

days but one nevertheless condemned and shunned by Malherbe. Long sounds are made to rhyme with short ones (*âme-flamme*). Facile rhymes abound. In short, as far as rhymes are concerned, *La Pucelle* is not Malherbian either. Its worst failing, however, is in its basically bad construction. Collas, usually kind to his subject, singled out the following lines as objects of scorn:

> *Par ces difficultés la princesse qui treuve*
> *Pour son évasion vain le secours du fleuve.*[22]

Unfortunately, in linear balance these lines are typical. Add to that bad puns, outlandish hyperboles, and absurd metaphors such as "sa couche est la scène où tonne son ennuy" and the picture is complete.

Several short poems of Chapelain accompanied his *Pucelle,* and they are instrumental in determining the poet's prosodic practice, for if a long epic poem can be excused for its many infractions, a sonnet cannot. Two of these sonnets are "Pour le Roy" and "La Pucelle au Roy." Both are somewhat more regular than the longer poem, at least insofar as linearity is concerned: there are no enjambments or badly unbalanced lines. On the other hand, inversions are very frequent, some with diastrous results: "Quel astre flamboyant sur nos provinces erre."[23] As in so many of his poems, the hiatus is not always excluded ("Quand la France abbatue à force d'attentats"[24]), some words are abused (*seul* occurs three times in seven lines), and the rhymes are as weak as in the longer poem: the *consonne d'appui* is neglected, and some rhymes are very facile (*mienstiens,* verb forms).

According to Chapelain, many of his sonnets were rushed, and for this reason he begged the reader's indulgence. "Sur la maladie et sur la guérison du Roy" (1663) is one such poem. One quatrain and one tercet should suffice to give an idea of Chapelain's critical acumen:

> *Dans sa riche fusée, attentive, remarque*
> *Que la soye et l'argent à l'or brillent meslés,*
> *Et que vingt lustres pleins doivent estre écoulés*

[22] *Jean Chapelain,* pp. 244–45.
[23] *Lettres,* 2:324.
[24] Ibid., p. 321.

Avant que de Caron le reçoive la barque.

. . . .

Tu feignois seulement l'attentat furieux
Pour mieux faire sentir quel Roy perdra la Terre,
Quand à la Terre enfin l'enlèveront les Cieux.[25]

Such a poem indeed needs the reader's indulgence.

In 1666, Chapelain contributed two long odes to the *Elogia Julii Mazarini Cardinalis.*[26] The "Ode à Mazarin" is composed of fifty ten-line stanzas, each composed of five octosyllabic and five decasyllabic lines, a structure opposed to Malherbe's basic concepts of strophic unity and balance. The rhymes are as un-Malherbian as can be imagined (*chants-champs, Sicile-Virgile*, verbs, adverbs, proper nouns abused for cheap rhymes), and the many hyperboles verge on the ridiculous ("D'avoir mis sans effort leur Mars sous notre Mars"[27]). The "Ode pour la paix" is shorter but somehow manages to contain as many flaws. Many more examples could be given of Chapelain's disregard for some basic rules of prosody. All his poems, from the *mort-sort-port-Nort* combination of "Sur la mort de Catherine de Vivonne" (1666) to the *âme-flamme* of the "Tombeau de Mme la Duchesse de Montauzier" (1671), lack decent rhymes, their attempts at balanced antitheses invariably fall flat ("D'une immortelle mesme a fait une mortelle"),[28] and many of the lines defy rhythmic analysis ("Pardon, je ne suis plus vaine, arrogante, ingrate"[29]).

The above are ample proof that Chapelain neither heeded Malherbe's admonitions nor followed his example. Boileau saw this, of course, and considered Chapelain "mad" to even wish to rhyme.[30] But Boileau was an "outsider." Within the Academy, Chapelain was respected and admired, and, as many a critic has stated, *La Pucelle,* although disappointing, did not get the reception it deserved. A look at the work of some of his colleagues may explain this phenomenon.

Of all the poets at the Academy since its beginning, Conrart and Godeau were most like Chapelain in their pronouncements on matters

---

[25] Ibid., p. 307.
[26] Pp. 13–29 and 115–26 of the French portion.
[27] P. 17.
[28] *Lettres,* 2:435.
[29] Ibid., p. 787.
[30] Sat. IV, *Œuvres complètes,* p. 28.

poetic, and were almost as influential. The important role of Conrart, his influence, the varied services he rendered, all that is common knowledge. Equally well known is Boileau's comment that Conrart, as far as his poetic production was concerned, kept a "silence prudent."[31] Opposed to this opinion is that of Kerviler and Barthélemy, who state that Conrart's lines equal those "de l'ode majestueuse de la prise de Namur."[32] Conrart had contributed to the *Guirlande de Julie* a set of madrigals that are typically graceful but extremely facile and so devoid of metrical integrity as to verge on the prosaic. The following lines from the fable "La rose et la violette" show that he had not changed:

> *Le soleil, dit-elle, est le maistre;*
> *C'est luy qui nous a donné l'estre,*
> *C'est luy qui doit régler nos honneurs et nos rangs.*
> *Qu'il parle, qu'il décide, et soudain je me rens.*[33]

In view of the influence he wielded, of his revered position as judicious animator of an illustrious gathering, his reluctance to publish such poems must indeed be considered "prudent."

Few poets of the seventeenth century changed as radically as did Godeau, and the period of this change more or less coincides with the transition from the reign of Louis XIII to that of Louis XIV. His conversion from the gallant *ruelliste* to the assiduous residing bishop is well known, but it must be remembered that this residence in no way hampered his influence at the Academy. What is interesting here, however, is not so much the change of character and of subject matter, but the change in his prosodic practice.[34]

Generally speaking, Godeau's religious poems use a more direct approach than his worldly ones; they have a more clearly defined "conduite" of ideas, but the technique is still far from Malherbian. The rhymes are

---

[31] Ibid., p. 104.

[32] René Kerviler and Edouard de Barthélemy, *Valentin Conrart* (Paris: Didier, 1881), p. iii.

[33] Ibid., p. 152.

[34] As I discussed earlier, the subject matter was not entirely new, and one should not think of an overnight revolution. For years the poet struggled with his former tendencies, and lines betraying this preciosity frequently occur in his transitional poems.

as bad as ever, and all too often the pompous effect of well-structured alexandrines is ruined by rhythmic variations difficult to explain. In the choice of forms, Godeau is far from Malherbian. Malherbe must have sensed that alexandrine *dizains* would be very heavy and never used them. Godeau, perhaps to achieve a feeling of *ampleur*, used them— quite advantageously at times. The "Assomption de la Vierge" uses this form. In most of the stanzas, the break is 4–6, with a secondary 3–3 cut:

> *Ainsi, quand sur un fleuve à la course rapide*
> *Quelqu'un a sans péril gouverné les vaisseaux,*
> *S'il se veut signaler sur l'empire liquide,*
> *Il tremble au seul aspect des abîmes des eaux.*
> *Chaque flot dans son âme élève mille craintes;*
> *Cent morts devant ses yeux au lieu d'une sont peintes;*
> *Il est bientôt surpris des calmes ou du vent;*
> *Il trouve dans le ciel de nouvelles étoiles,*
> *Et voit la différence en l'usage des voiles*
> *D'un batelier timide et d'un nocher savant.*[35]

Unfortunately, he did not always abide by this system, and many stanzas are broken in such a way as to ruin their intended majestic flow. By the same token, whereas the lines cited above flow smoothly and are properly combined, such is not always the case:

> *Aujourd'hui, mes enfants, j'ai peine à reconnaitre*
> *Si j'eus plus de plaisir lorsque je le vis naître,*
> *Que lorsque je me sens proche de le revoir.*[36]

This question of structure plagues the reader at every turn throughout this period. In 1644, Godeau published five psalms in various forms, none Malherbian. Typical is Psalm 19, written in 8–12–12–12–12–8, *a a b c c b* sestets, most without any break:

> *Que le Monarque des Monarques*
> *Qui fait en ta naissance éclater tant de marques*

[35] Cited by Faguet, *Histoire*, 3:155.
[36] Raymond Picard, ed., *La poésie française de 1640 à 1680* (Paris: SEDES, 1964), p. 56.

Des tendres soins qu'il prend de l'Empire François,
Lorsque tu le prieras d'écarter les tempestes,
De qui l'horrible bruit grondera sur nos testes,
    Aussi-tost responde à ta voix.[37]

This un-Malherbian stanza was changed in 1656 to read as follows:

        Qve le Monarque des Monarques
    Te donne et t'exauçant, de favorables marques
            De sa paternelle bonté;
    Que le Dieu de Iacob te couure sous son ombre,
    Et si tes ennemis te surpassent en nombre,
    Qu'il les fasse ceder à ton cœur indonté.[38]

Such a median break occurs in four of the nine stanzas, but that is as-suredly the only improvement, be they judged by Malherbe's standards or any other.

In 1648, Godeau published the entire set of Psalms of David. He had intended these poems to be lyrical, hoping that "quelqu'vn de ces excellents Musiciens qui honorent nostre siecle, seroit peut-estre poussé par l'esprit de Dieu à leur donner des airs agreables et faciles."[39] At least four composers accepted the challenge. Some of these psalms are of an earlier vintage and have already been discussed. Others are new and most of these show the author's facility and rapid composition, a phe-nomenon which he was quite aware of but did not consider a defect worthy of correction. Many of these poems are totally lackluster, particu-larly those which, like Psalm 77—a catalogue of benefits that Israel de-rived from God—are in alexandrine *vers suivis.* Certain generalizations can be made about the forms involved: the didactic poems are generally in quatrains, both isometric and heterometric, with a few composed of five- and six-line stanzas. Expletives are very frequent:

        Mais dans cette troupe éclatante,
        Vne, entre les autres charmante
        Paroist assise à ton costé;

[37] Cited by Leblanc, *Paraphrases,* p. 155.
[38] *Paraphrase des Pseaumes de David,* p. 57.
[39] Cited by Leblanc, *Paraphrases,* p. 157.

L'aiguille sur sa robe artistement desploye
Tout ce qu'elle sçait faire auec l'or et la soye,
Et sa riche couronne accroist sa Majesté.[40]

Furthermore, notice that the division here is not merely syntactical but metrical, a mistake which Malherbe allowed himself only once, in the early "Plainte sur une absence." Equally frequent among Godeau's errors are the "parallélismes synonymiques," another form of padding, and one for which Malherbe had a particular dislike:

Le Seigneur a pris ma defense,
Et sous ce puissant Protecteur,
Il n'est point de persecuteur,
Dont je redoute la puissance.

Le Seigneur pour moi se déclare,
Et cet appuy, qu'il m'a promis,
Me fait de tous mes ennemis
Mespriser l'audace barbare.[41]

In addition, as Paulette Leblanc has noted,[42] wherever Godeau uses a rhyme scheme other than *cc* in a sestet, the break is frequently 3–3; but when the last two lines rhyme (*cc*), they are generally further set off by a 4–2 break, with a disagreeable effect the inevitable result:

Il n'est crimes abominables,
Il n'est brutales actions,
Il n'est infames passions,
Dont les mortels ne soient coupables;
En ce siecle maudit, à peine vn seulement
A soin de viure justement.[43]

Not even the sonnets are exempt from censure. While their rhyme scheme and choice of meter are above reproach, the rhymes and the inner constructions are not. Some lines are badly balanced:

[40] Ibid., pp. 162–63.
[41] Ibid., p. 163.
[42] Ibid., p. 166.
[43] *Paraphrases,* p. 35. There are six more such examples in this collection alone.

Et tu leur reprochas que, du lieu d'oraison,
Leur commerce faisait une place de change.[44]

Long sentences run entire stanzas together:

Vous que touchent si fort de fabuleux romans,
Et qui par le bel art de leurs savantes feintes,
D'un véritable ennui ressentez les atteintes
Pour les fausses douleurs qu'y souffrent les amants,

Si vous aimez à voir de langoureux tourments,
Des désirs enflammés et d'amoureuses craintes,
Mais des désirs tout purs, des peines toutes saintes,
Je vous offre en mes vers tous ces objets charmants.[45]

These long sentences and badly balanced lines are omnipresent in all the later poems of Godeau. The "Hymne sur la naissance du Seigneur," written in ten-line stanzas, has sentences running to ten lines and shows every conceivable cut (2-6, 3-5, 4-4). In short, at no time during this period of his career could Godeau really have considered himself Malherbian. His tone had changed. His technique had not.

The rest of the poets at the Academy in 1643 who had been members since its inception—Desmarests de Saint-Sorlin, Bois-Robert, and Saint-Amant—did not even claim to be following in Malherbe's footsteps. It is therefore very interesting to see how their later poetic production compares with that of the poets just discussed.

Desmarests de Saint-Sorlin in these years concentrated on the composition of *Clovis* and other heroic poems. In the "Advis" of *Clovis*, he enunciated his literary ideas, which include a defense of archaic and technical terms and of the judicious use of enjambments and inversions. All of these, as well as padding, commonplace rhymes, and excessive conceits abound in his later works.[46] One glance at his works, be they the long or the shorter poems in quatrains, convinces any reader that he is indeed in the presence of a creator totally oblivious to the existence of

[44] Picard, *Poésie française*, p. 65.

[45] Ibid., p. 66.

[46] See William A. Goodman, "The Heroic Poems of Jean Desmarets de Saint-Sorlin" (Doctoral dissertation, University of North Carolina, 1966; Ann Arbor: University Microfilms, 1967), pp. 74-76.

Malherbe—or of Marot, for that matter: "Autant les vers de Marot semblaient un moule étroit, tout gonflé de sentiment et de pensée, autant les vers de Desmarests, remplis de suaves riens, coulent sans laisser derrière eux d'autre trace qu'un vague parfum de fade dévotion."[47] It would be difficult to find a trace of the Malherbe of "Lauda anima" in the following:

> Chantons donc sa bonté,
> Ses vertus, ses largesses;
> Et quelle verité
> Reluit dans ses promesses.[48]

Throughout these poems, long or short, one gets the impression that without the word "et" the lines would be more uneven still and the sentences more tortured, no mean feat:

> Et cent chandeliers d'or, à dix bras étendus,
> Sont devant les miroirs de la voute pendus.[49]

The ambiguous phrasings of *Esther*, its tortured syntax, are strangely suited to this anachronism. The palace of Vashti, partly described in the two lines above, is the epitome of baroque ostentation, complete with "un trône pompeux" where "un paon étend sa queue" decorated with "mille diamans," as is the queen herself.[50]

Unlike Desmarests, Bois-Robert never bothered to enunciate any of his literary principles, but they are not very difficult to derive from his production, the bulk of which is taken up by his *Epîtres*. In these, as in all his other poems, Bois-Robert shows himself to be, first and foremost, an accomplished *courtisan*. There has never been any doubt that his position at the Academy was due more to diplomatic than to poetic talents, but his influence, like that of Conrart, was not predicated on the latter and must not be minimized.[51] The *Epîtres*, from first to last, show little or no change. While they constitute the bulk of his poetic production, they

[47] Leblanc, *Paraphrases*, p. 137.
[48] Ibid., p. 138.
[49] *Esther* (Paris: Le Petit, 1670), p. 48.
[50] Ibid., pp. 48–49.
[51] See Adam, "L'école de 1650," passim.

need not delay us much here, for it is obvious that their author did not consider these "chatty," friendly letters as deserving careful redaction. Enjambments are frequent:

> *Quoy! tout de bon, ton amitié m'impose*
> *Cette loy dure? elle veut que j'expose*
> *Aux yeux malins des injustes Censeurs*
> *Les nuditez de mes neuf pauvres Sœurs?*[52]

Every conceivable rule of versification is broken, especially where rhymes are concerned: monosyllabic homonyms, "rimes de Chartres," simple-compound rhymes, facile and gratuitous rhymes, lack of homophony of the *consonne d'appui,* and so on. In this respect, as in the length of sentences, he was a fine match for Conrart, who answered in kind one of his *Epîtres.*[53]

In addition to these letters, Bois-Robert wrote several occasional poems, including several sets of *stances.* Considering their relatively small number, what is remarkable is the great diversity of forms involved and the freedom within the forms. "Au Soleil"[54] is written in alexandrine sestets, divided 2–4 and 4–2, with some badly balanced lines: "Soleil visible, autheur des charmes du Printemps." "Rossignols," having five octosyllabic lines followed by an alexandrine, and using the unusual *a b a b c c* scheme, has only a weak 2–4 break.[55] Several poems are written in seven-line stanzas, some in nine, all with the greatest diversity in heterometry and rhyme scheme. The second collection, that of 1659, accentuates the trend, with stanzas ranging from an 8–10–12–6–6–12 sestet to a 10–10–6–6–8–8–4 septet (*a a b b c c b*) to an 8–10–12–10–12–6–12–12–12–8–12–8 (*a b a b c c c d e d d e*) monstrosity.[56] Even in the simplest of these, the sestet, the very nature of the form is frequently hampered by a metrical 3–3 division already commented on elsewhere:

> *Comme si l'on ouuroit déja vostre cerceüil,*
> *Ie voy la Cour en pleurs, je voy la Ville en deüil,*

---

[52] *Epistres,* 1:35.
[53] Ibid., pp. 248–53.
[54] *Autres œuvres* (1646), p. 17.
[55] Ibid., pp. 18–19.
[56] Ibid. (1659), pp. 261, 262, 271.

Vos maux causent partout une douleur profonde,
Mais Iris, ce ne seroit pas
La plus belle moitié du Monde
Qui pleureroit vostre Trespas.[57]

Of all these poems, only one, "Sur le retour du Roy," can be considered a serious attempt at pompous occasional poetry. The form is orthodox (octosyllabic sestets, *a a b c b c*), but the rhymes and inner structure are beyond belief and the tone never rises above the insipid.

Normally, it is in sonnets that a poet displays his most careful craftsmanship. In Bois-Robert's case, the sonnets add further proof of his lack of discipline. The form (alexandrine or octosyllabic, *a b b a . . . e d e* or *e e d*) is orthodox, but nothing else is. The first rhymes that greet the reader of the 1646 collection are *François-Loix-voix-choix*[58] and the others are no better. The constructions often combine several violations in a single sentence:

Enten, Reine adorable, enten par moy la voix
De la France à tes soins pour iamais obligee.[59]

As time goes on, expletives become more and more obvious[60] as do cacophonic phrases.[61] Enjambments are numerous, and sometimes even tie stanzas together. In short, there is no trace of Malherbe in any of them.[62]

While Bois-Robert enjoyed a reputation for which he had worked but slightly, Saint-Amant had to work very hard without always getting his just reward. Everyone is familiar with the scorn unfairly heaped on him by Boileau, and many of his later poems, such as "La lune parlante," were of a kind which, "à la Cour et partout ailleurs, ne trouva personne quil l'approuvât."[63] On the whole, however, this period of Saint-Amant's productivity was one of relatively conservative versification and fine crafts-

---

[57] Ibid., p. 265.
[58] P. 6.
[59] Ibid.
[60] Ibid., p. 10.
[61] Ibid. (1659), p. 250.
[62] On the other hand, Corneille might have claimed one of Bois-Robert's lines: "Et que ses coups d'essay sont des coups d'Alexandre," ibid. (1646), p. 8.
[63] Urbain Chevreau, cited by Lachèvre, *Glanes,* 2:149.

manship. Generally speaking, he preferred isometric forms (even in his epigrams, the isometric outweigh the heterometric stanzas two to one), and short stanzas.[64] As a rule, the shorter stanzas are used for shorter poems, the longer stanzas in more ambitious works. Most of his sonnets are quite orthodox in form. Out of forty, thirty-six are in alexandrines, the same number have an *a b b a . . . e d e* rhyme scheme, two have *e e d*, one is unfinished, and only one is very free (*a b a b b a b a c c d e d e*). Viewed chronologically, these sonnets show a further trend toward conservative practice in that both *e e d* examples as well as the unfinished one are very early, and the free one dates from the 1640s; in other words, during this period all the sonnets have a conventional rhyme scheme and all but two are in alexandrines.[65]

Unfortunately, be it Boileau's fault or not, this period of Saint-Amant's productivity has all too frequently been associated with his *Moïse sauvé*, an un-Malherbian poem in many ways. Malherbe had warned against many flights of fancy, particularly in the composition of ambitious epics, yet Saint-Amant created new historic characters (Elisaph and Merari), personified abstractions (Antipathie, Renommée), and introduced pagan mythology into a biblical context (Thetis, Aeolus, Boreas), often to a ridiculous degree ("le saint Olympe,"[66] "un saint et vray Mercure"[67]). Some of his metrical liberties, such as the following enjambment, have a purpose:

> *Va donc à Pharaon, va de ma part luy dire*
> *Qu'il relasche Israël, esclave en son empire.*[68]

Such is not always the case, and the following periphrase is not only clumsy but, as Yves Le Hir has pointed out, ridiculous:[69]

[64] According to Gourier, *Etude de Saint-Amant*, p. 230, he used quatrains in thirty poems, sestets in twenty-three and *dizains* in only nineteen. However, he was not averse to using less popular forms such as eleven- or nine-line stanzas, the latter in ten poems.

[65] One exception is in decasyllabic lines and another in octosyllabic, neither being a rarity at the time, though Malherbe never wrote a decasyllabic sonnet.

[66] *Œuvres complètes*, 2:235.

[67] Ibid., p. 155.

[68] Ibid., p. 201.

[69] "Notes sur la langue et le style du *Moïse sauvé* de Saint-Amant," *Fr Mod* 19 (1951):100.

Et, telle que l'on void sur un bord aquatique
Se tourmenter en vain la mere domestique
Quand le fils adoptif sous sa chaleur esclos,
Comme d'une autre espece, entrecouppe les flots, ...[70]

The ridicule becomes obvious when, after many more lines of this, the reader realizes that he is viewing a mother hen worried by an adopted duckling taking a swim.

In all fairness to Saint-Amant, however, this period should be considered not as that of *Moïse,* but one of intensive activity in the realm of occasional poetry where comparison with Malherbe is especially valid. Saint-Amant might be considered Malherbian in this type of poem in that he demonstrated a keen sense of structure:

Irritez-vous mortels; liguez-vous, potentats;
Fondez sur cet estat avec tous vos estats;
Faittes par tout la paix pour luy faire la guerre.[71]

A closer look reveals a totally different—and un-Malherbian—attitude:

Depuis qu'un si beau champ nourrit un si beau germe
Neuf lunes sur neuf mois ont presque fait leur tour,
Et pour le grand moment déjà toute la cour
S'émeut, craint et fremit sous l'espoir le plus ferme.[72]

Noteworthy is not only the periphrase at the beginning of this quatrain, but the fortunate effect of the enjambment at the end, perfect in its union of form and content. We are not concerned here with the submission of the muses to an iron rule, but of the disciplined interplay of all the elements involved in the creation of a poem. This is even more obvious in some of his heterometric poems:

Il en menace les moins proches,
Il gronde, il ecume, il fremit,

[70] *Œuvres complètes,* 2:233–34.
[71] Ibid., 1:440.
[72] Ibid., 2:98.

L'echo des rives en gemit
Dans la concavité des roches.
Toutesfois sa fureur, terrible à voir marcher,
S'efforce en vain de detacher
Les sourds liens de ces grands arbres;
Leur pié fait teste aux flots, et, comme autant de marbres,
Rien ne sçauroit les arracher.[73]

"Le rythme même du vers, évoquant la violence de la tempête et le calme de la résistance qui lui est opposée"[74] shows a new—though still totally un-Malherbian—Saint-Amant. But care must be taken here not to treat such a passage as descriptive poetry: the storm is the storm of war, and the mighty tree represents the crown of Poland; this is not so much a descriptive poem as an occasional one making full use of the descriptive genius of the poet who, elsewhere, calls upon the evocative powers of pure sounds for the same purpose:

La tymbale, aux chefs glorieuse,
Tonnant dans son ventre d'airain,
Fait bruire en l'air doux et serain
Une musique furieuse.
La trompette éclatante et le tambour divers
Au fifre embouché de travers
Joignent leur brusque melodie,
Et tous ces instruments, en l'oreille estourdie,
Semblent confondre l'univers.[75]

In one other respect, one which has already been noted in Saint-Amant's earlier poetry, the poet differs radically from Malherbe: many of his occasional poems are marked "héroï-comique," and "La généreuse" (1656), a poem of well over 100 nine-line stanzas,[76] "idyle héroïque."

---

[73] Ibid., pp. 358–59.
[74] Gourier, *Etude de Saint-Amant*, p. 38.
[75] *Œuvres complètes*, 2:367.
[76] These are 8–8–8–8–12–8–8–12–8, a b b a c c d d c, with a consistently strong 4–5 main break and 3–2 secondary break, and with very rich rhymes marred only by an occasional lapse in the homophony of the *consonne d'appui*.

When such labels are in vogue and when "illustre Bourbon" supplies a rhyme for "le jambon,"[77] the "école de 1650" may be ruling but for at least some members of the republic of letters Malherbe is dead and Boileau not yet born.

Except for Baro, who had fallen silent, all of the poets discussed above had been Academicians since the inception of that body. Strangely enough, only one poet was added to their number in a dozen years, in 1639, when Salomon de Priézac was elected. He had written a fairly large number of poems but only two found their way into the various *recueils,* which leads one to believe that his poetry did not find universal appeal. His vocabulary (*nonpareilles, foleteau*[78]) is anything but *châtié,* his rhymes and rhyme schemes defy description, enjambments add to the already chaotic impression given by his forms—in short, everything about his poetry testifies to the truth of his claim that "mon travail ne fust iamais accompagné de sueur."[79]

Not until 1647 did the Academy add another poet to its ranks. The addition of Pierre Corneille must be considered historic not only because it righted a terrible wrong, but because he was the first real poet to be added to a rapidly aging group. He and Tristan L'Hermite formed the elite of this second wave, which also included Mézeray, Scudéry, and Charpentier.

In his choice of forms, Corneille is anything but Malherbian, though in his religious poetry he used so many diverse forms that some of them were bound to coincide with those of Malherbe. In the *Imitation,* stanzas range from the conventional alexandrine quartet to the rather unusual five-line stanza of three alexandrines separated by hexasyllabics. The sestets show varied breaks or none at all, as do the eight-line stanzas. Most ten-line stanzas, on the other hand, are split 4–6. The unfortunate conclusion to which the reader must eventually resign himself when reading Corneille's religious poems, particularly the numerous hetero-metric ones, is that this poet, who could be so lyrical in the *stances* of his dramas, was unable to carry this success over into the religious realm.

---

[77] *Œuvres complètes,* 1:396.

[78] Paul Lacroix, ed., *Ballets et mascarades de cour* (Geneva: Gay, 1868–1870), 6:128.

[79] *Poésies* (Paris: Martin et Sercy, 1650), "Lettre."

Thus the 12–6–12–6 stanza of Malherbe's "Consolation" became, in Psalm 112 ("Laudate, pueri, Dominum"):

> *Enfants, de qui les voix à peine encor formées*
> *Ne font que bégayer,*
> *C'est à louer le nom du Seigneur des armées*
> *Qui'il les faut essayer.*[80]

Leblanc is right to comment on the "pénible coup de reins" necessary to finish the stanza after the pause at the end of line 2.[81] The entire poem is dry, plodding, without life or breath. These are not quatrains, they are successions of distichs, and only the rhyme helps to tie the pairs together. When Corneille uses this form with an *a a b b* rhyme scheme, the problem becomes even more acute, and "l'oreille a grand peine à savoir où commence et où finit la strophe et la pièce n'est guère autre chose qu'une succession régulière de distiques":[82]

> *Enfin le Seigneur règne, enfin il a fait voir*
> *Son absolu pouvoir:*
> *Terre, fais voir ta joie en tes cantons fertiles,*
> *Et toi, mer, en tes îles.*[83]

This is at times aggravated by certain leonine qualities:

> *Anges, que dans le ciel vouv vous faites d'honneur*
> *D'adorer le Seigneur!*
> *Sion, que de douceurs, sitôt que ses merveilles*
> *Frappèrent tes oreilles!*[84]

What seems to have escaped Corneille in these poems is Malherbe's fundamental ability to maintain the unity of heterometric stanzas, a capital point of his doctrine and practice.

---

[80] *Œuvres,* 9:213.
[81] *Paraphrases,* p. 228.
[82] Ibid., p. 241.
[83] *Œuvres,* 9:115.
[84] Ibid., p. 117.

For his secular poetry, Corneille was even less prone to heed Malherbe's lessons as to the choice of forms. All but three of his poems in quatrains are alexandrine; there are few six- and ten-line stanzas, and these, except for the alexandrines of the 1649 "Triomphes de Louis le Juste," are all heterometric. Whereas the bulk of his poems are in alexandrines, many in *vers suivis,* there are some heterometric poems in six-, eight-, and ten-line stanzas, as well as sonnets and *vers suivis.* Of all of these, only two use forms that can be found in Malherbe, each one once and quite early. One of the irregular sonnets will give an ample idea of Corneille's independence:

> *Je vous estime, Iris, et crois pouvoir sans crime*
> *Permettre à mon respect un aveu si charmant:*
>   *Il est vrai qu'à chaque moment*
>   *Je songe que je vous estime.*
>
> *Cette agréable idée, où ma raison s'abîme,*
> *Tyrannise mes sens jusqu'à l'accablement;*
>   *Mais pour vouloir fuir ce tourment*
>   *La cause en est trop légitime.*
>
> *Aussi quelque désordre où mon cœur soit plongé,*
> *Bien loin de faire effort à l'en voir dégagé,*
> *Entretenir sa peine est toute mon étude.*
>
> *J'en aime le chagrin, le trouble m'en est doux.*
>   *Hélas! que ne m'estimez-vous*
>   *Avec la même inquiétude!*[85]

To such forms must be added the use of seven-, nine-, and eleven-line stanzas, and frequently of *vers libre.*

There is in Corneille's nondramatic poetry a certain quality which some critics simply label "baroque"[86] without trying to analyze it, but which can readily be traced to two basic causes. From the start, Corneille refused to adjust his muse to the fantasy of a "rêveur de musique,"[87] but

[85] Ibid., 10:163.
[86] See Walther Staub, *Pierre Corneille als religiöser Dichter* (Schwarzenburg: Gerber, 1926), passim.
[87] *Œuvres,* 1:74.

in his later life he went even further in that direction. Jules Ecorcheville hit the mark perfectly when he saw in Corneille one of those men who could not only keep himself from becoming subservient to music, but could make music serve a fundamentally nonmusical purpose, that is, enhance his poetry.[88] The second of these causes is the frequent use of enjambments and *rejets*. As in his theater, Corneille here relied on these procedures to break the linearity of his poems:

> *Aaron y joint la sienne; elle seule y produit*
> *Des feuilles, des fleurs et du fruit.*[89]

One may debate the wisdom of such practices, but there is no doubt about their being opposed to everything for which Malherbe stood.

In matters of rhyme, Corneille was equally un-Malherbian. He did shun in later years the simple-compound rhymes of earlier days, but this was probably because the Academy had censured him for it. Also he made use of *rimes normandes*, as had Malherbe, but this could have been more an ethnic matter than one of discipleship, for every other practice suggests that he was indeed very independent. Facile rhymes, even in the shortest poems, abound, as do associated commonplaces:

> *Tu peux bien, ô mon Dieu, me faire cette grâce;*
> *Tu peux m'en accorder l'abondante efficace.*[90]

In this particular case, the fault is compounded by the rhyming of long and short sounds, a common practice in Corneille, as Souriau has noted.[91] Souriau also noted many cases of diaereses rhyming with synaereses (*yeux-glorieux, tien-ancien*), but this type of rhyme became less and less frequent.[92]

[88] "Corneille et la musique," *CMT* 9 (1906), p. 449.

[89] *Œuvres*, 9:24.

[90] Ibid., 8:667.

[91] *L'évolution*, pp. 134–36.

[92] Philippe Martinon, in "Etudes sur le vers français: les innovations prosodiques chez Corneille," *RHLF* 20 (1913):65–100, has suggested that Corneille was a great innovator in this domain, but Souriau came to the heart of the matter when he concluded that here, as elsewhere, Corneille followed his ear rather than Malherbe (*L'évolution*, p. 122).

Equally unacceptable to Malherbe would have been Corneille's use of leonine rhymes and frequent lapses into cacophony. It is not rare to find a rhyme at the hemistich stronger than the one at the end of the line. This becomes particularly disconcerting in heterometric poems:

> Redonne l'innocence à nos lèvres coupables,
> Et nous inspire des ardeurs,
> Digne et saint précurseur, qui nous rendent capables
> De chanter tes grandeurs.[93]

No less disconcerting to the reader are cacophonic passages such as "Telle soit-elle," or "Marie est cette échelle; elle l'est, et la passe," or "qu'à vous, qui que ce soit que j'aime," all occurring in the religious poetry.[94] The same effect is frequently due to long series of monosyllables:

> Ne dis point que c'est peu de chose,
> Ne dis point que c'est moins que rien.[95]

The above is, unfortunately, typical of Corneille's nondramatic poetry. I indicate his faults not to negate his obvious good qualities nor to suggest that his election to the Academy was not long-overdue and just. They do indicate, however, that Malherbe had little or no influence on him, and that if Corneille had any influence on his colleagues, it could not have advanced the cause of Malherbe.

Tristan L'Hermite entered the Academy in 1648, one year after Corneille. In all of his works, Boileau never mentioned Tristan, and alluded to him only once in discussing the misery of poets.[96] The reasons for this silence will become obvious after a brief look at Tristan's later production which, for our purposes, must be divided into two parts, the "heroic" and the religious.

The theatrical and lyric poetry of Tristan no longer needs rehabilitation, but the same cannot be said for his "heroic," that is, occasional

---

[93] Œuvres, 9:543–44.
[94] Ibid., pp. 77, 18; 8:513.
[95] Ibid., 8:469.
[96] Œuvres complètes, pp. 866–67.

poems. Bernardin neglected them, calling one of the best "médiocre." Camo, in his edition of Tristan's poems,[97] proscribed them entirely. Only recently, after Amédée Carriat's *Eloge* and his *Deux poèmes oubliés*[98] and after Sister Grisé's excellent edition of the *Vers héroïques*, is that side of Tristan on its way to getting full justice. Some of these poems, by the nature of their subject, are very easy to date. Others, such as "Les forges d'Antoigné" are impossible to pinpoint. Publication dates, with Tristan, are of no value whatsoever.[99] But early or late, these poems have some characteristics basic to Tristan. One might almost speak of a "l'Hermitian" trend made particularly obvious in those few poems that were modified by the author. In "Eglogue maritime," first published in 1634 and revamped for the *Vers héroïques* (1648), many lines were given a smoother flow or better rhythmic force: "Faite d'algues et de roseaux" became "Faite de joncs et de roseaux."[100] Many *contresens* such as amber white as milk or wild beasts who "se font des tablettes" were removed.[101] "La mer" (1628) lost most of its archaisms in its later version, and some of its progressions were made more logical. The earlier

> *N'est-ce pas un des beaux sujets*
> *Que puisse prendre la peinture?*
> *N'est-ce pas un des beaux objets*
> *Qu'ait jamais formé la nature?*[102]

was inverted so that the creation of the sea preceded its acting as a model. In these poems, as in the "Peinture de S. A. Sérénissime,"[103] there is also a constant search for the *mot juste* and a pitiless hunt for the cacophonic and the expletive. (Tristan's rhymes were, with few lapses, always quite good, thus naturally few changes were made there.)

Are these reworkings to be construed as an attempt, on Tristan's

[97] *Les amours et autres poésies choisies* (Paris: Garnier, 1925).

[98] (Limoges: Rougerie, [1955]).

[99] Carriat, in *Deux poèmes oubliés*, has convincingly put forth the argument that "Les forges," published relatively late, were really of a much earlier vintage.

[100] P. 38.

[101] Ibid., pp. 39, 51.

[102] Ibid., pp. 57–58.

[103] Ibid., pp. 90–110.

part, to become "Malherbian"? Not at all. In the new poems, as in the re-workings of the older ones, the basic concern for form does not lead in that direction. Not a single change in the older poems' form is to be noted. In the new poems, the old virtuosity in heterometry, the clever use of enjambments, of varied breaks, all the procedures that have already been identified with Tristan's inimitable style are to be found again in equal profusion.

Nearly half the lines of the *Vers héroïques* are *stances,* and very few of these are truly "heroic" in nature, lacking the elevation of the odes. Twenty-five of these poems were definitely written after 1643, and the majority of them are isometric: octosyllabic quatrains, *a b a b,* are used four times; octosyllabic five-line stanzas, *a b a b a,* once; octosyllabic sestets, *a a b c b c,* six times; octosyllabic ten-line stanzas, once; alexandrine quartets, *a b a b,* three times. Except for the five-line stanzas and the rhyme scheme of the *dizains,* the basic forms used here are quite orthodox. What is not orthodox is their implementation. The longer stanzas have either varied breaks or none at all,[104] and a sentence begun in one stanza is frequently carried over into the next.[105] Generally speaking, the rhymes in these works are not as good as those in the heterometric poems, suggesting perhaps a more careless attitude on the part of the author.[106]

Two of Tristan's ten heterometric poems use quatrains, one uses octets, the rest, sestets. In all, only three reproduce a form used by Malherbe: 12–12–12–6 quatrains and 8–8–8–12–12–12 and 12–12–12–12–6–12 sestets, though the rhyme schemes reduce the parallel still further. What is perhaps even more interesting is the use Tristan made of these forms. Malherbe had used the 8–8–8–12–12–12 sestet only once, very early, probably because he felt that such an arrangement used in conjunction with a 3–3 break would destroy the unity of the stanza, setting

---

[104] The twenty-four lines of "A M. de Voiture" (pp. 88–89) being an exception.

[105] See stanzas 1–2 of "La gloire" (p. 213). The same phenomenon also occurs in heterometric poems, *viz.* stanzas 4–5 of "Sur la prise de Gravelines" (p. 72).

[106] In addition to lapses of a common type (*point-point, grace-glace, ame-flame,* [iø-jø]), a predilection for facile rhymes leads Tristan to some ridiculous phrases, including on at least two occasions "que je te die" (*Vers héroïques,* pp. 227, 285).

the octosyllabics against the alexandrines. Tristan, by allowing the syntax to cross this line of demarcation, solved the problem:

> Sous ses auspices bien-heureux,
> Nos conquerans avantureux
> Produisent de si belles choses
> Que les peuples d'Ibere et les peuples Germains
> Sont contrains d'avouer qu'à l'ombre de vos roses
> Les palmes tous les jours croissent entre nos mains.[107]

For better or for worse, the results are totally un-Malherbian. The four longest heterometric poems depart further from orthodoxy in that they combine lines of six, eight, and twelve beats. They are further irregular in the balance of their lines, which show varied divisions. The following example is taken from the longest of these poems, "La servitude":

> Nuit fraische, sombre, et solitaire,
> Sainte depositaire
> De tous les grands secrets, ou de guerre, ou d'amour,
> Nuit mere du repos, et nourrice des veilles
> Qui produisent tant de merveilles,
> Donne moy des conseils qui soient dignes du jour.[108]

Tristan's lyricism, as can be seen, does not allow the speech groups to coincide with the lines, a procedure even more manifest in his songs, which are totally un-Malherbian in every respect.

The Vers héroïques contains sixteen odes, eleven of which are post-1643. Generally, these are longer, more pompous, more "heroic," though one rather interesting one deals with the boy-king, Louis XIV, playing with toy soldiers, while another one, the brief "Manifeste de la belle ingrate," is purely erotic though the tone is mock-heroic. All but two are octosyllabic, the exceptions being the bantering poem for the boy-king (heptasyllabic) and a joyous one in honor of a convalescence (heterometric). Two use twelve-line stanzas, four use dizains, one is in eight-line stanzas, and four in sestets. Yet, taking the rhyme scheme also

---

[107] Ibid., p. 134.
[108] Ibid., p. 155.

into account makes it apparent that the bulk of these poems use forms seldom if ever to be found in Malherbe. Furthermore, the sestets vary widely in their breaks, some being without any, as are two of the three *dizains*.[109]

A third type of poem must be considered here, the isolated stanzas. Many of these are inscriptions or short commemorative works, and most are octosyllabic. The *dizains* are usually broken 4–3–3, but enjambments are frequent:

> *J'ay porté dignement le titre*
> *D'apuy, de vainqueur, ou d'arbitre*
> *De tous les plus superbes rois.*[110]

On the other hand, the alexandrine sestets are well constructed in every respect:

> *Eblouy de l'éclat de la splendeur mondaine,*
> *Je me flatay toujours d'une esperance vaine,*
> *Faisant le chien couchant aupres d'un grand seigneur.*
> *Je me vis toujours pauvre et tâchay de parestre,*
> *Je vequis dans la peine atendant le bon-heur,*
> *Et mourus sur un cofre en atendant mon maistre.*[111]

The same care was obviously lavished on the sonnets, which are, almost without exception, well-polished works of art. Equally obvious is that Malherbe was not the master whom Tristan followed in the composition of these gems. As Sister Grisé has stated in the introduction to her edition of the *Vers héroïques*, the topic of the first sonnet, "L'avanture d'un pescheur," as well as its position in the volume, may be as strong an indication of Tristan's marinistic tendencies as is the style of the poem itself: "En mettant ce sonnet ici, après 'L'Eglogue maritime' et 'La Mer,' Tristan a-t-il voulu imiter Marino qui mettait dans la première partie de ses *Rime* un groupe de *poesie marittime?*"[112] This octosyllabic sonnet

---

[109] "Le manifeste," ibid., pp. 323–24.
[110] Ibid., p. 268.
[111] Ibid., p. 279.
[112] Ibid., p. 11.

is far from Malherbian, as the rhyme scheme indicates: *jour-joye-Amour-proye, bateau-Elise-beau-franchise, beauté-inquieté, repose-esprits-dispose-pris*. In many of these sonnets, lines are frequently unbalanced, always for good poetic reasons but with results that Malherbe would not have approved: "Depuis, ta vertu jointe aux grands fruits de tes veilles."[113] By the same token, enjambments frequently make form and content go hand in hand, but they remain enjambments for all that:

> *Prince dont le merite heureusement surpasse*
> *L'effort de la creance . . .*[114]

As Philip Wadsworth has so aptly demonstrated, artifice and sincerity readily coexist in many creative minds, and in Tristan L'Hermite perhaps more than in others: "Artifice and sincerity, happily combined, give his verse a special quality which sets him apart from other writers of his age."[115] It must be added that in making his point, Wadsworth did not quote a single line of Tristan's religious poetry, and he did well not to. I am not attempting to reopen the question of Tristan's religious beliefs, for I wish only to discuss his artistic sincerity. Whether one sides with Lacôte's idea of a "façade poétique" or Leblanc's concept of a "dévotion, non dévorante sans doute, mais sincère,"[116] there is no doubt that time and time again, throughout the *Office de la Sainte Vierge*, in form and in content, Tristan falls short of the standard of excellence demonstrated in earlier collections. Whatever the sentiments of the poet may have been, a mixture of tones such as the following is unfit for the subject:

> *Diuin Autheur de toutes choses,*
> *A qui les ronces et les clouds*
> *Quand tu voulus mourir pour nous*
> *Estoient des œillets et des roses.*[117]

The artistic integrity of this quatrain is not advanced by the fact that it is not even a sentence, in spite of the punctuation.

[113] Ibid., p. 136.
[114] Ibid., p. 189.
[115] "Artifice and sincerity," p. 430.
[116] Leblanc, *Paraphrases*, p. 150.
[117] (Paris: n.p., [1646]), p. 118.

There are, to be sure, some fine poems in the *Office*. The sonnets are generally well crafted, with some very impressive passages:

> *On me mit sur la Croix comme sur un Autel,*
> *Et seul apres ta faute accepté pour victime,*
> *l'acceptay de mourir pour te rendre immortel.*[118]

The "De profundis" is equally successful, technically as well as in content:

> *Du gouffre des ennuis dont mon ame est remplie,*
> *Et du milieu des maux dont ie me sens presser,*
> *Ma voix s'adresse à toy, Mon Dieu ie te suplie*
> *De vouloir l'exaucer.*[119]

And surely, when Wadsworth spoke of those religious poems that are "très réussis,"[120] he must have included in his mind the massive "Miserere" which another critic called "les 17 lourds sixains du *Miserere*."[121] An oppressive feeling does, to be sure, permeate the poem, but is that not a measure of the poet's genius? It seems that Tristan's whole skill and his personal contribution lie in the fact that, with all the antitheses, abstractions, conceits, and other weapons in the arsenal of the popular poet, he still managed to give an impression of dedication, of peace, of harmony. The alexandrine sestets of the poem are invariably well cut, with three balanced lines in each half:

> *Seigneur, i'ay mon recours, abysmé dans les crimes,*
> *A vos hautes bontez à ces profonds abysmes*
> *Qui sont toûjours plus grands que nôtre iniquité:*
> *Encor que mes pechez meritent le suplice,*
> *Au lieu de me punir selon vostre iustice,*
> *Veuillez me pardonner selon vostre bonté.*[122]

---

[118] Ibid., p. 117.
[119] Ibid., p. 545.
[120] Tristan L'Hermite, *Poésies* (Paris: Seghers, 1962), p. 14.
[121] Leblanc, *Paraphrases,* p. 151.
[122] *Office,* p. 119.

Strong antitheses abound in the "Miserere," but fit in well with thought and structure:

> *Ie meritois la mort et vous m'auez fait grace,*
> *I'estois digne de haine et vous m'auez aimé.*[123]

Unfortunately, these poems are the exception rather than the rule. Many constructions make no sense at all, and their implementation does not help. Thus, "Contre l'horreur du Peché" is composed of seventeen quatrains (8–12–8–12, *a b a b,* not to be found in Malherbe, of course) and a badly connected octosyllabic *dizain.* The rhythms are difficult to fit into any pattern:

> *O mon Ame, fuy le Peché*
> *Fuy cette abominable et dangereuse Peste:*
> *Celuy qui s'en trouue taché*
> *Ne sçauroit éuiter la colere Celeste.*[124]

"A son bon Ange,"[125] in octosyllabic sestets, has almost no median breaks. "Prière à la Sainte Vierge,"[126] in 8–8–12–12–12–12 sestets, is full of paddings and long metaphors: in one line he speaks of "Mes pechez ont produit ulceres sur ulceres" and only five tasteless stanzas later does "ce Grand Medecin" cure his most desperate ills. Nowhere is this seemingly hasty workmanship more evident than in "Sur la Reception du Saint Sacrement,"[127] where "Ce merveilleux ouvrier" must take up only six beats, yet rhyme with a diaeresis. In all of these poems, the forms are varied—usually non-Malherbian—but all too frequently misused, and the rhymes are all too often inadequate.

What is obvious here is that the penurious Tristan had sold his pen to a commercial enterprise. Some good poems resulted, but they form a decided minority, an unusual phenomenon for Tristan. Here, more than anywhere else in the man's work, a good anthology would have to be a

---

[123] Ibid., p. 120.
[124] Ibid., p. 45.
[125] Ibid., pp. 66–69.
[126] Ibid., pp. 123–26.
[127] Ibid., pp. 135 ff.

very thin one. His contemporaries may have sensed this fact, for they did not judge him by this collection. Boileau, usually so unforgiving, made no mention of it. In fact, he never spoke of Tristan, possibly because Tristan was too unorthodox to set as an example, and too good a lyricist to mock.

Two years after the admission of Tristan, the Academy rewarded another poet known more for his lyricism than for his orthodoxy.[128] Scudéry, who had fought so violently against some members of the Academy in literary combats[129] and had caused the entire Academy no little embarrassment,[130] finally joined that august body in 1650, thus marking, with Charpentier, the end of that second wave of poets elected after 1647. It is difficult to see why the Academy had neglected him for such a long time, electing men of even lesser talents, but it is even more difficult to understand why it finally admitted him when it did, for there were few poets more unruly, less disciplined than he, and by 1650 there was definitely a trend which, while it may not be called "Malherbian," must nevertheless be considered as in the direction of orderly and measured "creative furor." Because Scudéry had excused one of his errors by quoting Malherbe, Fukui puts him among those who "étaient tous malherbiens; autant dire qu'ils avaient tous, pour souci primordial, le culte des formes poétiques."[131] As we shall see, such was simply not the case.

In 1636, Scudéry had spoken of a "branle éternel."[132] Nowhere is this more obvious than in his epic *Alaric* (1654), where we even see "un mort qui remue,"[133] but it is omnipresent in his other works as well. This desire for movement leads the poet on a constant search for new forms, or ways to innovate in the standard ones. Thus, of the 102 sonnets in the 1649 edition,[134] only 55 are "regular," and 25 of these are in *e e d*.

---

[128] Meanwhile it had elected Mézeray, but Chapelain only grudgingly conceded that this man was "néanmoins le meilleur de nos compilateurs" (*Opuscules critiques*, p. 357), while Boileau listed him among those for whom "Apollon de son feu leur fut toujours avare" ("Art poétique," II, *Œuvres complètes*, p. 165).

[129] See Chapelain, *Lettres*, 1:137, 138, 154, 156.

[130] Ibid., p. 156.

[131] *Raffinement précieux*, p. 142.

[132] *L'amant libéral* (Paris: Courbé, 1638), 1:4.

[133] Cited by Jean Rousset, *La littérature de l'âge baroque en France* (Paris: Corti, 1953), p. 113.

The linear restrictions are often broken with fortunate results, but not without going contrary to all that Malherbe stood for:

Partout on voit briller le cristal des fontaines
Qui bouillonne et qui coule, à sources toujours pleines,
Qui bondit, qui murmure et qui sur des cailloux
Gazouille et fait un bruit resveur, charmant et doux.[135]

More often than not, the very choice of forms is non-Malherbian. At least ten poems in the 1649 collection are written in heptasyllabic lines; several odes have twelve-line stanzas, including one with an *a b a b c c d d e f f e* rhyme scheme; many poems are in alexandrine *vers suivis*, with enjambments, poor rhymes and far-fetched hyperboles.[136] Only one trait could be considered Malherbian, that of usually, though far from always, dividing his ten-line stanzas 4–6.

Scudéry's poetry is characterized by a love of descriptions. At the end of *Alaric* there is a "table des descriptions contenues en ce volume," and it is a long one. These descriptions are usually quite good, though overlong, thus frequently snapping the main thread of the poem. Many of these are in the form of prolonged metaphors:

Beaux et sombres Soleils, qui d'vn feu vif et pur,
Enflammez tant d'esprits et consumez tant d'ames;
Astres clairs et brillans, dont le Celeste Azur,
Deuient par son esclat, vne source de flame,[137]

in this case, the blue eyes of a lady.

Another of Scudéry's non-Malherbian characteristics is his lack of restraint. Malherbe had used repetitions judiciously for some stunning effects, but Scudéry did not know how to limit himself:

---

[134] *Poésies diverses* (Paris: Courbé).

[135] Cited by Rousset, *La littérature*, p. 148.

[136] See, for instance, the description of Notre-Dame de la Garde. In addition to the many bad rhymes are those forever associated with one another. In a single passage, *flots* occurs several times, each time with *matelots*, as does *rocher* with *nocher*.

[137] *Poésies diverses*, p. 35.

Heureux, Doris, dans un séjour champêtre
Heureux celuy qui n'a sujet ni maistre!
Heureux, Doris, celuy qui comme vous
Peut, en repos, aller planter ses choux![138]

Malherbe had demanded realism, but in *Alaric*, "Parmy la pourriture, on voit groüiller les vers," and when Malherbe demanded a clear language understandable by all, he could not have meant the following:

Pourquoy veux-tu, ma farouche Isabelle,
Enfin m'occir et par ta course isnelle,
Toy dérobber de moy qui suy tes pas?
Je cherche un bien qui ne t'appauvrit pas,
Et tu voudrois l'avoir perdu, cruelle,
Longtemps y a.[139]

The fact that such archaic language may be well suited to a rondeau, an archaic form damned by Malherbe, does not remedy the situation.

And yet some passages of Scudéry are quite well done. Livet, in quoting some lines of *Alaric*, rightly considered them not only well crafted but having "une ampleur vraiment cornélienne."[140] Boileau made fun of the first line of this epic—"Je chante le Vainqueur des Vainqueurs de la Terre"—but only because it promised too much and delivered too little, admitting in a reluctant compliment that "ce vers est assez noble, et est peut-être le mieux tourné de tout son ouvrage."[141] As this indicates, the good lines are the exception, not the rule. This is just as true in the smaller genres. Scudéry's imitation of Tristan's "La belle esclave Maure," his "La belle Egiptienne," is quite successful:

Sombre divinité, de qui la splendeur noire
Brille de feux obscurs, qui peuvent tout brusler;
Le neige n'a plus rien qui te puisse égaller,
Et l'ebene aujourd'huy l'emporte sur l'ivoire.[142]

[138] Ibid., p. 254; see also pp. 118, 275.
[139] Ibid., p. 227.
[140] *Précieux et précieuses* (Paris: Didier, 1859), p. 252.
[141] *Œuvres complètes*, p. 497.
[142] *Œuvres diverses*, p. 59.

And another imitative poem, his "Pour une inconstante," is fittingly constructed:

> *Elle aime, et n'aime plus, et puis elle aime encore,*
> *La volage beauté que je sers constamment;*
> *L'on voit ma fermeté; l'on voit son changement;*
> *Et nous aurions besoin, elle et moy, d'ellebore.*[143]

Unfortunately, most of these attempts to equal Tristan are as abortive as those he made to equal Corneille:

> *Mille, et mille surgeons, et fiers, et courroussez,*
> *Font voir de la colere à leur beauté meslée;*
> *Ils s'eslancent en l'air, de leur source gelée,*
> *Et retombent apres, l'un sur l'autre entassez.*[144]

From the moving dead to the watery jets, from rhymes such as *Goths-propos* to technical and archaic terms, Scudéry not only was an anachronism in 1650, but had obviously not, some critics notwithstanding, gone to the school of Malherbe.

François Charpentier, some twenty years Scudéry's junior, was no less quarrelsome. In fact, many of his surviving poems are diatribes leveled against his contemporaries. He appointed himself the mouthpiece of the Academy in its fight with Furetière and, as a partisan of Perrault, had a long quarrel with Boileau, who to no one's surprise got the best of his adversary. The factums leveled at Furetière were written by many poets, most of whom remain anonymous, and their style is far from studied or polished.[145] Still, the Academy could not have been very proud of contributions by Charpentier such as:

> *Quand un Corps illustre te chasse,*
> *Se déchargeant de toi comme d'un sale étron,*
> *Pour en mieux nettoyer la place,*

---

[143] Ibid., p. 53.

[144] Ibid., p. 2.

[145] Antoine Furetière, *Recueil des factums* (Paris: Poulet-Malassis et de Broise, 1858), 2:233 ff.

Que tu lui fais de bonne grace
Offrir Epigramme et Factum.[146]

His much longer "Desaveu fait par les Muses, du placet au Roi sous leur nom par Furetiere" is no better, being written in stanzas whose length is determined solely by the thought and often containing but a single sentence. The first sentence, of twelve octosyllabic lines, contains unbalanced lines, enjambments, cacophony, everything except a decent rhyme. This, in fact, is characteristic of the entire poem:

Ny ne sera qu'un embrion
Décharné, sans force et sans nom.[147]

The first sentence of "Le disné du 22e janvier 1656" is twenty lines long with a majority of the rhymes lacking the proper *consonne d'appui* and many of the rest being facile.[148] His *stances* "De mon esprit asseurément" contain two stanzas, one of six and one of seven lines, neither having a single break, and with rhymes that are uniformly bad.[149] The rhyme schemes range from the barely orthodox to a ridiculous *a a b c c d d*.[150] Is it any wonder that Boileau, who, it must be admitted, was perhaps motivated by personal animosity as well as by literary judgment, compared his work to the Augean stables?[151] In an un-Malherbian sestet to be put under his own portrait, Charpentier asserted:

Le rang où je suis parvenu,
N'est pas d'un fort grand revenu,
Un doyen de l'Académie
Fait peu craindre son Tribunal:
Pour être estimé dans la vie
Il faut pouvoir faire du mal.[152]

[146] Ibid., p. 264.
[147] Ibid., p. 288.
[148] Etienne Martin de Pinchesne, *La chronique des chapons et des gélinottes du Mans* (Paris: Leclerc, 1907), pp. 35–39.
[149] Ibid., p. 152.
[150] Ibid., p. 154.
[151] See Boileau, *Œuvres complètes*, pp. 611, 678, 864–65.
[152] Lachèvre, *Bibliographie*, 3:256.

It may well be that Charpentier succeeded in doing some harm in the world of letters, but certainly not because of his "Tribunal."

After a five-year hiatus, the Academy elected another poet into its membership, and in the fifteen years that followed it added a dozen more, but the harvest was meager nevertheless, with very little talent involved. What interests us here, however, is not the merit of these poets but whether or not they tended to follow a doctrine or even an example.

Cotin was, in every respect, an *attardé*. He had frequented many of the salons for some time and was more than fifty years old when he was finally allowed to become an Academician in 1655. Although he would not have admitted it, he was "le plus précieux de nos petits poètes," one for whom poetry was "un jeu, où l'art compte plus que l'inspiration,"[153] a not totally un-Malherbian concept. Chapelain thought his to be a "plume forte et polie," with great purity, though only rarely endowed with any force.[154]

Cotin's earliest production had little to recommend it, but *La Jérusalem désolée* (1634), while not always free of *galimatias*, is quite good as far as rhyme, rhythm, and structure are concerned:

> *De tes vives clartés on ne voit plus que l'ombre;*
> *Où sont tes citoyens dont l'éclat et le nombre*
> *S'égalaient aux flambeaux qui brillent dans les cieux?*
> *Les filles ont suivi le trépas de leurs mères,*
> *Les enfants son liés aux chaînes de leurs pères,*
> *Et l'effroi seulement habite dans ces lieux.*[155]

This Jeremiac tone, unfortunately, was not suited to the *précieux* salons which he then began to frequent. At Rambouillet, it will be remembered, cleverness was prized above all, and striking images and ingenious antitheses were the hallmark of the successful poet. Cotin played the game as well as any, and in so doing forever left behind any Malherbian tendency he might have had. In his *Œuvres meslées*[156] he is witty, so

---

[153] Bray, *Anthologie*, p. 157.
[154] *Opuscules critiques*, pp. 359, 469, 472.
[155] Livet, *Précieux et précieuses*, p. 117.
[156] (Paris: Sommaville, 1659).

much so in fact that, carried away by the game, he frequently becomes obscure. Phrases such as "bouche d'enfer qui réduit tout en poudre" to designate a firecracker,[157] ambiguous inversions, and padding are very frequent. To make matters worse, one of the most popular games was that of the poetic enigma, and Cotin became its uncontested champion. While the vogue lasted it made his fortune; when he survived it, he became fair game for Boileau and Molière.

In his later years, Cotin made some definite attempts to correct his earlier lapses in a trend that must be considered Malherbian. This does not mean that he achieved a high level of art, but the attempt was there nevertheless. In the original version of the "Satire des Satires" (1668) there had been many hiatuses such as "une Elégie, un Sonnet, un Sixain," or the even less debatable "copie un,"[158] which the poet corrected in the later version, though occasional new ones crept in. He constantly improved his rhymes, though a good number of facile ones or some lacking the homophony of the *consonne d'appui* remained. His "Magdeleine," of some 600 alexandrines, has good caesuras and few enjambments, and could well be considered one of the more Malherbian poems not only of the collection[159] but of the period. Recalling his *Jérusalem désolée*, the "Imitation de Jérémie" is, in Cotin's own words, "ni version, ni paraphrase; mais un pur ouvrage de mon esprit" which, in view of the subject, he tried to endow with "magnificence et pompe . . . sans galimatias et sans obscurité."[160] This intention was obviously in keeping with the precepts of Malherbe. The 101 alexandrine sestets of the "Imitation" use the conventional *a a b c c b* scheme which, while not popular with Malherbe, had been used by him. The breaks are almost all 3–3, the rhymes quite rich, and the tone, as can be seen by two typical lines, is as promised:

> *Infortuné témoin des misères publiques,*
> *Je vois de toutes parts nos palais magnifiques.*[161]

Unfortunately, in this poem as in all the rest, Cotin quickly bores. He had wanted to touch, to "faire éclater la douleur," and he failed. Obscure in

---

[157] Ibid., p. 3.
[158] Lachèvre, *Bibliographie*, 3:274–75.
[159] *Poésies chrestiennes* (Paris: Le Petit, 1668).
[160] Ibid., pp. 61–64.
[161] Ibid., p. 65.

his cerebral witticisms, insipid in his personal lyricism, and boring in his religious outbursts, Cotin was doomed to await the barbs of the satirists and the laughter of the *parterre.*

Two other poets must be considered here along with Cotin, for they were the last of their generation to be admitted to the Academy: La Mesnardière, born in 1610 and elected in 1655, and Saint-Aignan, the famous duke, also born in 1610 and elected in 1663.

Saint-Aignan obviously knew the rules and took them seriously enough to compete in the Caen Palinod of 1667, where his ode won first prize, but he always wished to give the impression of a great lord who amused himself with such trifling games, cultivating a studied negligence that was much admired. As a result, most of his meager production is in the form of madrigals that defy analysis: the number of lines and the heterometry, as should be expected, are totally free of any set of rules, enjambments are many, and the rhymes are far from perfect.[162] Much the same could be said for his ballad "A Caution tous ne sont pas sujets," the answer to an analogous poem by Mme Deshoulières. It is composed of four nine-line stanzas, *a b a b b c d d c,* and a seven-line *envoi,* *a a b c b b c,* and is replete with deliberate archaisms, enjambments, inversions, and other faults:

> *Jeunes beautez qui tendez vos filets,*
> *Chassez bien loin cette engeance maudite*
> *De jouvenceaux, quand prés des beaux objets*
> *D'estre indolent chacun se felicite.*[163]

This poem led to a countercharge and a counterreply, all delightfully gallant jousting but hardly Malherbian in any way. Saint-Aignan is interesting to us here only insofar as he indicates, by his very presence in the Academy, that Malherbe was not always heeded. His election was undoubtedly based on criteria other than literary, just as these same factors undoubtedly made him the influential man he was.

Chronologically, La Mesnardière should be considered as the last of these *attardés,* and, in the preface of his *Poésies,* he indeed tells us that

---

[162] See the two madrigals in Pinchesne, *Chronique des chapons,* pp. 202, 205.

[163] Antoinette Deshoulières, *Poésies* (Paris: Mabre-Cramoisy, 1688), p. 60.

most of his works had been written much earlier. His concepts of poetry, spelled out in that preface, are a strange mixture of Ronsard and Boileau: "Tous les autres ouvrages de l'esprit se peuvent à la fin rendre excellents par le travail. Cette seule espèce [poetry] ne s'acquiert point par lui seul. Quelque châtiée que soit la poésie qui ne coule point de source, elle a toujours quelque chose de dur, de contraint, d'inégal, de froid et de languissant, à l'oreille des vrais enfants du Parnasse." But he considers "Ordre et Symmétrie" of equal importance: "L'artifice, qui est une pièce de l'entendement, conduit et l'imagination et le génie."

In practice, La Mesnardière wrote in every conceivable form, but only in a few unsuccessful eclogues, in alexandrine *rimes plates*, did he achieve any kind of linear regularity. In most of his works there is a "hostilité aux tracés linéaires, le refus de simplifier en éliminant."[164] In his "galanteries," his style is "mol et étendu,"[165] and the content invariably *fade*:

> *Amour, c'était bien ma créance*
> *Que les charmes de sa présence*
> *Conduiraient mes esprits de l'extase au tombeau.*
> *N'accusons point ses yeux, notre sort est trop beau;*[166]

and so on, with little relief. Unfortunately, some of the composers of the time, in setting this type of poem to music, made matters even worse. "Plaignez la rigueur de mon sort" originally read as follows:

> *Plaignez la rigueur de mon sort,*
> *Beaux yeux qui le voyez, et qui devez le plaindre.*
> *N'est-ce pas un cruel effort,*
> *Que mesme en soupirant il faille se contraindre.*
> *Et souffrir jusques à la mort*
> *La douleur de languir et la peine de feindre?*

Boesset, setting this stanza to music, put in repeats that only worsened the insipidity:

[164] Rousset, *La littérature*, p. 190.
[165] Chapelain, *Opuscules critiques*, p. 360.
[166] *Poésies* (Paris: Sommaville, 1656), p. 12.

Et souffrir et souffrir jusques . . .
La douleur, la douleur de languir, de languir . . .[167]

It should be noted that this form (with or without Boesset) was never used by Malherbe, a statement that holds true for most of La Mesnardière's choices.[168] At the other extreme, La Mesnardière used standard, though not necessarily Malherbian, forms, such as alexandrine *vers suivis*, for his many attempts at elevation. Unfortunately, "quand il se veut élever, il dégénère en obscurité et ne fait paraître que de beaux mots qui ne font que sonner et ne signifient rien."[169] Thus "Hymne de la Nature" is so obscure that even the poet himself deemed it necessary to add marginal notes.[170]

With all his limitations, La Mesnardière is perhaps at his best in his descriptive poems. "Le soleil couchant,"[171] the most famous of these, is reminiscent of the "paintings" of Tristan and of Saint-Amant, both in form and in content:

> *La pourpre qui luit soûs ses pas,*
> *En l'air s'escarte en mille pointes,*
> *Où parfois deux couleurs sont jointes,*
> *Et parfois ne se joignent pas.*

The key word is used by the poet himself:

> *. . . admirez la nüance*
> *De ce jaune clair, qui s'avance*
> *Soûs cet incarnat velouté.*

Throughout this poem, there is a shimmering, sparkling quality that defies linearity, as can be seen in the second quotation. Colors are forever changing, shapes losing their definition. The bad rhymes and enjamb-

---

[167] Verchaly, *Airs de cour*, pp. 198–99.
[168] "Follette," for example, is written in seven-line stanzas combining six octosyllabics and one alexandrine in an *a a b c b b c* rhyme scheme.
[169] Chapelain, *Opuscules critiques*, p. 360.
[170] *Poésies*, pp. 89–109.
[171] Ibid., pp. 155 ff.

ments, such as the ones illustrated here, are obviously not the only aspects of the work that are not Malherbian. La Mesnardière was indeed of the generation of Saint-Amant, though he certainly lacked his genius.

Gilles Boileau, elected in 1659, is most difficult to consider. Most critics from Chapelain on have decried his facility and his lack of control over his youthful exuberance. In truth, only a lack of discipline can explain lines such as "Au moment que je vous eus vue,"[172] or

> Ces quatre petits vers entrent dans votre chambre,
> Ces quatre petits vers vous donnent vos étrennes,
> Ces quatre petits vers vous demandent les miennes[173]

or nonsensical phrases such as "sans effort forcer," "traits de prudence," and "du faste insolent réprimer l'insolence."[174] It is also to this tendency that one may attribute some bad rhymes, for Gilles Boileau obviously had read Malherbe and been able to learn from him. Many critics have seized upon one of his drinking songs to show his lack of poetic talent:

> A quoi bon s'affliger tant
> Pour de l'argent?
> Le Tellier et Colbert
> Qui gouvernent la France
> Sont moins en assurance
> Que Boileau et Robert.[175]

But we must remember that, according to contemporary testimony, this was an impromptu composition. For many poems, some courtly songs in particular, Boileau chose forms that Malherbe had not, such as the 7–7–6–6–6–6 sestets of "Ah! que les yeux sont contens," but their inner coherence shows him to have been a careful craftsman when he was inclined to work. In these songs, the breaks are steady, rhythms regular, and rhymes good, and there are some very well-turned parallelisms, par-

---

[172] Allem, *Anthologie,* 2:285.
[173] Boileau, *Œuvres complètes,* p. 1030.
[174] Emile Magne, *Bibliographie générale des œuvres de Nicolas Boileau-Despréaux et de Gilles et Jacques Boileau* (Paris: Giraud-Badin, 1929), 2:318.
[175] Ibid., 2:313.

ticularly in "Je ne puis plus souffrir qu'Iris soit infidèle."[176] Here Gilles Boileau shows himself to be youthful and careless but not unaware of certain rules that Malherbe considered basic to good poetry. Unfortunately, he never lived to add discipline to his craft, and by the time his brother penned the *Art poétique,* Gilles was dead.

In the 1660s, the Academy added several poets to its ranks, most of whom have sunk into well-deserved oblivion. The next few paragraphs are meant as an attempt not to revive them but to look at their works to determine the extent to which they may or may not have been under the influence of Malherbe.

Segrais, if one judges by the number of his poems in the *recueils collectifs,* was quite popular, and Chapelain, who thought his prose mediocre, admired his poetry for its "génie, feu [et] douceur."[177] Segrais thought so highly of Malherbe that he had a monument erected to him engraved with the following:

> *Malherbe, de la France éternel ornement,*
> *Pour rendre hommage à ta mémoire*
> *Segrais enchanté de ta gloire*
> *Te consacre ce monument.*[178]

He repeatedly spoke of Malherbe as one of the glories of Caen, Normandy, and France, but these poems are never Malherbian:

> *Cette longue Cité qui, célèbre et superbe,*
> *Entre ses citoyens compte le grand Malherbe,*
> *Et qui peut-être encor (si je ne me déçoi)*
> *Pourra bien quelque jour se souvenir de moi.*

This city he describes in lines whose rhythmic originality would have made Malherbe shudder:

> *Quelques toits remassés vers cet endroit, où l'Orne*
> *Divise en deux canaux son eau paisible et morne,*

[176] Allem, *Anthologie,* 2:284.
[177] *Opuscules critiques,* p. 359.
[178] Lachèvre, *Bibliographie,* 2:353.

Sans ordre, sans hauteur, et se sentant encor
De la simplicité de l'heureux âge d'or,
Dont jusqu'alors ces lieux conservoient l'innocence
Composoient un objet sans aucune apparence.[179]

Segrais was, after Racan, *the* bucolic poet. "Que Segrais dans l'Eglogue en charme les forests," said Boileau,[180] and it is in the eclogue and the idyl that Segrais is at his best. These poems were written in alexandrine *vers suivis*, with frequently very long sentences loaded with expletives. The otherwise fairly good rhymes are marred by facility and a certain banality: *nous* always seems to rhyme with *vous*, *Orne* with *morne*, and this banality does not fail to pervade the content as well as the form:

> *Clarice aime mes vers, faisons-en pour Clarice,*
> *Qui peut rien refuser au beau sang d'Arténice?*
> *Le beau nom d'Arténice a volé jusqu'aux Cieux,*
> *Le beau nom de Clarice est aimé de nos Dieux.*[181]

The poet made some efforts to ameliorate some of his lines, but they were not successful, either in form or in content.[182] Ogier, in what is obviously an "éloge de commande" inserted in the works of Segrais, thought these eclogues were wonderful and that, their style "doux et facile" being perfectly suited to the subject, they should be taken as models of the form.[183] Fortunately, they were not.

In his sonnets and *stances*, Segrais knew how to be delightful, but with little care for what might be called the Malherbian doctrine. His "Stances sur un dégagement," inserted in the fourth Sercy *recueil* (1658), are replete with unbalanced lines such as "Faute d'espoir, enfin s'est esteint mon amour," and in a majority of the rhymes there is no homophony of the *consonne d'appui*. Many of these poems use forms totally

---

[179] Van Bever, *Poètes du terroir*, 3:460–61.
[180] *Œuvres complètes*, p. 184.
[181] Jean Regnault de Segrais, *Poésies* (Paris: Sommaville, 1661), p. 8.
[182] The BN copy has these manuscript efforts. See, for instance, the corrections on p. 4, which, if anything, make matters worse.
[183] *Poésies*, p. 51.

foreign to Malherbe: "Doux ruisseaux coulez sans violence" is in nine-syllable quatrains while the song "Depuis qu'à Philiste" combines two uneven lengths:

> Depuis qu'à Philiste
> Mon cœur j'engageai,
> Tantôt je suis triste,
> Tantôt je suis gai.
> Ainsi s'en vont mes amours
> Avecque mes plus beaux jours.[184]

These last two lines are the refrain of the song. The rhymes are typical. There seems to be, in fact, a marked liking for uneven lines in Segrais's "stances et vers irréguliers," as he called them.[185]

Segrais also wrote several odes, and here especially he is crushed by any comparison with Malherbe. His "Ode à M. Chapelain" (1646) is composed of twenty ten-line stanzas, 8–8–8–8–8–12–12–8–12–12, with varied breaks. His "Ode à M. Ménage" (1651) is composed of eighteen octosyllabic ten-line stanzas. The rhymes in both of these odes are barely satisfactory, but the basic flaw is that the tone is pedestrian, not very different from that of the pastoral poems. On the occasion of the battle of Mardik, he wrote an "Ode à M. le comte de Fiesque" of fifteen eight-line stanzas, 8–8–8–12–12–8–8–12, *a b b a c d d c,* a totally un-Malherbian form. The content speaks for itself:

> Futur ornement de l'histoire,
> Comte, qui suis tes grand Aïeux
> Dans le sentier laborieux
> Qui conduit les héros au temple de la gloire,
> De tes rares vertus je sens mon cœur charmé,
> Qui sans cesse me sollicite
> De consacrer à ton mérite
> Des Vers dignes du feu dont tu l'as consumé.[186]

---

[184] Allem, *Anthologie,* 2:238–39.
[185] *Poésies,* p. 213.
[186] Ibid., p. 204.

Jacques Cassagnes would be forgotten today were it not for Boileau's remark to the effect that there was plenty of elbow room at his sermons.[187] His poems were no better than his sermons, but more popular. Chapelain had great hopes for him and high praise,[188] and Colbert was instrumental in his getting a pension for his ode on Henry IV. Goujet, though not as enthusiastic as these two, spoke rather kindly of him, especially of his shorter *stances*,[189] about eleven of which still survive, thanks to the *recueils* of the day. They are invariably prosaic:

> *Roses, en qui je vois paraître*
> *Un éclat si vif et si doux,*
> *Vous mourrez bientôt: mais, peut-être,*
> *Je dois mourir plus tôt que vous.*[190]

The "Paroles chrétiennes," with an octosyllabic refrain particularly un-suited to the alexandrine couplets, are no better:

> *Seigneur, par votre amour, empêchez-nous de suivre*
> *Tous les autres objets qui nous pourraient charmer;*
> *Sans aimer on ne saurait vivre*
> *Ni bien vivre sans vous aimer.*[191]

In all fairness to Cassagnes, however, it must be said that his place in the Academy and in the general esteem was due to his odes. These are not lacking in majesty; their rhymes, except for some failings in the *consonne d'appui* and the rhyming of long and short sounds, are generally good; the variants[192] show that care was taken to remove a few cacophonic lines. Be that as it may, these odes are totally un-Malherbian; they are heavy and plodding, and much of this is due to the fact that Cassagnes chose forms which Malherbe had rejected for very good reasons. The 600

[187] Sat. III, *Œuvres complètes*, p. 21.
[188] *Opuscules critiques*, pp. 360–61.
[189] *Bibliothèque françoise*, 18:56.
[190] Allem, *Anthologie*, 2:310.
[191] Ibid., p. 311.
[192] Picard, *Poésie française*, pp. 223–32.

alexandrines of his ode on Henry IV, for instance, are arranged in *dizains* which, regardless of the varied breaks, are so heavy as to defy reading. The later "Ode sur la paix des Pyrénées" (1660) is in ten-line stanzas combining four octosyllabic lines with six alexandrines. The breaks here are much stronger (all but one of the twenty-eight stanzas are broken 4–6, and most of them have a good secondary 3–3 break) but they are detrimental, for they merely accentuate an already prosaic and heavy form. For his ten-line stanzas, Malherbe never used alexandrines alone, and combined them with octosyllabics only once, in a fragment dated 1596. He had obviously sensed what Cassagnes had not.

During these years, the Academy admitted several other writers of some merit in the realm of prose who also turned some of their efforts to poetry. Dangeau, the famous "journalist," occasionally amused himself with impromptus or ballet libretti;[193] Michel Le Clerc had many friends[194] and an impeccable prosody, but this did not keep the few odes he wrote from falling into immediate oblivion; Testu-Belval wrote several courtly songs which were set to music by Mollier, but the very nature of these works makes a valid comparison with those of Malherbe impossible; Paul Tallemant, during these years, wrote three poems, all dealing with the "Isle d'Amour," but all before his twenty-fourth birthday and all devoid of any prosodic discipline. Only Pellisson and Furetière deserve more than a passing word.[195]

Much of Pellisson's early poetry resulted from the assiduous court he paid the various *précieuses* of Paris, particularly Madeleine de Scudéry. As a result, it is always witty and refined, but seldom well-disciplined. The forms themselves vary, some having been used by Malherbe:

> *Qu'on en parle, et qu'on en gronde*
> *Chere Sapho, croyez-moi,*
> *Tout doit aimer dans le monde,*
> *C'est une commune loy.*[196]

---

[193] Edouard de Barthélemy, "Le Marquis de Dangeau, poëte," *RFr* 15 (1858–1859):54–60.

[194] Lachèvre, *Bibliographie,* 2:333.

[195] The dramatist Boyer was also admitted at that time, but he had only one poem to his credit, an ode consecrating the Peace of the Pyrénées.

[196] Cited by Fukui, *Raffinement précieux,* p. 284.

Most of them, however, can best be described as very free; note a typical example:

> *Adorable merveille*
> *De notre cour,*
> *Quoi que l'on me conseille,*
> *Je veux toujours*
> *Ne parler qu'à l'oreille*
> *De mon amour.*[197]

Supposedly, Mlle de Scudéry and Pellisson wrote to each other daily, and many of these letters contain poems typical of the bantering emitted by most of the faithful of the "Samedis," but they are of little interest to us here: the forms themselves, the rhyme scheme, the rhymes—none show any trace of discipline:

> *Aussitôt que je les vis*
> *Tous mes sens furent interdits:*
> *Elles étoient aussi fières que belles.*
> *Ce n'est pas sans raison; quelques-unes d'entr'elles*
> *Ont fait des coups bien hardis. . . .*[198]

While at the Bastille following Fouquet's demise, Pellisson wrote some serious poetry in various forms, most of them Malherbian. However, if the forms themselves can be considered orthodox, the execution cannot. The rhymes violate every rule, the sestets often lack syntactical breaks, and the lines are badly balanced. His prose earned him a seat at the Academy. His prosody did not earn him even a single comment from Boileau.

Furetière's poetic production is of an entirely different type, being devoted almost wholly to satiric works of varied length. Five long satires appeared in 1655, all "lâchement versifiées,"[199] some amplified for the 1664

---

[197] Mongrédien, *Madeleine de Scudéry*, p. 80.

[198] E. J. B. Rathery and Boutron, *Mlle de Scudéry* (Paris: Techener, 1873), p. 457.

[199] Goujet, *Bibliothèque françoise*, 18:259.

edition, but none really improved. The sentences tend to be very long and technical terms, especially for the sake of the rhyme, are plentiful, as are monosyllabic homonyms. The linearity is not to be believed:

> —*Je le sens, dis-je, assez.*—*Or il vous faudra prendre*
> *Souvent de la Ptisane, avec du Scolopendre.*[200]

The smaller satiric poems were no better, and got worse as time went on, especially as far as rhymes and hiatus were concerned.[201] The *Fables morales* were quite popular when they appeared (1671), but their *vers libres* are totally devoid of interest: their very nature makes them un-Malherbian, and their lack of life and genius makes any comparison with La Fontaine insulting:

> *Certain procès fut mis en arbitrage*
> *Qu'avaient le cygne et le corbeau*
> *Sur la beauté de leur plumage.*
> *Le cygne soutenait qu'il était le plus beau,*
> *Et que sa blancheur singulière*
> *Etait la première en valeur,*
> *Puisqu'elle avait l'éclat de la lumière*
> *Qui donne la naissance à toute autre couleur.*[202]

In short, whatever Furetière's influence may have been, in or out of the Academy, before or after his expulsion, it could not have advanced the cult of Malherbe in any way.

The same must be said of Bussy-Rabutin, whose "Maximes d'amour" were inserted into several *recueils* about the time of his election to the Academy, in 1665. These are very clever madrigals of very free form and facile rhyme. A few of them use forms and rhyme schemes that are Malherbian, but in view of their small number, this cannot be considered

---

[200] *Le roman bourgeois, suivi de satyres et de nouvelles allégoriques* (Paris: Club du Meilleur Livre, 1956), p. 247.

[201] See *Recueils des factums*, passim, but especially 2:242 ff., and Lachèvre, *Bibliographie*, 2:169.

[202] Allem, *Anthologie*, 2:165.

as anything but coincidence. The following will give an idea of the versification:

> *Quoi! serez-vous toujours contente?*
> *Ne vous plaindrez-vous point de moi?*
> *Ah! votre flamme, Iris, n'est pas fort violente,*
> *Car un grand amour nous tourmente,*
> *Et souvent sans raison nous donne de l'effroi.*
> *Enfin, l'extrême confiance*
> *Tient beaucoup de l'indifférence.*[203]

His Mazarinades are no better:

> *Si le roi venoit à mourir,*
> *Monsieur ne se pourroit tenir*
> *De dire, en chantant Libera:*
> *Alleluia!*[204]

These poems, like his epigrams, are nothing more than "fantaisies, rimées librement."[205]

In the last two years of this period, the Academy added two illustrious names to the list of its poets, Quinault and Perrault. But in each case there are negative factors as far as this study is concerned: Perrault's truly productive years had not yet come and Quinault's creativity was, for the most part, channeled elsewhere.

When Quinault was twenty-five, Chapelain considered him "un poète sans fond et sans art mais d'un beau naturel qui tourne bien les tendresses amoureuses."[206] Years later, Goujet was to report that "Lully . . . étoit charmé d'avoir trouvé un Poëte tel qu'il pouvoit le desire, qui avoit

---

[203] Roger de Bussy-Rabutin, *Histoire amoureuse des Gaules* (Paris: Jannet, 1856), 1:359.

[204] Cited by Jean Orieux, *Bussy-Rabutin, le libertin galant-homme* (Paris: Flammarion, 1958), p. 313.

[205] *Epigrammes inédites* (Paris: Sansot, 1904), p. 10.

[206] *Opuscules critiques*, p. 344.

une oreille délicate pour ne choisir que des paroles harmonieuses, . . . [qui] badinoit très-agréablement . . . [avec] beaucoup d'esprit et de délicatesse."[207] Etienne Gros, speaking of the libretti of Quinault, commented on their platitudes, commonplaces, and "mièvrerie."[208] These comments he also applied to the nondramatic poems, which, according to him, "ne méritent pas mieux qu'une simple mention," even in a volume entirely devoted to Quinault.[209] This poet, it must be kept in mind, was popular not only for his opera libretti but also for his songs. His four poems included in the *Recueil des plus beaux vers qui ont esté mis en chant*[210] had all been set to music by Lambert. In later years, he had some sixty songs published in the *recueils,* composers such as Lully, Lambert, and Le Camus being credited with the music.[211] What is one to make of such diverse public and critical opinions? The answer is really quite simple: Lully (and much of the public) was looking for words that would accompany his music without detracting from it. This is a far cry from the concept of lyricism or of the role of poetry advanced by either Malherbe, Chapelain, or Boileau. But, as Perrault so wisely saw, if Quinault had done what his critics were demanding, the results would have been disastrous: "On feroit des paroles que les Musiciens ne pourroient chanter, et que les auditeurs ne pourroient entendre." What Lully liked about Quinault was precisely his ability to "faire avec un certain nombre d'expressions ordinaires, et de pensées fort naturelles, tant d'ouvrages si beaux et si agreables et tous si differens les uns des autres."[212] Undeniably, Quinault's words are eminently singable, and that was the poet's main aim. But are they as flawless as Perrault suggests? Unfortunately, my own conclusion, in this respect at least, is much closer to that of Gros.

Fukui is right when he suggests that by the time Quinault wrote these songs, psychological interest had replaced the flashiness, the metaphors, the "images frappantes ou antithèses ingénieuses" of the baroque.[213]

---

[207] *Bibliothèque françoise,* 18:248–52.
[208] *Philippe Quinault* (Paris: Champion, 1926), p. 708.
[209] Ibid., p. xii.
[210] (Paris: Sercy, 1661).
[211] Lachèvre, *Bibliographie,* 3:494–96.
[212] *Parallèle,* 3:240–41.
[213] *Raffinement précieux,* p. 296.

The trouble here is that Quinault was no Racine, and that his psychological analysis was exceedingly shallow. Furthermore, his technique was frequently sloppy and his lines cacophonic and tortured:

> Quand ce qui nous plaist trop, ne sent point nostre peine
> Que pour toucher son cœur nostre tendresse est vaine;
>   Et qu'on voit que rien ne l'emeut:
>   Pour se venger de l'inhumaine,
> Doutez-vous si l'on doit aller jusqu'à la haine,
> Ha sans dépit on le doit, et le destin le veut;
>   Mais je ne sçay si l'on le peut.[214]

Obviously, neither the prosody nor the psychology of the above stanza is worthy of Perrault's praise, and one can readily imagine what Malherbe would have thought of it.

Whereas it is easy to dismiss Quinault as anything but Malherbian, it is not so easy to do the same for Charles Perrault. There is no doubt, as we shall see, that the bulk of this poet's production in the early years of his career was far from orthodox, but the subject—for the most part burlesque—must be considered. With the few examples of serious poetry produced in these early years, a generalization becomes impossible.

Perrault had a very high opinion, not only of Malherbe's talent, but of his influence. At the end of the century he spoke of him in these terms: "Son talent principal dans la Poësie Françoise, consistoit dans le tour qu'il donnoit aux Vers, que personne n'avoit connu avant luy, que tous les Poëtes qui sont venus ensuite, ont tasché d'imiter; mais où trés-peu sont parvenus. . . . Quoy qu'il en soit, la face de la Poësie changea entierement quand il vint au monde. Il fut reconnu le Maistre dés qu'il parut, et tous ceux qui se mesloient de ce bel Art n'avoient point de honte d'en recevoir des Leçons. La pluspart des regles qui s'observent aujourd'huy pour la belle versification, ont esté prises dans ses Ouvrages, dont les beaux endroits sont encore dans la bouche de tout le monde."[215] We have seen, I hope, that this opinion, though popular, is far from true, but what con-

---

[214] Cited, ibid., p. 296.
[215] Hommes illustres, 1:69–70.

cerns us here is the extent to which Perrault himself followed this master, particularly in his poetic début.

It is difficult to ascertain exactly what part Charles played in the writing of the family projects, "Les murs de Troye" and "L'Enéide burlesque," though it was undoubtedly a major part, especially in the final forms. Certainly the Perraults intended to belittle Antiquity, a fact which explains the profusion of words more fitting the "language des Halles" than that of Parnassus, and of constructions obviously taken from popular language:

> *Te feront partuot reconnaître*
> *Pour le valeureux Marcellus,*
> *Mais si valeureux que rien plus.*[216]

As Francis Bar has noted, be it as a convenience or another way to make the reader laugh, *commodité* or *bouffonnerie*, burlesque poets violated every rule of versification, and the Perraults were no exception: [ə] counting as a syllable (*musée* a trisyllabic) or being swallowed (*éprons*), archaisms, slang. In such a context, even rhymes become laughing matter:

> *Et sembloit avertir Gargare*
> *Et dire à ses bois: gare, gare.*[217]

An art is definitely involved here, a deliberate one, but not Malherbian for all that. Much the same can be said for the delightful stanzas which Charles Perrault wrote to Pinchesne in reply to a scolding by the latter. These two stanzas, one of sixteen and one of thirteen lines, are completely free in versification. Equally free are the poet's *précieux* attempts at eroticism:

> *Ni de deux rossignols l'un de l'autre jaloux*
> *Le concert agréable et doux;*

[216] Charles and Claude Perrault, "L'Enéide burlesque," RHLF 9 (1901): 142.

[217] Charles, Claude, and Nicolas Perrault, Les murs de Troye (Paris: Chamhoudry, 1653), p. 50.

Ni d'un cygne mourant la musique plaintive;
*   Ni le murmure d'une eau vive*
Qui roule en gazouillant sur de petits cailloux
*   N'ont point cette douceur naïve,*
L'oreille n'entend rien de si délicieux
Et telle est seulement la douceur infinie
Des airs qu'Apollon chante à la table des dieux,
*   Ou l'inconcevable harmonie*
*   Du juste mouvement des cieux.*[218]

Not even a correction of the whimsical punctuation would measurably help this stanza.

All these works, by their very nature, could be expected to defy orthodoxy. What of the more serious poems? Perrault, like all his colleagues, celebrated the Peace of the Pyrénées in an "Ode sur la Paix" which, in its outer form at least, is very Malherbian:

Les Nymphes effarouchées
Des tambours et des clairons,
Depuis si longtemps cachées
Sous l'écorce de leurs troncs,
Au lieu des aigres trompettes,
N'ayant plus que les musettes
Dont résonnent les hameaux,
De mousse et de fleurs parées,
Dansent toutes les soirées
Antour des sacrés ormeaux.[219]

Despite the choice of form, the rhyme scheme, and the rhymes themselves, all acceptable, the end product is far from Malherbian: the tortured sentences, the uneven rhythm, the most ordinary pastoral flavor, all are unsuited to the occasion. Perrault, however, could do better, and in "La peinture" his lines are as carefully crafted as if they were indeed an example of plasticity:

[218] Cited by André Hallays, *Les Perrault* (Paris: Perrin, 1926), p. 34.
[219] Ibid., p. 35.

Sur le mur opposé la lampe en ce moment
Marquait du beau garçon le visage charmant;
L'éblouissant rayon de sa vive lumière
Serrant de toutes parts l'ombre épaisse et grossière
Dans le juste contour d'un trait clair et subtil
En avait nettement dessiné le profil.
Surprise elle aperçoit l'image figurée,
Et se sentant alors par l'amour inspirée,
D'un poinçon par hasard sous ses doigts rencontré,
Sa main qui suit le trait par la lampe montré,
Arrête sur le mur promptement et sans peine
Du visage chéri la figure incertaine.[220]

From uncertain to definite, from mobile to fixed, is this "painting" not also the beginning of another transformation, one from baroque to classical? For some years, Perrault was to be silent, spending most of his time on the building of the Louvre, but his later poetry was to continue such a trend, and when, at the end of the century, he stated that "les vers ne sont qu'un ornement de la Poësie, tres-grand à la verité, mais ils ne sont point de son essence,"[221] had he not gone beyond the struggle between form and "essence" and, as a result, liberated himself from the yoke which, according to his own statement as well as that of Boileau, Malherbe had meant to impose? It would seem that, for Perrault at least, Malherbe was read and appreciated, that the lesson was then applied, in the serious poetry, at any rate, with increasing fidelity, but that no sooner was the "master" assimilated than he was *dépassé*.

What then was the position of the "cas Malherbe" at the Academy in the thirty years preceding the appearance of the *Art poétique*? In the early years, as we have seen, everyone admired him, or at least gave lip service to his cult. Only some, Perrault's statement notwithstanding, actually tried to imitate him. Aside from Maynard and Racan, these imitators were mediocre at best and, as Perrault said, failed in their attempts. The later years were very lean ones for the Academy. Of the older generation, the only remaining poet of any talent was Corneille, and the

---

[220] Ibid., p. 54.
[221] *Parallèle*, 3:148–49.

younger ones were inconsequential. Only in 1671, with the entrance of Perrault, did the Academy get that much-needed infusion of new blood, but his period of true productivity was not yet at hand. In one sense, then, old Corneille (and Chapelain, no doubt) along with this new-comer could be considered the embodiment of the Academy, regretting the good old days and waiting for a rebirth that was just around the corner. No one can deny that Boileau, recounting the advent of Malherbe, was historically correct. It may be, as Boileau put it, that Malherbe "enseigna le pouvoir," but, at the Academy at least, only a few re-calcitrant learners were taking notes.

Chapter Seven

'Attardés'

If one looks at the bibliography of *recueils collectifs* dealing with the thirty years that concern us here, it becomes apparent that the political situation was not the only unsettled one. To be sure, some famous salons, such as that of Mme de Rambouillet, continued, at least for the first decade, to draw the best poets to their *ruelles*, and the Academicians still poured out a flow of occasional poetry; but by and large, the literary climate must be considered as having been very much in a state of flux. Nowhere is this more obvious than in the works of those poets not tied to the Academy and its semiofficial patronage and who, reaching their maturity about the time of the *interregnum*, could neither entirely shake off the habits of the old days nor focus with clarity on the ideals that were about to be enunciated by the generation of Boileau. For these poets, "les grandes odes civiques, exploitées par l'école malherbienne, restent dans l'ombre."[1] Taking their place are facile poems of preciosity, of *badinage*, and, particulary during the unsettled years of the Fronde, a strong wave of burlesque poems.

As we saw in the previous chapter, some of the best poets at the Academy—Saint-Amant, Tristan, Perrault—indulged in burlesque verse but brought great skill to bear on these works. For the majority of burlesque poets yet to be discussed, such is not the case. While the *courriers* of Saint-Julien[2] may have some interest for the historian, no amount of analysis can turn them into poetry, and the gazette of Loret will never be considered anything but "de la prose mesurée et rimée."[3] This does not mean that all the burlesque poems written by men outside the Academy are artless. Some good poets writing in this vein had a certain awareness of rules of prosody, though the extent of their adherence to Malherbian principles and practice is another matter entirely.

According to M. I. Protzman, in his introduction to the *Illustres fous* of Charles Beys, that poet's "technique conforms in general to the principles of Malherbe."[4] Jean Marmier, on the other hand, claims that Beys "suit les maîtres du burlesque" in every way.[5] In my opinion, the truth is somewhere in between. To be sure, the language of Beys is as coarse, as replete with anachronisms, orthographic fantasies, and even inventions, as any. The general impression, however, is one of *badinage* more than burlesque, as seen in the *Odes d'Horace,* or in this drinking song:

> *Amis enivrons nous du vin d'Espagne en France,*
> *Il n'est pas bon dessus les lieux.*
> *Icy nous le buvons avec plus d'asseurance*
> *Qu'on ne boit le nectar à la table des dieux.*
> *Ne perdons point de temps à dire toppe et masse*
> *Laissons Boire GASTON, il revient de la chasse.*[6]

Of Beys's versification the verdict must remain very mixed. His rhymes are generally good, though with numerous exceptions, almost all dealing with the *consonne d'appui,* monosyllabic homophones, and long-short sound rhymes (*âmes-flames, ame-femme*). Enjambments are relatively few, but obvious:

> *Son soupçon se descouvre, et cette deffiance*
> *Sert, pour le mieux tromper, aux autres de science.*[7]

There are many *chevilles,* but they are used for the most part deliberately in order to achieve a certain effect, and Beys is quite proud of them.[8] Where the actual choice of forms is concerned, the verdict is far less ambiv-

---

[1] Jean Marmier, *Horace en France au XVIIe siècle* (Paris: Presses Universitaires de France, 1962), p. 213.

[2] *Les courriers de la Fronde* (Paris: Jannet, 1857).

[3] Goujet, *Bibliothèque françoise,* 17:117. Most of the Mazarinades, gazettes, and *courriers* are not only burlesque but so totally devoid of craftsmanship that they need not be discussed here.

[4] (Baltimore: Johns Hopkins University Press, 1942), p. 36.

[5] *Horace en France,* p. 238.

[6] Verchaly, *Airs de cour,* p. 176.

[7] Fleuret and Perceau, *Satires françaises,* 2:6.

[8] *Les odes d'Horace* (Avignon: Aubanel, 1963), p. 36.

alent. The thirty-eight *Odes d'Horace* (adaptations, not translations, therefore allowing Beys complete freedom as to form) use twenty-one different forms, only three of which can be found in Malherbe, octosyllabic stanzas of six, eight, and ten lines. These three forms account for ten odes, but when the rhyme schemes are considered, the number is reduced to six. Most of these are so capriciously divided as to be anything but orthodox stanzas. If one considers not only the choice of meters and the rhyme schemes but division of stanzas as well, only odes 2 and 35 meet even the least rigorous application of Malherbian modes, a small percentage indeed.

Etienne Martin de Pinchesne, nephew of Voiture, was capable of good rhymes even in his lightest verse:

> *La Déesse dont je t'écris*
> *Est une Vénus de Paris,*
> *Plus charmante que celle*
> *Qui fut le chef d'œuvre d'Apelle.*[9]

In a mock-heroic ode to Mlles Melson in heptasyllabic ten-line stanzas, he carefully maintained 4–6 breaks of varying degrees of strength throughout. Unfortunately that poem, like the one already quoted, does not show the best of linear compositions:

> *Pour voir se mes Paralelles*
> *Y sont bons, ou sont mauvais*
>
> . . . .
>
> *Et que ce que l'on admire*
> *De près, . . .*[10]

In all of his works, be they religious or bantering, Pinchesne sought a "beauté naturelle et naïve," remaining faithful to "un bon nombre de moyens d'expression qui avaient fait fureur trente ans plus tôt," with results that are often "rocailleux et rudes, négligés et incorrects."[11] In his

---

[9] Cited by Paul d'Estrée, "Une académie bachique au XVIIe siècle," *RHLF* 2 (1895):508.

[10] Lachèvre, *Bibliographie*, 3:396.

[11] Leblanc, *Paraphrases*, p. 245.

serious poetry, he was unable to maintain an elevated tone; the lapses are made even more apparent by the "rocailleux" lines:

> J'en voy degenerer mon sang en pourriture,
> Mon corps n'est presque plus qu'os, que corruption:
> Mais pour voler au Ciel sans vieillir dans l'ordure
> Seigneur, vienne ta Grace, et ta sainte onction.[12]

Such juxtapositions of the sublime and the trivial not only were out of date when they were written (ca. 1670), but had already been relegated to literary limbo by Malherbe.

Pinchesne's most famous work, *La chronique des chapons et des gélinottes du Mans,* is full of delightful poetry, much of it worthy of Voiture, none recalling Malherbe. True, there are some stanzas of standard lengths (four, six, eight, or ten lines), almost all of which are octosyllabic, with a few also including alexandrines. True also, there are four alexandrine sonnets with an orthodox rhyme scheme. That, however, is the full extent of Pinchesne's orthodoxy. Every conceivable rhyme scheme is represented in these stanzas, some poems having more than one. Breaks are varied, with many stanzas, including *dizains,* having none. Add to this the fact that these "standard" stanzas are in a small minority, surrounded by stanzas of five, seven, or eleven or more lines, isometric or wildly heterometric, and by some poems that are entirely free. As for the rhymes themselves, proper nouns and verbs are omnipresent, compound words rhyme with their simple form, long sounds with short ones, synaereses with diaereses. Obvious pairs (*bouche-touche*) tend to recur, and the *consonne d'appui* is frequently so unsatisfactory that the result is more an assonance than a rhyme. In short, Pinchesne had obviously come into contact with Malherbe's rules but chose to disregard them, with only rare "lapses" into orthodoxy.

Whereas in Beys and Pinchesne the relaxing of discipline led merely to the further degeneration of an already weak talent, such was not always the case. Dalibray, Scarron, Dassoucy, and in a lesser way Cyrano, Blot L'Eglise, and Le Petit had genuine though irregular and undisciplined talent. What Nodier said of Cyrano in 1838 is valid for all of

[12] Ibid., p. 246.

these: "C'étoit un talent irrégulier, inégal, capricieux, confus, répré-
hensible sur une multitude de points; mais c'étoit un talent de mouvement
et d'invention."[13]

Claude Le Petit and Blot L'Eglise were two of a kind, but while the
latter, even with Gaston d'Orléans's protection, decided to keep his muse
in check while Richelieu lived, Le Petit gave full vent to his at a time
when the central power was once again firmly established. As a result,
the early poems of Blot have disappeared, but he lived to delight his
master with his later songs. Le Petit died for having sung too late.

The verse forms of Blot range from relatively orthodox octosyllabic
sestets, cut 3–3, *a a b c b c*, to stanzas such as:

> *Mazarin, ce bourgeron,*
> *De Paris chasse les c. . . :*
> *C'est un renégat*
> *De les avoir en haine;*
> *Il n'eust jamais esté qu'un fat*
> *Sans celuy de la Reyne.*
> *Lon la*
> *Sans celuy de la Reyne.*[14]

These nine lines use five different meters. On the other hand, the rhymes
are quite good, unusually so for Blot. "A la santé de nos amis" has five
rhymes in *-mis*, three of which are *amis*. Long sounds rhyme with short
ones, and this is frequently made worse by inner rhymes:

> *Dieu me fasse tousjours la grâce*
> *D'avoir du bon vin à la glace.*[15]

It goes without saying that in this type of poem enjambments abound and
the stanzas are broken in every way imaginable.

Claude Le Petit, as can be seen by titles such as "Stances irrégulières,"

[13] Charles Nodier, "Cyrano de Bergerac," *BBB* 3 (1838): 344–45.
[14] Claude de Chouvigny, Baron de Blot L'Eglise, *Les chansons libertines*
(Paris: Champion, 1919), p. 19.
[15] Ibid., p. 8.

was no more troubled by metrical discipline than Blot. There is no evidence of careful craftsmanship in either the many *livraisons* of *La muse de la cour* or the light verses that are sprinkled throughout *L'heure du berger;* witness these two lines of the sonnet "A moy-mesme":

> *En vain on joint la force avecque l'industrie,*
> *La force et l'industrie y ploient tour à tour.*[16]

His *Bordel des muses,* to no one's surprise, is the same, and the first part of its "Paris ridicule" begins with:

> *Loing d'icy, Muse serieuse,*
> *Va-t'en chercher quelqu'autre employ!*
> *Je n'ay aucun besoin de toy.*[17]

Truer words were never spoken.

The poetic production of Cyrano de Bergerac was probably quite large but he published only a small fragment of it,[18] a regrettable fact, for in the few examples that remain he demonstrates a very firm grasp of the art. Four of the eight poems published by Lachèvre are carelessly done liminary poems for the works of friends, ranging from a banal *huitain* for Dassoucy to a purposefully burlesque rondeau for Le Vayer de Boutigny's *Le Grand Selim,* whose subject and language might have inspired Molière's *turqueries:*

> *Tant d'amitié qu'à moy toy fais paroistre:*
> *Escoute moy donc toy louer grandement.*[19]

The other four poems deserve closer examination. One of them, the famous "Ministre d'état flambé," like most Mazarinades, fails to demonstrate great craftsmanship. Written in octosyllabic seven-line stanzas, it has varied breaks and the rhymes are not always satisfactory (lack of *consonne*

---

[16] *Les œuvres libertines* (Geneva: Slatkine, 1968), p. 55.

[17] Ibid., p. 113.

[18] Georges Mongrédien, *Cyrano de Bergerac* (Paris: Berger-Levrault, 1964), p. 47.

[19] *Œuvres libertines* (Paris: Champion, 1921), 1:xlix.

d'appui, facile rhymes: *Vendredy-Samedy-Jeudy*), some with unfortunate echoes:

> *Ha! ha! je vous tiens, Mazarin,*
> *Esprit malin de nostre France.*[20]

"La maladie," on the other hand, although far from serious, is written in octosyllabic *dizains, a b a b c c d e e d,* all cut 4–6, with very regular versification and only an occasional *consonne d'appui* failing to conform to otherwise perfect rhymes. There remain two sonnets, both alexandrine, both with an *a b b a . . . d e d e* scheme, whose rhymes are marred only once, by a *jour-séjour* lapse.[21] These three poems, in other words, are quite Malherbian in every respect, with but one departure, a deliberate freeing from linearity to give the sonnet a very fortunate élan by breaking the shackles of line and stanza:

> *Effroyables Autheurs de nos calamitez,*
> *Ennemis de la paix qu'on nous faisoit attendre,*
> *Superbes criminels qu'on ne peut plus deffendre*
> *Des maux que nous souffrons, et que vous méritez,*
>
> *Quels désordres nouveaux aviez-vous méditez?*[22]

In a writer known principally for his prose and only occasionally for his "libertine" poetry, this is indeed a pleasant surprise.

The same cannot be said of Charles Dassoucy. Even when addressing the king he keeps tongue in cheek and refuses to bow to convention:

> *Grand Roi, l'honneur de l'Univers,*
> *Vous ressouvient-il de ma Lyre,*
> *Vous ressouvient-il de mes vers,*
> *Qui tant de fois vous ont fait rire,*
> *Quand plus beau que le Dieu du jour,*
> *Couché, vous me faisiez redire*

[20] Ibid., 2:238.
[21] Ibid., 1:lxxxix.
[22] Ibid., p. lxxiv.

Mes chansons, et me faisiez lire
Mes vers aux yeux de votre cour?[23]

This is typical of all his works. In his burlesque poems the vocabulary is frankly suited to the cause:

Arrestez, ô Nymphe follette,
En faveur de jambe mollette
De Phebus le Dieu Lasdaller.[24]

Inversions often verge on the grotesque: "Neuf collets blancs aux muses neuf."[25] Enjambments in such poetry can be even more violent than the above:

Ainsi le beau Iuppin qui la
Voit. . . .[26]

As for the rhyme, he simply made fun of it:

Et l'honneur de notre siècle

. . . .

Qui pourra rimer en yecle.[27]

His heterometric combinations are such that "il en est qui peuvent lasser par recherche systématique de la virtuosité."[28] He frequently indulged in out-and-out nonsense, compounding the felony, as in this case, by having the thought straddle two stanzas:

Oyseaux de nuit, poussés vos tristes hurlemens,
Volez de tous costez sur l'aisle des hibous.[29]

---

[23] Goujet, *Bibliothèque françoise*, 18:30.

[24] *L'Ovide en belle humeur* (Paris: Sommaville, 1653), p. 105.

[25] Ibid., p. 101. For further examples, see Bar, *Genre burlesque*, pp. 321–23.

[26] *L'Ovide*, p. 142.

[27] Cited by Bar, *Genre burlesque*, p. 335.

[28] Ibid., p. 338.

[29] *Poésies et lettres* (Paris: Chamhoudry, 1653), p. 99.

These lines, like so many of Dassoucy, are also badly cut, adding to the chaos created by the breakdown of the stanzas, a far cry from the results achieved by Cyrano. Is it any surprise then that even in his most serious poetry Dassoucy allowed countless enjambments, padding, and bad rhymes to occur?[30]

The near-total of Scarron's poetic production falls within the realm of the burlesque and, as such, needs little discussion here. In his *Gazette* he is no more hampered by stylistics than Saint-Julien or Loret:

> *Quoy, que moy-mesme j'eusse crû*
> *Qu'au grand jamais, vous n'eussiez pû*
> *Faire un objet digne d'envie*
> *D'un homme ennuyé de la vie.*[31]

The rhymes in all of his burlesque poems break every rule, and the vocabulary, the syntax, the choice of forms follow suit. For verification, one need only point to the "Epistre à Mr. Sarazin," which uses three-beat lines, since short lines were considered ideal for comic effects, or to the "Epitalame du comte de Tessé et de Madamoiselle de Laverdin," surely the epitome of irregularity.[32] The care he bestowed on some of these poems is made manifest by the last line of one of them: "Ne vous y fiez . . . Foin! mon Sonnet finit mal."[33]

Scarron was seldom if ever really serious, but there are some forty poems for which the word "burlesque" would be inappropriate. Nevertheless, even in these, little suggests Malherbian influence. While there are some isometric quatrains, they are more than matched by heterometric ones, never in a combination that can be found in Malherbe. Of the fifteen poems in sestets, only one (octosyllabic *a a b c b c*) duplicates a Malherbian example, and many of the heterometric poems are trimetric, a rarity with most other poets. All the *huitains* are heterometric, whereas Malherbe used only isometric ones. The only *dizain* is hexasyllabic, the sonnets use an *e e d* scheme as often as the standard *e d e* one, and there

---

[30] See, for example, Goujet, *Bibliothèque françoise*, 18:31.

[31] Frédéric Lachèvre, *Un point obscur de la vie de Scarron: Scarron et sa Gazette burlesque* (Paris: Giraud-Badin, 1929), p. 55.

[32] *Poésies diverses* (Paris: Didier, 1947–1961), 1:55–59, 301–04.

[33] Ibid., 2:142.

are also stanzas of five, seven, twelve, and fourteen lines, none of which, of course, can be found in Malherbe. As for the rhymes, every imaginable rule is broken: words rhyme with themselves or their derivatives, long sounds with short ones, diaereses with synaereses, and so on. Entire lines are frequently unabashed padding:

> *Par l'injure des ans vous êtes abolis,*
> *Ou du moins la plûpart vous êtes démolis.*[34]

In regard to the linearity, it is obvious that most of the trimetrical poems are intrinsically bad, but even the isometric poems fail all too frequently:

> *Mais, puisque nostre Roy veut bien qu'on désupprime*
> *Son pere, qui faillit. . . .*[35]

That the songs should suffer is perhaps natural, but less so the sonnets and even the odes.[36] To put it simply, at no time was Scarron ever Malherbian.

To be equally direct, Charles Vion de Dalibray was of the same caliber, an avowed foe of overzealous craftsmanship: "Pour ce qui est de l'affectation de science dont i'ay parlé, c'est vn defaut si veritable en cette Poësie, que de grands Maistres l'ont condamnée iusques dans les Poëmes Heroïques." Pointing out that even Malherbe and Maynard occasionally wrote "irregular" sonnets, he adds, "Cette liberté s'estend tous les iours dauantage dans la Poësie, et nous fait esperer, que moins nous serons retenus par l'art; et plus les choses que nous produirons, s'en trouueront belles et naturelles."[37] There is much in these statements that could be considered akin to what E. B. O. Borgerhoff has rightly called "the freedom of French classicism," but it is hardly Malherbian. Thus it is

---

[34] Georges Margouliès, "Scarron et Lope de Vega," *RLC* 8 (1928): 511–12. This poem is imitative of a Spanish one, but, as the article from which it is cited amply demonstrates, the faults are clearly Scarron's. For an analogous treatment of a poem by Gongora, see idem, "Scarron sonnettiste et ses modèles espagnols," *RLC* 13 (1933): 137–38.

[35] *Poésies diverses*, 1:9.

[36] For an example of songs, see ibid., 2:155. For sonnets or odes, see ibid., 2:88, 93, 306.

[37] "Observations sur le sonnet," *Œuvres poétiques* (Paris: Sommaville, 1653), pp. 15–24.

all the more surprising to find Maurice Cauchie attempting to demonstrate Dalibray's "perfection de forme" by quoting a sonnet that boasts a passage such as "Chez elle, elle est malade" and an *a b a b a'b'a'b'* rhyme scheme, and another with rhymes such as *donnois-doigts-quelquefois-loix, decrie-recrie;* and speaking finally of this "merveille":

> *Je fus hyer, chere Silvie,*
> *Pour vous rendre un de ces devoirs*
> *Que je vay rendre tous les soirs*
> *Et mesme au peril de ma vie.*
>
> *Mais en vain: je perdis mes pas,*
> *Car j'appris que, cette soirée,*
> *On ne voyait point vos appas*
> *Et que vous estiez retirée.*[38]

The real "marvel" is that the tercets are still worse.

In fact, it is almost impossible to classify Dalibray's form: the first five sonnets of the van Bever edition[39] illustrate four different rhyme schemes, none orthodox, and the rest of the sonnets keep pace. One sonnet is dialogued and one is heterometric, combining lines of eight and six syllables. Although most of the quatrains are octosyllabic, some are alexandrine, and quite a few are heterometric, with every rhyme scheme well represented. In the sestets, again, most are octosyllabic with almost all the rest heterometric. In these, as in the quatrains, none of the heterometric combinations Dalibray used can be found in Malherbe; in some cases, this should not surprise: one poem has four different meters and another, of two sestets, uses two different combinations.[40] In these poems, as in all the others, in fact, every imaginable rhyme scheme and break is used, making a meaningful classification all but impossible. Typical of this free spirit is the following heterometric *huitain:*

> *Toy que je voy d'un triste front*
> *Estre ennemy des gaillardises,*

---

[38] Cited by Maurice Cauchie, "Le sonnet sous Louis XIII et la régence d'Anne d'Autriche," *DSS* 38 (1958): 51–53.

[39] *Œuvres poétiques* (Paris: Sansot, 1906).

[40] Ibid., pp. 59, 72.

Et qui reçois pour un affront
Tous les mots que tu n'authorises;
Sçaches que j'eusse bien, comme les autres font,
Changé les vers que tu mesprises;
N'estoit que plus on veut corriger des sottises
Et plus sottises elles sont.[41]

The above linearity is average for Dalibray. More often than not his lines read like rhymed prose:

Mais Phyllis, cette vérité
Ne doit point s'entendre de celles
Qui, soit faciles ou rebelles,
Forcent d'adorer leur beauté.[42]

Equally frequent are enjambments:

Autrefois, Promethée ayant à donner l'être
A l'homme, l'abbrégé de tout ce qu'on void naître.[43]

The rhymes of Dalibray are no better: monosyllabic homonyms are very frequent, especially *vers, nue,* and *point;* synaereses rhyme with diaereses, and not infrequently a word must be pronounced one way in one line and differently in another; long sounds rhyme with short ones, words with their compounds; verbs are abused: *appaise-appaiser-baise-baiser* is one of the curious combinations.

What should be obvious after even such a cursory study of these poets is that, unlike those at the Academy, they were unwilling or unable to leave their burlesque muse behind when they turned to other poetry, and with the very brief exception of Cyrano (three poems), none can be considered Malherbian in any way, not even in that rudimentary way that dictates pride in craftsmanship.

At the opposite end of this particular spectrum were the poets of a more "élégant badinage," whose muse was invariably at the service of a

[41] Ibid. (1653), "Au lecteur."
[42] Ibid. (1906), p. 13.
[43] Fleuret and Perceau, *Satires françaises,* 1:270.

woman—or of women—and of a far more aristocratic mien. While they may or may not have been more aware of or subservient to the rules and examples of Malherbe, they were usually quite proud of the polish they could give to their lines. Many of these were reluctant amateurs who did not seek public acclaim. Thus Rifflé had twenty-five poems inserted in a single *recueil collectif,* then was never heard from again. Others, such as Rampalle, wrote languid idyls somewhat reminiscent of Marino, but without trying to impress the literary world. Still others, without even trying, and writing in what the century called a "naïve" style, "de toutes petites Piéces,"[44] were extremely popular, as were Cailly and Charleval.[45] For the most part, however, amateur or professional, they were assiduous *ruellistes.* Their lives and their poetry were echoes of each other, and like Oronte, many of them could not separate the two. It is ironic, of course, that Oronte, like Vadius and Trissotin, could write a relatively decent poem on occasion.

In these the last years of the Hôtel de Rambouillet, there were few circles that held the entire personal or literary allegiance of any poet. Most writers flitted from the "lundis" of one to the "samedis" of another, and it would be fruitless here to differentiate between an "Illustre berger" and a habitué of the Chambre Bleue, for all these groups were rather fluid. Many of these poets, born in the first decade of the century, had already acquired their literary baggage by the end of the reign of Louis XIII, and might therefore be considered vestiges of another period. While these may not necessarily have had less talent than others, as we shall see, they do recall many of the poets discussed in previous chapters. In fact, due to purely chronological considerations, some have already been partially discussed.

Chapelain, speaking of Frénicle, accused him of having a "veine aisée mais sans fond et élévation."[46] This was particularly obvious since Frénicle, racked by illness in his later years, turned to paraphrases of psalms and other religious *stances.* In these, the mythological allusions that had spoiled his earlier efforts are gone, a phenomenon due perhaps to Malherbe's influence but more likely to his own genuine religious feelings. Nor is the general tone of these poems very Malherbian, fluctuating from

---

[44] Goujet, *Bibliothèque françoise,* 17:323.
[45] See Lachèvre, *Bibliographie,* 2:193; 3:239.
[46] *Opuscules critiques,* p. 346.

excessive pomp to a "douceur paresseuse"[47] more fitting the pastoral frolics of days gone by. In one realm, however, that of strophic innovations, Frénicle can be said to have taken a lesson from Malherbe. In these poems, he used thirty-four different forms of quatrains, most of them heterometric, but involving only lines of six, eight, ten, and twelve syllables, with eight and twelve dominating, as they did in Malherbe.[48] Thus, even if the specific combinations are not always to be found in Malherbe, the idea of heterometric innovation within the framework of compatible meters is certainly Malherbian. By the same token, the rhymes are good, as is the linearity, and the rare lapses seem due more to the poet's limitations than to a spirit of independence, so that critics who have seen echoes of Malherbe in his work are probably right:

> *Ainsi la mesme matinée*
> *Void poindre une herbe tendre, et se passer soudain;*
> *Elle est morte aussi-tost que née,*
> *Et sa fraisle beauté n'a point de lendemain.*[49]

The same is true for his other stanzas. Although some of his experiments cannot be considered Malherbian (there are about a dozen different five-line stanzas), the sestets and ten-line stanzas, by including strong 3–3 breaks in the former and 4–3–3 in the latter, follow the patterns set by Malherbe. It is indeed unfortunate that Frénicle could not shake the yoke of the *salons,* for there is no doubt that "Malherbe, Godeau, Racan, Corneille, lui ont enseigné une technique pure. Il les suit de loin, mais il continue leurs expériences métriques avec une virtuosité réelle," doing his share to "assouplir le langage et les mètres."[50]

The "veine aisée" may have been detrimental to Frénicle's religious poetry, but it was particularly suited to the elegant eroticism of the salon poetry, where elevation would have been completely out of place. Thus the reason for the rapid decline of Bouillon's poetry after his death in 1662 was not so much his lack of elevation as the fact that his poems were "de la dernière platitude":[51]

[47] Leblanc, *Paraphrases,* p. 222.
[48] Ibid.
[49] Cited in ibid.
[50] Ibid., p. 224.
[51] Viollet le Duc, *Catalogue,* 1:513.

Avec luy dans le cercueil,
Sont les aimables chansonnettes,
Les vers doux et galans, les passions discrètes,
Et partout se font voir en deuil
Les chalumeaux et les musettes.[52]

As this example also shows, Bouillon's poetry often defies metrical analysis. This is even more obvious in "Pressé de la douleur,"[53] written in trimetric five-line stanzas with the worst linearity imaginable.

Much the same can be said of Ogier's sonnets. Although Maurice Cauchie categorically states that they are *"tous* d'une valeur technique qui étonne,"[54] Ogier, to the end of his days, allowed sentences to straddle stanzas, monosyllabic homophones to rhyme, and diaereses to rhyme with synaereses. But what really caused his decline[55] was simply that he was unable to find a tone appropriate to the *galanteries* he was trying to dispense. This is precisely what hampered Montausier who, in his later years, was guilty of many a "vers raboteux et sans éclat,"[56] and perhaps to an even greater extent the playwright Gabriel Gilbert whenever he tried his hand at lyric poetry.

In his odes, Gilbert tried to reach an elevated tone, and succeeded only in being long-winded. "A la Reine de Suède" has eighty-five ten-line stanzas, most with a 4–3–3 break, but all tedious, filled with obscure proper nouns, most of which are shameless padding. Verbosity and pompousness have replaced breadth and pomp, and if one insists on seeking, as some critics have done, a conscious imitation of Malherbe, it must be through a veritable labyrinth of mythological allusions and rambling platitudes. His lighter *stances* are even worse. Not content with Malherbe's concept of experimentation, Gilbert varies his stanzas within a single poem. Thus "A la Reine" has seven sestets: the first one is 12–12–12–12–12–10; the second, 12–12–8–8–12–8; the third, 8–8–12–12–12–8; and so on. To complicate matters further, the alternation of

---

[52] Lachèvre, *Bibliographie*, 2:496.
[53] Allem, *Anthologie*, 1:336.
[54] "Le sonnet," p. 41.
[55] Although he was well represented in earlier *recueils,* the number of his poems included dwindled to the point where only one appeared after 1658.
[56] D'Estrée, "A travers les manuscrits de Conrart," p. 95.

masculine and feminine lines is such that in several stanzas no two lines
have the same length. The following is taken from one of his lighter
efforts:

> Desjà le beau Printemps a pris sa robe verte
> Qu'il traisne avecque grace en pompe par les champs,
> Et Venus dans un char, la gorge découverte,
> Reveille les oyseaux et leurs amoureux chants.[57]

The inversion and the nonsense of the last hemistich, the *b* rhyme, the
ridiculous style of the entire quatrain, all this should amply demonstrate
that while the "veine aisée" may have been a derogation in Chapelain's
mind, those who lacked it were doomed to failure in certain genres.

Fortunately, there were several poets of the time who did not lack
that skill, and to these I will now turn to see whether or not such a style
could be compatible with Malherbian doctrine, whether the nonchalance
on display did not hide the labor of the *difficulté vaincue*.

In view of his relatively short life-span, Jean-François Sarasin must
be considered extremely versatile, his production ranging from the most
outlandish *bouts-rimés* to epic fragments that rank with the best of his
time (a mild accolade indeed). It is unfortunate that Sarasin's *précieux*
and *galant* aspects have been allowed to overshadow his more serious
efforts, for precisely these interest us most, since it would be foolish to seek
Malherbian traits in deliberately archaic ballads or willfully irregular
madrigals.

Sarasin, born near Caen when Malherbe was preparing to conquer
Paris, did not follow his famous compatriot to the capital until 1635 or
1636, at least seven years after the latter's death. Much of his serious
poetry did not see the light of day until still later, crammed, so to speak,
into the last ten years of the poet's life. His first ode, "A Monsieur de
Chavigny," written in 1637, is in octosyllabic *dizains, a b a b c c d e e d,*
a form particularly liked by Malherbe; but the similarity ends there. Of
the seven stanzas, three have no break at all; the others are divided 4–6,
but they fail to enter into the spirit of the structure in that the first part,
rather than being a stately introduction to any given theme, is merely a
chaotic prelude:

[57] Olivier, *Cent poètes lyriques,* p. 520.

Eloigne ces tristes pensées
Et reprends le soin de ton luth,
Muse, nos frayeurs sont passées,
Et nous voyons notre salut.[58]

Elsewhere, the tone is spoiled by the breathless outpouring of ten uninterrupted lines:

Qui n'eût pensé, voyant l'injure
D'un tel orage s'apprêter,
Qu'il n'était point de Palinure
Capable de lui résister,
Et que la mauvaise fortune
Dans notre ruine commune
Allait achever par nos mains
Ce dessein rempli de furie
Pour qui le Lion d'Hespérie
Se joint à l'Aigle des Romains?[59]

His second effort, a "description du Cabinet de M. D. C.," is no better, displaying the same form and giving rise to the same reservations: the first stanza is divided 1–1–1–1–1–5, the others are broken either in every way possible or not at all. There are several noteworthy enjambments and the allusions verge on the pedantic. The odes written in the last ten years of his life (1644–1654) are even more emancipated. In the ode "A Monseigneur le duc d'Anguien," sentences straddle stanzas and radical changes of tone occur within stanzas. "Sur la prise de Dunkerque" is written in nine-line stanzas, three of them being constructed of a single syntactical unit. Ironically enough, it is in this ode that he invokes ". . . la lyre qu'en mourant/ Malherbe nous a laissée,"[60] but there can be no doubt as to the reception Malherbe would have given the enjambments, the bad rhymes, and the very form of this ode or the one that followed, dedicated to Chapelain and composed of 8–12–8–6–6–6, *a b b c c a* sestets.

---

[58] *Œuvres*, 1:213.
[59] Ibid., p. 214.
[60] Ibid., p. 221.

A great many of Sarasin's poems are *stances* of medium length (about twenty lines) dealing with love. Although he experimented with some original structures (one poem has both a seven-line and a nine-line stanza, two others have five-line stanzas, while still another is made of alternating decasyllabic and octosyllabic isometric octets), half of his *stances* are isometric quatrains (neglected more and more by Malherbe) while most of the rest are taken up by heterometric sestets. Like Malherbe, Sarasin seemed to enjoy experimenting with the possibilities offered by heterometric sestets: one single combination was used more than twice by Malherbe, and only one combination was used more than once by Sarasin. Unlike Malherbe, however, Sarasin also experimented with the various breaks possible: of the sixty-five sestets he wrote, thirty-one are in one syntactical unit and nine more are broken unevenly (2–4, 4–2, 1–5, and 1–1–4).

Sarasin wrote only thirteen sonnets, all isometric except for an enigma which, as the genre demanded, has a single word as its last line. Ten of these sonnets use the preferred *a b b a* quatrain scheme, but only seven end *e d e* and six end with a feminine rhyme, both strong departures from Malherbian practice and dogma.

As may be expected in this type of poetry, the rhymes are not always satisfactory. Even if one discounts the profusion of *rimes normandes*, since both Sarasin and Malherbe came from Normandy, there are still far too many lapses for a poet of this quality. Most common here, as in the works of almost all his contemporaries, is the lack of homophony of the *consonne d'appui*. Almost as common, and far more difficult to explain, are the many words that rhyme with their derivatives (*dire-contredire, jure-conjure, voir-pourvoir*) and the abuse of verbs and adverbs. Long sounds rhyme with short ones—in some cases (*âme-flamme*) so frequently as to constitute a commonplace—and synaereses with diaereses. Ironically, while "norman rhymes" such as *mer-abîmer* may be excused, they make it very difficult to explain one like *regrets-éviter*. Monosyllabic homophones are also frequent, as are diminutives (*fleurette-amourette*). In short, while Sarasin, by his versatility, demonstrated what Pellisson called "la plus certaine marque de la grandeur et de la beauté d'un génie,"[61] he showed no affinity for the rigorous method demanded by his famous compatriot.

[61] "Discours sur les œuvres de M. Sarasin," ibid., p. 131.

Among the contemporaries of Sarasin who still warrant comment are the Abbé d'Aubignac, Madeleine de Scudéry, Jean de Bussières, and René de Bruc de Montplaisir. Some of these names have fallen into complete oblivion, but we must keep in mind that the seventeenth century did not always share our critical opinions. Thus Chapelain tells us that d'Aubignac's style "n'est pas des pires," and that his sonnets were "assez approuvés,"[62] faint praise indeed, but one that was still echoed as late as the nineteenth century when Livet judiciously concluded that the *précieux* abbé was in every way very much of his times.[63] This must remain the verdict, even where his metrics are concerned: facile rhymester, he commits no grave errors, but some of his lines are not as well balanced as others, and many of his rhymes show the little care he obviously lavished on them. All the usual abuses are here, and some lines leave little choice: "Tout cela fait et eux rassis"[64] is either cacophonic or imbued with two hiatuses. In only one respect is he even more un-Malherbian than most of his fellow *ruellistes*: his poetry has an unusual number of very long sentences, a habit that caused him to link stanzas together, even in sonnets where the quatrains often comprise one sentence and the tercets the second.[65]

Jean de Bussières was known more for his Latin than for his French poetry.[66] His French lines are colorless and insipid and interesting only because he took some of Malherbe's favorite forms to warp beyond recognition. Thus his poem on a budding rose is in octosyllabic *dizains* with 4–6 breaks, but lines such as

> *Est-ce une fleur? ou si la flamme*
> *Brusle les bords de ce rosier?*
> *Est-ce un rubis, que l'ouvrier*
> *Advantageusement entame?*[67]

[62] *Opuscules critiques*, p. 342.

[63] *Précieux et précieuses*, p. 149.

[64] Charles Arnaud, *Les théories dramatiques au XVIIe siècle: Etude sur la vie et les œuvres de l'Abbé d'Aubignac* (Paris: Picard, 1888), p. 70.

[65] See "Epitidès à Hermesile," cited in ibid., p. 69.

[66] Chapelain, *Lettres*, 2:122; *Opuscules critiques*, pp. 351–52; Goujet, *Bibliothèque françoise*, 18:13.

[67] Jean Rousset, ed., *Anthologie de la poésie baroque française* (Paris: Colin, 1961), 2:28.

Malherbe's cause was obviously much better served by René de Bruc de Montplaisir whose erotic poetry was considered by Costar[68] the best in France, an opinion shared by the compilers of *recueils*. He did not follow Malherbe's example as closely as Bussières in choice of forms, nor in his rhymes, which are generally mediocre, but his sense of balance and "juste cadence" is ever visible. Although in his sonnets he used the *a b a b* scheme as often as *a b b a,* and *e e d* as often as *e d e,* he was quite orthodox in his stanzas. Unfortunately, while his isometric poems are quite good, his heterometric ones show that he failed to grasp the reasons for most of Malherbe's practices. "L'hiver," for instance, is in ten-line stanzas composed of four alexandrines followed by six octosyllabic lines, a combination used only once by Malherbe (in a 1596 fragment) and never used again for the obvious reason that it breaks the unity of the stanza beyond reason. Montplaisir, to compound the error, puts a very strong 4–6 syntactical break in every stanza, further accentuating the rift.[69] Malherbe had been followed but not understood.

The poetry of Madeleine de Scudéry did not become popular until long after that of her brother, and the reason is readily found in the works that reflect the two contrasting personalities. Georges de Scudéry was, in life and on paper, a Matamore, and as such could not easily survive the Fronde. Madeleine was a *précieuse,* of course, but *tendre* rather than *coquette,* certainly not pedantic nor prudish, and far from ridiculous, Molière interpreters notwithstanding. As a result, judging not only by contemporary statements but also by the number of her poems included in the various *recueils,* her popularity grew as time went on. Since this popularity lasted into the following century, it is all the more important to ascertain the degree of her orthodoxy.

In her choice of forms, Madeleine de Scudéry was anything but Malherbian, but that is only half the story. Her quatrains are almost all isometric, and all her sestets heterometric with alexandrine or octosyllabic bases. None of the heterometric combinations can be found in Malherbe, and the rhyme schemes vary from *a a b b c c* to *a a a b a b* with only an occasional orthodox one. The breaks also vary from 3–3 to none, passing through every other type possible. What is unusual about all these deviations is that they seem to be neither conscious contradictions of Malherbe

[68] Lachèvre, *Bibliographie,* 2:388.
[69] For example, see Fukui, *Raffinement précieux,* p. 229.

nor lackadaisical disregard of any discipline, but the result of a totally different system. Whereas Malherbe had allowed basically external considerations (musical in the case of the breaks, for instance) to impose limits on the poetic mode, Mlle de Scudéry allowed the poem itself to dictate the form. Thus in the "Stances sur la paix," the punctuation would seem to indicate a 4–2 break, but the case is not that simple. The poem is one of theme and variations, the main theme being

> *Voici le règne des Amours.*
> *La paix s'en va bientôt rétablir son empire*
> *Et l'on ne verra plus de cœur qui ne soupire.*[70]

These are the last three lines of every sestet, and it will be noted that they are not limited by the break. In each stanza, the first three lines deal with a different facet of that time, which is then recapitulated in the fourth line, "Voici le règne des Amours," the last two lines acting as a further commentary on the happy tidings.

Even in the sestets that break in the standard way, Madeleine de Scudéry manages to maintain a flavor suggesting an essential rhythm rather than a form imposed from without:

> *Mon cœur que la raison éclaire*
> *Méprise de l'encens vulgaire,*
> > *N'en doutez point.*
> *Mais rejeter par modestie*
> *Le plus pur encens d'Arabie,*
> > *C'est là le point.*[71]

This consideration is undoubtedly to blame for the fact that the poetess reversed Malherbe's ration of preference, writing many poems in *huitains* while neglecting *dizains* and their formal rigidity almost entirely. This is also the probable reason for the overwhelming predominance of *vers suivis* and free verse in her production.

The linearity of her poems is invariably good, with few enjamb-

---

[70] Cited by Rathery and Boutron, *Mlle de Scudéry*, p. 509. For some interesting variants, see Mongrédien, *Madeleine de Scudéry*, p. 164.

[71] Cited by Rathery and Boutron, *Mlle de Scudéry*, p. 511.

ments, even in the free verse, and a fine sense of rhythm. The rhymes, on the other hand, are not on that level. As the above sestet shows, she was not averse to using monosyllabic homonyms; she also rhymes verbs and adverbs in quantity, diaereses with synaereses, long sounds with short ones, words with their derivatives, especially in the case of verbs (*durer-endurer, soutenir-retinir*), and *vous* invariably rhymes with *doux* or *vous*. It should be obvious by now, however, that she was not alone in this respect, and few of her contemporaries could have found fault with that aspect of her work without also damning the rest of the century. All this may explain Boileau's reaction to her poetry. He seems to have taken particular delight in mocking her novels, but he never used his pen against her verse. Could this be because, as an admirer of Malherbe, he could not praise works that did not fit the Malherbian mold, but as an honest and perspicacious critic he had to admit that the system was nonetheless viable and the results above average? Is this not the very position in which Boileau found himself vis-à-vis some of the better poets of his day?

Even more interesting than the poets just discussed are those who, somewhat younger, were truly transitional. Some, such as Benserade, had reached maturity by the time Louis XIII died, but continued to evolve; others, such as Pure, born in 1634, were truly *arriérés* immersed so to speak in the tastes of the previous generation. "Maturity" must here be taken as a relative term, since Benserade, the oldest of the poets to be discussed here, was only thirty years old in 1643.

There is a certain danger in attempting too close an analysis of the works of some of these younger poets precisely because of their reliance on the taste, and even on the actual help, of their elders. Pierre and Marie La Lane, Alexandre Campion, Madame de La Suze, and many of their friends not only formed a very close group but also assiduously frequented Lacger, Montplaisir, and others who not only advised them but, in the case of Madame de La Suze, even helped directly in the composition of poems.[72] As most critics have pointed out, the poems of La Suze, particularly her elegies, are heartfelt, direct outpourings of feelings almost totally devoid of craftsmanship. In many of these a certain pulsating rhythm undeniably enhances the expression of sentiment:

[72] Frédéric Lachèvre, *Nouvelles glanes bibliographiques et littéraires* (Paris: Giraud-Badin, 1933), p. 127. See also Goujet, *Bibliothèque françoise,* 17:314.

Mon cœur n'est plus mon cœur, il suit l'objet qu'il aime,
Pour luy seul il respire, il consent à ses vœux,
Il soûpire, il languit, il brûle de ses feux,[73]

but the technical skill is lacking. Like Madeleine de Scudéry, Madame de La Suze allows the content to dictate the form, but unlike her elder, she does not have a sense of composition, so that the form runs away from her:

Laisse-moy soûpirer, importune raison,
  Laisse, laisse couler mes larmes,
Mes déplaisirs sont doux, mes tourments ont des charmes
  Et j'aime ma prison;
Ah! puisqu'Amarillis me défend d'espérer,
Au moins en expirant laisse-moy soûpirer.[74]

More annoying here than the 4–2 break is the trimetric division of the stanza, the lone octosyllabic line having reached that length solely on the strength of a dithyrambic expletive. Her odes point up this tendency even more. Her ode to Christina of Sweden begins as follows:

Belle lumière vagabonde,
Mobile source de clarté,
Flambeau d'éternelle beauté,
Œil du jour qui vois tout le monde,
Soleil qui dans un char si pur
Te promeines dessus l'azur
Avec un appareil si superbe et si grave,
Vois-tu rien de si beau de ton Trône orgueilleux,
  Que la fille du grand Gustave?
Et le Ciel a-t-il rien qui soit si merveilleux?[75]

Even if one disregards the unusual heterometry of the stanza and the bad syntactical break, how could a careful poet allow the ludicrous succession of repetitions that begins this ode? It is unfortunate that her mentors could not tone down her lyricism.

[73] Cited by Fukui, *Raffinement précieux*, p. 289.
[74] Lachèvre, *Nouvelles glanes*, p. 128.
[75] Ibid., p. 143.

Fortunately, such was not the case with Marie La Lane. Amarante was one of the shining stars of *précieux* Paris of the mid-century, inspiring such poets as Campion and Saint-Amant. Like Madame de La Suze, she was far from coy or prudish, telling a suitor who had threatened to die,

> *Je t'ordonne de vivre; et veux qu'à l'avenir*
> *Le destin de nos cœurs n'ait qu'une même trame,*
> *Que notre embrasement ne pousse qu'une flame*
> *Qui ne puisse jamais finir.*[76]

Unlike her counterpart, Marie La Lane managed to keep a sense of proportion and balance.

It is impossible to determine who in her immediate entourage taught and who learned, but there can be no doubt on one score: her two most ardent admirers, her husband Pierre and the less fortunate Alexandre Campion, were as regular in their prosody as the most ardent of Malherbe's disciples. Campion, using a form made famous by Malherbe, produced quatrains that the master would not have denied:

> *Si son cœur qui partu toûjours inaccessible,*
> *S'estoit laissé toucher;*
> *Que l'on seroit heureux d'avoir rendu sensible*
> *Cet aimable Rocher.*[77]

Pierre La Lane's technique was no less rigorous, nor did he allow it to hamper his feelings. His keen sense of rhythm is made manifest in this answer to his wife's appeal:

> *J'aime et je suis aimé, j'adore et je possède*
> *Vne beauté divine, à qui tout autre cède.*[78]

These feelings are often translated into the most sensuous of lines without, however, sacrificing craftsmanship:

[76] N.-N. Condéescou, "Une muse du XVIIe siècle: Madame de La Lane," *RHLF* 46 (1939): 11.

[77] Ibid., p. 22.

[78] Cited by Fukui, *Raffinement précieux*, p. 235. Note the effect of this, one of his rare enjambments.

Quand je voy ces cheveux dont Amour m'entortille,
Ces longs serpents de soye, épars sur ces beaux yeux,
Ces palpables rayons . . .

. . . .

Floter lascivement.[79]

When his wife died prematurely, he poured out his grief in poems that have been unfairly neglected, for as far as the union of sincerity and craftsmanship is concerned they have few equals in the century:

Est-ce donc icy-bas une loi du destin,
Que la plus belle chose y passe en un matin?
Falloit-il en un jour voir Amarante naître
Et la voir disparaître.[80]

The sonnets written on that occasion are extremely regular, demonstrating unfailing rhymes, even in the matter of the *consonne d'appui* or synaeresis,[81] and an enviable sense of balance:

Tous vos conseils envain me veulent secourir;
S'ils n'ont pas le pouvoir de la faire revivre,
Ils ne peuvent aussi m'empêcher de mourir.[82]

None of the other *badins* poets approached this degree of technical excellence, though many were aware of the paths to take. Ménage and Chevreau were both avowed admirers of Malherbe, but neither drew the appropriate lessons from their readings of his works. Although a frequenter of the Hôtel de Rambouillet and a sometime friend of Chapelain, Sarasin, and Voiture, Gilles Ménage was doomed by his personality to be an outsider. His "Requête des dictionnaires"

A Nosseigneurs Academiques,
Nosseigneurs les Hypercritiques,
Souverains arbitres des mots,[83]

[79] Ibid., p. 234.
[80] Ibid.
[81] See Condéescou, "Une muse," pp. 24–25.
[82] Goujet, *Bibliothèque françoise,* 17:320.
[83] Furetière, *Recueils des factums,* 2:333.

delighted Balzac in his provincial retreat, but it certainly had something to do with the Académie closing its doors to Ménage. Chapelain had originally protected Ménage and introduced him to Madame de Rambouillet, but the younger poet soon alienated Chapelain to such an extent that the latter said of him, "aussi n'a-t-il jamais rien fait de lui-même qui ne fût ou imité, ou dérobé d'autrui."[84] The man may well have been a very unpleasant fop, but there were worse *précieux* poets.

If one judges by the rhymes, which contain every fault imaginable, Ménage paid but scant attention to his *vers suivis,* yet the syntactical units seldom extend beyond the two lines suggested by Malherbe. The linearity is generally good and the ideas are concisely presented. In his stanzas and sonnets, these qualities are again present, though without the excessive hindrance of bad rhymes. "Indifférence,"[85] in 12–6–12–6, *a b a b* quatrains, lacks some *consonne d'appui* homophony, and at least one rhyme (*pris-mespris*) is unacceptable, but it is hardly an "un-Malherbian" poem; his sonnet in the *Guirlande* is, except for one rhyme (*fleurs-sœurs*), completely orthodox; and the sonnet "Les vers du chantre de Thrace," a parody of Malherbe's "Plus Mars que Mars de la Thrace," is in every technical respect the equal of the model. This does not mean that Ménage always followed Malherbe slavishly. "Vous m'avez payé, Mélite" is in heptasyllabic seven-line stanzas and is by no means the only innovative poem he wrote.

Urbain Chevreau, considered by Chapelain as the best of the second-order poets,[86] was even more aware of Malherbian doctrine and practice. Where Ménage imitated, as in the hyperbolic line quoted above, Chevreau commented adversely whenever he felt the hyperbole to be excessive. He considered Malherbe a pioneer but one who had not gone far enough in ridding himself of "un vilain reste du siècle passé," also deploring the fact that, at times, "les Graces ont esté quelquefois chez luy en mauvaise intelligence avec les Muses."[87] He deplored the poor taste of "Les larmes de Saint Pierre" and was glad that Malherbe had later disowned it, but failed to follow that example: in sending "Myrrhe," a heroic poem, to a friend, he apologized for its not being "dans toutes les règles: j'ai quelque chose de meilleur à faire qu'à corriger les fureurs de ma

[84] *Opuscules critiques,* p. 343.
[85] *Poemata,* pp. 85–87.
[86] *Opuscules critiques,* p. 347.
[87] Malherbe, *Œuvres* (1722), 1:223.

jeunesse."[88] This raises two important questions: if the man was aware of the rules and knew that his early works violated them, why did he not correct or suppress them? Did his later works avoid these pitfalls?

The answers are not too difficult to find. Chevreau was an admirer of Malherbe; he was also a close friend and admirer of Tristan and, as indicated by at least two of his poems, "La belle gueuse" and "La belle en deuil," a Marinist of sorts. "La belle gueuse," written in nine-line stanzas, 12–8–12–8–12–12–12–8–8, *a b b a c d c d c*, is as far removed from Malherbian doctrine as are Chevreau's satires in free verse. The basic form of "La belle en deuil" is Malherbian:

> *Noire divinité qu'on ne peut assez craindre,*
> *Et qui faites qu'en vous on aime ce qu'on craint!*
> *Qui regarde ce crespe, et qui vous entend plaindre,*
> *Croit voir, et croit entendre une ombre qui se plaint.*[89]

As the rhymes of this stanza and the linearity of most of the others indicate, that was the full extent of the poet's orthodoxy. Generally speaking, Chevreau was a purist in language but not in matters of prosody, where wit is often allowed to replace discipline, as in this portrait done in 1661:

> *Elle a de l'embonpoint; son visage est ovale,*
> *Et son humeur est libérale.*
> *A la raison ses désirs sont soumis.*
> *Elle a l'air grand agréable et modest;*
> *Ne manque point à ce qu'elle a promis;*
> *Aime fortement ses amis,*
> *Et se moque de tout le reste.*[90]

The comtesse de Chalais, in 1663, received this equally prosaic sample of his poetry:

> *Je n'eus jamais l'honneur de vous connaître;*
> *Il se peut faire aussi que je m'en porte mieux;*

[88] Urbain Chevreau, *Œuvres meslées* (The Hague: Moetjens, 1697), 2:558.

[89] *Poésies* (Paris: Sommaville, 1656), p. 12.

[90] *Œuvres meslées*, 1:65.

> *Puisqu'il n'est point de cœur, quelque fier qu'il puisse être,*
> *Dont un certain enfant ne devienne le maître*
> *Par tout où brillent vos beaux yeux.*[91]

This is merely a small sample from a long letter, but it should suffice to show that while Chevreau the critic may well have been ultra-Malherbian, Chevreau the poet was anything but that.

Although not nearly as avowed an admirer of Malherbe as either Ménage or Chevreau, the Abbé de Pure nevertheless professed many ideas that can only be considered Malherbian. In 1668 he stated that "la mesure des vers n'est prise que de la justesse des chants. . . . De sorte qu'être poète et ne savoir pas chanter, c'est n'être qu'à demi poète."[92] While this recalls more Racan's musicianship than Malherbe's defective recitation, the latter could not have gainsaid any part of it in view of his own ideas concerning the relationship of poetry and music. But if Pure's theories can be thought of as Malherbian, his poetry cannot:

> *Les Dames, les Princes, les Roys,*
> *Et le Ciel, et la terre et l'onde*
> *Ne vous font que justice en vous donnant leur voix,*
> *Car pour des vers de si grands pois,*
> *Ce n'est pas trop que tout le monde.*[93]

In view of his many *pointes*, Georges Mongrédien is right in considering Pure's poems not satires but quite servile imitations of the *précieux*:

> *Tel pense deviner, qui n'est qu'un Allement;*
> *Tel qui pense sçavoir à fonds ce que je pense,*
> *Pense une extravagance,*
> *Car il ne pense pas que je pense qu'il ment.*[94]

As for the forms and technique, the above samples and especially the following trimetric stanza should dispel any doubts:

[91] Ibid., p. 80.

[92] *Idée des spectacles anciens et nouveaux,* cited by Winegarten, *French Lyric Poetry,* p. 111.

[93] Cited by Georges Mongrédien, *Libertins et amoureuses* (Paris: Perrin, 1929), p. 183.

[94] Ibid., p. 187.

Je ne puis accuser mes sens
Quoiqu'auteurs des maux que je sens;
Ils ont été surpris d'un objet trop aimable,
Mais, contre ma raison, mon cœur est animé
De voir que la coupable
Me fasse plus aimer que je ne suis aimé.[95]

However slight these poetic talents may have been, they were surpassed by only one of the other poets to be discussed, Isaac de Benserade. The rest—Tallemant des Réaux, Louis Petit, and Jacques Carpentier de Marigny—are mentioned here only because of their popularity in their day, not because of their obvious mediocrity.

Louis Petit wrote as frequently in his Norman *patois* as in French, but without ever taking himself seriously: "Chacun a sa sorte de génie, et le mien n'eût jamais rien d'amer. J'avoue qu'il n'est pas d'une grande élévation, ainsi ma Muse chante assez uniment."[96] Actually, his satirical vein situates him closer to Régnier than to Malherbe. When his friend and compatriot Corneille asked him to take greater care in the composition of his lines and to write more elevated poems, he answered as follows:

Damon, ma muse libertine
Ne peut s'assujettir aux loix
Des neuf sœurs de Mnémosyne
Quand elles marchent avec poids.

. . . .

Je renonce au style sublime;
Et quand avec succès je rime
En vérité, c'est par hazard.[97]

He carried this love of facility well beyond the realm of poetry:

Angélique, si je vous quitte,
Ce n'est point par aucun mespris;
Je sçay bien que vostre mérite

[95] Cited by Emile Magne, "L'Abbé Michel de Pure ou le confident des précieuses," *RParis* 2 (1938):835.

[96] *Discours satyriques et moraux* (Rouen: Lallemant, 1686), "Au lecteur."

[97] Lachèvre, *Bibliographie*, 2:414.

Surpasse celuy de Cloris;
Mais si vous estes la plus belle,
Ma Cloris est la moins cruelle,
Et paye mieux que vous mes veilles et mes soins;
Et comme je n'ay pas une ame trop hautaine,
Sans regret aucun, et sans peine
Je quitte le plus pour le moins.[98]

The above *dizain* is properly divided, but that is the extent of its orthodoxy. His rhymes, linearity, and choice of forms are invariably non-Malherbian. What his poems lack even more is the sparkle and urbanity demanded by the readers of the age of Louis XIV, and this defect, certainly more than his "libertinism," caused his rapid decline in popularity as demonstrated by the *recueils collectifs.*

Neither Tallemant des Réaux nor Marigny lacked that required de-degree of polish, though their poems were equally free, and they fared somewhat better as a result. In his early years, Tallemant indulged in many archaic forms then fashionable, such as rondeaux and ballads, without great care for either rhyme or rhythm:

Je ne m'attends d'avoir, pour le salaire
De tous mes maux, que l'honneur de vous plaire
Et qu'il me soit permis tant seulement
De vous aimer.[99]

Most of his satirical poems against his many foes are badly composed five-line stanzas:

La cardinal Mazarin
Fait Boislève évêque enfin,
Voyez le choix exemplaire!
Lère la, lère lan lère,
Lère, lère lan la. [100]

---

[98] Cited by Mongrédien, *Libertins et amoureuses,* p. 40.
[99] Cited by Magne, *La joyeuse jeunesse de Tallemant des Réaux* (Paris: Emile-Paul, 1921), p. 112.
[100] Cited by Magne, *La fin troublée de Tallemant des Réaux* (Paris: Emile-Paul, 1922), p. 143.

The later poems, of course, are more sophisticated, but their versification is ever free. His sonnets on the death of Mme d'Harambure range from the relatively orthodox one addressed to Malleville to the very free one (*a b a b a b b a*) to Gombauld.[101] In all of these, whether the scheme be orthodox or free, the rhymes are seldom disciplined, with most of the common faults enumerated elsewhere in this chapter well represented.

Much the same can be said of the poems of Marigny, who had a special predilection for forms shunned by Malherbe. In addition to the usual ballads and rondeaux, he also liked to write triolets, a form despised by Malherbe, undoubtedly because of its easy rhyme scheme. Enjambments are very frequent, even in songs where they invariably break the flow:

> *C'est la véritable effigie*
> *De Jules, ce fourbe éternel.*[102]

Even in his more serious poems, all sonnets, he shows no preference for any particular rhyme scheme, and his rhymes are frequently unsatisfactory. His popularity may well have equaled that of La Lane, but his pen was certainly not nearly as *châtié*. That in itself is remarkable.

One *badin* poet remains to be discussed, and he has been kept for last for a definite purpose. Today, Isaac de Benserade is remembered chiefly for a very clever sonnet that led to one of the livelier literary debates of the 1630s. While the sonnet is undoubtedly good, it should not blind us to those merits of the poet that maintained his popularity throughout the century. Corneille, Costar, Chapelain, all his contemporaries admired his *esprit* if not his *savoir* and *science* in matters poetic.[103] It was undoubtedly for his unusually sophisticated *esprit* that Benserade was esteemed. Even his ballet libretti were considered poetry, a definitely novel attitude on the part of critic and public alike. This is because until Benserade, ballets were either obscene or lifeless: "Aucune finesse, aucune grâce et, bien entendu, aucune poésie."[104] By his training, Benserade was

---

[101] Yoshio Fukui, "Sur la mort de Madame d'Harambure: sonnets inédits de Tallemant des Réaux, Chapelain, Gombauld," *RSH* 94 (1959):170–71. For other examples, see Lachèvre, *Bibliographie*, 2:666–67.

[102] Blot L'Eglise, *Les chansons libertines*, p. 71.

[103] For a sample of opinions, see Lachèvre, *Bibliographie*, 2:142–43.

[104] Mongrédien, *Libertins et amoureuses*, p. 280.

a contemporary of Voiture. Later he adapted his muse to the tastes prevalent at Versailles. Thus as a transitional poet he is of particular interest to us.

Even though Benserade brought the ballet verses to new heights, it would be unfair to judge his ability by them, for he had a just notion of the relative importance of the contributing artists. He did not consider ballets "ceux où les conviés recitent des ouvrages dressés selon les maximes des arts oratoire ou poétique." The spectators, he believed, came to admire "les merveilleuses dispositions et cadences regulieres des acteurs, qui est la seule fin pour laquelle les Ballets ont esté institués," and not some clever *pointe* invented by a poet.[105]

At first glance, the stanzas of Benserade involve every form imaginable and range from the carefully crafted to the awkward, from the lyrical to the prosaic. On more careful examination, a definite pattern evolves, with burlesque, or at least realistic, verse on the one hand and poems of a more aristocratic, *précieux* vein on the other. In the first category the greatest variety in the choice of forms exists. Here also the nature of these forms is most frequently warped:

> *Je puis chanter la grandeur et le nombre*
> *De vos hauts faits; mais pour y mieux resver,*
> *Il faut des bois, du repos, et de l'ombre;*
> *Et jusqu'icy je n'en ay sceu trouver.*[106]

As can be seen, the potential for gravity and elevation of the decasyllabic quatrain is completely annulled by the prosaic syntax. Heterometric constructions suffer in the same way:

> *Il n'en faut point rougir, si la pitié n'est pas*
> *Une qualité criminelle.*[107]

Most obvious of these deformations are those which, unlike the preceding examples, use forms found in Malherbe:

[105] Lacroix, *Ballets et mascarades*, 6:268.

[106] Cited by Charles I. Silin, *Benserade and his Ballets de Cour* (Baltimore: Johns Hopkins University Press, 1940), p. 56.

[107] Cited by Fukui, *Raffinement précieux*, p. 276.

Souffrez que je m'emporte, et que je vous confesse
  Que je suis très-mary,
Qu'il faille que je souffre, et de vôtre sagesse,
  Et de vôtre mary.[108]

In these poems, not only is the full value of the form far from properly exploited, but cacophonic lines such as "Elle me voudroit me voyant de tous mes sens perclus"[109] make them almost unreadable. Inner rhymes frequently add to the difficulties:

Et quand je suis sans bois, m'en promettre une Voye
C'est une douce voye à me gagner le cœur.[110]

Fortunately Benserade's badinage has its more elegant side. In this realm, he must be considered orthodox though not overly disciplined. His rhymes are all too frequently sloppy, showing a minimum of care. Every fault already discussed in relation to other poets is represented, and some rhymes (*autre-nôtre*) are annoyingly omnipresent. As for the form, Benserade had definitely read Malherbe and learned some lessons. On rare occasions he tried some new forms of his own; these are sometimes poorly structured, as is the case with the heptasyllabic seven-line stanzas to Manneville:

Toute la Cour est éprise
De ces attraits précieux,
Dont vous enchantez nos yeux,
Manneville;[111]

but for the most part, his stanzas are of standard length (four, six, and ten lines) and isometric (octosyllabic or alexandrine). In the heterometric poems, whether he uses forms already tested by Malherbe or not, the variations are used to good advantage:

[108] *Œuvres* (Paris: Sercy, 1697), 1:166.
[109] "Jalousie," ibid., pp. 40–42.
[110] Ibid., p. 71.
[111] Ibid., p. 340.

Un rival prend son temps, choisit son avantage,
Et vient voir la beauté qui cause mon ennui.
Il est sot et me fait ombrage,
Car elle est sotte comme lui.[112]

The metrical change coming on the heels of the syntactical break may be harmful to strophic unity, but it undeniably reinforces very well the change in tone, thus making for an inner harmony of form and content. This mastery of rhythm is also evident in the handling of clever *chutes:*

Que ce trait d'un esprit adroit comme le vôtre
Est délicat et doux!
Et que vous feignez bien de parler pour un autre,
Quand vous parlez pour vous![113]

Benserade was admired, by Balzac among others, for the rhythmic effects of which he was capable. His use of heterometry makes this skill manifest, but no more so than the perfect balance of almost every line:

Es-tu si tenebreux, toy qui fus si brillant?
. . . .
Le cœur vous apprendra qu'est devenu l'esprit.[114]

There are, to be sure, a few enjambments, but even they manage to exude an aura of deliberate craftsmanship:

. . . et qui sçavez
Si bien jouer de la prunelle.[115]

The choice of forms has already been commented on. Equally interesting is their inner structure, for here one can really determine the extent of Malherbe's influence. Ironically, that influence is least noticeable

[112] Ibid., p. 63.
[113] Ibid., p. 80.
[114] Ibid., p. 277.
[115] Ibid., p. 26.

in the sonnets. Unlike Malherbe, Benserade preferred octosyllabics to alexandrines and *a b a b* quatrains to *a b b a*. Equally un-Malherbian is the tendency to allow a sentence to run beyond the quatrain:

> L'autre jour, me sentant pressé
> D'écrire en vers avec un zèle
> Purement desinteressé,
> Et sur la laide et sur la belle,
>
> Des neuf sœurs je fus caressé.[116]

His *stances* are another matter entirely. With few exceptions, the sestets are symmetrically divided. The 3–3 break is not always strong and often gives the impression of no break at all, but it is present in even the lightest airs:

> Je vous le dis et le repete
> Que Marianne fut coquette
> Et n'a pû se passer d'Amans;
> Ce n'est point médisance noire,
> Et je m'en raporte aux Romans
> Où vous croyez mieux qu'à l'histoire.[117]

If one recalls the fundamentally lyrical reasons for the division, as proposed by Maynard and accepted by Malherbe, one can appreciate the importance of Benserade's carrying of the practice even to the lightest airs. By the same token, nearly all of his ten-line stanzas are divided 4–6 with a secondary break after the seventh line, although there are some variations in that secondary break. Racan himself, it will be remembered, was unwilling to adhere to the rigid demands of his master on that score.[118] There is little doubt that Racan, and perhaps even Maynard, understood the full implications of this system better than Malherbe himself. By his choice of forms and the implementation of them, Benserade showed that

[116] Ibid., p. 23.
[117] Cited by Mongrédien, "Vers inédits de Benserade," RHLF 30 (1923): 513.
[118] Racan, Œuvres complètes, 1:283.

while he may not have been the poetical peer of Racan, and while he obviously lacked the discipline required, he understood many of the Malherbian principles equally well. In the realm of *précieux* poetry there were better poets. There were no better Malherbians.

As I stated earlier, the great odes were not in vogue with the independent poets of this period. In the serious praise of State or God, in any form, the harvest was indeed meager. Only two poets of any merit, Brébeuf and Arnauld, were involved, the rest of the production coming from rather talentless poetasters or, as in the case of Benserade, from otherwise good writers who were misguided into thinking they could also succeed in these genres.

At various stages of his career, Benserade attempted to produce serious poetry. The results, violating every rule of prosody under consideration, are uniformly bad. The "Paraphrases sur les IX leçons de Iob" (1638) are replete with senseless enumerations, enjambments, and padding:

> *N'as-tu pas étendu sur toutes ses parties,*
> *Et des peaux, et des chairs?*
> *Et quel autre que toy les eust mieux assorties*
> *D'os, de muscles, de nerfs?*[119]

Most of the sestets, even those in alexandrines, are constructed of single syntactical units, and the sense is not always clear.[120] His serious secular poetry is no better. In 1658, on the occasion of the "Guérison de Sa Majesté," he wrote a long poem in octosyllabic *vers suivis* with very long sentences and rhymes that are bad even when compared to Benserade's own.[121] "Sur l'accomplissement du mariage de Leurs Majestez," in decasyllabic *vers suivis*, has many lines that defy rapid reading: "Muse, en un mot, je ne m'en puis plus taire," and frequent enjambments:

> *Et donne-moy le secret de pouvoir*
> *L'enveloper pour le faire entrevoir.*[122]

---

[119] Cited by Leblanc, *Paraphrases,* p. 118.
[120] See ibid., pp. 252–53.
[121] Mongrédien, "Vers inédits de Benserade," pp. 515–17.
[122] *Œuvres,* 1:1–2.

In all of these poems, the rhymes are very unsatisfactory, and entire lines verge on the cacophonic, one *chute* in a 12–12–12–4 quatrain reading "Mons en Hainaut."[123]

Several names must be mentioned here, not because they represent any great talent, but because they were held in esteem by the critics and readers of their days. Antoine Corneille, for instance, won several prizes at the Rouen *palinods*, perhaps because some of his poems had a familiar ring:

> *Percée au plus profond du cœur*
> *D'une atteinte imprévue aussi bien que mortelle,*
> *Droite au pied de la croix où son cher fils l'appelle,*
> *La Vierge, triste objet d'une injuste rigueur, . . .*[124]

The hiatus in the first line indicates, however, that neither his older brother nor Malherbe had taught him very much. Although the four lines above comprise the first stanza of a paraphrase of the *Stabat Mater*, they are far from containing all of the first sentence. The stanzas have neither the same length nor the same heterometry, yet several times there are sentences straddling stanzas. The poet may well have had a certain vogue in Rouen and Paris, but his brother's reputation probably had much to do with that.

The popularity of Le Maître de Sacy's poetry rests on equally shaky grounds. In his choice of forms, in the lack of discipline demonstrated by many of his rhymes, he is far from Malherbian.[125] The only claim to fame of the 2,000 octosyllabics of the *Enluminures* is that their structure "fût toute extraordinaire et n'eût jamais eu d'exemple."[126] The reputation which the author had earned through his other endeavors undoubtedly helped his poems to achieve their popularity.

More puzzling still is the fact that the slight reputation of Père Le

---

[123] Ibid., p. 53.

[124] Allem, *Anthologie*, 2:93–94.

[125] See Yves Leblanc, "Les enluminures de Le Maître de Sacy," DSS 32 (1956):475–501 passim.

[126] Godefroy Hermant, *Mémoires* (Paris: Plon-Nourrit, 1905–1910), 2:380.

Moyne did not die out completely as the century went on. Chapelain granted him a relative purity of style, but one which "tient de la déclamation, est guindé, diffus, enflé et rempli de figures vicieuses," and which, when trying to become sublime, invariably "dégénère en hyperbolique."[127] Costar readily agreed: "Ses vers sont si figurez qu'ils sont extravagants."[128] What makes his survival all the more surprising is that he is in many ways a transitional figure. We shall see in a moment how this affected his versification, but a more fundamental aspect of his poetry deserves first to be commented on.

Jean Rousset, in his *Anthologie de la poésie baroque française*, includes thirteen selections from Le Moyne, a number equaled only by Hopil and surpassed only by d'Aubigné, La Ceppède, and Saint-Amant. Nor can the judgment of the compiler be faulted, because in many ways Le Moyne is indeed "baroque." His descriptions are a phantasmagoria of light, color, movement, fire, water, all that Rousset sees as the very essence of baroque art.[129] In these poems, Le Moyne tried to do what Saint-Amant and Tristan L'Hermite were doing so well at the time. Unfortunately he failed, for two reasons. Whereas the two greater poets had a genuine sense of *coloris*, he did not. His paintings remain vague and even abstract:

> *Leur dehors pour un temps lumineux et doré*
> *Des faveurs du soleil nous paroist coloré;*
> *Elles sont à nos yeux des soleils elles-mesmes,*
> *De longs rayons de feu leur font des diadèmes;*[130]

But worse than this is his tendency to moralize. Somehow, the poet never seems able to get past the Jesuit, and what starts out as a beautiful description of water ends as a platitudinous sermon:

> *Et puis, voyant nager sur la face des eaux*
> *Les images du ciel, des arbres, des oyseaux,*

[127] *Opuscules critiques*, pp. 346–47.
[128] Lachèvre, *Bibliographie*, 2:335.
[129] For a thorough discussion of this aspect of Le Moyne, see the brilliant pages in Rousset's *Littérature de l'âge baroque*, pp. 125–51. For examples, see his *Anthologie*, 1:76, 179, 251–53; 2:14–15, 30–33, 52–53, 95–96, 149–51.
[130] Cited by Rousset, *Littérature de l'âge baroque*, p. 132.

Il est ainsi, dit-il, des plaisirs de ce monde,
Ce ne sont . . .[131]

and so on until the landscape is completely forgotten. In temperament, then, he is kin to neither Malherbe nor Saint-Amant. In matters of prosody, the verdict is equally mixed.

Although there are some sonnets and sestets, most of Le Moyne's lyric poems are in *dizains*. While the form of the hymns is far from Malherbian (seven octosyllabics followed by three alexandrines), the odes are all octosyllabic *dizains*. The hymns as well as the odes all use Malherbian rhyme schemes and are divided 4–3–3. The linearity is generally good and a comparison of early and later versions of poems shows that most of the changes improved it further. Unfortunately, the same comparison shows that Le Moyne never tried to improve rhymes which badly needed it. This is, in fact, the weakest part of his prosody. Even in the reworked odes, synaereses rhyme with diaereses, long sounds with short ones, monosyllabic homonyms abound, and the *consonne d'appui* is frequently unacceptable. In short, in the cut of his ten-line stanzas and in his linearity, Le Moyne constantly tried to improve his already Malherbian tendencies. In all other respects he seemed unaware of the very existence of concepts.

Des Barreaux and Patrix, both libertines in their early years and both reformed later on, were not unlike Le Moyne in many respects. The early poetry of des Barreaux, very free and un-Malherbian, has already been discussed. That of Patrix is no less unorthodox. Even in his occasional poetry, which might have been more carefully crafted than his bawdy songs, Patrix failed on many counts. "Sur le siège de Gravelines" (1645) is in octosyllabic sestets with varied breaks, *a b a b c c* rhyme scheme, and rhymes such as *inutilles-filles, prise-entreprise,* and monosyllabic homophones. Several lines verge on the cacophonic: "A qui sçait ce que c'est qu'amour."[132] His later poems, however, are quite different, and his belated popularity is entirely due to these. Except for some poems in *vers suivis,* the bulk of his production is in stanzas frequently used by Malherbe. The linearity is invariably good, as are the rhymes in all re-

[131] Rousset, *Anthologie,* 1:251.
[132] Blot L'Eglise, *Chansons libertines,* pp. 80–82.

spects excepting the eternal question of the *consonne d'appui*, although there too the lapses are less frequent than in most poems of the day. The balance of the isometric stanzas is above reproach:

> *Que deviendrai-je donc, ô pécheur misérable?*
> *Un état si douteux me doit bien étonner;*
> *Je pars tel que je suis, innocent ou coupable,*
> *Et Dieu me va tantôt absoudre ou condamner.*[133]

His heterometric quatrains frequently have *chutes* that recall the better efforts of Malherbe and Maynard:

> *Déjà de toutes parts, je sens venir l'orage;*
> *L'état de ma santé commence à s'empirer:*
> *Ma barque, en vieillissant, doit craindre le naufrage,*
> *Il s'y faut préparer.*[134]

Though des Barreaux did not try to destroy all his earlier poems, as Patrix did, he nevertheless abandoned the libertinism of his youth. It is difficult to date his poems with any degree of accuracy, but some twenty of them can be ascribed to this period of "assagissement."[135] All but two of these are sonnets, fifteen of which are in alexandrines. As far as the rhyme scheme is concerned, one is truly free (*a b b a b a a b c c d e e d*) and the others employ *a b b a* as often as *a b a b,* and the unorthodox *e e d* almost as often as *e d e.* The linearity of his earlier works had left much to be desired:

> *Nous n'appréhendons point la mort, mais le dommage*
> *Qu'apporte le non estre; et ce fatal moment*
> *Qui nous porte à la triste horreur du monument*
> *Doit estre justement appréhendé du Sage.*[136]

---

[133] Picard, *Poésie française,* p. 152.

[134] A. C. Lefort de la Morinière, *Bibliothèque poëtique* (Paris: Briasson, 1745), 1:451.

[135] Frédéric Lachèvre, *Jacques Vallée des Barreaux: Sa vie et ses poésies* (Paris: Leclerc, 1907), pp. 227 ff.

[136] Ibid., p. 251.

In his later efforts, he adhered to a very strict concept of linearity. As far as forms are concerned, then, it must be admitted that both choice and discipline improved but not rhyme schemes. As for the rhymes, they are as bad as those of Patrix, if not worse: in addition to the usual errors, there is the frequent recurrence of certain couplings (*vie-suivie, vie-envie, sort-mort*) and leonine rhymes ("Celuy qui vit pour l'autre vie"[137]). Looking at the growing popularity of these two poets late in the century, an interesting conclusion imposes itself: Patrix used Malherbian forms and rhyme schemes, des Barreaux ignored the latter consideration. Both took great care with inner structure but neither worried much about rhymes. As far as they were concerned, what Boileau called Malherbe's "juste cadence" was obviously important. The rest of Malherbe's concepts were not.

Georges de Brébeuf, although not a member of the Academy, was held in high esteem by most of his contemporaries, perhaps more so than any other poet discussed in this chapter. Corneille admired him, as did Chapelain, who considered his *Entretiens* not only saintly but full of poetic delights.[138] His poems in general and his epigrams in particular were frequently reproduced in the *recueils* until the end of the century. Boileau had some mixed opinions about *La Pharsale* but never mentioned Brébeuf's lyric poetry, though two centuries later René Harmand would consider Brébeuf worthy "d'être cité au premier rang parmi les contemporains de Corneille."[139]

In the early production of Brébeuf, badinage and burlesque consistently have the upper hand. With lines such as

> *L'ame bonne, l'ame blanche,*
> *L'ame droite, l'ame franche,*[140]

and the usual liberties in every aspect of prosody, the burlesque poems need not delay us here. The *précieux*, lighthearted ones deserve some comment. The *dizains*, many of which are heptasyllabic, always have a strong break after the fourth line and a weaker one after the seventh:

---

137 Ibid., p. 227.
138 *Lettres*, 2:87.
139 Lachèvre, *Bibliographie*, 2:171.
140 *Lucain travesti*, cited by Bar, *Genre burlesque*, p. 343.

Allez donc où vous engage
Votre léger ascendant.
Je n'y perds qu'une volage
Et j'y gagne en la perdant.
Une amitié plus durable
M'eût rendu plus misérable
Que m'ont fait vos changements,
Et dans ces vicissitudes
J'aime vos ingratitudes
Plus que vos ressentiments.[141]

Note in passing that the rhymes are quite good and the balance and linearity above reproach. Ironically, not all his sestets fared so well:

Quand de votre beauté je parle
Chez le droguiste, maître Charle,
Il me répond d'une fierté
Dont mon âme est tout effrayée:
"Ce sera, dit-il, sa beauté,
Lorsqu'elle me l'aura payée."[142]

Brébeuf also wrote a great number of heterometric quatrains of octosyllabic and alexandrine lines. In many of these he experimented, changing the combination several times within the same poem. The five stanzas of "Sur le portrait de l'Amour fait de sa main" are structured as follows: 8–12–12–8, 8–12–12–12, 12–12–12–12, 12–8–12–12, and 8–12–12–8, all *a b a b*;[143] "Sur un papillon qui était entré dans l'œil de Mlle ***" differs only in that several quatrains contain only one alexandrine, an unorthodox situation. Of course, while individual stanzas may be Malherbian, such a poem, lacking structural unity, is not.

As he grew older, Brébeuf abandoned preciosity and burlesque for the sake of occasional and religious poetry. One of the most interesting of these works is the epitaph of Elizabeth Ranquet.[144] Although Brébeuf

---

[141] Cited by Faguet, *Histoire de la poésie*, 3:281.

[142] Cited by Mongrédien, *Les précieux et les précieuses* (Paris: Mercure de France, 1963), p. 189.

[143] Ibid., p. 188.

hated to correct his work, he made several key changes in this sonnet, thus giving a good insight into his poetic principles. For instance, in its original version, the first quatrain read as follows:

Ne verse point de pleurs sur cette sépulture
Tu vois de Leonor le tombeau précieux,
Où gît d'un corps tout pur la cendre toute pure
Mais la vertu du cœur vit encore en ces lieux.[145]

In 1661, line four became "Mais l'éclat de son nom brille encore en ces lieux," and in 1662 the last two lines were changed to

Où gît de son beau corps la cendre toute pure
Mais sa rare vertu vit encore en ces lieux.[146]

The cacophonic "vertu du" was removed, but the balance and the skillful echo were lost in the process. At least as interesting is the fact that the unsatisfactory *b* rhymes were left unchanged, as they were in the second quatrain.

The *magnum opus* of this period is Brébeuf's *Entretiens solitaires*. In his introduction to the critical edition, René Harmand, commenting on the fact that many of the ideas of the *Entretiens* could be found in Racan and Malherbe, spoke of influence and even of "emprunts."[147] This is somewhat unfair and highly debatable, for we are dealing here with a prayerbook whose content could not be based on great flights of imagination and was bound to contain many commonplaces. If one is to seek influence and borrowing from a specific source, it must be in the realm of form, where the poet was free to select or to create.

Being a compatriot of Malherbe, Brébeuf saw nothing wrong with *rimes normandes*. Like most of his contemporaries, he was not nearly as

---

[144] Many critics have tackled the question of the authorship of this sonnet, the most cogent arguments being those of Kurt Wais, "Corneille oder Brébeuf," *Archiv* 169 (1936):213–23, and of André Blanchard, "Corneille et Brébeuf," *CS* 356 (1960):130–34.

[145] Blanchard, *Baroques et classiques*, p. 132.

[146] Ibid., p. 133.

[147] *Entretiens solitaires* (Paris: Cornély, 1912), pp. xxxix–xli.

rigorous as Malherbe where the *consonne d'appui* was concerned. In all other respects, lapses are few indeed, and most of these deal with the diaeresis-synaeresis rhymes which almost everyone allowed. The linearity of the *Entretiens* is nearly perfect, with few enjambments and well balanced lines. His choice of forms, however, demands a more detailed comment.[148] The book is divided into twenty-eight "chapters," twenty-four of which are composed of single poems, the rest being made of diverse smaller ones. Of the twenty-four, four are in alexandrine *vers suivis*, two in heterometric *huitains*, neither of which is a Malherbian form. The rest are either in *stances* to be found in Malherbe or experimentations in heterometric combinations that Malherbe never used but that are nevertheless not foreign to the spirit. By this I mean that all the heterometric stanzas are dimetric, all but four combining octosyllabics with alexandrines, the four having hexasyllabics with alexandrines. There is a greater variety in the many short poems composing the four remaining chapters, but here again, the vast majority are in no way contrary to Malherbian practice or theory. Furthermore, with only rare exceptions, the sestets are cut 3–3 and the ten-line stanzas 4–3–3 with a strong break after the fourth line.

What is even more remarkable is Brébeuf's good sense of rhythm, manifest even in forms that would seem to tax these powers in any poet:

> *O qu'une ame, Seigneur, contre vous revoltée,*
> *Est souvent inquiéte et souvent agitée,*
> *Que la paix dans son cœur sejourne rarement!*
> *Ses troubles sont frequents, son chagrin est extrême,*
>   *Et son crime est luy mesme*
>   *Son premier châtiment.*[149]

This skill is particularly obvious when it is put to balancing various thoughts, as he does in chapter 26, where he presents the "paradoxe de l'infini dans le limité, de l'essence dans la contingence":[150]

[148] René Harmand, at the end of his critical edition of the *Entretiens*, compiled a very complete table of the metrics of the collection. From that table the following figures are taken.

[149] *Entretiens*, p. 64.

[150] Rousset, *Anthologie*, 2:303.

Cette intelligence premiere,
Cette Essence infinie, et cet Estre constant,
Qui de vostre naissance a precedé l'instant
    D'une Eternité entiere,

    . . . .

    Cette Essence haute et profonde,
Qui demeure en soy-mesme, et se trouve en tous lieux,
Cet Estre qui remplit et la terre et les Cieux,
    Sans qu'il s'enferme dans le Monde;
    Luy qui par son immensité
Trouvant cet Univers un lieu trop limité,
Loin au-delà des Cieux habite dans soy-mesme:
Il semble dédaigner ces Palais éclatans,
    Et reduit sa grandeur suprême
    A se renfermer dans vos flancs.[151]

Malherbe never used a *dizain* containing five alexandrines, but it would be difficult to consider this stanza un-Malherbian.

Robert Arnauld d'Andilly wrote his "Ode sur la solitude" (1645) in ten-line stanzas of the same type, that is, combining five alexandrines with five octosyllabics:

    Affranchi de l'inquiétude
    Et des vains travaux de la Cour,
    Chante, mon ame, ton amour
    Pour ton heureuse solitude.
Chante l'aveuglement qui porte les mortels
A faire tant de vœux, et bâtir tant d'Autels
Au fantôme adoré sous le nom de Fortune.
Chante l'Astre éternel, dont la flamme reluit
    Dans ce Soleil et cette Lune
Qui regnent à leur tour sur le jour et la nuit.[152]

Throughout this ode, except for the *consonne d'appui*, the rhymes are good but the linearity, as can be seen, is not, and the total effect is cer-

[151] *Entretiens*, pp. 198–99.
[152] Goujet, *Bibliothèque françoise*, 17:333–34.

tainly not on a par with that achieved by Brébeuf. In two earlier works, "Vie de Jésus" (1634) and "Stances sur diverses vérités chrétiennes" (1642), Arnauld had relied on alexandrine *dizains*. In the first, the caesuras are very strong, as is the break after the fourth line, although the secondary break varies in both strength and location. In the second work, although the form is still basically un-Malherbian, a certain influence can be detected: the rhymes have fewer lapses, and the secondary break is, in almost all stanzas, after the seventh line. Thus Arnauld, who was held in very high esteem by all his contemporaries,[153] began by accepting some of the more important lessons Malherbe had to offer, only to forget them later on, and consistently shied away from Malherbian forms. In view of this, it is interesting to note that in only one anthology, the *Recueil La Fontaine*, is he well represented. This may have been due in part to the fact that, as he had said in stanza 83 of the "Stances sur diverses vérités chrétiennes," he believed in using poetry only to further religion. It may also have been due to the strong voice he had in the composition of that collection.[154]

That Malherbe was read at Port-Royal is also demonstrated by the poetry of Jacqueline Pascal, whose lyrical career was stopped by her spiritual guides at a moment when she was beginning to show some genuine talent. Born in 1625, Jacqueline Pascal made her literary debut twelve years later. Her earliest poems are remarkable for a child of her age but, in spite of what has been said, do not show a great command of prosody:

> *Cher pere, ne crains point l'effort*
> *Du temps, ni mesme la mort;*
> *C'est en vain qu'ils te font la guerre.*
> *Ils peuvent bien ravir ta presence à nos yeux;*
> *Mais ton ame à jamais vivra dedans les cieux,*
> *Et ton renom dessus la terre.*[155]

[153] See Gédéon Tallemant des Réaux, *Les historiettes* (Paris: Techener, 1854–1860), 3:266; Chapelain, *Lettres*, passim; Goujet, *Bibliothèque française*, 17:335–38. Arnauld had been invited to join the Académie but had declined.

[154] For details of his role, see Ferdinand Gohin, "La poésie à Port-Royal: La Fontaine et Arnauld d'Andilly," *MdF* 246 (1933):519–21.

No stanza is without its enjambment and the rhymes are quite bad. The various heterometric combinations seldom show a unity of form and content, a failing leading to some very unfortunate "chutes"; furthermore, very few of these combinations are Malherbian. What is remarkable is not the low quality of these precocious poems but that, as early as 1640, a definite improvement was to be noted. To be sure, most of the forms are still not Malherbian and the rhymes are far from satisfactory, but the difference is undeniable. At the age of fifteen, "la petite Pascal" won first prize at the *palinod* of Rouen with her "Sur la conception de la Vierge" in alexandrine quatrains. Within the next five years, her command of the art improved immeasurably and the "Consolation sur la mort d'une Huguenote" (1645) is a regular poem by almost any standards. After a silence of nearly five years imposed by her superiors, Jacqueline Pascal put the translation of a hymn into verse. While it shows that she had not yet mastered the art of rhyming, the balance of the lines is above reproach:

> *Jesus, digne rançon de l'homme racheté,*
> *Amour de notre cœur et desir de notre ame,*
> *Seul createur de tout, Dieu dans l'eternité,*
> *Homme à la fin des temps en naissant d'une femme.*[156]

Ironically, while Arnauld believed that poetry could be used to further religion, Singlin considered it only a vehicle for self-aggrandizement, and so he ordered the young poetess to cease her lyrical activities. Only once did she return to the craft, in 1656, writing twenty-five *dizains* on the miracle of the holy thorn.[157] Like Arnauld, she had forgotten everything: no two consecutive stanzas have the same breaks, and some have none at all; the rhymes are seldom good, and some of the worst combinations are repeated (*moy-toy, moy-soy, ame-flamme, choix-voix*).

It seems that at Port-Royal, as at the Academy, as almost everywhere in France, Malherbe's time had not yet come, and at least as far as the poets discussed until now were concerned, not "Tout reconnut ses loix."

---

[155] Blaise Pascal, *Œuvres complètes* (Paris: Hachette, 1904–1914), 1:207.

[156] Ibid., 2:424.

[157] Ibid., 6:103–14.

Chapter Eight

The New Wave

Whereas, in the Academy, the bulk of the poets may have been conservative, even *attardés*—and this is natural in an official group that has a tendency to perpetuate its tastes—it should be obvious that outside of this august body the proportions were not the same. While, as we have seen, there were many old poets still actively plying their trade under somewhat worn banners, there was also a rapidly increasing number of young and often iconoclastic poets anxious to prove their mettle. Their talents were very diverse, as were their tastes, but almost all had one thing in common: the desire to break with the trends that had sidetracked so many of their older fellow poets. Boileau, it is true, maintained that everyone followed Malherbe once he came, but one has only to look at the long list of poets Boileau ridiculed to realize that even the best of these (and they include some very good ones) had strayed from the narrow path.

Many of these younger poets appeared but briefly on the literary horizon. Among these, one might mention the Abbé de Baralis, who had twenty-eight poems in the 1658 Sercy *recueil* and was never heard of again; La Thuillière, whose airs enjoyed a brief popularity; and Madame de Lauvergne, whose poems were published posthumously even though the public had had a sample in the *recueil* La Suze:

> *Hélas! je me trahis quand j'agis autrement,*
> *Je ne sçaurois aimer sans l'aimer ardemment. . . .*[1]

There were also poets such as Benigne de Bacilly, whose airs were published only in his own anthologies, and the Président de Périgny, whose poems were only published during his brief reign as preceptor to the Dauphin. Still others owed what fleeting fame they had to important friends: Chapelain considered an ode by Louis de Francheville "forte et brillante,"[2] but few shared that opinion; Testu-Mauroy's reputation was due in large part to the protection of a powerful lord who eventually got him into the Academy.[3]

There were also writers who dabbled in lyric poetry but whose reputation was and remains based on other works. Some of these were mediocre at best: Pellisson, Somaize, Hauteroche, Métivier. Others were among the very great: Molière and Racine. In fact, what strikes even the most casual researcher is the tremendous number of poets active at that time, a phenomenon which goes a long way toward explaining the wide range of talent and taste. Furthermore, whereas the subjects of the previous chapter were men condemned to live and work on the fringe of the establishment, many of the young poets about to be treated were destined to enter—and radically affect—all sectors of that establishment.

To be sure, not all poets were dedicated to serious endeavors. There was a strong vogue of light poetry, of polymorphous genres which defy codification, just as there was still a strong current of "poésie galante [qui] ne veut pas être prise au sérieux."[4] Again, it must be stated that in such poetry there is no possibility of strict observance of Malherbian precepts, but a rapid glance may nonetheless be worthwhile. First, however, a distinction must be made between those poets who wrote light verse exclusively and were therefore never hampered by any care for form and those (La Fontaine and Boileau immediately come to mind) who were very conscious of their art but indulged at times in poetic badinage. At the outset, it must be understood that by "light" verse I refer not to content but to either form or a lack of serious regard for craftsmanship.

Some of these poets did not even take their craft seriously. Claude de Chaulne, for example, as Nodier noted and Lachèvre later confirmed, dictated his poems to a servant "à qui la prosodie était certainement étrangère."[5] It is therefore not surprising that every rule concerning rhymes is repeatedly broken and the linearity is marginal at best:

[1] Cited by Fukui, *Raffinement précieux*, p. 291.

[2] *Lettres*, 2:82.

[3] Jean Lerond d'Alembert, *Histoire des membres de l'Académie Française* (Paris: Moutard, 1787), 2:307–34.

[4] Victor Cousin, *La société française au XVIIe siècle* (Paris: Didier, 1858), 2:285.

[5] Frédéric Lachèvre, *Les derniers libertins* (Geneva: Slatkine, 1968), p. 260. See also Charles Nodier, "Notice sur les poésies de Claude de Chaulne," *BBB* 2 (1836):90.

> *Et ne croy pas de leur devoir céder*
> *Au Parlement, ni mesmes à la Chambre,*[6]

a fault compounded by rapid changes of tone and lapses into bad taste:

> *Loing de vous j'ay le groin plus blesme,*
> *Que celuy qui premier osa*
> *Chanter sur le ton du caresme*
> Stabat mater dolorosa.[7]

Much the same can be said of Edme Boursault, one of the "continuateurs de Loret." While some of his sonnets are relatively orthodox, most of his poems are not. His stanzas are anything but Malherbian in choice of form and execution:

> *Dans une officialité,*
> *Ces jours passez, une soubrette*
> *Passablement belle et bien faicte,*
> *Et d'une robuste santé,*
> *Avec la bienséance ayant fait plain divorce,*
> *Dit qu'un vieux médecin l'avoit prise par force,*
> *Qu'il falloit, ou le pendre, ou qu'il fût son mary.*[8]

His lines are badly balanced and invariably prosaic:

> *En faisant sa visite un Evêque assuré*
> *De l'ignorance d'un curé . . .*[9]

and the heterometry of some of his poems must be considered at least "libérée." For example, "Flore, la larme à l'œil et l'âme désolée" is in hetero-metric ten-line stanzas, combining lines of twelve and seven syllables in highly varied combinations with some very unfortunate *chutes* resulting:

[6] Cited in Lachèvre, *Derniers libertins,* p. 269.
[7] Ibid., p. 355.
[8] Olivier, *Cent poètes lyriques,* p. 519.
[9] Ibid., p. 518.

Et, voyant à présent quelle faute il a faite,
Le nigaud qui la regrette
Se souffle le bout des doigts.[10]

Such disregard for even the most basic rules of prosody should not surprise in poetry that was meant only to amuse and was undoubtedly written
as an amusement for the poet. This is most obvious in the works of Samuel
Ysarn, one of the wittiest of authors, who always sacrificed orthodoxy on
the altar of effect:

Tous les cœurs plus attiédis,
Tous les cœurs les plus refroidis,
Et dans la glace tout roidis,
Sont enflammés par vos beaux dits,
Et moy-mesme je me rendis
Dès lors que je vous entendis
Dans vos aymables Samedis.[11]

Not all the stanzas of this monorhyme poem to Madeleine de Scudéry
are of the same length. Equally clever, and equally unorthodox, is this
stanza of "galanterie":

Mais non, je ne m'en puis taire;
Dans vos vers remplis d'appas,
Je vous trouve à chaque pas
Et seulement pour vous plaire,
Je ne vous conoistray pas.[12]

Ysarn's most popular work is *Le louis d'or*,[13] a combination of prose and
poetry that defies prosodic analysis, but a single look at the rhymes will
show that the author had not even intended to follow any rules, and that
criticism along these lines would be senseless.

[10] Allem, *Anthologie*, 2:352.
[11] Cited by Mongrédien, *Madeleine de Scudéry*, p. 104.
[12] Ibid., p. 110.
[13] Fournier, *Variétés*, 10:235 ff.

Not all of these *badins* have fallen into complete oblivion, of course, and the madrigals of Antoine de La Sablière, in spite of their freedom and occasional cacophony ("Si je n'en eusse connu qu'une"[14]) still find their way into anthologies. In his own days, Etienne Pavillon was considered to combine the best of Voiture and Benserade, and he replaced the latter at the Academy in 1691. The eighteenth century quickly reversed that judgment, but Pavillon, despite his bad rhymes, his frequent lapses concerning hiatus, and his bad linearity, still manages to appear in an occasional anthology. Many other poets of that vein are remembered today, mostly because of their literary associations. Thus Montreuil is remembered mainly because Boileau made fun of his popular ditties,[15] and no one would mention Le Royer de Prade were it not for his attachment for Cyrano and his part in Cyrano's fight with Dassoucy.[16]

The most illustrious of these *badins* are undoubtedly Chapelle and Bachaumont, whose famous *Voyage* is still considered one of the best works of its type, combining as it does prose and poetry into a delightful whole. The verse, more akin to the poems of Chapelle than the *mazarinades* sometimes attributed to Bachaumont, makes no attempt at orthodoxy, as the first lines show:

> *C'est en vers que je vous écris,*
> *Messieurs les deux frères, nourris*
> *Aussi bien que gens de la ville.*[17]

Most of the poetry of Chapelle is in isometric (octosyllabic) *vers suivis* or, when heterometric, with a strong octosyllabic basis. Even his *stances* and odes are, by his own admission, "irregular," as are his somewhat more serious sonnets.[18] The linearity, recalling that of the *Voyage,* is anything but disciplined:

[14] Antoine de Rambouillet, sr. de La Sablière, *Madrigaux* (Lyon: Amaulry, 1681), p. 63.

[15] *Œuvres complètes*, p. 40.

[16] For details of this quarrel, see the Lachèvre edition of Cyrano, *Œuvres libertines,* 1:lxxxiv.

[17] Chapelle and Bachaumont, *Voyage* (Paris: Letellier, 1826), p. 1.

[18] Ibid., pp. 77, 106.

Cruelle princesse, qui fais
Que tous les jours je me retranche
Les longs dîners de la Croix blanche,
Et les charmants soirs du Marais,
Qu'absent tu me tourmentes! Mais
J'en aurai bientôt ma revanche.[19]

Few poems are without enjambments, some having several in rapid succession,[20] some extremely obvious:

. . . si vous demandez qu'est-ce
Qui cause. . . .[21]

As for his rhymes, they were of no concern to him, and he called one poem a "tirade d'adverbes en *ment.*"[22]

And yet Boileau considered Chapelle one of the two "plus beaux Esprits" of the century,[23] and Bernier, in his epitaph, said "Jamais la nature ne fit une imagination plus vive, un esprit plus pénétrant, plus fin, plus délicat, plus enjoué, plus agréable," considering him a sure critic of taste.[24] Neither Bernier nor Boileau considered him a great craftsman. Nevertheless, it would be wrong to think that Chapelle had no concern whatsoever for his art. There are two versions of a letter to "MM. de Nantouillet et de Sarcelles," one published by Barbin in 1692, and one autograph at Mariemont, and the variants are most interesting, for they show a "souci d'éviter les répétitions de sonorités à l'intérieur d'un même vers, . . . Souci également de supprimer quelques inversions."[25] There are also attempts to improve the rhyme scheme, though these are more comic than rigorous: the *épître* is in *vers suivis*, divided into what might

[19] Ibid., p. 81.
[20] See "A M. d'Assoucy" in ibid., pp. 125–26.
[21] Ibid., p. 91.
[22] Ibid.
[23] Letter to Brossette, 1 April 1700.
[24] Georges Mongrédien, "Le meilleur ami de Molière, Chapelle," *MdF* 329 (1957):259.
[25] Marie-Jeanne Durry, *Autographes de Mariemont* (Paris: Nizet, 1955), 1:17.

be termed paragraphs. One such paragraph has twenty-five lines all ending in either *ire* or *si,* a tour de force maintained in both versions where the *consonne d'appui* is so inadequate that one should speak of assonances rather than rhymes, a fact which made the removal of inner assonances all the more important. In both versions, enjambments are very frequent. So, while it must be admitted that Chapelle tried to improve sounds and syntax, he could not have been motivated by thoughts of Malherbe or of "juste cadence."

Ironically, there was one poet in this kingdom of badinage who had heard of Malherbe, Gaspard de Fieubet. The irony is that he took Malherbian forms and degraded them by the use he made of them. His song "Sur le raisin" is replete with errors in prosody and cacophonic passages: "S'il eut eu des muscats. . . ."[26] It is written in 12–12–12–12–6–6 stanzas, as is the song "Sur le cidre":

> O charmante liqueur, ô liqueur sans pareille,
> De combien vaux-tu mieux que le jus de la treille,
> Tu l'as sur tous les fruits de tout temps emporté,
> L'homme le plus parfait, Adam le premier homme
>   Renonça pour la pomme
>   A l'immoratalité.[27]

To fully appreciate the extent of the irony, it must be remembered that Malherbe used this form for a totally different purpose in the famous "N'espérons plus, mon ame, aux promesses du monde."

The above poets were given to writing light verse almost exclusively, and therefore could not be expected to be disciplined. Others, although known principally for their serious endeavors, occasionally indulged in more frivolous diversions. It could therefore be expected that the skill lavished on the masterpieces might also be present, although to a lesser degree, in these "petits riens," some of which I shall now examine.

François de Maucroix was born in 1619 and is considered here with much younger authors because of his late blossoming and close association with La Fontaine and his contemporaries. Very prolific, Maucroix used so many different forms that some of these were bound to coincide with those

[26] Lachèvre, *Bibliographie,* 3:333.
[27] Ibid.

used by Malherbe, but it is difficult to see in this anything more than co-incidence. Seeking *le naturel* above all else, Maucroix succeeded only in writing prosaic lines devoid of rhythmic character, a trait particularly obvious in the lighter poems, such as the hitherto unpublished ones of Reims, made available recently by René Kohn.[28] These are, for the most part, quite obscene, but even the others are far from regular. The sonnet "Quel bonheur est égal à mon bonheur extreme"[29] has an *a b b a c d c d e e f g f g* scheme and is replete with errors of prosody.

François Colletet, known today primarily for his arts of poetry, also indulged in more frivolous pastimes, but all are marred by bad rhymes, padding, and unbalanced lines; witness this excerpt from "Le tracas de Paris":

> *C'est une balle dans le corps*
> *Qui luy perce son juste-au-corps;*
> *Au meurtre! au meurtre! A l'ayde! à l'ayde!*
> *Secours! Un Prestre et du remede![30]*

This is obviously burlesque at its very worst.

Madame de Villedieu's most famous work is her delightful "Récit en prose et en vers de la Farce des Précieuses."[31] As with most works mixing prose and verse, the poetry is very light in tone and completely devoid of discipline. The stanzas are either isolated or, in the rare cases where there are more than one, "irregular." Few of the forms are Malherbian, and the rhymes, linearity, heterometry, and cuts of stanzas are haphazard at best. If, as critics have so often stated, Madame de Villedieu earned her living with her pen, and if this was her most popular work, then Malherbe had certainly not entrenched himself by 1660.

Much the same can be said of the popularity of Pierre Perrin, credited with having created French opera,[32] whose poems were set to

---

[28] *Lettres* (Paris: Presses Universitaires de France, 1962), pp. 205–35.

[29] Ibid., pp. 207–08.

[30] Paul Lacroix, ed., *Paris ridicule et burlesque* (Paris: Delahays, 1859), p. 211.

[31] Molière, *Œuvres* (Paris: Hachette, 1923–1925), 2:115–34.

[32] Arthur Pougin, *Les vrais créateurs de l'opéra français: Perrin et Cambert* (Paris: Charavay, 1881).

music by the best composers of his day. By 1645 he had composed a set of poems dealing with various insects. In these his vein, light and easy-flowing, is much better served than in the serious poems he occasionally wrote, but the results, for all that, cannot be considered orthodox. "La fourmi"[33] is written in 10–10–10–12, *a b a b* quatrains, has no concern for the *consonne d'appui,* and even uses rhymes such as *détourne-retourne* and *inégal-travail.* Although "Le papillon" uses a more orthodox form, its sentences run from one stanza to the next and its rhymes are no better. The forms used for these insects are very diverse, ranging from alexandrine *vers suivis* ("L'abeille") to octosyllabic ten-line stanzas used, ironically, for the most insignificant of all the creatures described ("Le moucheron"). However, this is not where Perrin's departure from Malherbian norms is greatest. While he lacks Saint-Amant's descriptive powers, his light poetry is nevertheless oriented toward the descriptive:

> *Observe une belle muance*
> *Dans ce petit cerne azuré,*
> *Et que ce verd et ce doré*
> *Font une discrette nuance.*[34]

To obtain the flitting effect of the butterfly, he radically alters the rhythm:

> *Beau Phœnix, Plante sans racines,*
> *Amour, Ange, discret voleur,*
> *Oyseau fleury, volante fleur,*
> *Petit paon, rose sans épines.*[35]

The results are indeed felicitous, but hardly Malherbian.

René Le Pays is another author involved in writing both serious and light verse. Many of his works, including *Zélotyde,* a novel recently examined by Maurice Cagnon,[36] are a mixture of prose and loosely rhymed free verse. Even the poetry written in stable forms defies analysis.

[33] Allem, *Anthologie,* 1:343–45.
[34] "Le papillon," Rousset, *Anthologie,* 1:153.
[35] Ibid., p. 154.
[36] "Zélotyde: un roman négligé du XVIIe siècle," *DSS* 79 (1968): 43–56.

The rhymes are seldom satisfactory, with inner rhymes often making the reading quite difficult.[37] Padding is omnipresent, even in the sonnets:

> *Vn jeune Matelot, Messieurs, le croirez-vous?*
> *Vn jeune Matelot, . . .*[38]

In short, these poems are far removed from the concepts espoused by the man Le Pays called "nôtre Pere Malherbe."[39]

Strangely enough, two clergymen, Esprit Fléchier and Pierre-Daniel Huet—both destined, because of their more serious works, to take their place at the Academy at the end of this period—began their careers with poetry that is anything but serious. The madrigals of Fléchier, like all those of the time, are extremely free,[40] but so are his stanzas: "Relation de l'autre monde," in octosyllabic quatrains, does not even maintain a single rhyme scheme, some stanzas being *a b b a,* others *a b a b.* The rhymes themselves are no better and the linearity still worse:

> *Tout le monde disait: "Voilà*
> *Cette âme triste et misérable";*
> *Et, quoiqu'elle fût fort aimable,*
> *Tout le monde la laissait là.*[41]

In some of his works there is a further departure from the chosen form. Although "Le terrible homme que Barbin" begins with octosyllabic sestets having either *b c b c* or *b c c b* rhyme schemes and varied breaks, it soon includes heterometric stanzas containing occasional decasyllabic or alexandrine lines.[42]

Huet's deviations from orthodoxy are more subtle and can more readily be defended, as the following "Chanson" illustrates:

> *Pour faire l'amour à Blois*
> *C'est trop d'un quand on est trois:*

[37] See his *Nouvelles œuvres* (Amsterdam: Hogenhuysen, 1690), 1:191.
[38] *Amitiez, amours et amourettes* (Paris: Sercy, 1667), p. 358.
[39] *Nouvelles œuvres,* 2:179.
[40] Antonin Fabre, *La jeunesse de Fléchier* (Paris: Didier, 1882), 1:44.
[41] Allem, *Anthologie,* 2:298.
[42] Lachèvre, *Bibliographie,* 3:336–37.

Et de l'avis de tous ceux
Qui débitent des fleurettes,
C'est assez quand on est deux.[43]

It is impossible to defend either content or style, but the choice of form (heptasyllabic five-line stanza) is quite appropriate though not Malherbian. Huet persisted in this vein late in life, writing a long poem in trisyllabic *vers suivis:*

Tu vas voir
Chaque soir,
Les beaux yeux
Dont les cieux
S'orneroient,
Se feroient
Des soleils
Sans pareils.[44]

Furthermore, his rhymes are seldom acceptable, his stanzas have varied breaks, and, like Fléchier, he frequently indulged in "liberated" stanzas similar to those written by his friend La Fontaine.

Three poets remain to be discussed in this classification, all worthy of the superlatives generally bestowed on them, yet who on rare occasions produced minor poems which show only the slightest trace of the skill they normally demonstrated. Much has been said about the relationship that may or may not have existed between Boileau, Molière, and La Fontaine. Their treatment together here should not be interpreted as an endorsement of any position regarding their friendship, but as simply a convenient way of dealing as rapidly as possible with a very minor part of their production.

Only a handful of nondramatic poems can be ascribed to Molière with any degree of certainty, and most of these can readily be dismissed, as far as this study is concerned. The ballet air "D'une brillante grâce," a twelve-line hexasyllabic ditty, the "Premier couplet d'une chanson de Dassoucy," the quatrains, all are in forms either unknown to

[43] Pierre-Daniel Huet, *Poésies françaises* (Paris: Dentu, 1881), p. 17.
[44] Ibid., p. 51.

Malherbe or badly implemented. The sonnets, excepting the one in *bouts rimés*, range from the orthodox *a b a b . . . e d e* to *a b a b a' b' a' b' . . . e e d* with the last line octosyllabic. The "Remerciment au Roi" is in *vers libres* with rather bad rhymes. It is a remarkably successful joke whose merits have not escaped the critics, from Robinet and Bayle down to our own times,[45] but nowhere in it can one detect Malherbe's influence.

Strangely enough, Boileau's "poésies diverses" are no better. The rhymes are not very good and even the sonnets rely heavily on unsatisfactory combinations such as *jours-toûjours, moy-toy,* and so on. The forms for most of the light poems are far from Malherbian, and the linearity is frequently bad:

> *Si Bourdaloüe un peu severe*
> *Nous dit: "Craignons la Volupté"*
>
> . . . .
>
> *Bacchus le declare héretique*
> *Et Janseniste, qui pis est.*[46]

It is obvious from the above example, with its cacophonic last line, that Boileau's light poetry was far removed from the precepts enununciated either by Malherbe or by himself in the *Art poétique.*

"Contons; mais contons bien; c'est le point principal; C'est tout."[47] With these words, La Fontaine was stating the case not only for his *Contes* but for many of his other creations as well. Bad rhymes, hiatuses, enjambments, all the faults are there, and piling on of evidence would be child's play for, as Pierre Clarac stated in his introduction to the *Contes,* "le vers des *Contes* en prend à son aise avec les règles essentielles de la versification."[48] The same must be said of the numerous madrigals, ballads, comic epitaphs, songs, and epigrams that flowed from his pen. The longer poems, in stanzas or *vers suivis,* are only slightly better. "Vous qui menez les Gripon," the only long poem by La Fontaine in isometric sestets, displays bad rhymes, padding, loose syntax and a horrible sense of humor:

---

[45] See the recent article by Benjamin Rountree, "Narrative Poetry as Drama: Molière's 'Remerciment au Roi,' " *RN* 9 (1968): 260–64.

[46] *Œuvres complètes,* p. 253.

[47] *Contes et nouvelles en vers* (Paris: Belles Lettres, 1961), 2:10.

[48] Ibid., 1:xv.

Vous qui menez les Gripon,
Dont l'œil a grippé, dit-on,
Tous les cœurs de Normandie. . . .[49]

Some of the light poetry in *vers suivis* is heterometric and as such is very difficult to categorize. In some cases, as in "Pension poétique," a pattern is easily discernible and the work appears to be more a set of *stances irrégulières* than free verse. Other works ("Le différend de Beaux Yeux et Belle Bouche," or "Les arrêts d'Amour," for instance) verge on the amorphous and cannot be considered Malherbian in any way, since only the rhymes bear comparison and these are seldom satisfactory. Most of the *vers suivis,* however, are isometric, thereby warranting a comment or two. The lighter poems shun the alexandrine, but the sentences, many running to well over a dozen lines, are still far too long. Enjambments are very frequent, both in the octosyllabic poems:

> *Vous ne daignâtes recevoir*
> *Le tribut, qu'il croit vous devoir,*[50]

and the decasyllabic ones:

> *En telles gens ce n'est pas qualité*
> *Trop ordinaire. Ils savent . . .*[51]

Rhymes are generally unsatisfactory (*pas-pas, nom-renom*) and careless craftsmanship is manifest not only in the numerous instances of padding, some of which might be excused since they help to establish an aura of lightheartedness, but also in the frequently chaotic lines, the result of piling on of monosyllabics: "Et moins pour moi que pour pas un."[52] As an accomplished artist, La Fontaine had few, if any, peers, but in the realm of the bantering poem he was indeed like all his contemporaries, not only free of Malherbian traits but oblivious to even the most basic rules of versification.

[49] *Œuvres diverses* (Paris: Gallimard, 1958), p. 513.
[50] Ibid., p. 503.
[51] Ibid., p. 578.
[52] Ibid., p. 504.

As I have already remarked, two genres really came into their own during the period under discussion: free verse and the narrative alternating prose and poetry. These two are not necessarily devoid of art; however, they obviously cannot be studied for adherence to rules of prosody as the more orthodox forms might be. In discussing seventeeth-century free verse, we must note that it was not the truly polymorphous or even amorphous thing that the nineteenth century was to make of it. It was, in the words of Mallarmé, "qu'un agencement, sans la strophe, de mètres divers notoires."[53]

The most famous of all practitioners of the *vers libre* was La Fontaine, of course, but while he brought the genre to heights it had not known before, he did not create it. Cyrano's friend, François Payot de Lignières, used it quite early in his poem "Pénitence," though without success. Jean Dehénault was another early practitioner of the form, and he too failed miserably, somehow managing to write lines totally devoid of rhythm and sporting the worst rhymes possible. Only one other writer can be considered as having any talent in the genre—Madame de Villedieu, whose *Fables* were obviously patterned after those of La Fontaine, though they fail to demonstrate the art, the vivacity, and the spontaneity of the master.

The art of La Fontaine in his *Fables* has been discussed very frequently, and usually quite well, though one might deplore the single-mindedness of some of the critics. Thus Antoine Albalat, who pointed out that few poets had managed to hide their arduous labor better than La Fontaine,[54] made very little of the fact that while the poet did not show his labors in his style, he spoke of them repeatedly. By the same token, Gohin is absolutely right when he describes the rhythmic richness of the *Fables*,[55] but it is not easy to follow him when he insists on combining hexasyllabic lines into alexandrines, or removing hemistichs to add them to adjacent lines. Granted, the *rejets* and *contre-rejets* are very numerous in these poems, but they all have a definite purpose that is defeated by the regrouping of rhythmic units. My complaint, though, is not so much that the criticism has done injustice to La Fontaine or that it

---

[53] "Variations sur un sujet," *Œuvres complètes* (Paris: Gallimard, 1956), p. 363.

[54] *Le travail du style* (Paris: Colin, 1911), pp. 178 ff.

[55] *L'art de La Fontaine dans ses Fables* (Paris: Garnier, 1929), passim.

has warped him at times, but that it has all too frequently missed its mark. The truth of the matter, as Odette de Mourgues has pointed out so clearly, is that the real art of La Fontaine is of an entirely different nature and has little to do with the standard patterns: "L'équilibre entre la régularité et l'irrégularité s'opère à l'intérieur d'une unité prosodique qui peut n'être ni le vers, ni le quatrain, ou le sixain, mais une sorte de paragraphe poétique ordonné par des éléments réguliers suivant un dessein qui ne coïncide pas nécessairement avec celui d'une strophe reconnue."[56] As de Mourgues puts it, to search for a succession of ten or twelve syllables or a rhyme scheme of sorts leads to conclusions not only debatable or arbitrary but, worse still, "en marge de ce qui constitue l'équilibre prosodique d'un passage."[57] In other words, the *Fables* do not illustrate so much what one critic called "a discriminate violation of the existing rules of the game,"[58] as a different game played with entirely different rules. "Le vers libre ne se justifiait nulle part mieux que dans ses *Fables*"[59] because this newly recreated genre demanded a variety of style that the old forms could not provide. This is made obvious by a look at the rhymes, whose insufficiency has frequently been studied,[60] and at many of the other instances of disregard for Malherbian concepts. Notable among these, for example, is La Fontaine's use of the hiatus for felicitous effects. Whereas Malherbe dreaded any occurrence of hiatus, La Fontaine found some that were perfectly expressive—"Le coche arrive au haut"—and many that were, in the word of Maurice Grammont, "délicieux."[61]

Thanks to *Psyché* and the *Voyage en Limousin*, La Fontaine must also be considered the foremost writer of serious works combining prose and poetry. The verse is sometimes free, often not, but is considered separately here because, alternating as it does with prose, it cannot be imbued with any élan or sustained mood, a prerequisite of "grande poésie." In the *Voyage*, La Fontaine, debating the pronunciation of a

[56] *O Muse*, p. 125.

[57] Ibid.

[58] Margaret Guiton, *La Fontaine: Poet and Counter-poet* (New Brunswick: Rutgers University Press, 1961), p. 44.

[59] Gohin, *L'art de La Fontaine*, p. 149.

[60] See Souriau, *L'évolution*; X. de la Péraudière, "Remarques sur les rimes insuffisantes de La Fontaine," *Mém. Soc. Angers* 2 (1899): 48–56; Gohin, "De la rime dans les Fables de La Fontaine," *Muse Fr.* 8(1929): 475–84.

[61] *Le vers français* (Paris: Delagrave, 1954), p. 336.

town name, says, "Est-ce Montléry qu'il faut dire, ou Montlehéry? C'est Montlehéry quand le vers est trop court, et Montléry quand il est trop long. Montléry donc ou Montlehéry, comme vous voudrez."[62] Borgerhoff sees in this a perpetual concern for his trade, a passion for versemaking.[63] But was La Fontaine really serious? Did he see a lesson in this town name or a joke reminiscent of Voiture's lines:

> La tour de Mont-le-Heris
> Qui pour regarder Paris. . . .[64]

If indeed it shows that art was ever-present in La Fontaine's mind, it must also demonstrate his willingness to bypass its thornier problems and to find facile solutions. An examination of the actual practice reinforces this impression.

The *vers suivis* of these works have bad linearity with frequent enjambments:

> Que vous en dirai-je? et comment
> En parler assez dignement?[65]

Some of these enjambments, encompassing an entire hemistich, are not as obvious, but the results are still far from felicitous:

> L'architecte y posa les vivantes images
> De ces objets divins.[66]

The rhymes are generally quite bad with every fault conceivable freely represented. The hiatus is carefully avoided, sometimes not without cost, for in avoiding it La Fontaine sometimes resorts to structures that verge on the cacophonic: "enfin l'on les."[67]

As for the stanzas, less than half the forms represented in these prose-verse works can be found in Malherbe, but these have good linear and

---

[62] Œuvres diverses, p. 536.
[63] Freedom of French Classicism, p. 133.
[64] Œuvres, 2:344.
[65] Œuvres diverses, p. 172.
[66] Ibid., p. 145.
[67] Ibid., p. 141.

syntactical structure, and were it not for the usually bad rhymes they would be quite Malherbian. Among the non-Malherbian forms are five- and seven-line stanzas and heterometric *huitains* and quatrains. The last two are particularly interesting in their deviations from accepted standards. One of the *huitains,* for instance, is tetrametric, with a 3–5 break and an *a a b b c d c d* rhyme scheme.[68] Another such stanza has four decasyllabic lines followed by four octosyllabic ones, a far too radical break as far as the strophic unity is concerned.[69] La Fontaine's predilection for unusual forms is best illustrated by the following trimetric quatrain:

> *De quoi je ne lui sais aucunement bon gré;*
> *Car d'autres gens m'ont dit qu'ils avaient admiré*
> *Ce degré,*
> *Et qu'il est de marbre jaspé.*[70]

The *Voyage* and *Psyché* remain two of the most enjoyable works of La Fontaine, but in spite of and not because of the quality of the verse.

Despite the vogue for free verse and works combining prose and poetry, it would be wrong to think that the "grands genres" did not hold their own. With these livelihoods were made and reputations established, and on these any attempt at gauging Malherbe's influence must be based.

Ironically, it was in this realm that some of the practitioners had the least talent for poetry, and Saint-Evremond was undoubtedly the most famous of these. On that point, most of his editors agree. Célestin Hippeau, in his introduction to the *Œuvres choisies,* calls Saint-Evremond's poetry "prose rimée."[71] René de Planhol, in his edition, calls it "caduque" because the author simply "n'était pas poète."[72] These prosaic poems are composed of sentences rather than lines, and with this author, the two seldom coincide. As Quentin Hope so aptly noted, the poet is "alien to Saint-Evremond's nature [because] . . . Saint-Evremond's response to literature is primarily intellectual,"[73] whereas, as the author himself said,

---

[68] Ibid., p. 129.
[69] Ibid., p. 548.
[70] Ibid., p. 555.
[71] (Paris: Didot, 1852), p. xxvi.
[72] *Œuvres* (Paris: Cité des Livres, 1927), 1:xvi.
[73] *Saint-Evremond: The Honnête Homme as Critic* (Bloomington: Indiana University Press, 1962), pp. 49, 80.

"la Poësie demande un génie particulier, qui ne s'accommode pas trop avec le bons-sens."[74] Small wonder then that the ornamentation, the artificiality that is the crux of poetry had but little appeal for him. Not only prosaic in origin, the poetry of Saint-Evremond is fundamentally devoid of rhythmic patterns with form ever subservient to content. As a result, there is little truly free verse, but even less rigidly structured poetry. The impression gathered most frequently is one of random construction. Thus, "Le bon vieux temps," in *vers suivis*, begins with four decasyllabics followed by four octosyllabics, then a decasyllabic, an alexandrine, and so on. On the other hand, the first six rhymes are in couplets, the next four are *embrassées*. The syntactical division of the poem is independent of either rhyme or meter.[75] Generally speaking, *stances irrégulières* and *vers suivis* account for most of his poems, and even some of his sonnets are heterometric. But in all of these, the lack of rhythm and strophic unity is apparent. They are indeed "rhymed prose."

Another failure, though in a different way, is Le Petit de Beauchasteau. The authenticity of the poems attributed to this author has been often debated, and while the arguments for are more convincing, they are not proof. What is interesting here is not the solution of the question of possible *supercherie*, but the nature and quality of the poems. Since Beauchasteau was attempting to earn a living with his pen, it is only natural that the bulk of the production was occasional poetry. Unfortunately (and this lends credence to the theory of a child-poet) while all the standard forms of occasional verse are present, what is lacking is the most basic understanding of them. Sixteen octosyllabic lines may be arranged so as to praise a ruler, but by being arranged in rhyming couplets with only one syntactical break, they are merely breathless;[76] by the same token, while five-line alexandrines are not a Malherbian form, we have seen that some poets used these advantageously. However, Beauchasteau was unable to bring two alexandrines together without a disruption of the rhythm:

> Par tes exploits on peut connoître ta vaillance,
> Par tes ayeux, on doit connoître ta naissance.[77]

[74] Cited in ibid., p. 80.
[75] *Œuvres mêlées* (Paris: Techener, 1865), 2:539–41.
[76] Goujet, *Bibliothèque françoise*, 16:227.
[77] Ibid., 17:309.

Cacaphony, bad inversions, long syntactical units, all these faults mar the lines of even his shortest poems. Child or adult, the author of these lines had obviously come into contact with all the commonplaces of French seventeenth-century poetry and had absorbed them without understanding any of their underlying principles. One may speak of blind imitation but hardly of meaningful influence.

Beauchasteau interests us less because he failed to understand the forms he used, than because he used so many. Some of these were Malherbian, others not. Generally speaking, his contemporaries were not always so adventuresome. To be sure, free verse was in full swing, but for serious poetry most authors refused to experiment quite as much as either a Malherbe or a Tristan had done in days gone by. Lignières, for instance, wrote some very free stanzas:

> *Nous attendions de Chapelain*
> *Une Pucelle*
> *Jeune et belle.*
> *Vingt ans, à la former, il perdit son latin*
> *Et, de sa main,*
> *Il sort enfin*
> *Une vieille sempiternelle.*[78]

These however, are the exception to an overwhelming number of isometric stanzas and *vers suivis*.

Lignières's rhymes are no worse than those of most of his contemporaries, which means that they are far from Malherbian. The *consonne d'appui* is the greatest villain but far from the only one. Long sounds rhyme with short ones (*grâce* always rhymes with *place* or *audace* or a like sound); obvious rhymes abound (*toy-moy*); synaereses rhyme with diaereses (*glorieux* is not only a frequent member of such a rhyme but usually occurs with a diaeresis in the middle of the line and a synaeresis at the end); other rhymes are completely unacceptable (*liez-deliez, point-point, famille-ville*).

As a whole, Lignières's linearity is sound; one may readily think of a certain cadence, though there are frequent lapses. Some lines are badly

[78] Cited by Magne, *Un ami de Cyrano de Bergerac: Le Chevalier de Lignières* (Paris: Chiberre, 1920), p. 64.

balanced: "Quoy que ses yeux ne soient pas trop à fleur de teste."[79] Enjambments also occur, some very obvious:

> *Je n'en veux plus parler, de crainte*
> *De réveiller le chat qui dort.*[80]

There are many instances of shameless padding, some of which contribute to a debatable rhythm: "Mon nez, mon nez qu'ici par deux fois je répète."[81] Last, but far from least for our considerations, is the fact that Lignières's strophic forms are far from Malherbian in spite of their relatively small number. His octosyllabic sestets have every cut and every rhyme scheme imaginable, as do the *huitains;* the alexandrine *vers suivis* have extremely long sentences; and even the sonnets, using very diverse rhyme schemes, are not free from censure.

Jean Dehénault, attending many of the circles frequented by Lignières, would naturally have much in common with him. The libertine tendencies of both have been amply discussed by Frédéric Lachèvre and I intend merely to dwell on the similarities in their prosody. The *vers suivis* of Dehénault can be readily divided into two types: long poems in alexandrines and shorter ones, usually heterometric, interspersed with prose. The latter frequently lapse into "rhymed prose," though the rhymes are hardly the most salient feature:

> *Ces beaux yeux, en public toûjours si retenus,*
> *En secret pour Daphnis perdront leur retenuë.*
> *Ils verront les amours tous nus:*
> *Et la volupté toute nuë.*[82]

The prosaic, unbalanced lines are clearly not unlike those of Lignières. Much the same can be said of the rhymes, adding to the list of faults a predilection for facility. In one poem, *généreux(se)* appears four times, each time rhyming with *(mal)heureux(se)*. In another, the rhyme *dégoûtent-coûtent* is immediately followed by *coûté-dégoûté.*

---

[79] Cited by Lachèvre, *Derniers libertins,* p. 36.

[80] Magne, *Un ami de Cyrano,* p. 110.

[81] Cited by Lachèvre, *Derniers libertins,* p. 9.

[82] Jean Dehénault, *Œuvres* (Geneva: Slatkine, 1968), p. 67.

If the *vers suivis* recall those of Lignières, the stanzas do not. Dehénault showed a strong predilection for heterometric stanzas with great variety, this liking for change shown by the fact that seldom do two stanzas of a single poem have the same heterometry. The breaks and the choice of meters are no more Malherbian than the rhymes and can best be described as chaotic:

> *Je perds en vostre amour un bien d'un si grand prix,*
> *Qu'il vous couteroit trop, Iris,*
> *De m'en rendre la joüissance;*
> *Mais laissez-moi du moins joüir de ma constance.*
> *Hélas si c'est un bien,*
> *Il ne vous coûte rien.*[83]

This love of metrical experimentation is also seen in some of his sonnets:

> *Toy qui meurs avant que de naistre,*
> *Assemblage confus de l'estre et du néant,*
> *Triste avorton, informe Enfant,*
> *Rebut du Néant et de l'Estre,*
>
> *Toy que l'amour fit par un crime,*
> *Et que l'Honneur défait par un crime à son tour,*
> *Funeste ouvrage de l'Amour,*
> *De l'Honneur funeste victime,*
>
> *Donne fin aux remords par qui tu t'es vangé;*
> *Et du fond du Néant où je t'ay replongé*
> *N'entretiens point l'horreur dont ma faute est suivie.*
>
> *Deux Tyrans opposés ont décidé ton sort:*
> *L'Amour, malgré l'Honneur, t'a fait donner la vie,*
> *L'Honneur, malgré l'Amour te fait donner la mort.*[84]

The metrics are not the only departure from orthodoxy: the rhyme scheme is "libertine" and the first sentence, with its eleven lines, is certainly unique in the annals of seventeenth-century sonnets.

Madame Deshoulières, a student of Dehénault, was very popular in her day with everyone but Boileau, Racine, and La Fontaine, exceptions

---

[83] Ibid., p. 59.   [84] Ibid., pp. xiii–xiv.

which in themselves cast much light on the limitations of Boileau's pronouncements.[85] For obvious chronological reasons, only her *vers de jeunesse* will be considered. Like those of her mentor, her poems are marked by very free use of heterometry in irregular stanzas that seldom have the same metrics or even the same number of lines. Reminiscent of Dehénault's, her poems have few enjambments and are very prosaic, despite the novel use of heterometry:

> *Livrons nos cœurs aux tendres mouvements;*
> *N'écoutons point la chagrine vieillesse;*
> *Si l'Amour est une foiblesse,*
> *On la doit permettre au printemps:*
> *Employons bien cet heureux temps,*
> *Il n'en reste que trop pour la triste sagesse.*[86]

The rhymes are not always above reproach and leonine rhymes are frequent: "Il semble que sans lui tout le bonheur nous fuie."[87] In view of these findings, which do not differ radically from those previously enunciated, and in view of Mme Deshoulières's popularity in the face of Boileau's contempt, what can one make of the critic's credibility as to what was acceptable to people of taste of his time?

Obviously much doubt existed in the minds of writers and readers alike as to what was good poetry. Remember how close the theories of men such as Chapelain were to those of Malherbe. But these theories were not always accepted without reservations, and François Colletet's *Parnasse françois,* a work that saw many editions, advanced far different views, more lax than those of Malherbe and generally more in keeping with the practice of the various poets: *consonne d'appui* lapses, rhymes of words containing the same stem, any rhyme scheme in sonnets or odes, all were allowed. Ten-line stanzas were to be divided 4–2–4, and the only difference suggested between *odes* and *stances* is that the latter be sadder. Most important of all, poetry is described as "vn don de Nature, per-

---

[85] For a complete discussion of Madame Deshoulières's popularity, see Mary E. Storer, "Madame Deshoulières jugée par ses contemporains," *RR* 25 (1934): 367–74.

[86] Antoinette Deshoulières, *Œuvres* (Paris: Prault, 1753), 1:94.

[87] Ibid., p. 9.

fectionné de L'Art."[88] *Le Parnasse* is an *art poétique,* but a practical one based on experience rather than a theoretical one based on ideals. Colletet's poetic production is nothing more nor less than the illustration of these very lax precepts. "Est-il rien de plus beau," for instance is written in 12–12–8–12–8–8–12–12–12–12, *a b a b c c d e d e* stanzas, with some very marginal rhymes, and the sonnet on the death of his father demonstrates some strange leonine rhyme patterns:

> *Jules, mon père est mort, la tristesse m'accable,*
> *Je perds en le perdant mon unique support,*
> *Et si tu n'es touché du malheur de mon sort,*
> *Je ne voy point de sort qui soit plus déplorable.*[89]

This doubt concerning tradition is nowhere more obvious than in the works of Madame de Villedieu. One modern critic has called her "arch conservative in letters, blindly following what she understood to be tradition."[90] But this statement suggests absolutes which the careful examination of any of her poems will not allow. From the early "Jouissance," a sonnet with unsatisfactory rhymes and rhyme scheme, to the later *vers irréguliers,* Mme de Villedieu is anything but orthodox. Many of her choices of forms are capricious, and the execution is seldom flawless, as the following trimetric stanzas show:

> *Quand vieux seigneur entreprend jeune dame,*
> *Il ne fait qu'applanir les chemins de son âme*
> *Pour un plus jeune qui le suit.*
> *Par ses sçavans conseils, ses ruses, son adresse,*
> *Il va semant les germes de tendresse,*
> *Dont un autre cueille le fruit.*

Or:

> *Mais si pour cette Bergere,*
> *J'avois de feintes amours,*

[88] *Le Parnasse françois ou l'Ecole des Muses* (Paris: Sercy, 1664), pp. 9, 24, 25, 43–48.

[89] Lachèvre, *Bibliographie,* 3:266.

[90] Cited by Bruce A. Morrissette, *The Life and Works of Marie-Catherine Desjardins* (St. Louis: Washington University Press, 1947), p. viii.

> *Et que mon âme sincere*
> *Pour vous eût brûlé toujours,*
> *Seriez-vous encor cette fidelle Amante,*
> *De qui je suis si tendrement épris?*
> *Et votre cœur feindroit-il pour Timante,*
> *Si le mien feignoit pour Miris?*[91]

The divisions, metrical and syntactical, of this stanza, the syllable count of the fifth line, and the last rhymes certainly do not betray unequivocal arch conservatism. Furthermore, as in the sonnet "Impétueux transports," her rhymes betray nothing less than careless composition by allowing words to rhyme with themselves (*puissants-puissants*). Mme de Villedieu, it has been charitably said, earned her living by her pen. It was not dipped in a Malherbian ink.

Such attitudes should not be thought to mean that Malherbe had been forgotten. As in the recent past, many poets still regarded him as a teacher:

> *C'est de nôtre Pere Malherbe*
> *Que nous avons appris cet agreable tour,*
> *Ce secret de placer et le Nom et le Verbe,*
> *Qui donne au style un si beau jour.*[92]

Several considerations must be kept in mind in pondering these lines, first and foremost of which is the fact that they are part of a ten-line stanza in which only the 4–6 break is Malherbian. Of great importance also is the fact that Malherbe's name is here associated with only one aspect of poetry, the importance of "un mot mis à sa place," not with versification as such. As a matter of fact, the author of these lines, Le Pays, is anything but Malherbian in his versification. His stanzas have highly varied breaks, when they have any; his choices of heterometric combinations verge on the ludicrous, one "air" combining lines of three, five, six, and eight syllables; enjambments and expletives are quite frequent; many of the forms deliberately rejected by Malherbe (alexandrine *dizains*, heterometric *huitains*) are used by Le Pays in his most serious works. The rhymes,

[91] Ibid., pp. 28–29.
[92] Le Pays, *Nouvelles œuvres*, 2:179.

however, are the most striking features of his poetry. In only one long poem in *vers suivis* is there any evidence of hard work, all the rhymes being in *-ence,* a tour de force indeed.[93] Otherwise the rhymes range from the mediocre to the unimaginative (*constante-constamment-amante-amant*), to the totally unacceptable (*attraits-traits-portraits-traits*), with several outlandish combinations (*tous-nous-coups-vous*) used several times.

For many of the minor writers of this period, one simply cannot speak of Malherbian versification unless considerations are limited to matters of rudimentary linearity. Thus the poems of Bonaventure de Fourcroy, one of the few writers of Mazarinades conscious of style, have few enjambments and even fewer unbalanced lines, though the exceptions cannot always be considered marginal: "J'aime, et j'aimerois mieux n'aimer pas ce que j'aime."[94] On the other hand, his rhymes are quite bad and his choice of forms far from Malherbian.[95]

The same concern for linearity is evident in Fléchier's "Le siècle d'or," which was long attributed to Huet but restituted to its real author by Lachèvre:

> Dès qu'ils estoient aimés, ils aimoient à leur tour,
> Et n'avoient d'autres loix que les loix de l'amour,[96]

but Fléchier's orthodoxy does not extend much beyond that consideration. The same balance and cadence are to be seen in the poems of Perrin, particularly in his occasional sonnets:

> En toy, Prince, Gaston reçoit un successeur,
> La ville vn Citoyen, l'Estat vn Defenseur,
> La Famille Royale vn Fleuron de sa tige.[97]

[93] *Amitiez,* pp. 6–7.

[94] Cited by Georges Mongrédien, "Un avocat-poète au XVIIe siècle: Bonaventure de Fourcroy," *RHLF* 33 (1926): 9.

[95] Many of his *stances* use heterometric combinations whose very constitution is opposed to Malherbe's basic concepts, but the extreme cases are mostly found in airs such as the "Air de M. d'Hotman," a 10–10–8–12–8–12 stanza, cited in ibid.

[96] Huet, *Poésies françaises,* p. 59.

[97] *Les œuvres de poésies* (Paris: Loyson, 1661), p. 138.

But these are the only sonnets that can rightfully be considered Malherbian.

Yet, Boileau notwithstanding, the "juste cadence" and the "mot mis à sa place" did not impress everyone as being of equal importance, and late in his life Maucroix was to say: "Puisque vous suivez Malherbe, songez une autre fois que c'est un guide qui peut égarer. Il a beaucoup d'élévation, mais il n'a presque ni douceur ni tendresse. Son grand travail, en quelques endroits qu'il a tâché de polir, ne sert qu'à mieux faire voir qu'il n'est point naturel."[98]

Maucroix's own attempts at elevation failed pitifully. His odes, seeking a happy medium between pomp and "naturel," are merely prosaic:

> Conrart, quand finiront ces guerres obstinées
> Qui depuis deux fois dix années
> Coûtent tant de pleurs à nos yeux?
> Entendrons-nous toujours l'aigre son des trompettes,
> Et les douces musettes
> Sont-elles pour jamais absentes de ces lieux?[99]

The form is only one of many unknown to Malherbe. The longest attempt at elevation is in an eclogue extolling the glory of Reims, but the following sample may lead the reader to wonder how Maucroix dared chastise Malherbe:

> C'est l'illustre cité du sacre de nos rois,
> Reims, la gloire et l'honneur du climat champenois.
> Vois-tu ce temple saint dont dont la superbe masse
> Dans le milieu des airs occupe tant d'espace?[100]

In spite of these isolated attempts at grandeur, the major objection to Maucroix must be directed at another aspect of his work. Be it due to a desire to seem natural or an aversion to a formalism he associated with Malherbe, Maucroix shunned consistent rhythms. This can be seen in the six-line stanza quoted above, but the results are frequently far more

---

[98] *Lettres,* p. 181.

[99] *Œuvres diverses* (Reims: Techener, 1854), 1:60.

[100] Ibid., p. 94.

drastic. Deliberately rejecting strong rhythmic expressions and well-balanced lines, Maucroix inevitably produced badly rhymed prose:

> *Que vous êtes heureux! Vous pourrez voir Iris,*
> *Tous les soirs vous irez chez elle.*[101]

To put it simply, the search for inner rhythm calls for genius. Maucroix lacked the genius of a La Fontaine, and the vehicle he chose could only crush him. It must further be argued that Maucroix tried these loose forms for all manners of expression, whereas La Fontaine, for his most ambitious endeavors, frequently reverted to forms that were tried and true if not always Malherbian. On these I now wish to comment.

La Fontaine had many masters. As Philip Wadsworth has so well shown, he was a great admirer of Marot and, to a lesser degree, of Voiture.[102] As for his relationship to Malherbe, there has been much debate over the famous "Je pris certain auteur autrefois pour mon maître."[103] Wadsworth[104] and Gohin[105] see in it a clear reference to Malherbe, whereas Clarac[106] disagrees. As for me, I consider the evidence supporting the first of these opinions overwhelming. La Fontaine's "wholehearted" admiration of Malherbe[107] is everywhere manifest in his works. Calling Malherbe and Racan "Ces deux rivaux d'Horace, héritiers de sa lyre,/ Disciples d'Apollon, nos maîtres, pour mieux dire,"[108] he never misses an opportunity to praise the master.[109]

We are told that "l'harmonie poétique de Malherbe" so struck the young La Fontaine that he immediately began not only to read him but to

---

[101] Ibid., p. 40.

[102] *Young La Fontaine* (Evanston: Northwestern University Press, 1952), pp. 88–99.

[103] *Œuvres diverses,* p. 646.

[104] *Young La Fontaine,* pp. 99–105; "La Fontaine as Critic and Student of Malherbe," *Sym* 3 (1949): 130–39.

[105] *La Fontaine: Etudes et recherches* (Paris: Garnier, 1937), pp. 167 ff.

[106] *Œuvres diverses,* pp. 935–36.

[107] Wadsworth, *Young La Fontaine,* p. 101.

[108] *Fables* (Paris: Belles Lettres, 1934), bk. III, f. 1.

[109] See "A Monseigneur le Prince de Conty"; his letter to Fouquet of 30 January 1663, in which he speaks of Malherbe's "traits de poésie"; or the panegyric in the "avertissement" of the *Poésies chrétiennes.*

write his first works "dans le goût de Malherbe."[110] In the "avertissement" to *Adonis*, La Fontaine tells of his preference for elevated, heroic poetry. However, it would be dangerous to take these statements at face value. First, these early Malherbian attempts have been lost and we shall probably never know how slavishly the pupil followed the master. Secondly, we do know that La Fontaine radically changed his views. I am not referring here to his admission that Malherbe "a pu faillir," as he claims in the "avertissement" of the *Poésies chrétiennes,* or to his corrections of Malherbe, for it is well known that these corrections deal mostly with "la construction et . . . l'harmonie de la phrase"[111] and with the removal of constrictive elements. Rather, I am speaking of the evidence in those works that have reached us that, as Renée Winegarten put it, La Fontaine "did not consider the idyll incompatible with the epic,"[112] a far from Malherbian attitude. This in itself is only one aspect of a broader question. Let us look once more at the quotation that began this discussion, but in a more complete form:

> *Je pris certain auteur autrefois pour mon maître;*
> *Il pensa me gâter. A la fin, grâce aux cieux,*
> *Horace, par bonheur, me dessilla les yeux.*
> *L'auteur avait du bon, du meilleur; et la France*
> *Estimait dans ses vers le tour et la cadence.*
> *Qui ne les eût prisés? J'en demeurai ravi;*
> *Mais ses traits ont perdu quiconque l'a suivi.*
> *Son trop d'esprit s'épand en trop de belles choses:*
> Tous métaux y sont or, toutes fleurs y sont roses.[113]

Times and tastes had changed; Malherbe's poetry could only be considered "tendue" and "forcée" by the younger generation.[114] The masters had indeed been great—"qui ne les eût prisés?"—but La Fontaine saw also

[110] Pellisson and d'Olivet, *Histoire de l'Académie*, 2:303–05.

[111] Gohin, *La Fontaine*, p. 197. See also Gohin's "La poésie à Port-Royal," *MdF* 246 (1933): 513–31.

[112] *French Lyric Poetry*, p. 98.

[113] *Œuvres diverses*, p. 646. This close paraphrase of Malherbe gives further credence to the theory that he is the abandoned master.

[114] Gohin, *La Fontaine*, p. 197.

that it would have been a grave error to "s'essayer sur leur lyre"[115] at a time when "la poésie lyrique" and "l'heroïque" had fallen from favor.[116] If La Fontaine refused to undertake

> . . . de chanter dans ces vers
> Rome ni ses enfants vainqueurs de l'univers,[117]

it was not because, as so many of his contemporaries suggested, he knew that his forte lay elsewhere, but because he no longer considered it profitable. "His attitude does not imply that he condemned Malherbe as outmoded or archaic; rather, he seemed to regret that styles had changed."[118] One need only look at La Fontaine's odes to see that this opinion is well founded. Those odes meant for publication quickly lapse into a bantering mood. Only the "Ode au Roi" maintains a properly elevated tone, "apparently because it was written for private circulation."[119]

Be it in the *Fables* or in more orthodox genres, in corrections of Malherbe or of Maucroix, La Fontaine repeatedly reveals that he knew the value of a "precise and technical approach to the problems of style."[120] Equally obvious is that his ideas concerning technique were not those of Malherbe.

The individuality of La Fontaine's art is, of course, manifest throughout the *Fables,* but no less so in some of the longer poems in alexandrine *vers suivis.* One of these, *Adonis,* elicited the highest praise from Valéry: "La nonchalance . . . est savante, la molesse, étudiée; la facilité, le comble de l'art."[121] It has been suggested repeatedly that La Fontaine, aware of his limitations, decided to shun the greater genres in favor of the shorter, lighter ones. This theory is given credence thanks to several remarks of the poet to the effect that he "lacked voice," as in the opening lines of *Adonis:*

[115] Ibid., p. 207.
[116] *Le songe de Vaux* (Geneva: Droz, 1967), p. 51.
[117] *Œuvres diverses,* p. 5.
[118] Wadsworth, "La Fontaine as Critic," p. 133.
[119] Idem, *Young La Fontaine,* p. 104.
[120] Jean D. Biard, *The Style of La Fontaine's Fables* (New York: Barnes and Noble, 1966), p. 13.
[121] "Au sujet d'Adonis," *Rev. Paris* 1 (1 Feb. 1921): 542.

Je n'ai pas entrepris de chanter dans ces vers
Rome ni ses enfants vainqueurs de l'univers,

. . . .

Ces sujets sont trop hauts, et je manque de voix.[122]

But there is at least as much evidence to the contrary. La Fontaine spent nearly three years on the *Songe de Vaux*, abandoning the fragments only because he no longer had "quelque esperance qu'il reüssist, et qu'un tel ouvrage pûst plaire," for he was convinced, as I said, that the poetry he was trying to write—lyric and heroic—had gone out of style.[123] His regrets are voiced in his introductions not only to the *Songe*, but also to *Adonis* and *Psyché*, among others.

There is internal evidence as well. One needs only to glance at the variants of *Adonis*, studied by Gilbert Guisan,[124] to be convinced of La Fontaine's total commitment to the creation of a masterpiece. As Guisan points out, there is a search for balance, fluidity, tightness of composition, a sense of direction. Thus lines 9–10, meaningless and aimless in 1658, eventually became:

C'est parmi les forêts qu'a vécu mon héros;
C'est dans les bois qu'Amour a troublé mon repos.[125]

Notice that the second of these lines is not balanced in the strict sense of the word, since syntactically the break is after *bois*. However, were this word at the hemistich, as in the original, there would be a simple repetition of the first hemistich quoted. The correction may have brought about a worsening of the linearity from the Malherbian point of view, but there can be no doubt that the progression was admirably served. Not all the changes are for the best, however. In the original, there were many unsatisfactory rhymes. Despite the many changes, the 1669 version demonstrates a complete disregard for these problems. The *consonne d'appui* is neglected, proper nouns are abused, rhymes such as *âme-flamme* and

---

[122] *Œuvres diverses*, p. 5.
[123] *Songe*, p. 51.
[124] "L'évolution de l'art de La Fontaine d'après les variantes de l'"Adonis,' " *RHLF* 42 (1935): 161–80, 321–43.
[125] *Œuvres diverses*, p. 5.

traits-attraits are not only frequent but occur in combinations that are often repeated. On the other hand, the reworking removed most instances of hiatus and padding, though some new ones were introduced.[126] Still, the result, though far from Malherbian, is impressive, and Valéry could only regret the time spent by La Fontaine in later years on the *Contes* and their "ton rustique et faux" in verses "d'une facilité répugnante."[127]

Generally speaking, the other long poems in *vers suivis* are somewhat more Malherbian than *Adonis*. In the elegies, in particular, the sentences seldom exceed the suggested four lines; the rhymes, except for the matter of the *consonne d'appui,* are quite good; and the linearity is nearly flawless. Only in the poem "De la captivité de saint Malc" are there frequent enjambments and badly cut lines.

In addition to "stances libres" such as the ones in the *Songe,* La Fontaine wrote quite a number of poems in the more standard forms. What is perhaps most remarkable about these is the preponderance of isometric stanzas. Discounting the light poems, there are only five occurrences of heterometric stanzas: 12–6–12–6, *a b a b* quatrains; 5–5–5–5–7–7 sestets; a single eight-line stanza alternating lines of six and twelve syllables; another *huitain* combining lines of eight, ten, and twelve syllables with an *a a b a b c b c* rhyme scheme; and the paraphrase of Psalm 17, sixteen *dizains* in which six octosyllabics are followed by four alexandrines, a form discussed in previous chapters. As can be seen from this list, only one instance, the fragment in quatrains from part VII of the *Songe,* is in a Malherbian form. Much the same must be said for the execution. While the linearity and the rhymes are generally good, there is little or no concern for those aspects of prosody that can be ascribed to Malherbe. The sestets are broken 2–4, 4–2, 2–2–2, or not at all; not one is 3–3. The last of the quatrains departs radically from form. Not only is there a change in meter from 12–6–12–6 to 12–12–12–8, but the linearity deteriorates and strange inner rhymes appear:

> *Mais n'avez-vous point vû dans Vaux une merveille,*
> *Qui fait ainsi que vous admirer son pouvoir?*
> *Si vous ne l'avez vûë, Acante vous conseille*
> *De ne point partir sans la voir.*[128]

[126] See Guisan, "L'évolution," pp. 323–43.
[127] "Au sujet d'Adonis," p. 560.

Perhaps most un-Malherbian of all these poems is the psalm. In addition to the basic departure occasioned by the 6–4 metrical division, there is the matter of frequent enjambments and *bourres* that completely destroy any semblance of strophic rhythm:

> *On vit et furent découverts*
> *Les fondements de l'Univers,*
> *Du liquide élément les canaux et les sources,*
> *Le centre de la terre; et l'enfer, obligé*
> *D'abandonner ces chars. . . .*[129]

The rhymes of this poem are very good, but it would be foolhardy to speak of Malherbe under the circumstances.

Although variety in form is naturally limited where isometric stanzas are concerned, several of La Fontaine's choices have no example in Malherbe (decasyllabic quatrains, heptasyllabic and hexasyllabic sestets, decasyllabic *huitains* and *dizains*). The quatrains are almost all relatively light in tone, which may also explain the little care obviously lavished on the rhymes. One such quatrain has *vous-avoue-doux-loue* rhymes with strong echoes within the lines. In the "Ode pour la paix," some sentences straddle stanzas, and in the "Stances sur [Escobar]," there is a plethora of enjambments. The sestets are somewhat more orthodox. Although some are made of single syntactical units, most of them have a median break, standard rhyme schemes, and decent rhymes. The only isometric *huitain*, on the other hand, is Malherbian in neither rhyme scheme nor meter and has bad rhymes and worse linearity:

> *Ils sont partis! et j'ai peu d'espérance*
> *De les revoir.*[130]

Malherbe had shunned *dizains* made of long lines, for such stanzas would inevitably seem heavy. La Fontaine wrote four poems in decasyllabic *dizains*, but three of these are single-stanza works. The breaks and rhyme schemes of all four are very capricious, enjambments numerous, and the

---

[128] *Songe*, p. 194.
[129] *Œuvres diverses*, p. 592.
[130] Ibid., p. 609.

rhymes bad. The octosyllabic efforts, including the "Ode au Roi," are much more orthodox, though there is variety in the breaks and the rhymes are far from perfect. The linearity is quite good, and I could detect only one case of hiatus: "Chassent le soin hoste des villes."[131] In the only work in heptasyllabic *dizains*, the long "Ode pour Madame," the linearity is equally good, but neither the rhymes nor the rhyme scheme is Malherbian.

La Fontaine wrote only four sonnets, all alexandrine, all with acceptable rhyme schemes. As in his other poems, the rhymes are seldom more than assonances (*amour-jour-Luxembourg-cour*). In most of these short poems, the structure leaves much to be desired, with enjambments such as

> *C'est le plus digne prix dont on puisse acheter*
> *Ce bien, . . .*[132]

or

> *Laisse en paix l'Univers; ne lui va point apprendre*
> *Ce qu'il faut ignorer, si l'on veut être à soi.*[133]

Many passages are quite prosaic:

> *Aussi bien manque-t-il ici je ne sais quoi*
> *Que tu ne peux tracer, ni moi te faire entendre.*[134]

In several instances two quatrains share a single sentence. In short, in the sonnets as in most of his other poems, La Fontaine did not remain faithful to the dicta of Malherbe. Unfortunately, in several cases, as in the ones quoted immediately above, some Malherbian rigor might have proved beneficial.

Boileau had mixed feelings about La Fontaine. I would now like to examine rapidly two authors whom he admired with little or no reservations, Molière and Racine. Molière wrote only one serious nondramatic

---

[131] *Songe*, p. 99.
[132] *Œuvres diverses*, p. 583.
[133] Ibid., p. 488.
[134] Ibid.

poem, the long "La gloire du Val-de-Grâce." Vauvenargues thought the poem full of "expressions bizarres et impropres," but Voltaire held a far different opinion.[135] Boileau, according to Brossette, considered the poem's versification to be "la plus régulière et la plus soutenue" of all of Molière's efforts.[136] The 366 alexandrines are, to be sure, imbued with a certain pomp. The caesura is invariably regular and there are no obvious enjambments. It would seem, then, that Boileau had found a work "soutenu" and "régulier," worthy of the standards of Malherbe. Unfortunately, such is not the case, for there are two serious flaws, concerning hiatus and rhyme. Molière seems to have made little or no effort to ban the former— "elle joue aux" (l. 96) or "D'une féconde idée étale" (l. 132) to name but two of many—and every violation imaginable is present in the latter. Among these, monosyllabic homonyms, short sounds rhyming with long ones, diaereses with synaereses, and words rhyming with their own derivatives are the most common. In short, Molière seems to have achieved an elevated tone and regular cadence, but little else. The "crocheteurs des Halles" would have gotten lost in the technical jargon and the long sentences, and neither the rhymes nor the frequent hiatuses would have passed muster.

Souriau, who neglected Molière's nondramatic poetry, treated Racine's with great care, distinguishing between the light verses of his earliest youth, replete with lines such as "J'ai aussi le manche agréable" or "Il n'y a tête . . . ,"[137] and the later, serious works: "bien entendu, on ne trouve pas dans ses œuvres sérieuses un seul hiatus."[138] This is only true to some extent; there are debatable cases concerning the ear.[139]

From first to last, the linearity of Racine's nondramatic poetry, even the lightest, is above reproach, and were it not for the uniformly unsatisfactory rhymes and the preponderance of *vers suivis,* the entire production might be considered quite Malherbian. Unfortunately, discussion of many good works must be limited here due to considerations of chronology. The hymns from the Roman breviary, for instance, were first written in 1655 or 1656, but the extant versions are ones retouched about

[135] Molière, *Œuvres,* 9:525.
[136] Ibid., p. 530.
[137] Racine, *Œuvres complètes* (Paris: Gallimard, 1964), pp. 1022–23.
[138] Souriau, "L'évolution," p. 416.
[139] Most frequent of these is the use of *un héros.*

1675, and it would be specious to draw conclusions from them concerning those years of Racine's life preceding the appearance of the *Art poétique.* If one discounts the "pièces juvéniles," there remain eleven poems definitely written during the period under consideration: "La Nymphe de la Seine à la Reine," "Ode sur la convalescence du Roi," "La Renommée aux Muses," "Stances à Parthénice," and the seven odes of "Le paysage." Of these, only the third and fourth, in *a b a b* quatrains, 12–6–12–6 and alexandrine, are Malherbian forms in meter and rhyme. "La Nymphe," a very early work, is in 8–8–8–8–12–12–12–12–8–12 *dizains,* without élan or elevation. The ode to the king fails only in the rhyme scheme and would be considered Malherbian by all but the most fanatic. "Le paysage" is composed of 8–8–8–8–8–8–6–8–6–8 *dizains,* a radical departure from Malherbian standards. On the other hand, the vast majority of the ten-line stanzas are broken 4–6 with a good secondary 3–3 break. It would thus seem that Racine had indeed learned from his readings of Malherbe, though he may not have been convinced of the necessity to limit himself to Malherbian forms.

Racine's rhymes are an entirely different story. Souriau suggested that only in the early works are the rhymes unsatisfactory.[140] Unfortunately, such is not the case. Rhymes remained the weakest part of Racine's art throughout his career, and even if one disregards the light verse it is only too easy to find numerous examples. The *consonne d'appui* is unsatisfactory more often than not; monosyllabic homonyms abound, particularly *pas-pas;* not only do words rhyme with their compounds, but some of these combinations are repeated quite often (*jour-séjour*); some combinations occur so frequently as to become commonplaces, and many of these are facile (*moi-toi, ombre-sombre*); *âme-flamme,* [jø-iø], and all the other rhymes proscribed by the ear are equally frequent. Strangely enough, these lapses bothered neither Racine nor Boileau (nor Souriau, for that matter), but they would certainly have bothered Malherbe.

"Enfin Boileau vint." It should go without saying that before one can really assess the merits of Boileau's "tout reconnut ses lois" it is essential to determine how strict an interpretation of these laws Boileau demanded. Marcel Hervier considered Boileau's statement an exaggeration since at

---

[140] "L'évolution," pp. 421–22.

least Théophile had to be exempted by Boileau's own admission.[141] As we have seen so far, the list of exclusions is very large indeed, and I would further suggest that it should include Boileau himself, both as practitioner and as critic.

R. A. Sayce sees in Boileau the literary embodiment of the anti-baroque reaction,[142] while Borgerhoff, in *The Freedom of French Classicism*, views Boileau as much more a part of that past he was trying to eradicate. The critical writings of Boileau are far from unequivocal on the subject. When he scorned those who preferred Théophile to Racan and Malherbe, he was not, to quote Sayce, indulging in a personal whim but making "a sharp distinction between two opposed conceptions of poetry."[143] Furthermore, since his militance never abated, we have every right to assume that the battle had not yet been won. What must be kept in mind, however, is not so much the contradiction of these two conceptions in their theoretical purity, but the stand taken by a critic, Boileau, vis-à-vis two different practices. In fact, his criticism of his contemporaries definitely shows that he was not a Malherbian in the strict sense of the word. For instance, he considered Bouillon's *Joconde* "moins à blâmer pour les fautes qui y sont, que pour l'esprit et le génie qui n'y est pas."[144] Are these the words of a disciple of an "arrangeur de syllabes"? At issue here is the basic fact that Malherbe believed in the primacy of rules and order. Boileau, on the other hand, did not. He was a hard worker, of course, but this did not keep him from voicing his envy of Molière's facility in his second satire. He believed in rules, but saw the sublime as being well outside that realm, suggesting that even in the ode, "Un beau desordre est un effet de l'Art,"[145] a precept "qui donne pour regle de ne point garder quelquefois de regles."[146]

It is evident that the poet faced the same problems as the critic. There must have been many moments of crisis in Boileau's breast. Fortunately, in most of these "le poète a vaincu le puriste."[147] Most of the rules

---

[141] *L'art poétique de Boileau* (Paris: Mellottée, 1949), p. 204.
[142] "Boileau and French Baroque," *FS* 2 (1948): 148–52.
[143] Ibid., p. 151.
[144] *Dissertation sur la Joconde* (Paris: Belles Lettres, 1942), p. 23.
[145] "Art poétique," *Œuvres complètes*, p. 164.
[146] "Discours sur l'ode," ibid., p. 227.
[147] Gustave Lanson, *Boileau* (Paris: Hachette, 1892), p. 48.

enunciated in the *Art poétique* are unquestionably in accord with those
stated and practiced by Malherbe. Ironically, the *Art poétique* itself is no
more Malherbian than Boileau's other poems which, as we shall see, are
far from orthodox.

Lanson, generally considered a critic of rare insight, said that "à
l'ordinaire, la fameuse loi de la consonne d'appui est observée" in Boileau's
poetry.[148] But a random sample shows that this is far from true. Of the first
ten rhymes of *Satire I*, only two abide by the rule, and one of these
(*front-affront*) is unacceptable on other grounds; of the first ten rhymes
of *Epître I*, only one passes muster; an equal sampling of the *Art poétique*
reveals only four passable rhymes, a better percentage, to be sure, but
hardly a rigorous application. Nor is the failing of the *consonne d'appui*
the only flaw in Boileau's rhymes. From the *Art poétique* to the odes,
there is little sign of strict adherence to Malherbian standards. The "Ode
de Sapho," for instance, has only one acceptable rhyme (*parler-égaler*),
flaws in the others ranging from *voix-vois* to *flame-ame*. In the *Art
poétique*, every deviation imaginable is profusely represented: monosyllabic
homonyms (*nüe-nüe*), abuse of proper nouns, long and short sounds
rhyming, synaeresis-diaeresis, words of the same stem, and so forth. Souriau
warmly defended Boileau's refusal to become the slave of rhyme. Whether
or not rhyme is the poet's friend or foe is not the question here. What is,
is whether Boileau was Malherbian in matters dealing with rhyme, and the
answer must be a firm "no."

Upon close examination, Boileau has been found to be one of the
least harmonious of French poets,[149] but Malherbe is not much better in
that area. As far as prosody is concerned, both Boileau and Malherbe
considered rhythm to be of prime importance, and in this domain,
Boileau is at least Malherbe's equal. True, Boileau demonstrated little
originality in his choice of forms. As Marguerite Durand has pointed out,
excepting the light poems, the near-total of his production is in alexandrines.[150] But he was a master in the art of uniting form and content,
making full use of rhythmic patterns within the framework of the
alexandrines. What is more expressive than the line in which four slow

---

[148] Ibid., p. 47.
[149] Grammont, *Vers français*, p. 436.
[150] "Essai sur le vers de Boileau," *Fr. Mod.* 6 (1938): 331–46.

oxen "Promenoient dans Paris le Monarque indolent"?[151] The linearity is nearly perfect in all but the lightest poems, with little cacophony, relatively short sentences, and few enjambments either at the hemistich or at the end of the line. Exceptions to this last consideration are always well founded. At the hemistich, the *rejet* is most often used for emphasis: "Vous? Mon Dieu, mêlez-vous de boire, je vous prie."[152] The *contre-rejet* brings about the same effect, setting off a word for additional force: "Vient de s'enfuir, chargé de sa seule misère."[153] At the line, there are some rare enjambments, but always with a "rejet très expressif,"[154] as in the "Discours au Roi":

> Soûtiens tout par Toi-mesme, et vois tout par Tes yeux,
> Grand Roi; . . .[155]

Nowhere is the mastery over form more obvious than in the lyrical fragment of the "Ode de Sapho":

> Heureux! qui prés de toi, pour toi seule soûpire:
> Qui jouït du plaisir de t'entendre parler:
> Qui te voit quelquefois doucement lui soûrire.
> Les Dieux dans son bonheur peuvent-ils l'égaler?
>
> Je sens de veine en veine une subtile flame
> Courir par tout mon corps, si tost que je te vois;
> Et dans les doux transports où s'égare mon âme,
> Je ne sçaurois trouver de langue, ni de voix.[156]

In these few lines one can see the entire relationship of Boileau to Malherbe: no influence whatsoever insofar as rhymes are concerned, but a sure mastery over words, sounds, syntax—in short, over all other aspects of prosody.

[151] "Le lutrin," *Œuvres complètes*, p. 200.
[152] Sat. III, ibid., p. 25.
[153] Sat. I, ibid., p. 13.
[154] Georges Ascoli, *Boileau: Satires de I à IX* (Paris: Centre de Documentation Universitaire, 1967), p. 12.
[155] *Œuvres complètes*, p. 9.
[156] *Odes, Poésies diverses* (Paris: Belles Lettres, 1941), p. 11.

It is quite possible that Boileau's "tout reconnut ses loix" was nothing more than wishful thinking or an attempt to lead poets back to a more rigorous discipline. The samplings presented here seem to indicate that Fukui was right when he stated that there was a "décadence à cette époque du sens aigu des formes poétiques," a proliferation of "stances libres," and of mixed forms.[157] A contemporary, Sorel, deplored the state of things, saying that "on ne voit plus que des vers irréguliers."[158] This does not imply a disregard for such basic elements of poetry as rhythm (a single glance at La Fontaine's work will suffice to assure us of that), but rather a divorce, in the mind of the poet, of outer from inner form. In the final analysis, in the 1660s, the "sens aigu" was quite out of style and Malherbe was far from popular as an example. Boileau was not ascertaining the omnipresence of the master: he was bringing him back.

[157] *Raffinement précieux,* p. 293.

[158] Charles Sorel, *De la connoissance des bons livres* (Amsterdam: Boom, 1672), p. 231.

Chapter Nine

Conclusion

The major problem in trying to ascertain the degree of influence of a man on his times is that if the man was also of his times, his personal contribution cannot always be easily distinguished from that of his contemporaries. There is no doubt that between Desportes and Boileau, poetry in France underwent a fundamental change, but who is to get the blame or the credit? As Philip Wadsworth recognized some years ago, "as one advances beyond the individual and into the channels and cross-currents of literary history, the problem becomes infinitely complex. The imprint of Malherbe is not always distinguishable from that of other poets, such as Corneille. And their successors were exposed to many other forces from all directions."[1]

One must therefore seek, in the practice of the poets, not so much the general trends of an evolutionary pattern as specific forms and norms which were created by, or got their impetus from, a single man. For instance, the French language at the turn of the century was receiving the attention of every intellectual, and with or without Malherbe the "classics" would have had their tool. In that realm Balzac and Pascal did far more than Malherbe ever dreamed of doing. On the other hand, Malherbe's influence on the popularity of the great ode is undeniable.

From the beginning, critics disagreed on the role played by Malherbe, or on the limitations of his influence. In 1688, François de Callières claimed that Malherbe had been chosen as the leader of lyrical poets because of "le defaut de dignes concurrens."[2] Huet, on the contrary, claimed that his compatriot "a mis nôtre siècle et nôtre nation en droit de disputer le prix de la Poësie Lyrique, à tous les autres siècles, et à toutes les nations."[3] Chapelain thought that Malherbe wrote rhymed prose,[4] and Fénelon thought little of his excessive discipline: "L'excez choquant de Ronsard nous a un peu jettez dans l'extremité opposée."[5]

Modern critics, often without giving full consideration to the actual practice of the poets, have not only echoed these contradictory sentiments but enshrined them as facts. On the very first page of *La formation de la doctrine classique en France,* René Bray, commenting on Balzac's "Primus Franciscus Malherbe, aut in primis, viam . . ." and on Faguet's categorical denial of any Malherbian influence, states that "l'enseignement de Malherbe a porté sur quatre matières, sur la langue, sur le vers, sur le style, sur ses prédécesseurs. Sur les deux premiers points, personne ne niera que sa leçon a porté."[6] The second of these points is the subject of this study, and there is little doubt in my mind that, especially in the years 1615–1660 discussed by Faguet, the influence of Malherbe on "le vers" was, at best, negligible.

René Bray is by no means alone. Fukui, speaking of the "generation of 1630," categorically states that "parmi les poètes alors vivants, l'autorité de Malherbe n'est contestée par personne. Sa doctrine, plus cohérente et plus exigeante que celle de ses prédécesseurs, devint maintenant la base de toutes les productions poétiques."[7] Gohin goes still further: "L'influence de Malherbe s'étend sur tout le XVIIe siècle et domine le mouvement poétique. . . . Non seulement on cultive les genres chers à Malherbe, en particulier l'ode et les stances, mais encore on pratique les règles de versification qu'il a établies."[8] Allem, in an introduction to the poems of Malherbe, is not quite as enthusiastic but no less wrong: "Ce n'est guère qu'en 1660, c'est-à-dire après la venue de Boileau, que la victoire de Malherbe fut complète."[9] As we have seen, the authority of Malherbe was all too frequently contested, "his" rules were seldom followed to any noticeable degree, and by 1660 his victory was far from complete; and

---

[1] "Malherbe and His Influence," in *Studies in Seventeenth-Century French Literature Presented to Morris Bishop* (Ithaca: Cornell University, Press, 1962), p. 34.

[2] *Histoire poétique de la guerre . . . entre les Anciens et les Modernes* (Paris: Aubouin, 1688), p. 59.

[3] *Origines de Caen,* p. 364.

[4] *Lettres,* 1:637.

[5] *Reflexions sur la rhétorique et sur la poétique* (Amsterdam: Bernard, 1717), p. 33.

[6] P. 7.

[7] *Raffinement précieux,* p. 108.

[8] *La Fontaine,* p. 187.

[9] (Paris: Garnier, 1926), p. xvii.

Boileau, at the ripe old age of twenty-four, was anything but "arrivé." It is therefore quite unfair for a critic to state that after Malherbe "French poetry suffered from the eminence which he had attained, in that this ignorance of poetry was perpetuated in his successors, and fortified by continued imposition of restrictions for which he was originally responsible."[10] Such condemnations were the rule during the last century but make little sense in view of the evidence, and Antoine Adam was right in questioning them.[11] Malherbe did have a tremendous personal following and received great critical acclaim. Du Ryer was certainly not alone when he spoke of Malherbe as "un homme que j'aime et que je révère."[12] But as we have seen, "le critique a ses raisons que le poète ne connaît pas," and Du Ryer was not alone either in neglecting to imitate his idol.

"Ni l'école de du Bartas, ni celle de Desportes ne répondaient plus au goût des courtisans."[13] Malherbe came because he was long overdue. But just as he erected the desires of an age into a doctrine, so did the Boileaus, the Rapins, the Bouhours; only the tastes had radically changed in the meantime. In the eyes of the seventeenth century, Malherbe was the man who had brought poetry out of the dark ages. Ronsard, in the beginning, opened the way, but it was Malherbe who showed to all "le caractère et la majesté de l'Ode" by giving it "la pureté, la clarté, l'harmonie et la magnificence."[14] But the same critic also stated that the ode's elevation "paroît plûtôt l'effet de l'inspiration et de l'enthousiasme, que du sens rassis,"[15] and with this statement he was echoing the sentiments of an entire century. Malherbe had come at the right time and had diagnosed the illness correctly, but his remedy was unsatisfactory, relying as it did on "exigences techniques . . . trop raffinés."[16]

From the beginning, poets and critics praised his achievements while also voicing their disagreement. The "mais il a fait pour lui" of Théophile shows the latter to have had a clearer vision of the classical age that was

[10] Borgerhoff, *Freedom of French Classicism*, pp. 38–39.
[11] *Théophile de Viau*, p. 221.
[12] Malherbe, *Œuvres*, 2:260.
[13] Brunot, *Doctrine de Malherbe*, p. 563.
[14] André Dacier, ed., *Horace: Œuvres en latin et en français* (Paris: Ballard, 1709), 1:li.
[15] Ibid., p. xci.
[16] Fromilhague, *Technique*, p. 627.

to come than had Malherbe himself. Long before Boileau or Rapin, critics such as Méré and Pascal were to speak of *agréments inexplicables, grâces secretes, un je-ne-sais-quoi. Honnêteté* was urbanity, grace, bound to be "set against those forces which work too ardently for the establishment of obvious order and convention."[17] One need only remember Molière's most obvious lessons to see that pedantry was as much anathema to the *honnête homme* as ignorance. Malherbe's concern for technique could not possibly appeal to the poets who followed. To be sure, there were cases of "Malherbianism," such as La Lane and Campion, or even on occasion Ménage and Benserade, but they were few indeed. Huet, in spite of his admiration for Malherbe, saw the difference between the Malherbian ideal and the classical: "Ceux qui n'ont point le sentiment de la belle poësie, en ont renfermé toutes les régles dans celles de la versification."[18] Fénelon, in his *Réflexions sur la rhétorique et sur la poétique* and his *Jugement sur un poète de son temps,* said no less. Dacier blamed the "gênante servitude des pieds et des mesures reglées" for many of the woes of poetry.[19]

Must one then speak of classicism as the opposite of Malherbianism? Far from it. One must simply keep in mind that the *Art poétique* was written by a very young and militant poet, one who would eventually write the "Discours sur l'ode" and the "Traité du sublime." I do not wish to suggest here that Boileau denied himself; merely that we have all too often neglected his later, considered dicta to revel in the absolutism of the *Art poétique,* although the former reflect a view generally held at the time whereas the latter's "Enfin Malherbe vint" is little more than a hasty judgment of the past. Classicism is neither over-rational nor anti-rational, nor is it a simple compromise, a wallowing in some kind of nebulous *aurea mediocritas.* Rules are, of course, necessary, and they must be understood. But the true artist must be willing to go beyond them and, as Bouhours's Ariste suggests, to admire rather than merely understand. "Enfin Malherbe vint" is legitimate only if viewed as a springboard, for the century viewed Malherbe as nothing more nor less than a great teacher from whom all could learn, but who could be—and had to be— *dépassé.*

[17] Borgerhoff, *Freedom of French Classicism,* p. 236.
[18] *Huetiana* (Paris: Estienne, 1722), p. 177.
[19] *Horace,* pp. xi–xii.

Bibliography of Works Cited

Abraham, Claude. *Gaston d'Orléans et sa cour: Etude littéraire.* Chapel Hill: University of North Carolina Press, 1963.

[Académie Française.] *Trois siècles de l'Académie Française, par les Quarante.* Paris: Firmin-Didot, 1935.

Adam, Antoine. "L'école de 1650." *Revue d'Histoire de la Philosophie* 29–30 (1942): 23–53, 134–52.

―――. *Histoire de la littérature française au XVIIe siècle.* Paris: Domat, 1948–1956.

―――. *Théophile de Viau et la libre pensée française en 1620.* Geneva: Slatkine, 1966.

Albalat, Antoine. *Le travail du style.* Paris: Colin, 1911.

Alembert, Jean Lerond d'. *Histoire des membres de l'Académie Française.* Paris: Moutard, 1787.

Allais, Gustave. *Malherbe et la poésie française à la fin du XVIe siècle.* Paris: Thorin, 1891.

Allem, Maurice, ed. *Anthologie poétique française: XVIIe siècle.* Paris: Garnier, 1914.

Angot de l'Eperonnière, Robert. *Le chef d'œuvre poétique.* Rouen: Boissel, 1872.

Arnauld, Charles. *Les théories dramatiques au XVIIe siècle: Etude sur la vie et les œuvres de l'Abbé d'Aubignac.* Paris: Picard, 1888.

Ascoli, Georges. *Boileau: Satires de I à IX.* Paris: Centre de Documentation Universitaire, 1967.

Asselineau, Charles. *Notice sur Jean de Schelandre.* Alençon: n.p., 1856.

Aubigné, Théodore Agrippa d'. *Œuvres complètes.* Paris: Lemerre, 1873–1892.

Auvray, Jean. *Le banquet des Muses.* Edited by E. H. Balmas. Milan: La Goliardica, 1953.

Bailbé, Jacques. "La couleur baroque de la langue et du style dans les premières œuvres de Saint-Amant." *Français Moderne* 28 (1960): 171–80, 287–96; 29 (1961): 43–61.

Balzac, Jean-Louis Guez de. *Lettres.* Paris: Toussainct du Bray, 1624.

―――. *Lettres choisies.* Paris: Courbé, 1647.

―――. *Œuvres.* Paris: Billaine, 1665.

Balzac. *Œuvres*. Paris: Lecoffre, 1854.

Banville, Théodore de. *Cariatides*. Paris: Charpentier, 1879.

Bar, Francis. "Fins et moyens de l'archaïsme chez les burlesques du XVIIe siècle." *Cahiers de l'Association Internationale des Etudes Françaises* 19 (1967): 39–58.

———. *Le genre burlesque en France au XVIIe siècle: Etude de style*. Paris: D'Artrey, 1960.

Baro, Balthasar. *A Monseigneur le Duc d'Alvin . . . Ode*. N.p., n.d. [1633?].

———. *Contre l'auteur d'un libelle*. Paris: Camusat, 1637.

Barthélemy, Edouard de. "Le Marquis de Dangeau, poëte." *Revue Française* 15 (1858–1859): 54–60.

Bataille, Gabriel. *Premier livre d'airs*. Paris: Ballard, 1611.

Baunier, André. "Un grand poète Louis XIII: Saint-Amant." *Revue des Deux Mondes* 43 (1918): 210–21.

Bénichou, Paul. *Morales du grand siècle*. Paris: Gallimard, 1948.

Benserade, Isaac de. *Œuvres*. Paris: Sercy, 1697.

———. *Poésies*. Edited by Octave Uzanne. Paris: Librairie des Bibliophiles, 1875.

Bergounioux, Louis-Alexandre. *Marc-Antoine Dominici*. Paris: Boivin, 1936.

Berthelot, [N.?]. *Œuvres satyriques*. Paris: Bibliothèque Internationale d'Edition, 1913.

Bever, Adhémar van, ed. *Les poètes du terroir*. Paris: Delagrave, 1920.

Beys, Charles. *Les illustres fous*. Edited by M. I. Protzman. Baltimore: Johns Hopkins Press, 1942.

———. *Les odes d'Horace*. Edited by André Lebois. Avignon: Aubanel, 1963.

Biard, Jean D. *The Style of La Fontaine's Fables*. New York: Barnes and Noble, 1966.

Blanchard, André. "Corneille et Brébeuf." *Cahiers du Sud* 356 (1960): 130–34.

———, ed. *Baroques et classiques*. Lyon: IAC, 1947.

Blot L'Eglise, Claude de Chouvigny, baron de. *Les chansons libertines*. Edited by Frédéric Lachèvre. Paris: Champion, 1919.

Boileau-Despréaux, Nicolas. *Dissertation sur la Joconde*. Edited by C.-H. Boudhors. Paris: Belles Lettres, 1942.

———. *Odes, Poésies diverses*. Edited by C.-H. Boudhors. Paris: Belles Lettres, 1941.

———. *Œuvres complètes*. Edited by Françoise Escal. Paris: Gallimard, 1966.

Boisard, François. *Notices sur les hommes du Calvados*. Caen: Pagny, 1848.

Bois-Robert, François le Metel de. *Autres œuvres poétiques*. Paris: Besongne, 1647 [*sic*: read 1646].

———. *Autres œuvres poétiques*. Paris: Courbé, 1659.

———. *Epistres en vers*. Paris: Hachette, 1921–1927.

Borel, Eugène. *Des réformes littéraires opérées par Malherbe.* Stuttgart: n.p., 1857.

Borgerhoff, Elbert B. O. *The Freedom of French Classicism.* Princeton: Princeton University Press, 1950.

Borton, Samuel L. *Six Modes of Sensibility in Saint-Amant.* The Hague: Mouton, 1966.

Bouhours, P. Dominique. *La manière de bien penser.* Paris: Mabre-Cramoisy, 1687.

Bray, René. *La formation de la doctrine classique en France.* Lausanne: Payot, 1931.

———, ed. *Anthologie de la poésie précieuse.* Paris: Nizet, 1957.

Brébeuf, Georges de. *Entretiens solitaires.* Edited by René Harmand. Paris: Cornély, 1912.

Brunetière, Ferdinand. "La réforme de Malherbe et l'évolution des genres." *Revue des Deux Mondes* 6 (December 1892): 660–83.

———. "Maurice Souriau: L'évolution du vers français au dix-septième siècle." *Revue d'Histoire Littéraire de la France* 1 (1894): 497.

Brunot, Ferdinand. *La doctrine de Malherbe.* Paris: Masson, 1891.

Bruzzi, Amelia. *Il barocco nella poesia di Théophile de Viau.* Bologna: Pàtron, 1965.

Buffum, Imbrie. *Studies in the Baroque from Montaigne to Rotrou.* New Haven: Yale University Press, 1957.

Bussy-Rabutin, Roger de. *Epigrammes inédites.* Paris: Sansot, 1904.

———. *Histoire amoureuse des Gaules.* Paris: Jannet, 1856.

Le cabinet des Muses. Rouen: Du Petit-Val, 1619.

Le cabinet satyrique. N.p., 1864.

Cagnon, Maurice. "Zélotyde: Un roman négligé du XVIIe siècle." *Dix-Septième Siécle* 79 (1968): 43–56.

Callières, François de. *Histoire poétique de la guerre . . . entre les Anciens et les Modernes.* Paris: Aubouin, 1688.

Carriat, Amédée. *Deux poèmes oubliés.* Limoges: Rougerie, [1955].

———. *Tristan: Ou l'éloge d'un poète.* Limoges: Rougerie, 1955.

Cauchie, Maurice. *Documents pour servir à l'histoire littéraire du XVIIe siècle.* Paris: Champion, 1924.

———. "Les églogues de Nicolas Frénicle et le groupe littéraire des 'Illustres Bergers.' " *Revue d'Histoire de la Philosophie* 30 (1942): 115–33.

———. "Les premières poésies de Scudéry (1631–1636)." *Mercure de France* 299 (1947): 58–73.

———. "Le sonnet sous Louis XIII et la régence d'Anne d'Autriche." *Dix-Septième Siècle* 38 (1958): 40–54.

Chandeville, Eléazar de Sarcilly, sr. de. *Diverses poésies.* Paris: Courbé, 1639.

———. *Poésies.* Edited by Armand Gasté. Caen: Le Blanc-Hardel, 1878.

Chapelain, Jean. *Lettres.* Edited by Philippe Tamizey de Larroque. Paris: Imprimerie Nationale, 1880–1883.

Chapelain. *Miserere*. Paris: Camusat, 1637.

———. *Ode à Mgr le Cardinal Duc de Richelieu*. Paris: Camusat, 1633.

———. *Opuscules critiques*. Edited by A. C. Hunter. Paris: Droz, 1936.

———. *La Pucelle*. Paris: Flammarion, 1891.

Chapelle, C.-E. Lhuillier, dit, and Bachaumont, François Le Coigneux de. *Voyage*. Paris: Letellier, 1826.

Charmois, Alain. "Ogier de Gombauld." *Mercure de France* 305 (1949): 647–53.

Chevreau, Urbain. *Œuvres meslées*. The Hague: Moetjens, 1697.

———. *Poèsies*. Paris: Sommaville, 1656.

Clavelier, G. "Œuvres inédites de François Maynard." *Annales du Midi* 20 (1908): 225–36, 392–401, 500–511; 21 (1909): 77–85, 338–50.

Collas, Georges [Carl Felix von Schlichtegroll]. *Jean Chapelain*. Paris: Perrin, 1912.

Colletet, François. *Le Parnasse françois ou l'Ecole des Muses*. Paris: Sercy, 1664.

Colletet, Guillaume. *Poésies diverses*. Paris: Chamhoudry, 1656.

———. *Le trébuchement de l'yvrongne*. Paris: n.p., 1627.

Colomby, François de. *Discours presenté au Roy avant son partement pour aller assiéger Sedan*. Paris: Prevosteu, 1606.

———. *Les plaintes de la captive Caliston à l'invincible Aristarque*. N.p., 1605.

Colotte, Pierre. "Malherbe et Deimier." In *IVe centenaire de la naissance de Malherbe*, pp. 77–88. Gap: Orphrys, 1956.

———. "Notice sur Pierre de Deimier." *Dix-Septième Siècle* 17–18 (1953): 30–32.

———. *Pierre de Deimier, poète et théoricien de la poésie: Sa carrière à Paris et ses relations avec Malherbe*. Gap: Orphrys, 1953.

Condéescou, N.-N. "Une muse du XVIIe siècle: Madame de La Lane." *Revue d'Histoire Littéraire de la France* 46 (1939): 1–32.

[Conrart, Valentin.] Manuscrit Conrart. Vol. 22. Paris: Bibliothèque de l'Arsenal.

Corneille, Pierre. *Œuvres*. Edited by Charles Marty-Laveaux. Paris: Hachette, 1862–1868.

Cotin, Charles. *Œuvres meslées*. Paris: Sommaville, 1659.

———. *Poésies chrestiennes*. Paris : Le Petit, 1668.

Counson, Albert. *Malherbe et ses sources*. Liège: Liège University, 1904.

Cousin, Victor. *La société française au XVIIe siècle*. Paris: Didier, 1858.

Cyrano de Bergerac, Savinien de. *Œuvres libertines*. Edited by Frédéric Lachèvre. Paris: Champion, 1921.

Dacier, André, ed. *Horace: Œuvres en latin et en français*. Paris: Ballard, 1709.

Dalibray, Charles Vion de. *Œuvres poétiques*. Paris: Sommaville, 1653.

———. *Œuvres poétiques*. Edited by Adhémar van Bever. Paris: Sansot, 1906.

Dassoucy, Charles Coipeau. *L'Ovide en belle humeur*. Paris: Sommaville, 1653.

———. *Poésies et lettres*. Paris: Chamhoudry, 1653.

Dehénault, Jean. *Œuvres*. Edited by Frédéric Lachèvre. Geneva: Slatkine, 1968.

Deimier, Pierre de. *Académie de l'art poétique*. Paris: Bordeaulx, 1610.

———. *La royale liberté de Marseille*. Paris: Perier, 1615.

Les délices de la poésie françoise ou recueil des plus beaux vers de ce temps. Paris: Toussainct du Bray, 1615.

Le second livre des délices. . . . Paris: Toussainct du Bray, 1620.

Les délices de la poésie françoise ou dernier recueil des plus beaux vers. Paris: Toussainct du Bray, 1620.

Delplanque, Albert. *La Marquise de Rambouillet et Malherbe*. Paris: Lethielleux, 1925.

Deshoulières, Antoinette. *Œuvres*. Paris: Prault, 1753.

———. *Poésies*. Paris: Mabre-Cramoisy, 1688.

Desmarests de Saint-Sorlin, Jean. *Esther*. Paris: Le Petit, 1670.

———. *Œuvres poétiques*. Paris: Le Gras, 1641.

———. *Prières et œuvres chrestiennes*. Paris: Thierry, 1669.

Desonay, Fernand. "La réputation littéraire de Ronsard au XVIIe siècle." *Bulletin Bibliographique et Pédagogique du Musée Belge* 27 (1924): 141–60.

Drouhet, Charles. *Le poète François Mainard*. Paris: Champion, 1909.

Du Bois-Hus. *La nuict des nuicts. Le jour des jours. Le miroir du destin ou la nativité du Daufin du ciel*. . . . Edited by Annarosa Poli. Bologna: Pàtron, 1967.

Dulorens, Jacques. *Satyres*. Paris: Villery, 1624.

———. *Satyres*. Paris: Alliot, 1633.

———. *Satyres*. Paris: Sommaville, 1646.

Du Perron, Jacques Davy *Perroniana*. Geneva: n.p., 1667.

Durand, Etienne. *Méditations*. Edited by Frédéric Lachèvre. Paris: Leclerc, 1906.

Durand, Marguerite. "Essai sur le vers de Boileau." *Français Moderne* 6 (1938): 331–46.

Durry, Marie-Jeanne. *Autographes de Mariemont*. Paris: Nizet, 1955.

Ecorcheville, Jules. "Corneille et la musique." *Courrier Musical et théâtral* 9 (1906): 405–12, 438–49.

Elogia Julii Mazarini Cardinalis. Paris: Vitré, 1666.

Esternod, Claude d'. *L'espadon satirique*. Paris: Fort, 1922.

Estrée, Paul d'. "Une académie bachique au XVIIe siècle." *Revue d'Histoire Littéraire de la France* 2 (1895): 491–522.

———. "A travers les manuscrits de Conrart." *Revue d'Histoire Littéraire de la France* 2 (1895): 89–107.

Fabre, Antonin. *Les ennemis de Chapelain*. Paris: Fontemoing, 1897.

———. *La jeunesse de Fléchier*. Paris: Didier, 1882.

Faguet, Emile. *Histoire de la poésie française de la Renaissance au Romantisme.* Paris: Boivin, 1923–1936.

———. "La poésie de Malherbe à Boileau." *Revue des Cours et Conférences,* ser. 3, 6 (1894).

Fénelon, François de Pons de Salignac de la Motthe. *Reflexions sur la rhétorique et sur la poétique.* Amsterdam: Bernard, 1717.

Fleuret, F., and Perceau, L., eds. *Les satires françaises du XVIIe siècle.* Paris: Garnier, 1923.

Fournier, Edouard. *Variétés historiques et littéraires.* Paris: Jannet [et Pagnerre], 1855–1863.

Françon, Marcel. "La renommée de Ronsard au dix-septième siècle, d'après les recueils collectifs du temps." *French Review* 32 (December 1958): 144–46.

Frénicle, Nicolas. *Premières œuvres poétiques.* Paris: Toussainct du Bray, 1625.

Fromilhague, René. "La création poétique chez Malherbe." *Dix-Septième Siècle* 31 (April 1956): 247–68.

———. *Malherbe: Technique et création poétique.* Paris: Colin, 1954.

———. *La vie de Malherbe.* Paris: Colin, 1954.

Fukui, Yoshio. *Raffinement précieux dans la poésie française du XVIIe siècle.* Paris: Nizet, 1964.

———. "Sur la mort de Madame d'Harambure: Sonnets inédits de Tallemant des Réaux, Chapelain, Gombauld." *Revue des Sciences Humaines* 94 (1959): 169–77.

Furetière, Antoine. *Recueil des factums.* Paris: Poulet-Mallassis et de Broise, 1858.

———. *Le roman bourgeois, suivi de satyres et de nouvelles allégoriques.* Edited by Georges Mongrédien. Paris: Club du Meilleur Livre, 1956.

Fussel, Paul, Jr. *Poetic Meter and Poetic Form.* New York: Random House, 1965.

Garapon, Robert. *La fantaisie verbale et le comique dans le théâtre français . . . .* Paris: Colin, 1957.

Gay, Lucy M. "Sources of the *Académie de l'Art Poétique* of Pierre de Deimier." *Publications of the Modern Language Association* 27 (1912): 398–418.

Gilbert, Gabriel. *Poésies diverses.* Paris: Luyne, 1661.

Godeau, Antoine. *Institution du Prince Chrestien.* Paris: Camusat et Le Petit, 1644.

———. *Œuvres chrestiennes.* Paris: Camusat, 1633–1637.

———. *Paraphrase des Pseaumes de David.* Paris: Camusat et Le Petit, 1648.

———. *Poésies chrestiennes.* Paris: Le Petit, 1660.

Gohin, Ferdinand. *L'art de La Fontaine dans ses Fables.* Paris: Garnier, 1929.

———. *La Fontaine: Etudes et recherches.* Paris: Garnier, 1937.

———. "La poésie à Port-Royal: La Fontaine et Arnauld d'Andilly." *Mercure de France* 246 (1933): 513–31.

————. "De la rime dans les Fables de La Fontaine." *Muse Française* 8 (1929), 475–84.

Gombauld, Jean-Ogier. *Epigrammes.* Paris: Courbé, 1657.

————. *Poésies.* Paris: Courbé, 1646.

Goodman, William A. "The Heroic Poems of Jean Desmarets de Saint-Sorlin." Doctoral dissertation, University of North Carolina. Ann Arbor: University Microfilms, 1967.

Gosse, Edmund. *Malherbe and the Classical Reaction in the Seventeenth Century.* Oxford: Clarendon Press, 1920.

Goujet, C.-P. *Bibliothèque françoise.* Paris: Mariette, 1740–1765.

Gourier, Françoise. *Etude des œuvres poétiques de Saint-Amant.* Geneva: Droz, 1961.

Grammont, Maurice. *Le vers français.* Paris: Delagrave, 1954.

Grisé, Catherine M. "The Poetry of Tristan L'Hermite." Doctoral dissertation, University of Toronto, 1964.

————. "Towards a New Biography of Tristan L'Hermite." *Revue de l'Universite d'Ottawa* 36 (April–June 1966), 294–316.

————. "La vraie source de 'L'ambition tancée' de Tristan L'Hermite." *Revue de Littérature Comparée* 41 (1967): 585–88.

Gros, Etienne. *Philippe Quinault.* Paris: Champion, 1926.

Guedj, Hélène. "Théophile de Viau, poète baroque, et le Sud-Ouest." *Actes des Journées Internationales d'Etudes du Baroque* A2 (1963): 143–52.

Guéret, Gabriel, ed. *Le parnasse réformé.* Paris: Osmont, 1674.

Guisan, Gilbert. "L'évolution de l'art de La Fontaine d'après les variantes de l'"Adonis.' " *Revue d'Histoire Littéraire de la France* 42 (1935): 161–80, 321–43.

Guiton, Margaret. *La Fontaine: Poet and Counter-poet.* New Brunswick: Rutgers University Press, 1961.

Habert, Germain de Cerisy. *La métamorphose des yeux de Philis en astre.* N.p., 1639.

Habert, Philippe. *Le temple de la mort.* N.p., n.d. [Bound with above.]

Hallays, André. *Les Perrault.* Paris: Perrin, 1926.

Hermant, Godefroy. *Mémoires.* Paris: Plon-Nourrit, 1905–1910.

Hervier, Marcel. *L'art poétique de Boileau.* Paris: Mellottée, 1949.

Hill, Robert E. "In Context: Théophile de Viau's *La Solitude.*" *Bulletin d'Humanisme et de Renaissance* 30 (1968): 499–536.

Hope, Quentin M. *Saint-Evremond: The Honnête Homme as Critic.* Bloomington: Indiana University Press, 1962.

Huet, Pierre-Daniel. *Huetiana.* Paris: Estienne, 1722.

————. *Les origines de Caen.* Rouen: Maurry, 1706.

————. *Poésies françaises.* Edited by Gaston Lavalley. Paris: Dentu, 1881.

Jodelle, Estienne. *Les amours et autres poésies.* Edited by Adhémar van Bever. Paris: Sansot, 1907.

Kastner, L. E. *A History of French Versification.* Oxford: Clarendon Press, 1903.

Kerviler, René, and Barthélemy, Edouard de. *Valentin Conrart.* Paris: Didier, 1881.

Lachèvre, Frédéric. *Bibliographie des recueils collectifs de poésies publiés de 1597 à 1700.* Geneva: Slatkine, 1967.

————. *Les derniers libertins.* Geneva: Slatkine, 1968.

————. *Disciples et successeurs de Théophile de Viau: La vie et les poésies libertines inédites de des Barreaux.—Saint-Pavin.* Paris: Champion, 1911.

————. *Glanes bibliographiques et littéraires.* Paris: Giraud-Badin, 1929.

————. *Jacques Vallée des Barreaux: Sa vie et ses poésies.* Paris: Leclerc, 1907.

————. *Nouvelles glanes bibliographiques et littéraires.* Paris: Giraud-Badin, 1933.

————. *Un point obscur de la vie de Scarron: Scarron et sa Gazette burlesque.* Paris: Giraud-Badin, 1929.

————. *Le procès du poète Théophile de Viau.* Paris: Champion, 1909.

Lacôte, René. "Tristan L'Hermite et sa façade poétique." *Lettres Françaises* 584 (8–14 September 1955): 5.

Lacroix, Paul, ed. *Ballets et mascarades de cour.* Geneva: Gay, 1868–1870.

————, ed. *Paris ridicule et burlesque.* Paris: Delahays, 1859.

Lafenestre, Pierre. "François Maynard." *Revue d'Histoire Littéraire de la France* 10 (1903): 457–77.

La Fontaine, Jean de. *Contes et nouvelles en vers.* Edited by Pierre Clarac. Paris: Belles Lettres, 1961.

————. *Fables.* Edited by Ferdinand Gohin. Paris: Belles Lettres, 1934.

————. *Œuvres diverses.* Edited by Pierre Clarac. Paris: Gallimard, 1958.

————. *Le songe de Vaux.* Edited by Eleanor Titcomb. Geneva: Droz, 1967.

Lagarde, André, and Michard, Louis. *Les grands auteurs français du programme: XVIIe siècle.* Paris: Bordas, 1961.

Lagny, Jean. *Le poète Saint-Amant.* Paris: Nizet, 1964.

La Mesnardière, Jules de. *Poésies.* Paris: Sommaville, 1656.

Lanson, Gustave. *Boileau.* Paris: Hachette, 1892.

La Sablière, Antoine de Rambouillet, sr. de. *Madrigaux.* Lyon: Amaulry, 1681.

La Serre, Jean Puget de. *Le secrétaire de la cour.* Lyon: Muguet, 1646.

Leblanc, Paulette. *Les paraphrases françaises des Psaumes à la fin de la période baroque.* Paris: Presses Universitaires de France, 1966.

Leblanc, Yves. "Les enluminures de Le Maître de Sacy." *Dix-Septième Siècle* 32 (1956): 475–501.

Lefort de la Morinière, A. C. *Bibliothèque poëtique.* Paris: Briasson, 1745.

Le Hir, Yves. "Notes sur la langue et le style du *Moïse sauvé* de Saint-Amant (1653)." *Français Moderne* 19 (1951): 95–108.

————. "Sur un poème d'Auvray." *Etudes Classiques* 35 (1967): 335–44.

Le Pays, René. *Amitiez, amours et amourettes.* Paris: Sercy, 1667.

————. *Nouvelles œuvres.* Amsterdam: Hogenhuysen, 1690.

Le Petit, Claude. *Les œuvres libertines.* Edited by Frédéric Lachèvre. Geneva: Slatkine, 1968.

Lierau, Maximilian. *Die metrische Technik der drei Sonettisten Maynard, Gombauld and Malleville, verglichen mit derjenigen Fr. Malherbes.* Greifwald: Abel, 1882.

Lingendes, Jean de. *Œuvres poétiques.* Edited by E. T. Griffiths. Manchester: Manchester University Press, 1916.

Livet, Ch.-L. *Précieux et précieuses.* Paris: Didier, 1859.

Magne, Emile. 'L'Abbé Michel de Pure ou le confident des précieuses." *Revue de Paris* 2 (1938): 819–43; 3 (1938): 156–85.

————. *Un ami de Cyrano de Bergerac: Le Chevalier de Lignières.* Paris: Chiberra, 1920.

————. *Bibliographie générale des œuvres de Nicolas Boileau-Despréaux et de Gilles et Jacques Boileau.* Paris: Giraud-Badin, 1929.

————. *La fin troublée de Tallemant des Réaux.* Paris: Emile-Paul, 1922.

————. *La joyeuse jeunesse de Tallemant des Réaux.* Paris: Emile-Paul, 1921.

————. *Voiture et les années de gloire de l'Hôtel de Rambouillet.* Paris: Mercure de France, 1912.

————. *Voiture et les origines de l'Hôtel de Rambouillet.* Paris: Mercure de France, 1911.

Malherbe, François de. *Œuvres.* Edited by Gilles Ménage. Paris: Barbou, 1722.

————. *Œuvres.* Paris: Hachette, 1862–1869.

————. *Poésies.* Edited by Maurice Allem. Paris: Garnier, 1926.

Mallarmé, Stéphane. *Œuvres complètes.* Paris: Gallimard, 1956.

Malleville, Claude de. *Poésies.* Paris: Courbé, 1659.

Margouliès, Georges. "Scarron et Lope de Vega." *Revue de Littérature Comparée* 8 (1928): 511–15.

————. "Scarron sonnettiste et ses modèles espagnols." *Revue de Littérature Comparée* 13 (1933): 137–38.

Marmier, Jean. *Horace en France au XVIIe siècle.* Paris: Presses Universitaires de France, 1962.

Marolles, Michel de. *Mémoires.* Amsterdam: n.p., 1755.

Martinon, Philippe. "Etudes sur le vers français: les innovations prosodiques chez Corneille." *Revue d'Histoire Littéraire de la France* 20 (1913): 65–100.

————. "La genèse des règles de Jean Lemaire à Malherbe." *Revue d'Histoire Littéraire de la France* 16 (1909): 62–87.

Maucroix, François de. *Lettres.* Edited by Renée Kohn. Paris: Presses Universitaires de France, 1962.

————. *Œuvres diverses.* Reims: Techener, 1854.

Maurice-Amour, Lila. "Musique et poésie au temps de Malherbe." *Revue d'Histoire Littéraire de la France* 56 (1956): 204–20.

————. "Les poésies de Malherbe et les musiciens de son temps." *Dix-Septième Siècle* 31 (1956): 296–331.

Maynard, François. *Lettres.* Paris: Quinet, 1653.

————. *Poésies.* Paris: Garnier, 1927.

Mazzara, Richard A. "Saint-Amant, Avant-garde *Precieux* Poet: 'La Jouyssance.'" *Ball State Teachers College Forum* 4 (1963): 58–63.

Ménage, Gilles. *Poemata.* Paris: Courbé, 1656.

Méziriac, Claude Gaspar Bachet de. *Chansons devotes et sainctes.* Dijon: Guyot, 1615.

Minogue, Valerie P. "Tristan L'Hermite in the Context of the Seventeenth Century." Master's thesis, University of Cambridge, 1957.

Molière. *Œuvres.* Paris: Hachette, 1923–1925.

Mongrédien, Georges. "Un avocat-poète au XVIIe siècle: Bonaventure de Fourcroy." *Revue d'Histoire Littéraire de la France* 33 (1926): 1–13.

———. *Cyrano de Bergerac.* Paris: Berger-Levrault, 1964.

———. *Etude sur la vie et les œuvres de Nicolas Vauquelin.* Geneva: Slatkine, 1967.

———. *Libertins et amoureuses.* Paris: Perrin, 1929.

———. *Madeleine de Scudéry et son salon.* Paris: Tallandier, 1946.

———. "Le meilleur ami de Molière, Chapelle." *Mercure de France* 329 (1957): 86–109, 242–59.

———. *Les précieux et les précieuses.* Paris: Mercure de France, 1963.

———. "Vers inédits de Benserade." *Revue d'Histoire Littéraire de la France* 30 (1923): 513–19.

Moréas, Jean. *Œuvre en prose.* Paris: Valois, 1927.

Morel, Lydie. *Jean Ogier de Gombauld: Sa vie, son œuvre.* Neuchâtel: Delachaux et Niestlé, 1910.

Morrissette, Bruce A. *The Life and Works of Marie-Catherine Desjardins.* St. Louis: Washington University Press, 1947.

Motin, Pierre. *Œuvres inédites.* Paris: Librairie des Bibliophiles, 1882.

Mourgues, Odette de. *O muse, fuyante proie. . . .* Paris: Corti, 1962.

———. "Reason and Fancy in the Poetry of Théophile de Viau." *Esprit Createur* 1 (1961): 75–81.

Müller, Gerhard. *Untersuchung des poetischen Stils Théophiles de Viau.* Munich: Huebner, 1968.

Les Muses en deuil en faveur du sieur Brun. Paris: Toussainct du Bray, 1620.

Nelson, Lowry, Jr. *Baroque Lyric Poetry.* New Haven: Yale University Press, 1961.

Nervèze, Antoine de. *Essais poétiques.* Paris: Dubreuil, 1605.

Nodier, Charles. "Cyrano de Bergerac." *Bulletin du Bibliophile et du Bibliothéquaire* 3 (1838): 343–57.

———. "Notice sur les poésies de Claude de Chaulne." *Bulletin du Bibliophile et du Bibliothéquaire* 2(1836): 87–90.

Nouveau recueil de divers rondeaux. Paris: Courbé, 1650.

Nouveau recueil des plus beaux vers de ce temps. Paris: Toussainct du Bray, 1609.

Nouveau recueil des plus belles poésies. Paris: Loyson, 1654.

Les nouvelles Muses des Sieurs Godeau, Chapelain, ... Paris: Bertault, 1633.

Olivier, Paul, ed. *Cent poètes lyriques, précieux ou burlesques du XVIIe siècle*. Paris: Havard, 1898.

Orieux, Jean. *Bussy-Rabutin, le libertin galant-homme*. Paris: Flammarion, 1958.

Paquot, Marcel. "Les 'Vers du Balet des Nations' de Guillaume Colletet." *Revue Belge de Philosophie et d'Histoire* 10 (1931): 53–68.

Parker, Richard Alexander. *Claude de L'Estoile, Poet and Dramatist, 1597–1652*. Baltimore: Johns Hopkins Press, 1930.

Le Parnasse des plus excellens poëtes de ce temps. Paris: Guillemot, 1607.

Le Parnasse des poètes satyriques. Paris: Sommaville, 1622.

Le Parnasse Royal. Paris: Cramoisy, 1635.

Pascal, Blaise. *Œuvres complètes*. Paris: Hachette, 1904–1914.

Peiresc, Nicolas-Claude de Fabri, sr. de. *Lettres*. Paris: Imprimerie Nationale, 1888–1898.

Peletier du Mans, Jacques. *L'art poëtique*. Paris: Belles Lettres, 1930.

Pellisson, Paul, and d'Olivet, P.-J. Thoulier. *Histoire de l'Académie Française*. Paris: Didier, 1858.

Péraudière, X. de la. "Remarques sur les rimes insuffisantes de La Fontaine." *Mémoires de la Société d'Angers* 2 (1899): 48–56.

Perrault, Charles. *Les hommes illustres*. Paris: Dezallier, 1696–1700.

———. *Parallèle des anciens et des modernes*. Paris: Coignard, 1688–1697.

———, and Perrault, Claude. "L'Enéide burlesque." Edited by Paul Bonnefon. *Revue d'Histoire Littéraire de la France* 9 (1901): 110–42.

———, and Perrault, Claude and Nicolas. *Les murs de Troye*. Paris: Chamhoudry, 1653.

Perrin, Pierre. *Les œuvres de poésies*. Paris: Loyson, 1661.

Petit, Louis. *Discours satyriques et moraux*. Rouen: Lallemant, 1686.

Petit de Julleville, Louis. *Histoire de la langue et de la littérature françaises*. Paris: Colin, 1897.

Picard, Raymond, ed. *La poésie française de 1640 à 1680*. Paris: Société d'Edition d'Enseignement Supérieur, 1964.

Pinchesne, Etienne Martin de. *La chronique des chapons et des gélinottes du Mans*. Edited by Frédéric Lachèvre. Paris: Leclerc, 1907.

Pizzorusso, Arnaldo. "Sulla poesia di Etienne Durand." *Letteratura* 4 (1956): 34–47.

Poésies choisies de Messieurs Corneille, Bensserade, ... Paris: Sercy, 1653–1660.

Pougin, Arthur. *Les vrais créateurs de l'opéra français: Perrin et Cambert*. Paris: Charavay, 1881.

Priézac, Salomon de. *Poésies*. Paris: Martin et Sercy, 1650.

Racan, Honorat du Bueil, sr. de. *Œuvres complètes*. Paris: Jannet, 1857.

———. *Poésies*. Paris: Hachette, 1930.

Racine, Jean. *Œuvres complètes*. Edited by Raymond Picard. Paris: Gallimard, 1964.

Rapin, René. *Réflexions sur la poétique*. Paris: Barbin, 1675.

Rathery, E. J. B., and Boutron. *Mlle de Scudéry*. Paris: Techener, 1873.

Raymond, Marcel. *Baroque et renaissance poétique*. Paris: Corti, 1955.

———. *L'influence de Ronsard sur la poésie française*. Paris: Champion, 1927.

Recueil des plus beaux vers de Messieurs de Malherbe, Racan, ... Paris: Toussainct du Bray, 1627–1630.

Recueil des plus beaux vers qui ont esté mis en chant. Paris: Sercy, 1661.

Ronsard, Pierre de. *Œuvres complètes*. Paris: Gallimard, 1950.

Rosset, François de. *Les douze beautés de Phyllis et autres œuvres poëtiques*. Paris: L'Angelier, 1604.

Rountree, Benjamin. "Narrative Poetry as Drama: Molière's 'Remerciment au Roi.' " *Romance Notes* 9 (1968): 260–64.

Rousset, Jean. *La littérature de l'âge baroque en France*. Paris: Corti, 1953.

———. "La poésie baroque au temps de Malherbe: la métaphore." *Dix-Septième Siècle* 31 (1956): 353–70.

———, ed. *Anthologie de la poésie baroque française*. Paris: Colin, 1961.

Roy, Emile. "Un pamphlet d'Alexandre Hardy." *Revue d'Histoire Littéraire de la France* 22 (1915): 497–543.

Le sacrifice des Muses. Paris: Cramoisy, 1635.

Saint-Amant, Marc-Antoine Gérard de. *Œuvres*. Edited by Jean Lagny. Paris: Didier, 1967.

———. *Œuvres complètes*. Paris: Jannet, 1855.

Saint-Evremond, Charles de. *La comédie des académiciens* [sic]. Paris: Charavay, 1879.

———. *Œuvres*. Edited by René de Planhol. Paris: Cité des Livres, 1927.

———. *Œuvres choisies*. Edited by Célestin Hippeau. Paris: Didot, 1852.

———. *Œuvres mêlées*. Paris: Techener, 1865.

Saint-Julien. *Les courriers de la Fronde*. Edited by M.-C. Moreau. Paris: Jannet, 1857.

Saint-Pavin, Denis Sanguin de. *Recueil complet des poésies*. Paris: Techener, 1861.

Sarasin, Jean-François. *Œuvres*. Paris: Champion, 1926.

Saulnier, V. L. "Malherbe et le XVIe siècle." *Dix-Septième Siècle* 31 (1956): 195–229.

Sauval, Henri. *Histoire de Paris*. Paris: Moette et Chardon, 1724.

Sayce, R. A. "Boileau and French Baroque." *French Studies* 2 (1948): 148–52.

Scarron, Paul. *Poésies diverses*. Edited by Maurice Cauchie. Paris: Didier, 1947–1961.

Schelandre, Jean de. *Mélanges poétiques*. Paris: Micard, 1608. [Bound with *Tyr et Sidon*.]

Scudéry, Georges de. *L'amant libéral*. Paris: Courbé, 1638.

———. *Le cabinet de M. de Scudéry*. Paris: Courbé, 1646.

———. *Poésies diverses*. Paris: Courbé, 1649.

———. *Le trompeur puni*. Paris: Sommaville, 1635.

———. *Le vassal généreux*. Paris: Courbé, 1636.

Scudéry, Madeleine de. *Artamène ou le Grand Cyrus*. Paris: Courbé, 1650–1653.

———. *Clélie*. Paris: Courbé, 1660.

Segrais, Jean Regnault de. *Poésies*. Paris: Sommaville, 1661.

Seznec, Alain. "Saint-Amant, le poète sauvé des eaux." *Studies in Seventeenth-Century French Literature Presented to Morris Bishop*, pp. 35–64. Ithaca: Cornell University Press, 1962.

Silin, Charles Intervale. *Benserade and his Ballets de Cour*. Baltimore: Johns Hopkins Press, 1940.

Sorel, Charles. *De la connoissance des bons livres*. Amsterdam: Boom, 1672.

Souriau, Maurice. *L'évolution du vers français au dix-septième siècle*. Paris: Hachette, 1893.

Staub, Walther. *Pierre Corneille als religiöser Dichter*. Schwarzenburg: Gerber, 1926.

Stone, Donald, Jr. "Théophile's 'La Solitude': An Appraisal of Poem and Poet." *French Review* 40 (1966): 321–28.

Storer, Mary Elizabeth. "Madame Deshoulières jugée par ses contemporains." *Romanic Review* 25 (1934): 367–74.

Tallemant, Paul. *Le retour de l'Isle d'Amour*. Leyde: Elzevier, 1666.

———. *Le second voyage de l'Isle d'Amour*. Paris: Billaine, 1664.

———. *Le voyage de l'Isle d'Amour*. Paris: Billaine, 1663.

Tallemant des Réaux, Gédéon. *Les historiettes*. Edited by Gaston Paris and L.-J. Monmerqué. Paris: Techener, 1854–1860.

———. *Les historiettes*. Paris: Gallimard, 1960–1961.

Tardieu, Jean. "Etienne Durand, poète supplicié." In *Le préclassicisme français*, edited by Jean Tortel, pp. 189–95. Paris: Cahiers du Sud, 1952.

Testi, Fulvio. *Rime*. Modena: Cassiani, 1617.

Tortel, Jean, ed. *Le préclassicisme français*. Paris: Cahiers du Sud, 1952.

Tristan L'Hermite. *Les amours*. Paris: Billaine et Courbé, 1638.

———. *Les amours et autres poésies choisies*. Edited by Pierre Camo. Paris: Garnier, 1925.

———. *La mer*. Paris: Callemont, 1627.

———. *L'office de la Sainte Vierge*. Paris: N.p., [1646].

———. *Plaintes d'Acante et autres œuvres*. Paris: Billaine, 1634.

———. *Poésies*. Edited by Philip A. Wadsworth. Paris: Seghers, 1962.

———. *Les vers héroïques*. Edited by C. M. Grisé. Geneva: Droz, 1967.

Valéry, Paul. "Au sujet d'Adonis." *Revue de Paris* 1 (1 February 1921): 540–62.

Varga, A. Kibédi. "Enfin Du Perron vint: Malherbe ou le sens de la publicité." *Revue d'Histoire Littéraire de la France* 67 (1967): 1–17.

Varga, S. A. "Un poète oublié du XVIIe siècle: E. Durand et les 'Stances à l'inconstance.'" *Neophilologus* 39 (1955): 249–58.

Verchaly, André. *Airs de cour pour voix et luth* (*1603–1643*). Paris: Heugel, 1961.

Viau, Théophile de. *Œuvres complètes*. Paris: Jannet, 1856.

———. *Œuvres poétiques*. Edited by Jeanne Streicher. Geneva: Droz, 1951–1958.

[Viollet le Duc.] *Catalogue des livres composant la bibliothèque poétique de M. Viollet le Duc*. New York: Franklin, 1965.

Voiture, Vincent. *Œuvres*. Edited by J.-H.-A. Ubicini. Paris: Charpentier, 1855.

Wadsworth, Philip A. "Artifice and Sincerity in the Poetry of Tristan L'Hermite." *Modern Language Notes* 74 (1959): 422–30.

———. "Form and Content in the Odes of Malherbe." *Publications of the Modern Language Association* 78 (1963): 190–95.

———. "La Fontaine as Critic and Student of Malherbe." *Symposium* 3 (1949): 130–39.

———. "Malherbe and His Influence." In *Studies in Seventeenth-Century French Literature Presented to Morris Bishop*, pp. 20–34. Ithaca: Cornell University Press, 1962.

———. "Marin Le Roy de Gomberville: A Biographical Sketch." *Yale Romantic Studies* 18 (1941): 49–100.

———. "The Poetry of Tristan L'Hermite." *Kentucky Foreign Language Quarterly* 4 (1957): 205–11.

———. *Young La Fontaine*. Evanston: Northwestern University Press, 1952.

Wagner, R.-R. "Le langage poétique." *Dix-Septième Siècle* 31 (1956): 269–95.

Wais, Kurt. "Corneille oder Brébeuf?" *Archiv* 169 (1936): 213–23.

Winegarten, Renée. *French Lyric Poetry in the Age of Malherbe*. Manchester: Manchester University Press, 1954.

———. "A Neglected Critic of Malherbe: Jacques Favereau." *French Studies* 6 (1952): 29–34.

Wright, K. C. "Tristan et l'évolution de la poésie lyrique française entre 1620 et 1650." Doctoral dissertation, Edinburgh University, 1958.

Index

Malherbe's name appears on nearly every page and has therefore been omitted. Wherever a poet gets more than passing mention, those page numbers are in italics.

Fieubet, Gaspard de, 296
Fléchier, Valentin-Esprit, 299, 300,
　314
Flotte, 21, 24, 32, 37, 39, 50
Fouquet, Nicolas, 234, 316
Fourcroy, Bonaventure de, 314
Francheville, Louis de, 290
Françon, Marcel, 6
Frénicle, Nicolas, 150, 151–53, 255–
　56
Fromilhague, René, 1, 4, 5, 7, 8, 20,
　32, 33, 34, 35, 36, 37, 38, 40, 41,
　44, 46, 60, 93, 116, 168, 331
Fukui, Yoshio, 113, 114, 145, 149,
　152, 167, 168, 176, 218, 237, 328,
　330
Furetière, abbé Antoine, 103, 221,
　222, 233, 234–35, 267
Fussel, Paul, Jr., 168

Garapon, Robert, 125
Gassendi, Pierre, 51
Gaston d'Orléans, 86, 112, 170, 244,
　247, 314
Gay, Lucy M., 46
Gilbert, Gabriel, 257–58
Godeau, Antoine, 48, 58, 59, 70, 71,
　75, 82, 85, 86, 88–92, 187, 194–
　99, 256
Gohin, Ferdinand, 288, 303, 304,
　316, 317, 330
Gombauld, Jean Ogier de, 63, 85, 86,
　96–99, 102, 103, 187, 273
Gomberville, Marin le Roy de, 85,
　86, 92–96, 153, 187
Gongora, Luis de, 252
Goodman, William A., 199
Gosse, Edmund, 3, 4, 6
Goujet, C.-P., 80, 88, 92, 93, 94,
　108, 117, 145, 170, 176, 232, 234,
　236, 244, 255, 264, 288
Gourier, Françoise, 123, 130, 203,
　205

Gournay, Marie le Jars de, 72, 80,
　125
Grammont, Maurice, 304, 326
Grancé, Mme de, 58
Grisé, Catherine M., 165, 167, 211,
　214
Gros, Etienne, 237
Grünewald, Mathias, 138
Guedj, Hélène, 163
Guéret, Gabriel, 22, 23, 82
Guisan, Gilbert, 319, 320
Guiton, Margaret, 304

Habert, Germain, 48, 62, 63, 80–84,
　117
Habert, Philippe, 48, 62–63, 117
Harambure, Mme d', 273
Harcourt, comtesse d', 70, 129
Hardy, Alexandre, 22, 66
Harmand, René, 283, 285, 286
Hauteroche, Noël le Breton de, 291
Henri IV, 26, 31, 38, 42, 149, 232,
　233
Hermant, Godefroy, 279
Hermite. See Tristan L'Hermite
Hervier, Marcel, 324
Hesnault. See Dehénault
Hill, Robert E., 160, 164, 165
Hippeau, Célestin, 306
Hope, Quentin M., 306
Hopil, Claude, 280
Horace, 244, 245, 316, 332
Hotman, François de la Tour, 314
Houdar de la Motte, A., 90
Huet, Pierre-Daniel, 58, 59, 73,
　299–300, 314, 329, 332

Isar. See Ysarn

Jodelle, Estienne, 110

Kastner, L. E., 169
Kerviler, René, 195
Kohn, Renée, 90, 297